IN THE Beginning
WAS THE Meal

IN THE **Beginning** WAS THE **Meal**

SOCIAL EXPERIMENTATION & EARLY CHRISTIAN IDENTITY

Hal Taussig

FORTRESS PRESS
MINNEAPOLIS

IN THE BEGINNING WAS THE MEAL
Social Experimentation and Early Christian Identity

Cover photo: © Erich Lessing / Art Resource, NY
Cover design: Ivy Palmer Skrade
Book design: Jessica A. Puckett
Interior illustrations (pp. 24–25) are by Romney Oualline Nesbitt and are copyright © 2002 Romney Oualline Nesbitt and Dennis E. Smith.

Library of Congress Cataloging-in-Publication Data
Taussig, Hal.
  In the beginning was the meal : social experimentation and early Christian identity / Hal Taussig.
    p. cm.
  Includes bibliographical references and index.
  ISBN 978-0-8006-6343-8 (alk. paper)
  1.   Fasts and feasts. 2.   Dinners and dining—Religious aspects—Christianity.
3. Dinners and dining—Social aspects. 4. Lord's Supper—History. 5. Church history—Primitive and early church, ca. 30-600. I. Title.
  BV43.T38 2009
  270.1—dc22
                                                                                    2008043285

The paper used in this publication meets the minimum requirements of American National Standard for Information Sciences—Permanence of Paper for Printed Library Materials, ANSI Z329.48-1984.

Manufactured in Canada

13   12   11   10   09   1   2   3   4   5   6   7   8   9   10

For Markus

Table OF Contents

Abbreviations

BTB	*Biblical Theology Bulletin*
Eth. nic.	Aristotle, *Ethica nichomachea*
GThom	*Gospel of Thomas*
JBL	*Journal of Biblical Literature*
NASB	New American Standard Bible
NJB	New Jerusalem Bible
NRSV	New Revised Standard Version

Preface

In the beginning was the meal.

The ironic affirmation of this book's title concerning Christian beginnings cannot be overlooked. It is, of course, a complete contradiction in terms. The title and the book itself do propose a hypothesis for the beginnings of Christianity, even while they undermine the idea of Christian origins itself. But a meal can never be a pure beginning, even as Christianity's beginnings can never be pinpointed. A meal is always derivative of a complex set of prior events: food preparation, relationships, invitations, and locales, to name a few. To assert that Christianity—or anything—began with a meal begs too many questions.

Yet many things are generated at meals—ideas, additional relationships, new intentions, more communal fabric. The value in conceiving Christian beginnings in terms of the meals that first- and second-century "Christians" ate is that it taps a generative social practice for early Christians while avoiding much of the pretense of previous proposals about how Christianity began. Like a meal itself, this work assumes a complex combination of ongoing dynamics, prior initiatives, social interaction, previous histories, overlapping ideas, and ambiguous intentions at work in the process of Christian identities emerging. It is not possible to account for Christian beginnings by identifying who the founding figure was, what the essential beliefs were, what the guiding social principles were, or what transformative event triggered it all. What is done here is the mapping of one of the primary social practices during Christianity's emergence: the meals that they shared. Instead of producing a definitive origin, this project analyzes the intersection of this important social practice and early Christian literature. It does not abandon the task of thinking about how Christianity began, but rather seeks to understand a range of early Christian identities as they partially appeared within one of the major social practices of the first two centuries, the Hellenistic meal. In this, the task is less the establishment of some early Christian "essence" and more what Judith Lieu has called the articulation of "a grammar of practice" in the study of early Christian identities (for more details, see chapter 6 of Lieu's book *Christian Identity in the Jewish and Graeco-Roman World* [2006]). As such, it means to lay crucial groundwork for the next stages of study of Christian beginnings.

This book has been actively in the making for twenty years. Hence my indebtedness for its completion is immense and broad. My primary intellectual debts are indeed multiple. Dennis Smith, with whom I have already written one book on early Christian meals, has provided the key research breakthroughs for this work as well as loyal collegiality, good humor, and genuine friendship. Although the length of time spent with Matthias Klinghardt has not spanned the same two decades, his brilliant research, conversational partnership, and emerging friendship have meant a great deal to me. The methodological and conceptual gifts of Burton Mack, my graduate school mentor, are too numerous and complex to name. Karen King's intellectual companionship, friendship, and international leadership in rethinking the history of early Christianity have deepened and guided this entire work. I cherish the constancy, insight, and friendship of Brigitte Kahl and Janet Walton, my two teaching colleagues at Union Theological Seminary in New York, in inestimable ways.

As I enter my tenth year of teaching at Union, I am aware of my gratitude for the support of this institution. I am especially indebted to the advanced students in the four different versions of my course in ritual meals. I owe especially significant debts to Davina Lopez, Lillian Larsen, Velma Love, and Jae Won Lee. The support of the administration, especially Deans Euan Cameron and Jim Hayes, and President Joe Hough was crucial to this work. Among my Ph.D. students, Maia Kotrosits and Celene Lillie have been inspirational conversational partners and valuable copy editors.

My partner, Susan Cole, has given me deep friendship, wonderful critique, intellectual companionship, important distraction, and valuable perspective on the twenty years of work on this book. My friends Clyde Flaherty, David Tatgenhorst, Cathy Nerney, Jim McIntire, and David Eckert make whatever I do better and more fun. The members of the Society of Biblical Literature's Consultation and Seminar on Meals in the Greco-Roman World have been invaluable in their critique and support. I also thank my friend Heath Allen, who first called the idea of this book into being.

I dedicate this book to my son, Markus Taussig, who started talking to me about these matters when he was seven years old and who has been important to me ever since as a rigorous intellectual partner and affectionate companion.

CHAPTER ONE

Experiencing THE Meal

IT WAS AN AMAZING MOMENT FOR INARUS. *Even though he had only moved to Thessalonica from his native Egypt four years ago, the merchant Suetonius now had invited many of his neighbors to a meal in honor of Inarus' birthday. And now he was reclining in the dining room Suetonius had rented for the occasion, and watching as many of his new friends and neighbors entered the space.*

Inarus was relatively sure that something like this would not have happened in his native Egyptian village. Perhaps it could have happened in the big city of Alexandria, where the mix of people was greater. And it was true that he was not at all the only one in the room who had moved from someplace else to his Thessalonican neighborhood.

In between the hearty greetings of those gathering and the placing of bread, vegetables, and fruit on the small tables around the room, Inarus continued to marvel. Here he was an ordinary laborer from a foreign country, and they were honoring him with a meal.

Of course, he also knew the subtext of this. Suetonius in many ways was his patron and the patron of many other invitees. He depended on Suetonius for much of his work. And this display of a festive meal in honor of Inarus was also indeed a reminder that many of the invitees were in social debt to Suetonius. Nevertheless, he felt happy and honored to have this meal upon the occasion of his birthday.

Then his musing halted as his neighbor, Eli, rose to begin the meal: "It is our pleasure to be together in affection for our neighbor Inarus, in honor for his patron god Osiris, and in the debt of our neighbor Suetonius. The flute girls will be arriving after the food is finished, and we have plenty of songs and games to play during the symposium. So blessed be the One who gave us all of this and this occasion for festive joy."

Eli lay back down on the dining couch. The other 15 in the room cheered. And before he could take it in, he, Eli, and Suetonius were served some delicious lamb flank. For a moment, Inarus was embarrassed that only these three would receive any meat. But then he realized that this is what was meant to happen to honored guests.[1]

The festive meals of the Hellenistic Mediterranean were almost everywhere. The wealthy, the poor, the elite, the merchants, and the laborers all had some occasion to recline for festive meals. Indeed, in this period after classical Greece's cultural dominance, these festive meals had spread into societal locations that included a wide range of people not part of the former classical versions. Although not always the norm, both slaves and women now often participated, sometimes even reclining.

Although these gatherings were known for their conviviality, they often also were the occasion for spontaneous address of controversial issues. Here is another imagined example:

It's true that they were all tired. They had been working in the port all day. The ship they were building would only need two or three more days before it was finished. And now they had been dining for over an hour. The food had been put away, several rounds of wine consumed, and a couple of rowdy songs accomplished.

Several of those reclining near the door were in an animated conversation about the mast of the ship and how it was to be finished. A flute girl had now begun to dance in front of the couches across the room. And even though the work of the day had been difficult, life was returning to most of the group.

But when the man with graying hair raised his question, all 18 men in the room came to attention.

"Why didn't we raise a cup to the emperor this evening?" he said, loud enough so that everyone could hear him, but still with a plaintive curiosity.

For a moment, there was silence.

It was clear that the president for this evening's meal did not know what to say. He knew that every meal of their shipyard guild was supposed to drink a cup in honor of the emperor, but he also knew that a number of the men at tonight's meal had recently been beaten by soldiers.

Then one of those men spoke: "We work so hard, and what does the emperor care? We raised a cup to Apollo last week. Apollo and the emperor are family. That's good enough."

Several others mumbled approval.

The man who had raised the question spoke again. "It's not that I care that much. I was just worrying that they might try to close our supper club down, if we didn't do it."

A man who had been beaten replied, "They won't know, if we skip it once in a while."

Several men spoke at the same time, so that no one was heard. Each of them then turned to those on the couches in their respective corner of the room, and started talking about the issue of raising a cup to the emperor. The discussion proceeded in several groups with great intensity.

Then the president saw his chance to change the subject. He placed a bowl in the middle of the room, and proposed to everyone a round of their favorite game of kottobos, which involved flicking the last bits of wine from their smaller bowls into the larger bowl in the center of the room. Everyone burst out laughing when the short man in the corner overshot his goal and hit the graying man across the room right in the face with a few drops of wine.[2]

While these meals all had an intense level of give-and-take, every meal also had its religious dimension. And many religious groups at this time claimed these meals as their primary moment together. As in the following sketch from Hellenistic Egypt:

The older man had been reading the Torah for a long time. With the food already digesting well for everyone, there was a moment of pause. From the way they had listened, it was clear that some others wanted to speak about what had just been read. Indeed, a younger man near the door seemed to be climbing to his feet. But perhaps because of the length of the reading combined with the comfort of good food, the silence sustained itself a bit. The lamps flickered around the room, adding an additional aspect to the mesmerizing moment.

So before one of the men was able to add a thought to what had been read, one of the women started humming. Above that hum, another woman started improvising on the words in the reading about the Red Sea. Her voice grew stronger, as she rose to a seated position from her reclining. Another woman also sat up and followed the improvisation with harmony. A few others joined the initial humming, while the two improvisations rose and fell, and the words took on a firmer pattern: "The waters parted, and the people walked through."

Almost as one, the men, who were still reclining on their side of the room, joined in, both in improvising and keeping the humming strong. After a while, most of the voices died down, with only the two women and three men still harmonizing and improvising about the path through the Red Sea. Until finally there was silence again.

This time the silence was strong and long, as the group savored both the beauty of the music and the implications of the words.

Finally, the younger man who had stirred earlier, said, "I've often wondered why they call us 'The Healers.' And tonight reminds me of how much better I feel, when we gather on the seventh day. G-d leads us too out of the desert of our aloneness. It could be that the healing is this sense of belonging to G-d and to one another. Perhaps when guests come here, they sense for themselves some healing of spirit. Or is it, of mind? On the other hand, I may be on the wrong track. When others outside our group talk about the healers, I always have the impression that they are talking about their bodies. Do they think we heal their bodies? Do some of us heal their bodies?"

Some silence. Then one of the older women spoke.

"Our founders of this way told us stories of healings of blindness and lameness. But then they always connected it to this gathering, especially on the seventh Sabbath, like today, when we celebrate more fully."

Again a bit of silence. Then an older man: "I have never healed anyone directly that I know of. But I feel that I have been healed many times here. I cannot tell whether the healing is of mind, body, or spirit."

Then longer silence.

At some point the younger man said, "Thank you."³

These meals were semipublic in nature. Often they were occasioned by someone's arrival or a family occasion in the town or neighborhood. Some—like the shipbuilders' regular monthly meal together described above—were mostly full of games and raucous songs. Others with some regularity had an interesting cross between entertainers and teachers as special guests. As in this sketch from Galilee:

Most everyone was reclining on their straw in the makeshift village dining room, although there was still one person washing his feet. But the dark skinned man decided it was time to begin anyway.

Raising his voice, he welcomed everyone, and went on to say, "I've invited you here this evening, to enjoy one another and this evening. There are two special things about tonight's banquet. First, Menachem has just returned from his trip to Jerusalem. It's great to have him returned safely to Cana. And secondly, we've been able to snag one of the traveling sages who are telling clever stories about the "realm of God" for tonight's entertainment. Now, of course, he's going to be doing that later, after we eat. So for now, please welcome Menachem back and let's hope that there is enough food to go around."

He started to lie back down on the straw. But suddenly stood up again, as if he had just remembered something.

He went over to the small table in the center of the room, and took a piece of bread. He then said in a similarly loud voice, quieting most of the chatter that had started back up, "Blessed are you, O G-d, ruler of the universe, who brings forth good things from the earth. Amen." The "Amen" with which everyone responded was almost within the same breath as the resumption of conversation.

Two of the younger men jumped up for some pieces of bread. A few moments later some vegetables arrived. Then some olive oil for the bread. A chickpea mix came in after the vegetables and most of the bread were almost all distributed. It looked as if there would be no meat tonight.[4]

This book explores the intersection of these festive meals with the beginnings of what came eventually to be called Christianity. Since the first 150 years of the early "Christian"[5] movements came together through the already established convention of these meal gatherings, this work looks to what can be learned about early Christianity through examining one of its major social practices. One sketch of ways the diverse forms of first-century "Christianity" worked at meals on their group identity follows:

The dogs were finishing up the scraps of bread on the floor. Most of those on the couches around the outside walls of the rented dining room were now stretched back in an almost exaggerated reclining position, letting the food they had just ingested settle. The one servant for this ragtag group was lugging in several large containers of wine, accompanied by one of those who had been reclining, who was carrying the bowls for the wine. The servant started trying to chase the dogs out of the room. Several others reclining seemed vaguely interested in the sunset over the famous mountains around Philippi, partially visible through the door.

The bowls landed on several small tables in front of the couches and the wine containers themselves were put on the floor between the tables and the couches. The president for the evening tried—first clumsily and then with a bit of flare—to mix the wine with the water in a large container. Several of those reclining—wanting to move as little as possible, but also wanting the wine about to be poured—reached for the bowls on the table, with one of the recliners barely avoiding knocking a bowl off the table in front of him. And now, the evening's president and the servant—after having pushed the last dog out of the room—were beginning to pour the wine for each person. The nine men received their wine first, followed by the two women.

The president—now back on his couch with his bowl of wine in hand—raised his bowl and spoke: "I dedicate this evening, actually I dedicate my whole life and the rest of this evening to . . ." Realizing that he wanted to be standing for the rest of his statement, he set his bowl on the small table for a moment, and struggled to his feet. "I dedicate this evening to the Christ. May he receive the honor and glory and power he deserves." He then took the bowl and made the traditional libational gesture of pouring a portion of the wine on the ground, while the rest of those reclining found their bowls of wine and began drinking in honor of the Christ.

The reclining man on the couch to the right of the president and the reclining woman on the other side of the room started singing, "Christ Jesus . . ." The rest of those reclining lifted their bowls in salute and joined in "Christ Jesus, who had the form of God, did not try to grasp equality with God." At this point, one of the dogs bolted back in the room, trying for another piece of bread that had just been thrown on the floor, and was chased out by the servant. The libational singing continued amid laughter about the dog: "Yes, Christ emptied himself, taking the form of a slave, becoming like people, and being in every way like us, Christ was even more humble . . ." The voices rose: "Having accepted death, yes, death on a cross." The man with a Macedonian accent then took a lead, almost a solo for a few words: "And because of this . . ." Everyone joined in: "God raised him very high, and gave him a name higher than any other name." The two women jumped on the next lines, leading everyone for a few phrases: "So that every being, all those in the skies . . ." Again the rest of the group caught up: "On the earth and in the underworld, should bend the knee at the name of Jesus." Everyone stopped for a moment and drank a big gulp, and then almost together sang: "That all tongues acknowledge Jesus as Lord, to the glory of God, the Father."

Some finished their glasses and went for more wine. Others repeated part of the song. A few others also poured a bit of wine on the ground. The Macedonian and the president started talking. Then one of the women wondered out loud: "Is there anyone here tonight who can read?" A couple more echoed her question. It turned out that no one could. "Well," the president concluded, "I think we will read that letter from Paul next time. Tonight we can talk about what Epaphroditus has to say, after his visit." The man at the right of the president poured his own wine, and started to sing another song. It was about Homer.[6]

As the ensuing chapters will show clearly, there were astonishing similarities in the basic structure and flow of these festive meals. There was indeed a common cultural form and norm for what one did at the meals.[7] However, within the general form, there was generous room for improvisation. And as is also demonstrated in later chapters, while following the overall meal conventions, the meal gatherings of early "Christians" varied substantially in their own content and character, depending on where the gathering happened and who attended. As the following example shows, the diversity often was both among those who ate together and between various groups eating in different places:

The dining room was already crowded, with almost every couch occupied with at least one person. But still a few more people from the group were coming in. The blessing had actually been said over the bread before the last group had even come. So the food was also being eaten and passed.

Two slaves were carrying large baskets of bread, fruit, and vegetables around to each couch. Bowls of olives seemed perched everywhere. Some of those reclining were able to see into the courtyard, and beyond. Because of their size, portions of both the temple of Diana and the synagogue were visible beyond the courtyard.

Then two other servants of the villa came with large platters of lamb and pork. The aroma of the meat wafted into the room, and several of those reclining clambered up to grab a piece as soon as possible, even before the platters arrived in front of the president and those reclining to his right.

The president rose quickly to receive the meat and to head off any dispute about who would get portions and who would not. Because of the size of the platters, it was clear to him that there would be enough for everyone. But he decided to make another point:

"Because we are all brothers and sisters in the Christ, we share this bounteous feast equally. Remember that we share this meat, and make sure that each one receives a healthy portion. We are grateful to our host for this good food which we divide among ourselves as God's people," the president declared.

A number murmured approval, as the platters started being passed around and the president reclined again on his couch of honor.

But suddenly a young man who lived near the synagogue was standing and asking for people's attention.

"Excuse me," he pleaded, "I do not approve of this meat. It is pork. G-d's people are not to eat pork. How can we celebrate our community in the Christ, when we are not one in our eating?"

The room fell silent. The president rose from his reclining, nervous and unsure of what to do or say.

In any case, he did not have time to gather his thoughts, since his own uncle was now speaking against the Jew who had objected to the meat. Without getting up from his reclining position, he said loudly, "This is despicable. We cannot refuse the generosity of our host. And in any case, all food is clean, when we are together in Christ. Just as we are both slave and free, men and women together, our food customs no longer matter."

The young Jewish man responded quickly, "Of course, we are all one in Christ. But Christ is a Jewish title. I know that in Christ, you are not required to eat like we are. But the Christ did not eat this kind of meat. Why should we? And didn't Paul write a letter twenty years ago to the Romans that said in fights about food like this, we should all respect the Jewish way?"

Quickly, a woman from just outside the city spoke: "I was not raised in the ways of Israel, as you were. But I also am not comfortable with eating this meat. I suspect that it may come from the temple of Diana. That means that it was probably also sacrificed in honor of the emperor. We know that the Christ is our leader, not the emperor. So I do not want to take the cruelty and dominion of the emperor into myself."

By now the president had realized that the group was in full debate. Such debate would be fine later in the meal, during the symposium, where debate, reading, singing, and prayer were all appropriate. But this food part of the meal should not be interrupted like this. So he raised his voice above the growing din.

"Brothers and sisters in Christ, it is not appropriate for us to have this debate now. I propose to discuss and decide this later after the supper and the raising of the cup to Christ. So, for now, let everyone eat what they wish, and we will honor the objection about the meat after we have raised the cup and sung our praises."

With some grumbling, each of the parties returned to the couches and began to eat.[8]

Based on a wide range of relatively new research, this book examines the major social practice of early Christians eating festive meals together.[9] Since the portrait of these meals has already been drawn by significant scholars, this book examines the implications of such important knowledge about the early Christians' social practice of the first 150 years. It shows how knowledge of such a major social practice can help us understand the social dimensions of early Christianity itself. It notices how understanding the meal as a primary location for social gatherings clarifies key questions about early proto-Christian identity. What were their social values? How did various such groups understand their relationships among themselves? Among men and women? Jew and Greek? Patron and client? Roman occupier, colonized people, and those caught in the middle? Slave, free, and master? Those in positions of honor and those shamed? What comes to life from the New Testament and other early Christian texts in different ways when one thinks socially about them, especially as revealed in the dynamics of the meal? What important hopes appear in light of knowing the contours and content of the meals in which early Christians so regularly participated? What new conflicts come into focus? What theological principles take on new importance, and what others recede in emphasis?

This book approaches these questions with a sense that much more can be said about Christian beginnings than before, now that a primary—and, in many ways, the first—social practice of early Christians can be elucidated. To do this, chapter 2 briefly reviews the study of Christian origins in our day. It critiques the conventional imagination of Christian origins and uses the work of Karen King, Burton Mack, Judith Lieu, Jonathan Z. Smith, and others to propose some new conceptualities. In chapter 3, the scholarly framework for the meal experiences sketched above is summarized, reviewed, and related to Christian beginnings. Here, the category of social experimentation at the meal is introduced. Chapter 4 then draws on contemporary social theory, primarily that of ritual and performance theory, to analyze Hellenistic and early Christian meals socially.

Chapter 5 shows how socially ambitious and widespread early Christian meals were. Building on this expansive picture of the meals, chapter 6 examines early Christian meals in terms of resistance to Roman imperial power, and chapter 7 outlines additional social experiments under way in the meal. Noticing how these analyses of the intersections of early Christian literature and Hellenistic meals break open new ways of understanding Christian beginnings, chapter 8 concludes that these are best understood as performances of early Christian identities. The epilogue reflects on implications of the early Christian meals for contemporary Christian worship.

CHAPTER TWO
New Paradigms FOR THE Study OF Early Christian Identities

B EFORE PROCEEDING WITH THE STRIKING WAYS early Christian meals help reshape the study of Christian beginnings, it is important to review what has been called the field of "Christian origins."

The study of "Christian origins" has surfaced from time to time in the history of modern scholarship.[1] It came into being mostly by virtue of the failure of what is now often called "the master narrative" of Christian beginnings to account for much of what had been learned in the late nineteenth century and the twentieth century about early Christianity.[2] This master narrative was the story that Christendom proposed as the way Christianity came into being. The study of Christian origins has attempted to provide alternatives to this master narrative that take more seriously historical-critical scholarship.

The Master Narrative

The master narrative goes something like this:

> Jesus was a great man. Perhaps the best human ever. Perhaps a god in human form and someone in direct and unique contact with God. Almost certainly perfect. Such a great person that the world was changed forever just by virtue of his extraordinariness. Jesus passed down his message successfully to his apostles, and they in turn passed it down to the church "fathers" (bishops, theologians, saints).[3] These church "fathers" successfully received the essence of Jesus' message and put it in the form of several creeds ("Apostles' Creed," Nicene Creed) that capture this Christian essence for all time. The essentials of Christian practice were also successfully transmitted in the sacraments of communion/eucharist

and baptism. In this way, Christianity today has direct authority from God and Jesus.

The disciplines of historical-critical and literary studies of the New Testament and early Christianity over the past two hundred years have raised many questions about the reliability of elements within this master story. But overall, most scholars operated within the master narrative paradigm, even while participating in technical scholarship that did not mesh with it. In the 1970s and 1980s, a number of scholars challenged the master narrative on the following bases:

1. The Third Quest for the historical Jesus emphasized the humanity of Jesus and the specific historical roots of his consciousness in first-century Galilee. It was less possible to hold him up as the quintessential human, since his own historical contingencies came more clearly into focus.

2. Increasingly, the diversity of various kinds of early Christianity began to be acknowledged. Both divergences within the canon and discovery of new literature beyond the canon underlined this diversity.

3. Evidence that the world had changed in a definitive, positive way because of Jesus seemed increasingly shaky in the wake of several holocausts and world wars, for which Christianity bore significant responsibility.

4. It was acknowledged more explicitly that the Apostles' Creed and the Nicene Creed do not actually contain teachings from Jesus but rather present cosmic images about him.[4] Hence, the idea that Jesus' teachings were passed down to the apostles and church fathers was much less demonstrable.

5. The ancient meanings and practices of baptism and communion/ eucharist appeared increasingly to be different than those of the twentieth century.

So most of the elements of the master narrative seemed less able to be trusted than previously assumed. The need for other ways to think about Christian beginnings again became evident and occasioned a new discourse about "Christian origins." Obviously, even though it covers a relatively short period of time, this master narrative took a long time to come into being. It depends not only on unquestioned and covert mythical thinking but also on cunning calculations that simultaneously preserve, hide, and rationalize the prerogatives of Christian dominance in our day. It is told today—at least in part—to compensate mythically for the messy situation in which Christianity finds itself as a worldwide dominant culture.

These reasons to challenge the master narrative remain today in place. Indeed, the need for new paradigms in thinking about Christian beginnings has been underscored by nonscholarly rejection of Christian authority in the general public. Other basic failures of Christianity to provide sufficient authority for negotiating (post)modern life have underlined the need to rethink the standard way Christian beginnings have been assumed. Perhaps most illustrative of this larger doubt about Christian authority and the master narrative of Christian beginnings was the enthusiastic public reception of a poorly researched novel, *The DaVinci Code*, which questioned the master narrative and proposed an alternative story. Much of the attraction to this novel had to do with the general population's suspicion that Christian authority in the twenty-first century was lacking. The connection between contemporary Christian authority and the master narrative became obvious as the public was fascinated by *The DaVinci Code*'s speculation of how the "real" story of Christian beginnings had been suppressed in favor of a self-justifying master narrative by church fathers.

Nevertheless, the field of Christian origins per se has not fared particularly well. Several weaknesses in the search for the "origins" of Christianity have become apparent. First, the contingencies of alternate imaginations of how Christianity began have been all too obvious. The flaws and biases of alternate trajectories have been fairly easy to spot.[5] Second, the hesitancy of scholars to propose grand alternative reimaginations for Christian beginnings has made the broad scope of the master narrative seem more comprehensive and allows it to continue as a default picture. Often, this has allowed the public and other scholars to revert to the master narrative, since its story is more comprehensive.

Third, and perhaps most important from this book's perspective, the notion itself of the "origins" of early Christianity has been increasingly contested.[6] This notion has been challenged on at least two levels. While clearly affirming that the master narrative itself is manipulative and illusory, some scholars doubt whether one can ever discover or decipher the actual origins of Christianity.[7] This worry that such origins cannot be uncovered comes mostly from a postmodern suspicion that any objective historical perspective is impossible, and partly from the recognition that the evidence one currently has for how Christianity began is far from comprehensive. Others see the idea of Christian origins itself as the production of originary truth, meant to privilege one perspective or another. These scholars see Christian origins scenarios that are meant to be alternatives to the master narrative as also functioning for ideological, not historical, purposes.[8] Just as the master narrative is a construction to defend Christian orthodoxy, alternative Christian origins schemes have their own ideological purposes, according to this growing critique.

Karen King—even as she challenges the master narrative—concisely puts these two critiques of the idea of Christian origins together:

The beginning is often portrayed as the ideal to which Christianity should aspire and conform. Here Jesus spoke to his disciples and the gospel was preached in truth. Here the churches were formed in the power of the Spirit and Christians lived in unity and love with one another. . . . But what happens if we tell the story differently? What if the beginning was a time of grappling and experimentation? What if the meaning of the gospel was not clear and Christians struggled to understand who Jesus was . . . ?[9]

Whether it is *The DaVinci Code*, the master narrative, or some halting scholarly alternatives, imaginations then of how Christianity began are deeply flawed at this juncture. It has become apparent that to think more clearly about Christian beginnings, one cannot simply have the "facts" straight. One must also shift one's method. Given this impasse, some important new approaches have surfaced in the last decade or so. These new, mostly methodological, departures form an important dimension to this book's effort to use the social practice of early Christian meals in reimagining ways Christianity began.

Recent Initiatives in Rethinking Christian Beginnings

Even for those who question the feasibility or integrity of alternatives to the master narrative for Christian origins, the need to challenge the master narrative seems pressing.[10] This imperative comes not only from the need to have a more honest picture of Christian beginnings. The role the master narrative plays in reinforcing the status quo of contemporary Christianity and the arbitrary authority of institutionalized Christendom also raises ethical issues about how contemporary Christianity might claim more integrity. That the master narrative tends to legitimize power from above as being ordained by Jesus, the apostles, and the church fathers marginalizes the voices of subaltern Christians and limits democratic processes for change within Christianity.

The need both to present a more coherent alternative portrait and to counter the hegemony of the master narrative has led to some important shifts in perspective and method, even if it has not produced viable counternarratives. These shifts include the following.

SEEING CHRISTIAN BEGINNINGS AS INHERENTLY DIVERSE

The idea of a straight trajectory of thought, practice, and authority from Jesus to the Nicene Creed is now in tatters. A variety of scholarship in the past twenty years has shown that throughout the first two centuries many different movements flourished in the name of Jesus. More to the point, the categories of orthodoxy and heresy have been shown to be inadequate to characterize these differences.

At first, as noted above, this discovery of Christian diversity occasioned challenges to the master narrative. In the past decade, the assumption of early Christian diversity has become a constituent part of rethinking Christian beginnings. Burton Mack, for instance, has sketched five distinctly different "Jesus movements" in Israel in the first generation of his followers in Israel and has shown that another "Christ" movement existed simultaneously in Syria and Asia Minor.[11] Similarly, Karen King has shown how the Nag Hammadi documents illustrate that a much broader range of early "Christianities" existed in both the first and second centuries.[12] Even more standard presentations of these first two centuries, such as Helmut Koester's two-volume *Introduction to the New Testament* and Bart Ehrman's *Historical Introduction to the New Testament*,[13] assume a wide variety of early "Christianities." All of these scholars have come to assume that the diversity of early Christianity existed also within the New Testament itself.[14] In the post–New Testament eras, James Carroll's groundbreaking study *Constantine's Sword* and Averil Cameron's *Christianity and the Rhetoric of the Roman Empire* complement the more extensive scholarship on the first century.

UNDERSTANDING EARLY "CHRISTIANITY" AS A SOCIAL MOVEMENT

Basic to the master narrative has been the assumption that proper belief was the crucial way that early Christianity maintained its integrity and unity. So, for instance, the "belief" in Jesus as the Son of God has often been posited as a core characteristic of early Christianity. Derivative of this tendency has also been an emphasis on what early Christians thought. In these versions of early Christian history, the ideas—if not the beliefs—have been portrayed as the heart of the matter.

The master narrative also structures itself around heroic individual personalities (for example, Jesus, Paul, particular church "fathers"). Although Christian beginnings did involve a number of important individuals (for example, Jesus, Paul, Mary Magdalene, Ignatius of Antioch), recent studies make clear that what early Christianity became cannot be accounted for by simply identifying one or more founder figures.[15] Rather, intense, prolonged, and complex social give-and-take occurred in this emergence. These social interactions and the communities they produced are at least as important as any early Christian founding heroes for the shapes of early Christianity. This emerging new principle of historical investigation is anti-heroic. It assumes that history is made through intricate and extended social processes and that early Christianity was no exception.

Studying belief and focusing on heroic persons, as the master narrative encourages, leaves huge gaps in how social and religious movements come into being. Such focus on belief and heroes also reinforces the values of contemporary Christian authority.

Given these problems, a range of studies in the last generation has concentrated on social stances that might better characterize the various early Christianities of the first two centuries than the search for guiding belief or heroic paradigms.[16]

Currently, the most influential scholarship in this vein is the characterization of early Christianities as resistant to the oppression and theological presumption of the Roman Empire. In this imagination of Christian beginnings, it has been the social stance of early Christians over against Rome (rather than some creedal conviction) that contributed greatly to what early Christianity was becoming. Here the case for these various early Christianities perhaps being best characterized as a spectrum of protests against Rome has been coherently made by such leading scholars as Richard Horsley, Brigitte Kahl, and Warren Carter.[17]

The master narrative of Christian origins has paid little attention to the emergence of early Christianity under the Roman Empire. For this conventional picture of how Christianity began, it hardly mattered that the entirety of Christian beginnings occurred within the huge "world" created by Rome's military, political, and economic domination. In this picture, Jesus' brilliant teachings and heroic deeds were mostly done in a fairy tale atmosphere. In its versions with the most ambitious frame of reference, the larger frame of the master narrative has the backdrop of Jesus opposing a "corrupt" Judaism.[18] No attention is paid to the fact that Judaism is living under, and in some cases collaborating with, Roman oppression. But, of course, since the master narrative finally serves as a justification for Christian religion (over against other religions) and global dominance, address to the political dynamics of the Roman Empire does not fit well.

Burton Mack's crucial notions of "social formation" and "social experimentation" have also enabled a trajectory of scholarship identifying the various social expressions in early Christianity. Mack writes of this effort:

> Work in this area provides a most welcome corrective to traditional preoccupations with the history of ideas and texts alone. How groups formed, defined their boundaries, elaborated activities, selected authorities, remembered experiences, forged social markers, created codes, and adjudicated conflict now are recognized as having had as much to do with the origins of Christianity as the thoughts that were thought and the literature produced. . . . The goal must be to bring these social histories together with what is known of textual traditions and seek to understand each in the light of the other.[19]

Social experimentation is a central notion of Mack's, although he has not described it very explicitly. He describes pre-Pauline community as "a novel experiment in social inclusivity,"[20] and the early Jesus movements as "arenas for social experimentation."[21] He describes his study of the Q people in *The Lost Gospel* as the tracing of "one tradition of social experimentation."[22] And in this same book, he seems to be describing the process of Q social experimentation in the following manner:

> To explore human community based on fictive kinship without regard to standard taboos against association based on class, status, gender, or ethnicity would have created quite a stir, and would have been its own reward. Since there was no grand design for actualizing such a vision, different groups settled into practices that varied from one another. Judging from the many forms of community that developed within the Jesus movement . . . these groups continued to share a basic set of attitudes. They all had a certain critical stance toward the way life was lived in the Greco-Roman world. They all struggled not to be determined by the emptiness of human pursuits in a world of codes they held to be superficial. And they all learned to apply the concept of the kingdom of God to the ethos that developed their own community.[23]

This work has been complemented by earlier work of historian of religion Jonathan Z. Smith[24] and by two generations of national seminars of the Society of Biblical Literature.[25]

Much of this new scholarship on the social dimension to early first- and second-century Christianity has based itself methodologically within the larger social sciences of sociology and anthropology. As scholars of early Christianity have in the past twenty years turned increasingly to broader social science fields, more and more theoretical attention has been paid to the study of social "practices" and behavior.[26] The first initiatives in examining social practices and behavior have focused on particular milieus of early Christianity, such as the character of urban life in Asia Minor or of village life in Galilee. However, specific social practices of early Christians have yet to be examined in any sustained manner. The most sustained theoretical work on this question has been done by Judith Lieu, who has called for the development of a "grammar of social practice" in relationship to early Christian identity.[27]

CONCENTRATING ON THE PROCESS OF THE EMERGENCE OF CHRISTIAN IDENTITY

Some new scholarship has met the above-mentioned inhibitions to finding the origins of Christianity with some key alternative methods of working on the character of the early stages of Christianity. Rather than trying to find originary moments of Christianity that somehow account for all that follows (and perhaps subliminally provide ideological models), this scholarship has focused on how early Christian identity was constructed over a period of several hundred years.[28] As Judith Lieu observes: "Christian 'identity' is not something which appears clearly as such at a given moment; in one sense it emerges through the centuries in ways which are difficult to plot clearly."[29] Such an approach rests neither on finding core beliefs of Christianity nor even on associating Christianity with particular social causes.

Rather, the questions of this task concentrate more on the ways sometimes tensive values and behaviors coalesce over time within a particular identity. Nor is early Christian identity seen as a final product or spiritual essence. It varies— sometimes incrementally and sometimes wildly—according to time and place. Such focus on identity accounts for the diversity of Christianities as well as the complex interplay of behavior, belief, and social bonds. Christian beginnings are, then, the stuff of negotiated identities within particular sets of social circumstances. In this way, one can see larger coherences, as well as complexities and digressions, without appealing to such wooden categories as orthodoxy-heresy, heroic models, or social programs. Scholarship on early Christian identity has been undertaken by several different clusters of scholars with different theoretical frames of reference.[30]

INVESTIGATING THE DYNAMICS OF IDENTITY FORMATION

Although to some extent simply a subset of the previous shift, special attention has begun to be paid to how identities were formed in the ancient Mediterranean. Two particular sets of studies are now in process relative to identity formation at that time. Both are derivative of social scientific study from beyond the study of early Christianity. These two new trends have studied collective memory and performance.

Collective memory studies are more than a century old and base themselves primarily on the work of Maurice Halbwachs. Collective memory, according to these studies, has more to do with the process of culture and identity formation than with what happened. Memory functions primarily to shape the identity of those remembering, rather than to report what happened. Collective memory is an ongoing process of appropriating the "past" to shape identities of peoples. This approach to identity formation is now being explored by a number of scholars of Christian beginnings. The works of Elizabeth Castelli, Alan Kirk, and Tom Thatcher have used collective memory studies in specific case studies of early Christianity. In the hands of these scholars, early Christian identity formation is relatively easily studied through existing traditions of textual criticism. Early Christian texts have already been shown to have layers of composition. Collective memory method can use this textual layering as a way of thinking of groups of people (re)casting their identity through the appropriation of past tellings. Castelli's study is particularly evocative because it examines the gripping phenomenon of early Christian martyrdom as it is framed and reframed to construct social identity.

Performance studies from beyond New Testament studies are also now enhancing understanding of early Christian identity formation. Among others, Richard Horsley,

John Dominic Crossan, and Stanley Stowers have studied the impact of performance on the emergence of first-century Christian identities. Performance shows a more dynamic approach to identity in that it demonstrates how identity is neither static nor universal. As Crossan notes, each time a parable was "performed," its meaning shifted, depending on its context. As Stowers notes, early Christian worship allowed the participants to improvise their own identity from time to time and place to place. Performance and ritual theory play a key role in this book's treatment of Christian beginnings and is examined closely in chapters 4 and 8.

These recent shifts in the study of Christian beginnings have not produced large new pictures of early Christianity. But they have continued to challenge the master narrative by advancing new methods for thinking about these beginnings.

The Meal and the Performance
of Early Christian Identities

Chapter 1 has already proposed that early Christian meals based themselves in a larger Hellenistic social practice. Chapter 3 lays out in some detail this social practice both within the Greco-Roman world and in "Christian" literature in the first two centuries. This book depends on the recent shifts in the study of Christian beginnings listed here in order to take a next step toward a larger portrait of Christianity in the first two centuries. That next step is to study a major social practice of early Christians and ask what that social practice says about early Christian identities.

Festive meals are that social practice. When the relatively new information about early Christian meals is examined through the recent shifts in methodologies of Christian beginnings, a substantive next step can be taken. That next step is the study of one major social practice of first- and second-century Christians. Such a next step does not resolve the question of how Christianity began; it does not find the essential belief or identify the crucial founding heroes; and it does not crystallize early Christianity in one social program. Rather, it takes the intermediate step of portraying the dynamics of a widespread early Christian social practice. From the perspective of Judith Lieu, it works to produce a major element for a "grammar of social practice."

The festive meals of early Christianity were a social stage on which early Christian identity was elaborated. Thus, studying them participates in the methodological shifts from heroic figure to social formation, from belief to social practice, from origins to identities, and from essence to performance.[31] Perhaps one reason that the festive meals of the Hellenistic Mediterranean have not been recognized as a central social practice of early Christianity is that such study has been segregated into the much narrower field of early Christian worship. So most analysis of the early Christian meals has asked only liturgical questions, leaving their social analysis aside. Since these early meals—Christian and otherwise—did contain ritual elements (especially those at least superficially connected to contemporary Christian worship gestures), the fact that the meals were also the main venue for the emergent Christian social dynamics was overlooked.

This book means to pull the analysis of these meals back from relatively obscure and liturgical scholarship into a fuller, more central discussion of what the social vision and practices of early Christians were. After such a reorientation, what becomes quickly evident is that the New Testament and other early Christian texts' treatment of meal gatherings are loaded with proclamation and contestation of social dynamics. In addition, the academic field of ritual studies has in recent decades shown how to think about ritual as expressive of social dynamics and formation. In other words, rituals per se may indeed have a great deal to do with social order and change. Chapter 4 analyzes this ritual dimension of these meals. Ritual analysis shows that these meals were helping other groups elaborate their identities prior to the emergence of Christianity. In this way, study of these meals has a respect for diversity built into it. Early Christian meals as social stage were a frequent place in which the performance elaborated identity.[32]

It is a rarity that historians have access to social practices of the ancient world. Usually, there is simply not enough information to make conclusions about what the practice might have been like. As chapter 3 shows, key research and analysis have been done in the past twenty years that make the festive meals of the Hellenistic era an exception. Through complex analysis of texts and discovery of key archaeological sites, the meal of that time is available to study. And by virtue of that access, important new access to Christian beginnings is now available.

This book pictures the first century of early Christianity as a series of bold social experiments. A variety of groups around the Mediterranean all gathered in that century around meals. These meals—because of their already established socially formative place in the Hellenistic world—evoked social experimentation. They allowed early Christians to try out new behaviors in dialogue with their vision of the realm of God. The meals became a laboratory in which a range of expressive vocabularies explored alternative social visions.

CHAPTER THREE

THE Hellenistic AND Early Christian Social Practice OF Festive Meals

A PRIMARY WAY FIRST-CENTURY "CHRISTIANS" spent time together was at meals. There they made decisions together about their inner workings and their relationship to the broader world. Meals were the place where they taught and learned together and where they worshipped, prayed, and sang their songs together. This was the time that they had arguments, sorted out differences, went their own ways, and reconciled with one another. It was a central community event. These meals provided the primary experiential evidence for those who opposed them, those who dropped in for visits, and those who were curious about them.

There is little argument about this within scholarship on the New Testament and early Christianity. Unfortunately, there is also little attention paid to it. The master narrative of what happened in the first century of the movement, and what matters about it, is so dominant that few people ask about the significance of the social practice of early Christianity. Instead of issues around who early Christians were as a social formation, the dominant questions have remained those of the master narrative. The new possibility of asking questions about this primary social practice of early Christianity and what it means for thinking about the emergence of the new movement has come into view much more clearly because of scholarship that has been accomplished in the past twenty years.

Two major books have been written on opposite sides of the Atlantic Ocean almost simultaneously with very similar and pivotal content. These two books, Dennis Smith's *From Symposium to Eucharist: The Banquet in the Early Christian World* and Matthias Klinghardt's *Gemeinschaftsmahl und Mahlgemeinschaft: Soziologie und Liturgie fruehchristlicher Mahlfeiern*, both independently established early Christian meals as a part of a much larger phenomenon in the first-century Mediterranean world, that of the Greco-Roman banquet.[1] They discovered a huge trove of literary and archaeological evidence that demonstrated a common pattern of behavior and meaning throughout the Hellenistic Mediterranean world when a wide variety of groups convened for meals. Both Klinghardt and Smith have proceeded to show thoroughly how early Christian literature's portrait of Christians eating together fits this larger Hellenistic pattern.[2] This material will be summarized in this chapter.

Following the summary of the new research, the place of early Christian meals within the larger Hellenistic meal convention is situated in the corpus of New Testament and other early Christian texts. The chapter then considers the social significance of these meals—both "Christian" and other—for the innovative and controversial Greco-Roman era, a consideration that chapters 4–7 take on in its full implications for a new sketch of early Christianity.

The Meal as a Central Element of Hellenistic Mediterranean Society

When people gathered for meals in first-century Mediterranean cultures, the event was laden with meaning. Meals were highly stylized occasions that carried significant social coding, identity formation, and meaning making. Participating in a meal entailed entering into a social dynamic that confirmed, challenged, and negotiated both who the group as a whole was and who the individuals within in it were.

That is, meals in general were about much more than eating.[3] This, of course, is true of most societies. But it was elaborately the case for the first-century Mediterranean in ways that surpass meal significance in many other cultures. The role meals played in the convergence of a number of different cultures in the first-century Mediterranean and a long historical continuity of meal practice within several of these cultures—as will be discussed later in this chapter—heightened the meanings of meals substantially at this time and place.

One distinction—already footnoted in chapters 1 and 2—makes the place of "meals" even clearer. This book, in keeping with already established vocabulary within scholarship about the ancient Mediterranean, uses the word *meal* to denote the frequent occasion of people gathering from different residences to eat festively. In other words, for our purposes a meal is not to be understood as the twice- or thrice-daily occasions for eating. Eating several times a day occurred in the ancient world in quite informal and varied manners that were not primarily social. Or, as Plutarch noted in this same era: "A witty and sociable person said after a solitary meal, 'I have eaten, but not dined today,' implying that a dinner always requires friendly sociability for seasoning."[4]

On the other hand, quite frequently—but not several times a day—people of various stripes gathered from various households to eat festively while reclining. This event has been called alternately a "meal" or a "banquet." There are advantages to both terms. The major disadvantages to the term *banquet* are that it connotes infrequency and wealth, neither of which characterizes the social occasions for eating so prevalent in the Hellenistic Mediterranean. The term *meal* is also not perfect because it connotes ordinariness, and the widespread Hellenistic eating practice referred to here was explicitly designed to be special. Keeping the tension between "not ordinary" and "frequent" indicates best the character of these meals. They were indeed a regular part of the daily rhythm of life, although it was not usual for a particular person to participate in such a meal every day. Rather, the possibility of being a part of such a gathering existed every day and was most likely realized up to several times a week by numerous persons, depending on one's social standing.[5]

If not so obtuse, the best word for this "meal" practice would be the literal meaning of a form of the Greek word *kline* used for the occasion in much of the literature, the "reclining" or the "couch." Using "reclining" for this Hellenistic meal/banquet would almost perfectly connote the appropriate meaning in that it would suggest both leisure and eating without the implications of luxury or ordinariness of the other terms.

The Basics of the Hellenistic Meal

Congruent with their wide meaning-making functions, the meals served a variety of other purposes. A gathering of friends, a birthday, a school session, a religious celebration, a club meeting, the anniversary of a death, a wedding, and a visit from out of town were among the formal and informal occasions for gathering at a meal. Often, the many clubs or associations existing in this era (as discussed in chapter 5) would have meals on a regular basis of every several weeks or monthly. Schools organized around a particular teacher or teaching would often meet more than once a week for a meal. Meals on specific religious occasions were also frequent, with hosts not being particularly loyal to just one god or set of gods. The gathering of friends at meals was considered a noble occasion on its own without need for any further outward occasion.

One striking aspect of Smith's and Klinghardt's respective volumes on these meals is that, despite the very diverse occasions for these meals and the relatively wide range of cultures around the Hellenistic Mediterranean, all the meals looked very similar. As Dennis Smith summarizes: "Formal meals in the Mediterranean culture of the Hellenistic and Roman periods, the period encompassing the origin and early development of Christianity, took on a homogeneous form. Although there were many minor differences in the meal customs as practiced in different regions and social groups, the evidence suggests that meals took similar forms and shared similar meanings and interpretations across a broad range of the ancient world."[6] Matthias Klinghardt notes clearly that this conclusion (with which he agrees) stands over against earlier scholarship's division of meal types between both Jewish and Hellenistic and private and associational meals. He insists that there is "no difference between Hellenistic-pagan and Jewish community meals" and that "it is not advisable to separate the consideration of private and association mealtimes."[7]

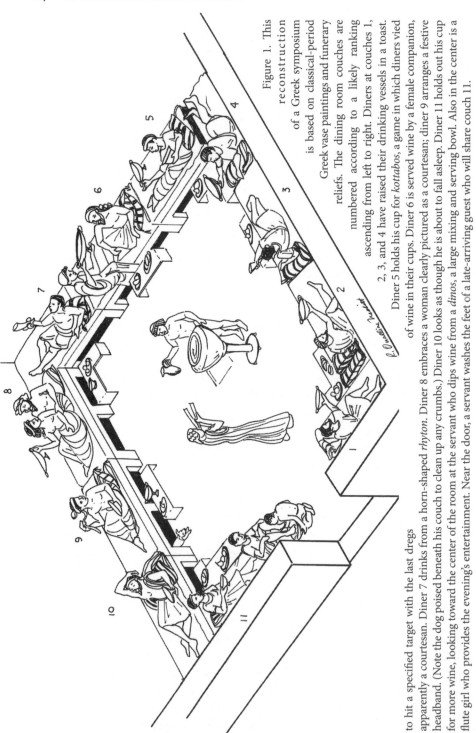

Figure 1. This reconstruction of a Greek symposium is based on classical-period Greek vase paintings and funerary reliefs. The dining room couches are numbered according to a likely ranking ascending from left to right. Diners at couches 1, 2, 3, and 4 have raised their drinking vessels in a toast. Diner 5 holds his cup for *kottabos*, a game in which diners vied to hit a specified target with the last dregs of wine in their cups. Diner 6 is served wine by a female companion, apparently a courtesan. Diner 7 drinks from a horn-shaped *rhyton*. Diner 8 embraces a woman clearly pictured as a courtesan; diner 9 arranges a festive headband. (Note the dog poised beneath his couch to clean up any crumbs.) Diner 10 looks as though he is about to fall asleep. Diner 11 holds out his cup for more wine, looking toward the center of the room at the servant who dips wine from a *dinos*, a large mixing and serving bowl. Also in the center is a flute girl who provides the evening's entertainment. Near the door, a servant washes the feet of a late-arriving guest who will share couch 11.

Figure 2: This reconstruction of a Roman banquet in a triclinium is based on a Roman-era mosaic floor (now on display at the Pergamon Museum in Berlin). The mosaic's design marked the area along the dining room walls where three couches were to be arranged in the typical Π shape, holding a total of nine diners. As in the Greek symposium, the couches generally marked rank ascending from the left to the right; but the custom evolved of placing the highest-ranking guest at position 6, where the middle couch joined the lower couch. This position was designated *locus consularis*, "the consul's position" (Plut., *Quaest. Conv.* 1.3). The host could be placed either at position 1 at the highest table (as in Petronius's depiction of the banquet of Trimalchio, *Sat.* 31.8; Smith, *Cena Trimalchionis*, 66–67), or, more commonly, at position 7 at the lowest table (and thus close to *locus consularis*). Here the three diners at the low table are all women, following a reference in Lucian's Symposium in which the women at a wedding banquet all reclined on the same couch (Luc. *Symp.* 8). The musicians in the center of the room providing the entertainment and the style of the tables in front of the couches are based on a fifth-century-C.E. Roman banquet scene.

Both Klinghardt and Smith detail how meals around the Mediterranean shared a very similar order and sequence of the evening, food types, invitations, dining rooms, leadership, placement of guests and participants, entertainment, and ceremonial and informal drinking.[8] As will be examined later, both also find quite similar social dynamics at the meals for the diverse occasions and in their various cultural settings.[9]

Although this chapter cannot dwell on all the specifics of these studies, it is important to note the basic dimensions of what Smith and Klinghardt's studies propose as a clear typology of the Hellenistic meal. They include the following:

- the reclining of (more or less) all participants while eating and drinking together for several hours in the evening
- the order of a supper (*deipnon*) of eating, followed by an extended time (*symposion*) of drinking, conversation, and performance
- marking the transition from *deipnon* to *symposion* with a ceremonial libation, almost always wine
- leadership by a "president" (*symposiarch*) of the meal—a person not always the same, and sometimes a role that was contingent or disputed
- a variety of marginal personages, often including servants, uninvited guests, "entertainers," and dogs.

So although the occasions for these meals ranged greatly, the shape of the meal was strikingly similar for all of the meals.[10] These five central characteristics of the Hellenistic meal are extensively analyzed in terms of ritual theory and elaborated in chapter 4.

The Social Dynamics of the Hellenistic Meal

Participating in these meals was a significant part of shaping many people's place in society. They provided social structure and processes for identity formation, distinctions or conflations of status, and articulation of meaning. Consideration of some of the more complex ways the Hellenistic meal configured social roles and meaning must await chapter 4's consideration of how recent ritual and performance theory illuminates some of the meal dynamics. The main outlines of the social dynamics of the meal, however, have been clearly identified by Klinghardt and Smith.

Klinghardt approaches this issue by identifying the social "values of the meals."[11] For him, the Mediterranean-wide agreement about how a meal occurred and its clearly articulated order of events and persons reflect an "indissoluble" connection to a set of clear social values expressed and consolidated in the meal.[12] These values are as follows:

- community (*koinonia*)
- equality and friendship (*isonomia* and *philia*)
- grace/generosity/beauty (*charis*) expressed as utopian political values

In establishing each of these as social values of the meal, Klinghardt takes pains to connect them to specific larger social (and sometimes political) realities. His arguments are worth summarizing.

According to Klinghardt: "There is absolutely no question that 'community' is the one central value and the decisive category" for understanding Hellenistic meals.[13] He writes: "In the major meal texts the problem for meal participants' *koinonia* is time and again social prestige, which endangers *koinonia* itself. It is important to remember the problem of the order of those reclining, the division of the food portions, the sequential order of the honors and toasts, the question of who is the president for the evening, the issue of who provides financial support for whom. All of these details were regulated in order to enable, or even to guarantee, community."[14]

In other words, the social value of community/*koinonia* was reinforced through the appropriate arrangements of food, reclining order, shared leadership, and finances of the meal itself. Klinghardt observes that during the last stages of classic Hellenic culture and the early moments of the Hellenistic era, the idea that the institutions of the classical Greek city-states would themselves enact the social value of community/ *koinonia* deteriorated and was finally abandoned.[15] So all of the wider hopes for the enactment of community within broader society then narrowed in on the meal itself. As the political ideals of classical Greek city-states faded, the meal became the Mediterranean's main hope for community.[16]

The character of community at the meals was posed pointedly in the Greco-Roman literature in its consideration of the values of equality/*isonomia* and friendship/*philia*. The explicit ranking of those reclining (the honored places were to the right of the president) and the frequent practice of giving those of higher rank more food usually reflected the order of the community or of the larger society. But since the meal was to express and extend community, how was one to understand the ranking of those reclining or when some meal participants received more or better food than others? Did not the close relationship between community and friendship stand in tension with such ranking and privilege? And, according to some of the wisest philosophers, did not friendship necessitate equality?[17] The intense claim of community in the shape and stability of the Hellenistic meal pushed those at the meals toward more explicit values of equality of food portions and interrogation of reclining rankings.

The term *philia* is translated equally well as "friendship" or "love." In any case, *philia* became a commonly asserted value of those who reclined together at meals. From Plato to Plutarch,[18] the challenge of the relationship between friendship and equality was worked out most directly in terms of how everyone ate together, who reclined where, and whether everyone received equal portions of food. So in the cases of the social values of friendship and equality, the meals exhibited them without resolving some of the implicit tensions of these values with larger societal codes of honor and prestige.

Klinghardt entitles his section on the social value of *charis* as "*Charis* as Expression of Symposial-Political Utopia." The term *charis* is used extensively as a primary descriptor of the intended spirit of the Hellenistic meal. But as Klinghardt notes:

> The field of meaning of "*charis*" is so broad that it is hardly possible to translate in one single German[19] idea (the best derivation seems to be "grace" or "charm"). *Charis* includes most of the values associated with the symposium. Festivity and joy (*thalia, euphrosune*) belong to these values as much as cheerful rest does. Reflectivity (*sophrosune*) and order for the good (*eukosmia, kosmos*), peace and riches (or at least prosperity) are connected to *charis*. Also the opposite end of giving and receiving, *pistis* (trust) and *koinonia* (community), as well as *eusebeia* (godliness), can be synonyms of *charis*.[20]

Such a strange and extensive set of synonyms for one notion might at first seem confusing or vacuous, but Klinghardt's keen social reading makes sense of the wide-ranging composite of *charis* as meal value: "The meal is a concrete utopia for community. The idealization of the meal becomes the basis for blueprints of governmental theory."[21] But it was not just the rhetoric about and within the meal that made the meal a major social paradigm, according to Klinghardt. The way these meals emphasized the richness and extensiveness of the food available represented a society that had all it needed. Providing meal participants with all they desired to eat was a way "to identify the basics of the ideal society with the symposium."[22]

It is in this section on *charis* as utopian value within the meal that Klinghardt also treats the plethora of literary references associating peace with these meals. Meals became particular moments for rhetoric against the evils of war.[23] Indeed, it was considered a violation of the meal ethos to recite legends of war. Among others, Klinghardt quotes Anakreon: "I do not love the one, who while drinking, when the cup is full, speaks of fighting and tear-rich war."[24] He also cites Theognis's meal portrait to this effect: "The lyre should play a holy melody, as well as the flute. We bring the gods offerings here. To drink, to talk about lovely things with one another, not fearing the warring of the Medes."[25]

Here, too, it was not just the speeches at the meals praising the meal for its value of love and peace among its participants. Rather, the behavior of the participants itself symbolized a perfect world. This, of course, was remarkable, since meals—especially during the wine-dominated symposium—were often occasions for rowdiness and disputes. The meals' leaders and commentators were vigilant against such disturbances, since, as Homer put it, inebriation creates conflict, which "disgraces the festive meal."[26] Associations, as we will see in chapter 5, also took pains to regulate meal disturbances through both rules and rhetoric about the virtues of peace and the vices of war.

Klinghardt's explicit social and even political reading of *charis* as meal value is telling. It connects directly to three matters considered later in this book: (1) chapter 4 returns to what Klinghardt has called the social idealization of these meals, when it considers the ways rituals negotiate social order; (2) chapter 5 notices how Jewish monotheism and particularly a Hellenistic Jewish understanding of scriptures (e.g., Isaiah 25) reinforced and complemented what Klinghardt calls the "utopian" picture enacted at meals; and (3) chapter 6 portrays many of these meals—especially, but not only, the early Christian ones—as acts of sociopolitical resistance against Roman imperial oppression.

Klinghardt's identification of social values at the heart of the Hellenistic meal opens up new horizons for thinking about the place of the meal in that larger set of ancient cultures. It is especially impressive in its methodology in that Klinghardt uses indigenous Hellenistic terms to describe the social values of the meals. Later in this chapter, this identification of social meal values helps us to rethink the role of meals in Christian beginnings. However, as chapter 4's examination of the social negotiating dynamic of rituals will show, framing the social character of meals by considering the values therein may oversimplify somewhat the social dynamic itself of these meals.

Dennis Smith's discussion of the social dynamics of the meals is somewhat less static. Instead of identifying social values, Dennis Smith proposes five different actions that the meals effect:

- social boundaries
- social bonding
- social obligation
- social stratification
- social equality

One notices the more dynamic and less ideological character of Smith's analysis in that some of these actions are in tension with one another. So, for instance, that meals simultaneously can effect social boundaries and social bonding, or social stratification and social equality, could be seen as ideologically incompatible. Yet these categories of analysis highlight the meals' attention to the dynamics of bonding and boundary setting, of stratification and equality.

In discussing social boundaries within meals, Smith refers to anthropologist Mary Douglas (whose work is discussed in chapter 4 of this book) and concludes: "As Mary Douglas notes, the defining of boundaries is primary to the social code of banquets. That is to say, whom one dines with defines one's placement in a larger set of social networks. . . . The social code of the banquet represents a confirmation and ritualization of the boundaries that exist in a social situation."[27]

But this replication and reinforcement of social boundaries in no way minimizes the ways the meal connects people. Smith writes: "The act of dining together is considered to create a bond between diners. In the ancient world this symbolism was carried by various elements of the banquet, such as the sharing of common food or sharing from a common table or dish."[28] Indeed, the social connections were sometimes innovative and creative: "The banquet could also create ties that did not previously exist. One example is the Greek tradition of *xenia*, or the extending of hospitality to a stranger or foreigner, which usually meant inviting the stranger to one's table."[29] Chapter 7 discusses a similar creative dynamic in the meals as they elaborated different practices for relating to the uninvited guests.

Related to (but not the same as) social bonding for Smith is social obligation—in both the practice of and the rhetoric about the meal. This analysis focuses on what today's culture might simply call etiquette.

> But for the Greeks, what we moderns refer to as etiquette was part of the larger category of social ethics. While we tend to view etiquette as a convention of culture without significant connection to morality or ethics, the Greeks addressed banquet rules in the context of serious ethical discussion. They presented philosophical dialogues on "symposium laws" and catalogued meal behavior under ethical categories such as friendship, joy, or pleasure.[30]

Here Smith intersects with Klinghardt's attention to the social values of the meal.

Of great interest to this book's larger hypothesis of Christian meals as social experiments is Smith's analysis of the Hellenistic meals' simultaneous embodiment of social stratification and equality. This is a tension already encountered in Klinghardt's discussion of the values of *isonomia* and *philia* (equality and friendship).

Smith has carefully remained true to the meals' interest in "social ranking." He writes: "The banquet provided a significant means for one's status in society to be formally recognized and acknowledged."[31] Perhaps most dramatic as a social stratifier is the definitive act of the Hellenistic meal, the "reclining." According to Smith: "The act of reclining itself was a mark of one's rank in society: only free citizens were allowed to recline."[32] That one reclined made that person different and more honored than someone who did not have the time, occasion, or social station to do the same. As later chapters in this book explore, the general taboo against women and slaves reclining seems to have been quite regularly violated in a kind of social experimentation. But even the idea that a woman or slave may have reclined was based on reclining as a position of social leisure and privilege. On the one hand, Smith asserts that "the banquet provided a means to honor" the patron-client system of privileged persons, and on the other, he notes that in the Hellenistic era "clubs and associations were organized in such a way that individuals from a lower status in society could achieve a higher status designation at the club banquets based on their rank within the club."[33] The socially coded, symbolic significance of reclining in a defined group functioned then as a way of elaborating and experimenting with who had social status.

No wonder that this special privilege of reclining together both complements and stands in tension with the meals' interest in social equality. As Smith explains:

> Those who dined together were to be treated equally. This was a standard feature of ancient dining protocol. It functioned as an elaboration of the concept of social bonding at the meal and was a strong feature of banquet ideology at all levels of the data. The idea was that a meal that was shared in common and that created a sense of community among the participants should be one in which all could share equally and with full participation. In essence, then, a meal conceived in this way had the potential to break down social barriers and allow for a sense of social ordering internal to the group.[34]

The expansive and sometimes transgressive experimentation with who reclined and who did not made the meal a primary location for exploring new kinds of equality. This exploration was underlined by the new mix of social backgrounds among those who reclined together. Smith's categories of analysis help us understand this exploration. He characterizes the Hellenistic meal not just as exhibiting social values but also as negotiating the related but tensive meal actions of bonding, setting boundaries, being obliged, stratifying, and becoming equal. Chapter 4 places this extended exploration of equality in a theoretical frame of reference that makes sense of the spectrum of socially coded actions within the larger ritual vocabulary of the meal system itself.

It is astounding how both Smith's research and Klinghardt's research on the social dynamics of these meals have discovered an intense social meaning making. At one point, even their analytical vocabulary merges. Although Smith does not use the Klinghardt term *utopian*, he points to a very similar dynamic, and both share the use of the term *idealized* to refer to the social significance of the meal. Both Smith and Klinghardt refer to "the messianic banquet" as an earlier Israelite version of such politically relevant meal idealization.[35]

Even though each of these scholars uses somewhat different categories of social analysis, they point to very similar social dynamics in the meal. After encountering their research, one cannot avoid the conclusion that meals in the Hellenistic Mediterranean overall had strong social significance. As to the somewhat different analytical approaches, Klinghardt's has the strong advantages of staying within the actual ancient vocabulary of social values and of making—as is seen in the next section of this chapter—the socially creative character of early Christian meals obvious. Smith's analytical categories, on the other hand, do more justice to the meals' social dynamics.

Together (and astonishingly independent of each other), Smith's and Klinghardt's research provide information that in this book shifts some basic understandings of social identity in the Hellenistic age. Their work establishes (1) the clear picture of the Hellenistic meal as a major practice of that era and (2) the important social dynamics these meals fostered in relationship to the larger societal, cultural, and political formations of the time. It swings open a door into new social understandings of how early Christianity emerged.

Religious Dimensions of Hellenistic Meals

Since the role of religion in Hellenistic culture was quite different from religion in the twenty-first century, it is necessary to sketch the ways religious expression was a part of all Hellenistic meals. Whereas contemporary America tends to see meals as religious or secular, Hellenistic meals had a much more nuanced and complex relationship to religion. On the one hand, it is fair to say that all Hellenistic meals contained a relatively strong dose of religious vocabulary and behavior. For instance, all of them included the central libation, which divided the *deipnon* from the *symposion*. This libation was always dedicated to a god and served in many regards as a way of dedicating the whole evening. Similarly, it was rare that these meals would not include some kind of singing expressive of gratitude to or admiration of a god.

On the other hand, only in a minority of the cases did these religious expressions represent exclusive devotion to a particular god. They did, rarely, oblige the meal participants to ongoing relationship to the particular religious activities, and often those dining would switch religious loyalties from one meal to another. In addition, the meals were also full of what moderns would see as completely secular and often sacrilegious speech and behavior. It was not unusual for prayers to a god, sexual licentiousness, conversation about ordinary daily routines, and parlor games to occur side by side at the meals. Religious expression belonged to every meal, but so did a whole range of what moderns would consider secular activities.

Philip Harland summarizes this very nonmodern mix of religious and nonreligious behavior in the Hellenistic world in his work on Greco-Roman (meal) associations (to which chapter 5 will return in some detail):

> We need to realize that in employing terms such as "religious" and "religion" we are dealing with abstractions that allow us to conceptualize our subject; we are not dealing with objective realities that the groups and persons we are studying would necessarily isolate from other aspects of life. The modern compartmentalization of life into the political, economic, social, and religious does not apply to the ancient context, where "religion" was very much embedded within various dimensions

of daily life of individuals, whose identities were inextricably bound up within social groupings or communities. Within the Greco-Roman context, we are dealing with a worldview and way of life centered on the maintenance of fitting relations among human groups, benefactors, and the gods within the webs of connections that constituted society and the cosmos. To provide a working definition, "religion" or piety in antiquity had to do with appropriately honoring the gods and goddesses (through rituals of various kinds, especially sacrificial offerings) in ways that ensured the safety and protection of human communities (or groups) and their members. Moreover, the forms that such cultic honors (or "worship" to use a more modern term) could take do not necessarily coincide with modern or Western preconceptions of what being religious should mean.[36]

So Hellenistic meals' complex mix of what twenty-first-century Westerners would regard as religious and secular needs to be taken into account. Characterizing meals of that era as religious or secular would be a modern caricature and therefore would miss much of what these meals have to say about the social identities of the complex variety of persons in the Greco-Roman epoch.

The Societal Role of Hellenistic Meals in the Larger Greco-Roman Mediterranean

Smith and Klinghardt, however, do not address issues of the growing importance the meal had in the societal and political realms of the Hellenistic Mediterranean. This too deserves description to do justice to the role of meals in the development of early Christianity.

As is obvious from both Klinghardt's and Smith's citations, much of the meal customs were in place, at least in Greece, prior to the Hellenistic age. Both authors cite a number of Hellenic and classical Greek sources for the values and dynamics of the later Hellenistic meal. This is appropriate in that the Hellenistic era was in many ways derivative of the Hellenic and the classical. However, the larger place of the meal was much more important in the Hellenistic era, for two main reasons. First, the Roman Empire undertook successfully to spread "Greek" culture throughout the entire Mediterranean. Second, what was most likely an almost exclusively upper-class meal phenomenon in classical Greece spread substantially during the Hellenistic era to nonelite classes. This was most evident in the spread of these meals through the growth of Hellenistic associations (as will be detailed in chapter 5). So the meals' form, values, and dynamics were quite similar in the two eras, but the meal was both more widespread and socially dominant as a form in the Hellenistic period.

This larger importance of the meal in the Hellenistic era can also be examined from several other perspectives. The meals of the associations (discussed more expansively in chapter 5) intersected with larger political realities in crucial ways. I summarized this interaction in a 2002 book as follows:

> This culture-wide innovation of voluntary associations was precipitated by the long-term dominance of imperial rule in the Mediterranean. Tribal and national cohesion and identity entered a dramatic period of decline after Alexander the Great conquered so much of the Mediterranean and Near East and the subsequent invasions and rule of the Seleucids, the Egyptians, and, then most ambitiously, the Romans. These centuries of imperial domination dealt mortal blows to many of the ways extended families, clans, tribes, and nations gathered people together. The oppression of the various empires seriously undermined the ways people gathered in traditional associations based on blood and geography.
>
> Many of the empires attempted to replace traditional social groupings with their own organization. There were constant attempts to impose new kinds of social organization on the conquered peoples. Perhaps the most dramatic example of this in the long Roman rule of the Mediterranean was the wildly ambitious attempts of Rome to build complete new cities, based supposedly on the ideals and values of classic Greece and imposed on almost every area by conquest. These imperial attempts to replace many traditional groups of kinship and nationality with their own constructs had limited success.
>
> The combination then of the destruction of traditional groups and the resistance to imperially imposed institutions resulted in a lack of social cohesion and identity among the populace throughout the Roman Empire. In the wake of these combined forces of social chaos, a new kind of social association emerged. This was the voluntary association, in which an individual chose[37] to belong to a group in contrast to being forced by the empire to be a part of some grouping or being able to claim a decimated family, tribal, or national social grouping.[38]

This cultural emergence of the associations in the Hellenistic era cannot be separated from the Hellenistic meal. The associations' main activity was the meal together. The meal constituted a major component of the social bonding for the association. (This very important development of associations as a dominant social organization is discussed in much greater detail in chapter 5.) To a certain extent, then, the Hellenistic meal itself became a replacement for the tribal, extended familial, and national assemblies. Similarly, the meal emerged in some quarters as an expression of resistance to Roman imperial institutions (see chapter 6 for a more detailed examination of this).

The semiprivate character of these meals proved to be a particularly evocative dimension of their societal and political influence in a world militarily occupied by an imperial power. To a certain extent, these meals were private in that a private individual almost always hosted them and the invitations were directed to either private individuals or members of an association. On the other hand, people from the public sphere permeated the meals with relative ease, and there was often a certain element of display inherent in the meals themselves. For instance, regularly these meals had to contend with uninvited guests, who often actually successfully negotiated staying for the meal. In addition, as has already been demonstrated by Klinghardt, the meals were often seen explicitly as models for larger society. The more private aspect of the meal served as a protection against the empire intervening in this social (and sometimes anti-imperial) experimentation.[39] At the same time, the semipublic aspect of the meal made it into an occasion for display of its social values. In the rhetoric of and about the meal, in the performances at the meal, and in the porous boundaries of the meal attendance, the meal was projected onto society as a model, or at least an event, in which societal issues were at stake in symbolic terms.[40]

The semiprivate nature of the meals suggests that they were in some ways social laboratories. They were protected enough to allow for real experiments yet open enough for the larger society to notice what occurred within them. Hellenistic society straddled an historical gap in which neither the artificially and forcefully imposed social institutions of Rome nor the decimated social remains of national or tribal associations held sway. In this gap, the meal developed a strong loyalty and an extended field of influence.

Methodological Issues in Using Ancient Texts to Describe Ancient Social Practices

It is important now to address briefly a clear methodological difficulty for any effort to discuss social dynamics and practice in the ancient Mediterranean world. Scholarship in the past twenty years has become much more careful in deriving social descriptions from ancient texts. This justifiable care results mostly from several hard-earned lessons concerning problems with taking ancient texts' representations of social practice at face value. These lessons are as follows:

1. Many texts portray social practice in certain ways for ideological purposes. The texts often idealize, vilify, and contort practices in order to impose the authors' own opinions on the reader.

2.   Often, texts refer to only one particular class or region's social practice but do not say so. The variation in social practices according to class and region is then often intentionally or unintentionally concealed.
3.   For some social practices, there are not enough texts to obtain a thorough enough description.

Because these lessons seem hard-won and clear, it is my general opinion that describing ancient social practice based on ancient texts is unreliable.

There are two reasons for taking seriously the body of ancient literature purporting to describe Hellenistic meal practice. First, the scope of literature surveyed by Smith and Klinghardt (and their scholarly predecessors) is deep and broad, spanning a variety of regions, classes, and circumstances with multiple versions from multiple perspectives.[41] Second, the ancient literature about meals has been supported by discoveries of artifacts, epigraphs, and archaeological dining sites. Both Smith and Klinghardt discuss this evidence in detail.

Of course, the result of this discovery of extensive ancient literature, artifacts, epigraphs, and sites is not a completely unified one. It is, however, the common virtues of both Klinghardt's and Smith's standards of investigation and assessment to take seriously the complexity of the evidence and nevertheless to produce an overview. In other words, the works of Smith and Klinghardt take the hard-earned lessons about the problematic character of ancient literary descriptions into account, achieving in this way a rare, thick description of an ancient social practice.

The Pervasive Place of Meals in the First Hundred Years of Christian Literature

The relationship between meals and the first hundred years of Christian literature is multifaceted and extensive. These documents—most of which are in the New Testament—both depend on and are replete with references to the meals of early Christians.

Perhaps the most overlooked and the most basic relationship between this literature and meals is that the meals provided a primary location for the reading of the early Christian documents. Again, there is little dispute in scholarship that the writings of the first hundred years were read primarily at the meals of these communities. It is just that scholarship has not noticed that this location for reading the early Christian literature both confirms the social significance of the meals and frames in an important way the meanings of the writings themselves.

The most obvious kind of document read at the meals was the letter. This most frequent genre of early Christian writing was explicitly written for the meals. The letters of Paul were written to communities of mostly illiterate persons. These people gathered in the name of Christ almost exclusively at meals. It is very clear from Paul's letters that he is not writing to a small, exclusively educated or representative subset of the communities in Corinth, Galatia, Philippi, Rome, or Thessalonica. Rather, he means his letters to be heard by all of the members of the communities. This could have been accomplished only by reading the letters at the variety of meal gatherings in each of the cities. The same applies to the letters of "Peter,"[42] "John,"[43] and Ignatius of Antioch.

Other documents, like the Didache, were written explicitly as manuals of behavior for local communities. The Didache, in contrast to the letters of Paul and others, seems to have targeted not one particular community but rather a larger set of such communities. Here also, the preponderance of meal gatherings, recognized in the Didache itself, provided the perfect set of audiences for such early Christian manuals.

For the past century, New Testament scholarship has been identifying a number of hymns or songs imbedded within the texts of particular letters, gospels, and apocalypses. This has been mostly a matter of literary study identifying hymnic patterns in fragments within the overall texts, without reflecting on the question of where such hymns or songs would be sung. The studies of Klinghardt and Smith now make it clear that these hymns were sung by those attending meals. From their studies, it is obvious that when Paul writes to the Corinthians, "When you come together, each one has a hymn, a lesson, a revelation, a tongue, or an interpretation" (1 Cor. 14:26), he is referring to standard behavior at a *symposion*. Or, as Dennis Smith comments on this text: "This is reminiscent of the philosophical banquets attended by Aulus Gellius where each guest brought a topic for discussion at the symposium."[44] So it is now possible to understand the hymns that occur in Luke, John, Romans, 1 Corinthians, Ephesians, Philippians, Colossians, 1 Timothy, Hebrews, and the Revelation to John as socially located within the meal gatherings of early Christians.

When the social location of both the many letters of early Christianity and the plethora of hymns is identified as the meal, the classic identification of Phil. 2:6-11 as a hymn becomes all the more interesting. Most scholars assume, with good reason, that verses 6-11 were a hymn already written and which Paul quotes in chapter 2.[45] When one takes seriously the meal as the location for both the letter and the hymn, however, one has to wonder whether, when Paul's letter was read at meals, the hymn of 6-11 was sung when the reading came to that part of the letter.

Still other writings, such as the Revelation to John, had a propensity for drama and performance. Adela Yarbro Collins has proposed that the Revelation to John was performed for the different communities it addressed in western Asia Minor.[46] This was not at all an unusual thing to occur at meals. Indeed, performances of some kind were the norm during the *symposion* part of the meal. Such performances were not limited just to the playing or singing of music. Rather, especially in the meals of the associations, relatively elaborate theatrical productions were frequent. These productions often featured dance[47] or pantomime.[48] Central to such productions were dramatic enactments of the deeds and relationships of the gods. The Statutes of the Iabakchoi describe members and perhaps performers in such a symposial drama.[49]

In *Crisis and Catharsis*, Yarbro Collins has charted how the drama within the text of the Revelation to John could have functioned for the members of the Christian communities of western Asia Minor to help them reorient themselves under a variety of imperial and societal pressures. This nuanced study of Revelation came before some of the recent sensitivity to the presence of drama at Hellenistic meals. Although Yarbro Collins does not seem to be particularly aware of performances at meals, her study of the Revelation text has developed a communal rationale for members performing the cosmic drama when they gather.

As Klinghardt and Smith's research paints the clear picture of early Christian hymns and performances at meals, the creative role of meals in the composition of the gospels opens up. This comes into focus through several research lenses. First of all, of course, it coheres with the larger picture of the Hellenistic meal in which different individuals bring a variety of stories, sayings, songs, and speeches during the *symposion*. Second, when one asks the question where early Christian gospels were read, the meals are the most plausible location. The same rationale applies to the gospels as to the letters and instruction manuals—that is, since these documents were obviously written for a broad spectrum of people, including a very substantial percentage of poorer people who did not themselves know how to read, the regular meal gathering of the various early Christian communities became the main place for the audience to hear the gospels. This was all the more the case since the porous boundaries of the meals also allowed for some people beyond the core meals community to hear the gospel stories, and at least some parts of the gospels display an interest in an audience beyond the primary community membership.[50]

Third, the past thirty years of research on how gospels were composed points toward the meal as well. The discovery and analysis of Hellenistic rhetorical manuals in the last scholarly generation has helped scholars understand some of the (especially pregospel) composition process of the first-century documents like the gospels. These manuals, called *Progymnasmata*, detail how people learned to elaborate short sayings into lengthier stories and treatises.[51] This elaboration occurred orally in school-like settings. It involved taking an inherited short, clever saying, called a *chreia*, and adding rationale, contrast, comparison, rephrasing, and other details to the saying in a set of oral exercises. When one asks where such oral exercises occurred, the evidence is almost singular in its suggestion.

The classical literature on the *symposion* portrayed this extended meal setting as a school setting.[52] That is, although the image of the meal as a school is counterintuitive for twenty-first-century sensibilities, the meal was a primary school location for the ancient Mediterranean. Once this setting is understood, the enormous creative potential for such learning comes into view. The combination of the structured learning exercises of the *Progymnasmata* and the lively repartee of the symposial atmosphere certainly allowed both a framework for composition and an improvisational and elaborative creativity, as the *chreiae* were reworked into longer units. When applied to gospel material, it becomes quite clear that the meals provided the conventional location for the communal and school-like composition of subgospel units.

So, for instance, the Matthean elaboration of the Beatitudes, in which four blessings drawn from Q become nine, would have been a classic exercise/interaction at the early Christian meals where schools met. Similarly, the ways various conflict stories became vehicles for a clever *chreia*-like saying (e.g., Mark 2:15-17 is a story of a conflict of Jesus and Pharisees *at a meal* in which the conflict is resolved with the *chreia* about how the sick, not those who are well, need a physician) would have happened organically within a "school" meal following *Progymnasmata* structure and carrying the meal energy of social experimentation. That is, the *symposion* would have begun with the *chreia* about the physician, the well, and the sick; and then those reclining would have elaborated—per the *Progymnasmata*-prescribed exercises—the *chreia* into the story about the meal controversy.

This same pattern also occurs less than a chapter later where a story of the healing of a man with a withered hand seems to have been elaborated out of first a *chreia* about the Sabbath being made for humankind and not the inverse, and a controversy story about picking grain (Mark 2:23—3:5).[53] This elaborative process also could very well have been projected into units as long as Mark 4:1-33, the majority of which has been seen by many scholars as a pregospel unit on parables and parabolic units.[54]

Much of first-century Christian literature, then, was intensely related to the meal gatherings of early Christians as a primary location for reading to the community. The scope of this "reading" at meals, as has been noted above, was broad in that it involved not simply the reading of the finished documents but often some kind of performance of the texts and the actual composition of many of the gospel subunits. Although one can feature some other locations at which some of this literature may have been occasionally read (e.g., single literate persons reading it alone or occasional rhetorical readings in an agora or forum), the meals were by far the most likely location for such "reading." Given this centrality of meals in Christian articulation and in the reading of important writings to the communities, the significance of this formative event becomes all the more important. Not only did the meal play an important role in social experimentation, but it also shaped the writings and provided a primary contextual framework for their meanings.

In optics slightly different from those of Smith and Klinghardt, several other scholars in the past thirty years have seen the centrality of meals for reimagining early Christianity's emergence. James Breech's pivotal work *The Silence of Jesus* saw the meals of the historical Jesus as the primary datum one has about who Jesus of Nazareth was. Breech's radical minimalism in terms of what the historical Jesus may have taught was offset by his interest in the meaning of Jesus' meals. Breech indeed saw the social framework of Jesus' meals as the only Jesus primary datum but also the primary meaning of the historical Jesus.

In a similar but less minimalist manner, John Dominic Crossan proposed the term *commensality* as key to understanding the activity, the teachings, and the vision of the historical Jesus. In *The Historical Jesus*, Crossan used "commensality"[55] to describe a social program of Jesus in which an open meal was one of two[56] primary examples of "the kingdom of God." It was a radically inclusive meal where all were welcome and in which food was shared with everyone; Jesus promoted it as the place where God's new reign of unmediated justice became evident.

Finally, Burton Mack, in both *A Myth of Innocence* and *Who Wrote the New Testament?* proposed the meal as the place where teachings by the early Galilean Jesus movements, the pre-Pauline and Pauline communities, and the later gospel communities were elaborated, and where crucial new social experimentation occurred.[57] Mack is especially interested in how the martyr mythology of the Hellenistic Mediterranean was enacted at the meals with reference to the person of Jesus.

Perhaps at least as significant as the meal as the location for early Christian literature and articulation is the plethora of references to meals within the early Christian letters, gospels, manuals, and apocalypses—that is, it is not just that meals provide the crucial context for early Christian articulation and meaning making. The centrality of meals as an early Christian social institution also becomes apparent from the many different kinds of references to meals within the literature itself. Indeed, one can find the entire scope of meal activity and meaning making within the first one hundred years of Christian literature. What follows is an overview of early Christian literature in terms of the basics of the common meal tradition outlined by Klinghardt and Smith. This overview shows how the literature addressed the following issues: the food and drink of the meals, the location of the meals, behavior at the meals, the constituency of the meals, and the ethics of the meal. As each issue is examined, it becomes clear that the early Christian literature not only takes food, drink, location, and behavior of these meals seriously as realia in its world. Rather, these dimensions of meals have for this literature important and often disputed social significance for the larger society and the self-understandings of early Christians themselves.

THE FOOD AND DRINK OF THE MEALS

A variety of New Testament texts display a concern for what one does and does not eat at meals. This concern for what food was appropriate to eat was not by and large in terms of health concerns. Rather, in each case, the food that is forbidden or permitted has a social and sometimes religious significance.[58] This attention to what to eat is not just an early Christian concern but is reflected in much of Hellenistic literature in which the amounts and kind of food are discussed and debated extensively.

The focus of Romans 14 and 15 is a controversy about which people in that community ate meat and which did not. Paul asserted that those who ate meat considered themselves superior ("strong") compared to those who did not: "Some believe in eating anything, while the weak eat only vegetables. Those who eat must not despise those who abstain, and those who abstain must not pass judgment on those who eat; for God has welcomed them" (14:2-3). Most commentators see this dietary debate as related to Jewish restrictions about the eating of certain meat. In particular, this meat could have been pork or shellfish, forbidden as foodstuff by the Torah, or any meat that had not been properly slaughtered, according to one or another Jewish interpretation of the day. In the meals of those addressed by Paul in this letter, there seem to have been people who did not abide by these restrictions on eating meat as well as persons who did. Paul's letter shows concern about how what people were eating and not eating affected their sense of community at the meals. His advice to these diners appears to have been that, for the sake of meal community, everyone at these meals should refrain from eating meat: "Let us therefore no longer pass judgment on one another, but resolve instead never to put a stumbling block or hindrance in the way of another. I know and am persuaded in the Lord Jesus that nothing is unclean in itself; but it is unclean for anyone who thinks it unclean. If your brother or sister is being injured by what you eat, you are no longer walking in love. Do not let what you eat cause the ruin of one for whom Christ died" (14:13-16).

Acts 15 tells a story of a meeting in Jerusalem among Paul, Peter, James, and others to think about a similar set of tensions at meals, experienced—according to Acts 15—by a relatively wide range of meal gatherings of early Christians. In this story, differences between Jews and Gentiles in "Christian" community were to be addressed by the meeting at Jerusalem.[59] Primary among the disagreements had been circumcision. But the main "solution" for these differences turned around what early Jewish and gentile Christians should eat when they gather together, and this solution was different from Paul's recommendation in Romans. Acts 15 has James having proposed the following compromise: "Therefore I have reached the decision that we should not trouble those gentiles who are turning to God, but we should write to them to abstain only from things polluted by idols and from fornication and from whatever has been strangled and from blood" (15:19-20). In other words, the main practice all Christians were to have in common was eating together, and their food included a wide variety but abided by certain limitations of Torah.

It may be that the controversy Paul discusses in 1 Corinthians 8 and 10 was related to the debates in Acts and Romans about what to eat. In 1 Corinthians, what is at stake is whether the Corinthians for their meal gatherings should have bought meat that had been slaughtered in temples of various gods. It is clear from the several treatments of this issue in 1 Corinthians that a number of Christian meal gatherings in Corinth did serve such meat. It is not quite so clear what Paul's recommendation was. Indeed, it appears that he recommended different approaches: (1) do not purchase or eat such meat for the community meals because that implies worship of the gods to whom the animals were sacrificed (see 10:14-21); (2) eat the meat so as not to offend those who have purchased it, and thus risk rupturing the meal community (see 10:31-33); and (3) if you do not know that the meat has been sacrificed to such a god, it is permissible to buy and eat it, but if you do know that is has been sacrificed to such a god, out of consideration for others one should not eat it (see 10:23-30). For this survey, making sense of Paul's various proposals is less important than noting that here, too, these New Testament texts consider what food the communities ate to be very important. In direct parallel to Romans 14 and 15 and Acts 15, the food issues in 1 Corinthians 8 and 10 are immediately related to the quality and character of relationships in the meal community.

Drinking wine and eating bread at the same meal is mentioned in the four "Last Supper" texts of the New Testament and in the instructions of the Didache. Wine is the basic "food" element of the *symposion*. The earliest of these texts, 1 Cor. 11:24-25, which Paul may have understood as a formula handed down to him by his teachers, explicitly evokes the patterns of the Hellenistic meal.[60] It calls for a blessing over the bread during the *deipnon* and the dedicating of the first cup of the *symposion* to a god, both of which are standard at the Hellenistic meal. Bread was standard and central fare for the *deipnon*, both as a food and as "napkin" and "utensil" to clean one's hands and to pick up food. Mark's and Matthew's accounts follow the same meal order in their Last Supper pericopes. Luke's Last Supper text is garbled and has substantial manuscript problems. The earliest Lukan manuscripts have a cup before the bread. The later Lukan manuscripts have two cups, one on either side of the bread. The Didache, without reference to any Last Supper setting but referring for the first time in Christian literature to the meal as "eucharist" (9-10), has the cup of wine with a prayer preceding the prayer over the bread.[61] In all of these texts, the eating of bread and the drinking of wine were described in highly religious and social terms.

Other texts refer to bread and wine separately. John 2's story of the wedding at Cana refers to the participants drinking all of the wine that was available and then Jesus turning other water into wine. Susan Marks has shown that this kind of wine drinking at wedding feasts fit the general picture of Hellenistic meals.[62] Luke-Acts refers to what it calls the "breaking of bread" three explicit times, once at the end of the story when the disciples encounter the risen Jesus at a meal (Luke 24:30-35), again in a picture of the early postresurrection believers in Jerusalem gathering for meals (Acts 2:46), and in a story about Paul at meal on the first day of the week in Troas. In Acts 27:35, Paul is portrayed as convening a meal on a threatened ship, wherein only the breaking of bread is portrayed as an official act. And, without the verb "to break," Luke 14:1 uses *phagein arton* (to eat bread) to designate an entire meal. These Lukan portraits do fit the general Hellenistic meal pattern but may also reflect a technical Lukan usage of "breaking of bread" as a specific term for their community meal gathering.[63] Although not quite explicitly about bread and wine, the Q-based characterization of Jesus as a "glutton and drunkard" (Matt. 11:19; Luke 7:34) certainly connects to wine and food, the Hellenistic banquet, and a wide range of Hellenistic critique of those who were thought to be abusing the banquet tradition.[64]

Finally, in the gospels, we have six different, relatively parallel stories of Jesus miraculously feeding thousands of people at a time. Both Mark and Matthew have parallel stories of five thousand and four thousand, while Luke and John both only have one story each. The food in these stories is bread and fish. These texts seem to place little emphasis on the significance of the food itself. Dennis Smith notices that even though these feedings are pictured as outside events, "when Jesus hosts the miraculous meals outdoors, they become reclining banquets as well."[65] In a footnote to this, Smith studies the various uses of reclining verbs to indicate that the gospels mean these outdoor meals of fish and bread to be understood as commentaries on actual Hellenistic meals indoors.[66] As commentary, Paul Achtemeier has noted that these stories are pre-Markan and signify a connection between meals of pre-Markan meal gatherings and inclusion of marginalized populations in the meals themselves.[67]

All of these passages clearly belong to the portrait of Hellenistic meals sketched earlier in this chapter. Not only do the particular drink and foodstuffs fit, but so does the intense interest in reading social and ethical significance into the particularities of how the meals happened. Moreover, the breadth of mention of food and drink that references the meal gatherings of the early Christians testifies to the intense interest in these meals as a central social institution for early Christianity.

THE LOCATION(S) OF THE MEALS

The New Testament and other first-century Christian literature pay a good deal of attention to where meals were held. Their pictures of meal location fit the larger picture of where Hellenistic groups banqueted together. One location used by many Hellenistic groups does not seem to have been used by early Christians. The dining rooms that encircled almost all Hellenistic temples and were used by a wide variety of Hellenistic associations were almost certainly not locations for early Christian meals.[68]

With this one exception, the New Testament portraits of meal locations do cohere with the larger picture. These locations were primarily the dining rooms of relatively wealthy persons (since poor people's houses did not have dining rooms) and dining rooms that were rented out for a variety of groups.

Typical of the meals hosted by the wealthy in their own homes are the stories of Jesus eating at the homes of Zacchaeus (Luke 19:6-7), a leader of the Pharisees (Luke 14:1), Levi (Mark 2:15), Simon the leper (Mark 14:3), and Mary and Martha (Luke 10:38-40). Almost certainly, this arrangement was also envisaged in the sending out of the twelve (Mark 6:7-13 and parallels) and seventy (Luke 10:1-16), and the Didache's instructions for prophets wishing to speak to the community (13:1). In each of these cases, wandering sages were pictured as arriving at houses where they could announce their message during a meal of the host. Perhaps the most prominent rented location for a meal in the gospel stories is the so-called upper room (Mark 14:12-16 and parallels). Similar arrangements seem to have been the case regarding the meal encounter between Peter and Paul at Antioch (Gal. 2:11-14)[69] and in Corinth (11:34).[70] Meals texts like the wedding at Cana,[71] the gathering of the "weak" and the "strong" in Rome (Romans 14 and 15), and the Emmaus breaking of bread (Luke 24:28-30) are ambiguous as to whether there is a wealthy host or a rented facility.

BEHAVIOR AT THE MEALS

There is a wide swath of early Christian writing about what exactly people (should) do and say at their community meal gatherings. These writings are quite diverse, indicating most likely a relatively wide span of practice and perhaps even some disagreement about what was to be done and said. On the other hand, this diversity of practice among the different Christian meal gatherings represented in the various writings does fit within the overall behavioral patterns of the Hellenistic meal—that is, the places in the meals where there were differences in what the various early Christian communities did or said were the same places where we observe a variety of words and behavior in the Hellenistic meals in general. So, for instance, the variations in what different Hellenistic meal leaders said over the cup at the beginning of the *symposion* (e.g., on one occasion, a group might dedicate the evening to one god; on another occasion, to another god) are analogous to the variations in the Christian meals (e.g., at the beginning of the *deipnon*, Paul blesses the bread by calling it the body of Christ, whereas at the same point the Lukan gatherings have a special blessing and breaking of the bread without evoking the body of Christ at all).

It is, of course, important to understand that the texts do not necessarily represent actual meal behavior. On several levels, this reservation must be taken into account. Scholarship on the primary texts about ancient Mediterranean meals has been clear for some time that these texts cannot be taken at face value. They were often written in fictive voices, were mostly representative of only aristocratic socioeconomic settings, and participated in a range of literary hyperbole.[72] It is also the case that the historical accuracy of gospel texts has been long called into question, and this questioning of the gospel representations applies to at least two-thirds of the gospel texts about meals.[73] Even when scholars examine gospel texts about meals in terms of what information they might provide concerning the meals of the community to or from which the texts were authored, literary hyperbole, multiple social locations for the ancient document itself, and complex literary agendas and motivations must also be taken into consideration.

Even with these important cautions, however, this book suggests that these texts can be taken seriously as indirect historical sources about early Christian meals. Although every text must be cross-examined for the above reasons, there are two motivations for looking seriously at their historical value. First, the density of mention made of meal behavior in first-century Christian literature is impressive. Once one realizes the broad spectrum of meal motifs in the New Testament, it is difficult to dismiss them out of hand. For instance, the portrayal of meals and the use of meal metaphors are far more frequent than other equally everyday institutions in the Hellenistic Mediterranean, such as the home or commerce.

Second, and newly determinative since the research of Smith and Klinghardt, the ways that the early Christian discussion of meals fit the model of Hellenistic meal customs overall are striking and consistent—that is, the meal behavioral patterns in a wide range of Hellenistic literature, murals, vases, and archaeological sites researched by Klinghardt and Smith are consistently found in the early Christian literature. This indicates that the early Christian literature took seriously the social institution of meals of its day in the way it signified meaning for its audiences. This match between the established institution of the Hellenistic meal and the early Christian meal references makes them more valuable as historically significant documents relative to meal behavior itself. It is still mandatory to analyze these texts critically in terms of the above listed challenges to their historical reliability, but within that complex discipline, they potentially can add greatly to an approximate description of early Christian meal behavior.

This examination of meal behavior in early Christian literature is organized around the larger patterns of the Hellenistic meal. The meal behavior found in the first one hundred years of this literature can be understood as part of one of three dimensions of the standard Hellenistic meal: (1) general tasks or stances of the meal, (2) the *deipnon*, and (3) the *symposion*. Each set of early Christian references is surveyed under each of these dimensions.

First, the early Christian literary references to the general tasks or stances at meals need to be considered. As noted earlier, the standard word in the Hellenistic world for the meal is one or another form of "reclining." *Reclining* is the definitive word for Hellenistic meals and, indeed, the definitive behavior. As described earlier, reclining signified both leisure and status. To recline was an indication of privilege. It is this word that the New Testament uses so consistently to characterize the primary behavior of early Christian gatherings.

The participial, nominal, and regular active and passive verb forms of this root "to recline" crowd the New Testament and early Christian literature.[74] They are—with very few exceptions—all referring to dining. Curiously, they do not have a standard English translation. Most often, they are translated "at table," which adequately conveys the sense, if not the mood, of the Hellenistic meal. Less adequate, but still plausible, is the translation of "sitting" (Matt. 14:19 NJB). Unfortunately, often the translation of "sit" voids the action of a meal, which is clear in the Greek meaning of "recline." At other times, these root words meaning "to recline" are translated as "guests" (Mark 6:22 NRSV), "place" (Luke 14:8 NASB), and "were at home" (Mark 2:15 THE MESSAGE), obscuring the idea of a meal.

This obscuring of the prevalence of meals through translation of the early Christian texts also occurs in the Coptic. For instance, the *Gospel of Thomas*'s picture of a dispute between Salome and Jesus has Salome asking Jesus: "Why do you climb up on my couch?" In our day, this would surely imply a sexual encounter in bed, whereas in the ancient Mediterranean the issue was about a man and a woman eating together (see GThom 61).

In an ironic twist on the emphasis on reclining, there are also a few meal-related verbs that indicate a meal in the Greek but do not connote a meal in the English translation. Perhaps most classic in this absence of a meal connotation for a text of great importance in the history of Christian interpretation is the portrait in Luke 10:39 of "Mary, who sat at the Lord's feet and listened to what he was saying" (NRSV and almost all other translations). As is discussed more thoroughly in chapter 7, the practice of women sitting at the feet of those (men) reclining at a meal was a compromised position in some Hellenistic Mediterranean meals in which women participated in the symposial give-and-take without directly challenging the patriarchal privilege of reclining meals.

The other general task or stance in the Hellenistic meal that was treated at length in the New Testament and other first-century "Christian" literature was serving those who were reclining. This general task at the meal prompted a wide variety of reflection and social experimentation. In a number of cases, mention of serving at the meal was simply part of an overall description of one particular early Christian meal or another. But in even more cases, reference to service was the occasion for contemplating a reversal of status, in which serving others becomes as much a sign of the meal community as reclining does. For instance, Mark 10:43 portrayed Jesus as saying: "But it is not so among you; but whoever wishes to become great among you must be your servant."

The second kind of meal behavior found in the New Testament is that related to the specific actions done during the *deipnon*. That these meals described in the New Testament knew of the *deipnon* as the first part of the meal followed by the drinking *symposion* is obvious from one of the earliest texts, which is perhaps even earlier than Paul: "In the same way he took the cup also, after the *deipnon*, saying . . ." (1 Cor. 11:25).

The primary *deipnon* activity described in early Christian texts is the blessing of the bread. For instance, the passage just cited from 1 Corinthians 11 has Jesus giving a blessing over the bread. Similarly, in Mark 14:22 (and its Matthean and Lukan parallels), Jesus was pictured as blessing the bread and distributing it during the *deipnon*. The Didache (from the late first or early second century) instructed early Christians to give thanks for the bread at the *deipnon* (9:5). It is probably something akin to these blessings that the Lukan literature refers to as "the breaking of the bread"

(Luke 24:30, 31; Acts 2:46; 20:7, 11; 27:35), which would have also taken place during the *deipnon*.

The other *deipnon* activity discussed in early Christian literature is foot washing. John 13 not only portrays Jesus washing his followers' feet but also has him showing it as an action to be repeated by his followers for one another at their meals. Similarly, 1 Tim. 5:10 and Luke 7:36-50 speak of women washing feet at the *deipnon*. This location of foot washing during the *deipnon* is somewhat curious in that it was generally an activity that happened before the Hellenistic meal began and was accomplished by servants.[75] However, in both Luke 7 and John 13, it is an activity during the meal.[76]

Third, and most present in early Christian texts, are the activities of the *symposion* part of the meal. A number of these texts will be discussed in the section on the ethics of the meals below. Indeed, since the *symposion* was the part of the meal where most of the social interaction, community discussion, singing, and teaching occurred, almost all of what is examined in chapters 4–7 occurred during the *symposion* part of the meal. The Hellenistic *symposion* typically began with a wine libation to a god. This pattern's presence in the early Christian writings has been one of the keys to the discovery that early Christians understood themselves to have been taking part in a *symposion*. The classic text here—also mentioned above—is 1 Cor. 11:25: "He took the cup also, after the *deipnon*, saying, 'This cup is the new covenant.'" Similar references are found in both the Synoptics' story of the Last Supper and the Didache's instructions for a meal that was not meant to memorialize the Last Supper.[77]

As discussed earlier in the chapter's situating of the presentation of much (if not most) early Christian literature at meals, the *symposion* entailed much singing. The existence of early Christian songs embedded in the letters and gospels has already been noted above. But that is not the only way these songs and their place in the meals are known. For instance, that early Christians sang in the *symposion* is dramatically illustrated in Ephesians 5:19, which warns: "Do not get drunk with wine, for that is debauchery; but be filled with the Spirit, as you sing psalms and hymns and spiritual songs among yourselves, singing and making melody to the Lord in your hearts." Similar references are found in Matt. 23:28; Mark 26:30; 1 Cor. 14:26; Acts 16:25; and Col. 3:16.

The other *symposion* activity is discussed in the treatment by 1 Corinthians 14 of the speaking in tongues. This activity was clearly occurring during the *symposion* by virtue of the way Paul compares and contrasts this activity to other symposial behavior like singing (vv. 15 and 26), teaching (vv. 6, 19, and 26), and prophesying (vv. 4-6, 29, 31, 32, and 39). Nor were ecstatic experiences at the *symposion* a uniquely Christian activity. Although the specific experience of the spirit of (the Jewish) God enabling people to speak ecstatically may have been unique to the Corinthian assemblies, ecstatic expression also occurred in Dionysian and other symposia.[78]

The Constituency of the Meals

Although there were some debates in the larger corpus of Hellenistic literature about who should eat with whom,[79] the New Testament literature is especially charged with such discussions. Much of these considerations were part of the larger intellectual and relational labor of early Christianity in which the constituency (especially the new openness to marginalized people) of the meals became a symbolic assertion about the nature of the world itself.

Whether in the form of stories about Jesus or letters to specific communities, the Christian literature of the first century regularly advocated for inclusion at meals of people who for one reason or another had been kept outside. Invitation to meals of marginalized people in this literature addressed poor people, the lame, the blind, women, tax collectors, Jews, and gentiles.[80] By and large, each text focused on one specific inclusion.

Perhaps the earliest reproach to the Jesus movement relative to meal constituency was the accusation to have eaten "with tax collectors and sinners." In Q 7:34, Jesus' association with these two groups was directly paralleled with the allegation of his being "a glutton and a drunkard." Mark 2:15-17 was a controversy story, picturing Jesus among these two groups at a meal in Levi's house. Eating with tax collectors was a meal association with a group of outcasts of Galilean society. The meaning of eating with sinners has been much debated, with the major proposed scholarly interpretations being women, prostitutes, gentiles, and the ritually impure. In any case, it stands as one of the earliest characterizations of the Jesus movement's interest in inclusive meals, or what John Dominic Crossan calls "commensality."[81]

Attention to women's participation in meals includes the several different stories of a woman anointing Jesus while dining (Matt. 26:6-13; Mark 14:3-9; Luke 7:36-50; John 12:1-8); the table service of Simon's mother-in-law (Mark 1:31; Matt 8:15; Luke 4:39); Mark's story of the Syrophoenician woman (7:24-30);[82] and Thomas's dialogue between Salome and Jesus (GThom 61).[83]

The presence of poor and hungry people at meals was clearly a deeply held position by a number of early Christian communities, as testified to by the presence in all four canonical gospels of miraculous feedings of thousands of hungry peasants.[84]

Although perhaps surprising to some, a New Testament work also advocated strongly against the exclusion of Jews from early "Christian" meals. In Romans 14 and 15, Paul critiqued gentiles who were objecting to dietary limitations that their Jewish companions at meals brought with them. More pervasive was the advocacy for gentile participation at meals meant initially perhaps for Jews alone. Galatians 2:1-14, Mark 7:24-30;[85] Matt. 8:11/Luke 13:28 (and therefore most likely Q 13:28); Matt. 22:1-14;[86] and Didache 9:4[87] all advocated for gentile inclusion over against various opinions that saw benefits in uniquely Jewish attendance.

Even though these texts urging inclusion at meals were very prevalent and strongly worded, other first-century texts made a very different point. In these texts, participation of certain marginalized people in early Christian meals is discouraged. Three primary examples are Paul's silencing of women at meals in Corinth (1 Cor. 14:34-35) or alternately limiting their speaking to those with heads covered (1 Cor. 11:5-16); Paul's instruction not to eat with "sexually immoral persons" (1 Cor. 5:9-11); and Jude's condemnation of the inclusion of false teachers in their meals (v. 12).

Although, in some ways, the emphasis on inclusion of women, foreigners, and poor people seems quite different from the texts urging exclusion of certain people, chapter 4's presentation of ritual theory analysis of these meals places all of these texts along a continuum of social negotiation through ritual. Such a spectrum of negotiating participation at meals is illustrated by a third kind of text, which accepts marginalized people at the meal under certain conditions. Two of the texts—already mentioned in other respects—are the Didache's limited access to meals for wandering prophets (13:1) and Luke's positioning of Mary at Jesus' feet as an acceptance of her participation in the teaching at the meal but a denial of her right to recline (13:29 NJB).

So the constituency at meals was a matter of strong interest in early Christian texts. This interest confirms intimations that these meals were both at the heart of the emergence of early Christian identity and a major social institution in which ambitious social experiments were taking place. Chapters 4–7 pursue the analysis of these texts in relationship to meals.

The Ethics of the Meal

Earlier in this chapter Klinghardt's typology of the ethics of the Hellenistic meal identified its commitment to community (*koinonia*), equality and friendship (*isonomia* and *philia*), and utopian grace/generosity/beauty (*charis*). Here the spectrum of early Christian meal texts affirming these central values will be sketched.

Koinonia is an explicit value of these texts, shown regularly with direct use of the word and often with standard images of community. First John (1:1-3) frames its entire agenda in terms of *koinonia*:

> We declare to you what was from the beginning, what we have heard, what we have seen with our eyes, what we have looked at and touched with our hands, concerning the word of life—this life was revealed, and we have seen it and testify to it, and declare to you the eternal life that was with the Father and was revealed to us—we declare to you what we have seen and heard so that you also may have *koinonia* with us.

As noted earlier in the chapter, the word *koinonia*, along with its root and derivative forms, was often synonymous with—indeed the name for—associations that met together for meals. In other words, given the connotations of *koinonia*, a paraphrase of 1 John 1:3 would be as follows: We are telling you about all of our experience in meals associations so that you may experience community and God as we experience them at our meals.

Acts 2:42 placed *koinonia* directly next to the breaking of bread in its picture of early Christians together. First Corinthians 1:9 characterized what later parts of the letter explicitly describe as community meals as the "*koinonia* of God's Son" into which "you [*humon*/plural] were called." The reference in Gal. 2:9 to James and Cephas giving the right hand of *koinonia* to Paul and Barnabas may be misread by Western moderns as a handshake. It is at least as likely that this right hand of *koinonia* refers to having a meal together where—according to standard practice—one ate only with the right hand, especially given the larger set of issues around meals in Galatians 2.

In addition to these explicit evocations of *koinonia*, there are central concepts and images in the early Christian meal texts that affirm the ethics of *koinonia*. The images of drinking from the same cup and eating the same bread, which have been so theologized and liturgized in ways foreign to their initial Hellenistic settings, were primary expressions of *koinonia*. The symbolic communal character and pivotal dramatic gesture of the cup, of course, was there before the early Christians used it. As noted earlier in this chapter, the dedication of a cup of wine to a particular god after the *deipnon* and at the beginning of the *symposion* was a central gesture of all Hellenistic meals.

This *koinonia* reading of the cup appeared throughout first-century "Christian" meal practice, even in texts that otherwise have marked differences in their interpretations. In 1 Corinthians, Mark, Matthew, and Luke all saw the drinking of a cup together as an agreement (covenant) among those drinking. All four of these sources also have a martyrological dimension to this drinking together in that the cup is associated with Jesus' blood.[88] So the drinking of the cup binds those at the meal together with one another but also with Jesus' loyalty to them to the point of death.

The sharing of bread together also represented a commitment to *koinonia*. Also in 1 Corinthians, Mark, Matthew, and Luke's Last Supper portrayals, the bread was designated as the body of Jesus. First Corinthians made the communal link explicit with the added phrase (not in Mark or Matthew) "which is for you" (11:24). The Greek term *humon* made it clearer than the English translation that "you" was plural. Luke had a similar communal tag: "which is given for you" (22:19). Earlier in 1 Corinthians, Paul made the group-solidarity meaning of the shared bread straightforward: "The bread that we break, is it not a sharing in the body of the Christ? Because there is one bread, we who are many are one body, for we all partake of the one bread" (10:16b-17). The *koinonia* roots of the "body of Christ" imagery are striking. First Corinthians is the earliest existing literary reference to the body of Christ, and in 1 Corinthians Paul explicitly interpreted this body of Christ imagery in direct relation both to the meal and to communal belonging (at the meal).

The interest in the complexities of meal *koinonia* came to expression in several different gospel treatments of denial and betrayal. In all four canonical gospels, *koinonia* was processed in images of shared bread and cup. Mark and Matthew portrayed Jesus as challenging his followers first with "Are you able to drink the cup I drink?" (Mark 10:38/Matt. 20:22), whose meaning is later elaborated in both Mark and Matthew as meaning Jesus' death (Mark 14:36/Matt. 26:39). Both gospels then had Jesus answering in the affirmative: "The cup I drink you will drink" (Mark 10:39/Matt. 20:23). That is, drinking the cup together was explicitly seen in Mark and Matthew as a commitment of *koinonia* solidarity, even to the point of death.

All four canonical gospels mapped out a narrative version of the same link between broken *koinonia* and disruption of the meal. Jesus predicts Judas's betrayal at the Last Supper in each of these gospels. Clearly, here the gospel narratives used the obvious association of *koinonia* with the meal ethos to highlight the irony and tragedy of the broken *koinonia*. Luke and John made use of the *koinonia* meal ethos similarly in their presentation of Peter's denials. In those two gospels, Peter's denials are predicted at the Last Supper.

The overall rootedness of early Christian *koinonia*/community of shared bread and cup in the longer tradition of the Hellenistic meal was ironically acknowledged by Justin in his testy reinterpretation of this resemblance:

> For the apostles in the memoirs composed by them, which are called gospels, thus handed down what was commanded them: that Jesus, taking bread and having given thanks, said, "Do this for my memorial, this is my body"; and likewise taking the cup and giving thanks he said, "This is my blood"; and gave it to them alone. This also the wicked demons in imitation handed down as something to be done in the mysteries of Mithra; for bread and a cup of water are brought out in their secret rites of initiation.[89]

That is, Justin accounted for the similarity in meal *koinonia* by alleging that others had copied the gospel practice. What is obvious from this book's perspective is that the gospels, Justin, and Mithra all saw eating and drinking together as an ethical commitment to *koinonia* (and that Justin's apologetic ignored the bigger picture).

It is probable that the ways some of the early Christian groups reconstructed the standard meal activity of service also was seen as a measure of *koinonia*. Mark 10:43 and its Matthean parallel characterized their communal life together with an inversion concerning service according to Jesus: "But it is not so among you; but whoever wishes to become great among you must be your servant." If this service were not described explicitly in terms of meals, Luke made it explicit: "For who is greater, the one who reclines or the one serves? Is it not the one who reclines? But I am among you as one who serves" (22:27). John narrativized this same point by having Jesus take the role of the foot-washing servant at the Last Supper and explicitly made it a matter of *koinonia* values at the meal with Jesus saying: "So if I, your Lord and Teacher, have washed your feet, you also ought to wash one another's feet. For I have set you an example, that you also should do as I have done to you" (13:14-15). Again, here these Christian texts did experiment with a new kind of meal *koinonia*, but they were not the only ones. Philo's treatise on the (Jewish) Therapeutae made similar note of their exceptional custom of serving one another at meals.[90]

Certainly, this same *koinonia* meaning of the meal applied to the surprising constituencies at meals in the gospels sketched earlier. In most cases, the gospel narratives emphasized the experimental or offensive character of this heterogeneous kind of *koinonia*. Again, as noted earlier and elaborated in later chapters, this experimentation with a risky version of meal *koinonia* had both roots in some segments of the broader Hellenistic meal practice and tension with other segments' images of meal bondedness.

The second major ethic of Hellenistic meals in general, as identified by Klinghardt, is equality and friendship (*isonomia* and *philia*). The above discussion of the value of *koinonia* in early Christian meal texts has already identified some dimensions of equality/*isonomia*. For instance, both the valuing of a meal constituency of women and men, Jew and gentile (Gal. 3:26-28), rich and poor (Luke 14), and the ironic value of service (Mark 10) also pointed toward equality.

The texts also demonstrated a keen appreciation of the friendship/*philia* ethic. Perhaps the most classic was John's portrait of Jesus reclining next to the "one Jesus loved" (13:23 and 21:20). Complementing this picture in John were three assertions from Jesus in his Last Supper discourse that his disciples were his friends (15:13-15). This typical symposial value of reclining together as friends appeared also in a more eschatological image—that of the poor man Lazarus reclining in the bosom of Abraham in the reign of God (Luke 16:23). With the more ironically redefining twist already observed in these texts, the Q passage that celebrated Jesus as eating and drinking with the undesirables explicitly evoked this meal ethic of friendship/*philia* when it termed Jesus a friend (*philos*) of tax collectors and sinners (7:34).

The third ethical principle of Hellenistic meals, according to Klinghardt and outlined earlier in this chapter, is utopian grace/generosity/beauty (or *charis*). As noted earlier, *charis* was a complex Hellenistic value that elicited generosity and grace from people as an expression of their participation in a larger utopian imagination of society. The generosity and hospitality of the meal participants was actively understood as a way of participating in an ideal society. It was this *charis* of the meals that made for much of their Hellenistic success, in that it called forth generosity and grace from participants and simultaneously filled the void of viable societal associations caused by the disintegration of the institutions of the city/*polis*, family, tribe, and nation. As chapter 6 illustrates, this meal *charis* was also experienced as an alternative to the imperial social vision imposed by Rome.

In his article "Table Fellowship as a Literary Motif in the Gospel of Luke," Dennis Smith has shown that Lukan literary activity around meal themes focused on the meals of Jesus as images for a utopian society. The Lukan assembly of "the poor, the crippled, the blind, and the lame" happens at meals (e.g., 14:21) as a reflection of the larger socially inverted vision of the coming age. Similarly, 13:27-30 draws on the Q passage to picture people coming "from east and west, from north and south, and will recline" together. Although Smith uses the—to my mind unfortunate—terminology of "messianic banquet," his point still holds that Luke's framing of the Last Supper of Jesus "is primarily eschatological in focus."[91]

Luke's portrait of the *phagein arton* in Acts (2:44-47), where the early post-resurrection followers of Jesus in Jerusalem sell all they have, hold all things in common, and gather daily for meals, exemplifies this meal *charis*'s utopian claim. Not only did the meal ethos picture a utopian sharing of all goods, but this was imagined in Jerusalem itself, underlining the utopian character of eating together.

The "wedding feast of the lamb" in Rev. 19:9 is for "a great multitude in the sky" (19:1), pictured proleptically in relationship to 3:20's promise to the assembly at Laodicea that the Christ figure "will come into you and eat with you." Massey Shepherd's larger analysis of the book itself in the form of a meal shows the *charis* values of the book in its overlay of meal and cosmic resolution.[92] Similarly, Didache's prayer over the bread at meals that was "scattered upon the mountains, brought together, and became one" (9:4) is explicitly made parallel with "your *ekklesia* gathered together from the ends of the earth into your realm." The *charis* of the meal occurred in both the generosity of the bread eaten by all and the utopian vision of a "worldwide" gathering. Subsequent eucharistic theologies notwithstanding, surely the images of the body and blood of the anointed one in 1 Corinthians and the Synoptic Gospels must be understood similarly to the Didache's prayer, which combines the elements of the meal with the picture of a larger utopian social body.

Early Christian Meals as Significant Social Experiments

Once the broad social convention of meals in the Hellenistic age and their powerful social coding are evident, much of the early Christian literature sounds quite different. When one knows the structure of the Hellenistic meal and the intrinsic and pervasive social meaning inherent in it, much early Christian language quickly takes on new (social) significance. Not only is it clear that meal vocabulary permeates early Christian literature, but when the social coding of the Hellenistic meal is acknowledged, the standard elements of this meal in early Christian contexts become dynamics of social negotiation and experimentation.

From this perspective, the meals of early Christians (and other Hellenistic groups) appear as a series of bold social and spiritual experiments. They allowed early Christians to try out new behaviors in dialogue with their social visions. On one level, these social visions were described at meals as participating in "the realm of God," "the body of Christ," "koinonia with God," "the heavenly court," or "the heavenly city." On another level, as noted in this chapter's close assessment of meal gestures and constituencies, the meals became a laboratory in which a range of expressive nonverbal "vocabularies" explored alternative social visions. The vocabularies consisted of alternative social relationships at the meals, complex ritual gestures, body postures, and actual food elements.

These meals need to be conceived as spiritual experiments as well. By this is not meant that they were occasions for mystification of real-life issues, retreat from social realities or intellectual quests, or some kind of prototype for later Christian liturgy. Rather, the meals enacted the new social alternatives so vividly that the meal participants experienced themselves as actually a part of a new social order. Both as groups and as individuals, many of those at the meal felt as if they were living in a different world. The ingestion of the food and all its communal dynamics internalized the social values and vision. It is this obviously simultaneous fantasy and transformation inside of the meal participants that made the meals themselves spiritual and enhanced them as social experiments. The extent and complexity of these nonverbal vocabularies can be fully explored only within the larger project of chapter 3's ritual analysis of these meals.

This survey of the pervasive social practice of Hellenistic meals and of the dense set of references within early Christian literature to this social practice establishes a framework for analyzing social dimensions of early Christianity in a way that places the actual social practice in creative dialogue with the texts themselves. With this framework established, this book now turns to theoretical categories for such analysis.

CHAPTER FOUR
Ritual Analysis: A New Method
FOR THE Study OF Early Christian Meals

U NDER CLOSE EXAMINATION, the Hellenistic meal demonstrates a dynamic structure that addressed extremely important social issues of that era. With principal aid from the field of ritual studies, this chapter shows how the meal carried so much social freight for that time period. In describing the ways in which these meals effected a wide range of intricate social transactions and relationships, this chapter also lays open the dynamics of the early Christian meals and their central role in the emergence of the early Christian movement itself.

It is important not to misunderstand this application of ritual theory to Hellenistic meals. Two pitfalls must be negotiated. The first pitfall is that "ritual" in common parlance often connotes an esoteric set of gestures or symbols practiced by strict adherents to religious or social cults. This turns out to be a caricature of ritual as it has come to be understood in the scholarship of the past two hundred years. Ritual applies in this more recent and studied optic to a wide variety of human behavior, much of it practiced by people not at all involved in esoteric practice or cultlike settings. This misunderstanding of ritual can dovetail harmfully with some inaccurate representations of early Christian gatherings.

In particular, conventional pictures of the early Christian groups often portray those early churches as participating in some early form of the Christian mass, eucharist, or communion service. Even when most historians acknowledged that the early Christians gathered for meals, they carelessly superimposed an anachronistic medieval rite of eucharist on a portion of those meals. It has only been the scholarly generation of Matthias Klinghardt,[1] Dennis Smith,[2] and Andrew McGowan[3] that has substantially corrected this impression in some scholarly circles.[4] Although Smith has made a major contribution by showing that these meals effected social bonding and boundaries, and Klinghardt similarly helped by connecting a series of social values to the meal, neither of these scholars has explained how the Hellenistic meal achieved these social effects. This has allowed the conventional pictures of early Christian meals to assume that the eucharistic gestures of the Middle Ages or contemporary America somehow existed within the meal. The conventional idea of ritual as esoteric gesture (in this case, a medieval eucharist) remained intact and unconnected to social structures and experimentation.

Picturing early Christians as participating in the highly stylized rite of taking one sip from a wine glass and sharing a tiny wafer only compounds the error in thinking that "ritual" is esoteric and cultlike. Since medieval (and, to a certain extent, modern) eucharists do indeed trade in esoteric meaning and practice, this picture fits with the caricature of ritual itself. So this chapter's ritual analysis of Hellenistic meals would be devastatingly misunderstood if its readers thought of ritual in the narrow esoterica of the contemporary imagination or of the ancient meals as having the medieval mass as a component part. Ritual theorization makes sense of the actual Hellenistic meal, showing how the formulaic behavior identified by Klinghardt and Smith effects social stability and experimentation. At the same time, this understanding of ritual as a broader set of human behaviors provides a technical analysis of how the social values of *koinonia*, *philia*, and *charis* and the tensive dynamics of social bonding, boundaries, obligation, stratification, and equality were negotiated at the Hellenistic meal.

The second pitfall in applying ritual theory to the Hellenistic Mediterranean is the inherent difficulty in studying social practices of the ancient world. We cannot know ancient society in ways similar to how ritual theorists have been able to study contemporary African, American, or Indian rituals. One cannot appropriate Hellenistic meal texts as directly representative of the meals themselves. As the Society of Biblical Literature's Seminar on Meals in the Greco-Roman World has demonstrated over the past three years, the relationship between text and meal in Hellenistic society must be treated as volatile, illusive, and complex. Even though a text in Luke or Plutarch claims to represent what happened, that is almost never the case. Texts often used meals "to think with"—that is, texts regularly, both today and in the ancient world, portrayed meals in order to make ideological points, to support and subvert existing values and institutions, and to promote and vilify personages and communities. So ancient texts cannot provide real meals for ritual theorizing. Indeed, texts often obscure and deform the meals themselves in order to make their point. It is only by virtue of the massive compilations of texts made by Smith and Klinghardt,[5] the careful analysis of archaeological sites, and the complex attentiveness to epigraphic material by the likes of Philip Harland[6] that some provisional notion of Hellenistic meals as events to be ritually analyzed can emerge.

Summarizing Contemporary Ritual Theory

With these preliminary cautionary notes consistently in view, the next step toward ritual analysis of Hellenistic meals is to summarize some key ritual theory of the past forty years. Only within these last forty years has theorizing about ritual (re)focused on the social power of ritual rather than the metaphysical, psychological, or institutional meanings of ritual.[7] Although the major theories of this recent period do differ in some regards, they all convincingly provide reason to see rituals contributing substantially to social stability and social change. In other words, ritual—thanks to these recent thinkers—now is seen as social negotiation rather than simply a set of cosmically or inwardly directed gestures.

With these theories briefly summarized, it is then possible to ask more specifically what the ritual-like dimensions of Hellenistic meals accomplished for the larger society and how. The larger patterns of the meal—identified by Smith and Klinghardt and summarized earlier[8] —present for ritual studies a clear set of gestures, relationships, and symbol sets for analysis. The social emphasis of recent ritual theory provides a way of thinking about Hellenistic meal patterns as socially productive for both the immediate communities and the larger society.

Although the field of ritual studies of the past forty years is very rich, this chapter concentrates on five major figures: Catherine Bell, Pierre Bourdieu, Mary Douglas, Jonathan Z. Smith, and Victor Turner. All are deeply indebted to anthropological study of ritual, but just two, Mary Douglas and Victor Turner, investigate as anthropologists per se. Bourdieu is a social philosopher. Douglas is the only theorist of the five to write directly about meals, although not specifically about Hellenistic meals. Bourdieu, Douglas, Turner, and Jonathan Z. Smith (to be listed in the rest of this chapter as J. Z. Smith in order to distinguish him from Dennis Smith, since both authors play a substantial role in the rest of the chapter) have a lifetime of theorizing behind them and in some ways represent diverse bodies of work on ritual already in a somewhat complete form.[9] Catherine Bell produced several important works in the past fifteen years that provide by far the most eloquent summary of the field. This makes Bell both the most useful for an overview of the current state of ritual studies. This chapter uses Bell and J. Z. Smith as primary theorists but consults substantively the work of Turner, Bourdieu, and Douglas to elucidate and extend the perspectives of Bell and J. Z. Smith.[10]

Catherine Bell

It is Bell who has attended most seriously to defining "ritual" for contemporary study. However, her rigorous attention to making clear what is (and is not) meant by "ritual" does involve both complexity and an eventual dissatisfaction with the term itself for defining the field.

For Bell, assuming that "ritual" is "an intrinsic, universal category or feature of human behavior" would be a mistake.[11] She insists on noticing that scholarly discussion of "ritual" has had a particular set of assumptions and intentions. Ritual as a term "is a cultural and historical construction that has been heavily used to help differentiate various styles and degrees of religiosity, rationality, and cultural determinism."[12] However, just because discussion of ritual has had its own "rather particular way of looking at and organizing the world" does not mean that there is nothing to it.[13]

In order to get at the phenomenon behind the scholarly agendas, Bell proposes shifting the focus from "ritual" as a thing in itself to "ritualization" as cultural practice. She explains:

> Basic to ritualization is the inherent significance it derives from its interplay and contrast with other practices. From this viewpoint, there would be little content to any attempt to generate a cross-cultural or universal meaning of ritual. Likewise, this view suggests that the significance of ritual behavior lies not in being an entirely separate way of acting, but in how such activities constitute themselves as different and in contrast to other activities. . . . Acting ritually is first and foremost a matter of nuanced contrasts and the evocation of strategic, value-laded distinctions.[14]

An example of acting ritually in this regard is contrasting "the routine activity of buying some regularly used article of clothing for a spouse or child (such as gym socks) and the ritualized version of buying a similar but different article (argyle socks) and giving it as a gift."[15] Positioning ritualization in this way shows that similar differences between eating bread for breakfast every morning and eating bread at a eucharist, or killing an animal in the wild and sacrificing one on an altar, are continuums whose intracontinuum relationships are crucial to the significance of ritualization.

Giving the argyle socks as a gift is a ritualization of the routine activity. Bell writes: "These activities are differentiated in the very doing and derive their significance from the contrast implicitly set up between them. Routine giving plays off ritualized giving and vice versa; they define each other."[16] It is not that the gift of argyle socks is a model for family shopping. It is a strategic version of family shopping whose meaning derives from its interactivity with the routine activity. Bell continues: "Yet this is not to say that ritualization is simply acting differently. Otherwise, buying mismatched socks at a bargain table—an act that may communicate simply insofar as it differs from a routine set of expectations—would qualify as a ritual."[17]

Ritualization then is "the ability to deploy, play, and manipulate basic schemes in ways that appropriate and condition experience effectively."[18] Ritualization is "the production of ritualized acts,"[19] and as such is more definable than trying to identify "ritual" as a universal thing in itself, since the thing in itself only exists in its relationship to a variety of "basic schemes."

Bell notes that this production of ritualized acts results in elaborate constructed realities: "Ritualizing schemes invoke a series of privileged oppositions that, when acted in space and time through a series of movements, gestures, and sounds, effectively structure and nuance an environment. . . . This environment, constructed and reconstructed by the actions of social agents within it, provides an experience of the objective reality."[20] This means that for those experiencing this ritualization, "the environment appears to be the source of the schemes and their values."[21]

Critiquing and appreciating some 150 years of ritual theory before her, Bell sees "ritualization" as most understandable within the larger significance of practice. Ritualization is not just esoteric gesture as a part of religious fervor, as unreflective traditionalists would have it. Nor is it necessarily a key human act in establishing a sense of cosmic order, as the likes of Mircea Eliade or C. G. Jung explained in the mid-twentieth century. Rather, it is a specifically modulated pattern of human actions within a highly constructed and differentiated environment that helps sort through basic social and cultural schemes. Ritualization "is a focus on the physical mind-body holism as the primary medium for the deployment and embodiment of everyday schemes of physical action and cultural values—as in the arrangement of a home or the orchestration of a game—that are the means by which culture is reproduced and individual categories of experience are forged."[22]

Later in this chapter, Bell's ritual theory breaks open the relationship between seemingly mundane actions in the Hellenistic meal and key social negotiations of the larger Hellenistic society. The activity of eating at the Hellenistic meal becomes a complex rhythm of social gestures, relational patterns, and subtle oppositions to what ordinary eating would be in and of itself. Adding reclining, libation, and symposial activities to eating per se interweaves a number of basic human schemes of eating and drinking, leisure, ranking, and speaking in order to "provide a sense of objective reality" that allows the appropriation of some experience, the rejection of other experience, and the conditioning of still other experience. The interweaving of these basic schemes creates an environment that is experienced as both an objective reality of something larger and a source of important values.

Jonathan Z. Smith

Although the ways Bell integrates the history of ritual theory meticulously into her own and this summary makes most sense (and critique) of ritual theory per se, it has been the work of J. Z. Smith[23] that has framed for my previous writings[24] ritual theory in ways that most clearly address the social dynamics of Hellenistic meals. An overview of his ritual theory creates a perspective in which Turner and Bourdieu can be useful in making social sense of Hellenistic meals. Not at all far from the perspective of Bell, J. Z. Smith also resists a universal meaning for rituals per se. Rather, he sees ritual as creating order and meaning within the specific and relative symbol sets of particular situations.

In an earlier study I have summarized J. Z. Smith's ritual theory as it relates to Hellenistic meals as having three "overlapping effects on the people involved."[25] These three dimensions of his theory are as follows:

1. A marking or noticing of an occurrence, pattern, or dynamic within a situation.[26] According to J. Z. Smith, rituals generally call attention to a problematic event or pattern in the lives of a particular people. Rituals make pointed—although, in most cases, symbolic and indirect—references to these difficulties. This ritual marking of such aspects of life for the ritual participants "does not solve the problem, overcome the incongruity or resolve the tension. Rather it results in thought. It is a testing of the adequacy and applicability of traditional patterns and categories to new situations and data in the hopes of achieving rectification."[27] In this way, ritual serves as a "focusing lens" in order to mark these problematic phenomena.[28]

2. A perfecting or rationalizing of such noticed phenomena.[29] As Bell characterizes J. Z. Smith in this regard: "Most simply, for Smith, ritual portrays the idealized way that things in this world should be organized."[30] In the constructed environment of the ritual, the problematic phenomena are explained away or made to look better. In his essay "The Bare Facts of Ritual," J. Z. Smith challenges a number of previous analyses of a Siberian ritual in which a bear cub is captured, raised by a village, and then ceremonially slaughtered. Instead of seeing this ritual as archetypal of sacrificial rites, J. Z. Smith sees it as a perfecting of the bear hunt, which so often tragically goes wrong for the Siberian people, who are so dependent on successful bear hunts. For him, ritual "provides the means for demonstrating that we know what ought to have been done, what ought to have taken place. But, by the fact that it is ritual action rather than everyday action, it demonstrates that we know 'what is the case.' Ritual provides an occasion for reflection and rationalization on the fact that what ought to have been done was not done, what ought to have taken place did not occur."[31]

3. An assertion of difference within a social body.[32] Sometimes the problematic phenomenon marked by the ritual is a significant difference for the society or community in question. Typically in this case, different symbolic actions stand side by side in ritual to represent the particular differences within the population itself. J. Z. Smith takes care to note that this marking of difference among a certain people rarely means to overcome the difference but rather simply to work with the difference in ways that the different parties all are recognized. His extended study of ritual in ancient Near Eastern temples explicates this dynamic of ritual.[33] The social difference that Near Eastern peoples needed to address regularly, he says, is the contending powers of king and priest and, by derivation, the power struggles between the priestly and monarchical

classes. J. Z. Smith shows how choreographed movement and the seating assignments of the king and priest in the temples marked their different claims in the society. These ritual movements and seating arrangements did not so much adjudicate the power struggles as recognize the ongoing contestation. I have commented elsewhere on the breakthrough accomplished in J. Z. Smith's understanding of the ways ritual creatively addresses social differences:

> Ritual symbols allow for groups to recognize these differences without necessarily trying to resolve them. This, of course, is a very different means of nourishing the group in which differences exist. Rather than try to come up with a common and final solution to the differences, the multivalent symbols of ritual keep allowing for indirect recognition of those differences. This allows each different sub-group to be recognized and for the group as a whole to work regularly on non-final, adaptive and constantly revised compromises. Final solutions to differences almost always lead to the elimination of valued different perspectives. Ongoing ritual recognition of differences tends to nourish the particular sub-groups.[34]

As noted earlier, J. Z. Smith's ritual theory proves especially illuminating for addressing the social functions of Hellenistic meals. This is the case in part because his approach assumes that ritual is not reductionist and accomplishes more than social functions. More specifically in this essay, his theory's emphasis on ritual as "focusing lens" allows attention to the specific relationships between the Hellenistic meal and a variety of issues of that era—that is, this theory facilitates asking questions about the particulars of the Hellenistic era and its meals. In addition, this theory's interest in provisional "perfection" of problems engaged by the ritual has particular relevance to the experimentation already observed in the Hellenistic meal. For instance, the issue of poverty as a larger societal phenomenon was "perfected" by the meal in several ways. Some groups went out of their way to make sure that everyone at the meal received the same portion of food.[35] In addition, many Hellenistic meals made a point of distributing the leftovers to people in need.[36] Finally, his concentration on how ritual marks difference within groups is crucial in denoting how Hellenistic meals addressed the broad mix of populations in the Greco-Roman Mediterranean. This makes much clearer how the Hellenistic meals themselves became social experiments.

Pierre Bourdieu

In his pursuit of an "Outline of a Theory of Practice," Bourdieu has centered upon the notion of *habitus* used by earlier sociologists and historians but reframed by Bourdieu for the pursuit itself.[37] *Habitus* helps Bourdieu give prominence to an analysis of society without primary recourse to the more common and problematized notions of historical causality or structural determinism. *Habitus* is the set of human habitual behavior and practice that "give[s] shape and form to social conventions." It is not one kind of behavior or practice but the entirety of them all. It both shapes social conventions and in turn as a whole is shaped by them.

Although he has not written a great deal on ritual, it is a specific and crucial element in the ongoing development of *habitus*. Ritual forms cultural wholes that constitute *habitus*. This is a major skill inasmuch as society contains so many irreconcilable differences. In his study of the Algerian Kabyle people, Bourdieu shows how rituals in relationship to marriage and plowing "have the function of disguising and thereby sanctioning the inevitable collision of two contrary principles."[38] Rituals are ways people negotiate social and cultural power by the way their performance brings tensive dynamics together. They are an ongoing practice by which social and cultural categories are challenged and reorganized. In the relatively small amount of time rituals take, the perceived differences and boundaries of one larger societal moment dissolve so that the next societal conventions can emerge. In other words, rituals are a primary way in which the *habitus* evolves.

Bourdieu's sense of ritual as an ongoing practice rather than a structure meshes well with both Bell and J. Z. Smith. The process dimension of Bell's "ritualization" and the ongoing marking of difference in Smith's theory correspond to Bourdieu's interlooping of ritual, practice, and *habitus*. Similarly, Bourdieu's understanding that ritual practice is in itself an ongoing adjustment complements J. Z. Smith's notion of the way ritual perfects and Bell's picture of ritual deploying social schemes. And although—as Bell has noted[39]—both Bourdieu's ritual and *habitus* can easily be romanticized or mystified, Bourdieu's own rigorous interrogation of the power ritual brings to those in charge of it mitigates this tendency. And although Bourdieu's conscious effort to think without recourse to notions of history could lead to a dehistoricized understanding of identity, Bourdieu's emphasis on complex and unending social process can itself be seen as a recognition of what many consider the historically located character of human consciousness.

In relationship to this chapter's interest in Hellenistic society's strong attraction to meals as a way of constructing tenuous human identities, Bourdieu's situating of ritual within a larger societal dynamic of compensation and integration offers important theoretical framing. Here, too, ritual theory shows how Hellenistic meals contained a ritual and socially coded vocabulary that allowed for ongoing construction of self-understanding in a very complex social era. From this theoretical perspective, the meal of that historical era becomes a laboratory of elaborative identity. The meals negotiated the emerging influences to form a cultural whole where there had not been one before. They were ongoing practice.

In addition, Bourdieu's appreciation for ritual's skill in holding contradictions together fits the portrait of meals in the Hellenistic Mediterranean. His theory shows ritual to be a human nonlinguistic skill of integrating competing values or even competing realities. This chapter poses the question of why Hellenistic meals simultaneously enabled social bonding and social boundaries (or social stratification and social equality). Bourdieu helps see the ritual dimension of Hellenistic meals as a negotiating skill for integration of such complexity or contradictions in the life of a particular ritualizing group.

Victor Turner

Similarly, Turner provides two concepts that complement J. Z. Smith's portrait of ritual as the work of a particular social body on a particular set of issues and as an always fluid process.[40] Drawing conclusions from his long set of ethnographic observations in southwest Africa, Turner's notions of "liminality" and *communitas* provide additional conceptualities for more thorough application of both Bell's and J. Z. Smith's theories to Hellenistic meals. This use of Turner within a broader Bell and J. Z. Smith framework does have its ironies in that both Bell and J. Z. Smith have been critical of Turner.[41] But Turner's "liminality" and *communitas* do indeed help understand how ritual effected social negotiation in Hellenistic meals, if this application is done within the sharper frames of reference of Bell and J. Z. Smith.

Turner observed how several key rituals of the Ndembu people of southwest Africa became occasions for the blurring of boundaries that otherwise were clear and firm in the rest of Ndembu society. In the middle of these rituals, which commonly lasted days or even weeks, social norms were often dropped and titles and rights of individuals explicitly confused or reversed, allowing for freer and less socially inhibited relationships and behavior.[42] Turner described this blurring of social boundaries as a "liminality" inherent in all ritual.[43] These liminal moments, for Turner, exhibit particularly clearly the ways ritual helps a group or society claim and situate basic values of mutual recognition and respect and basic affirmations of both individual expression and communal loyalty. The structured character of ritual provides those participating with a window through which they can enter liminal moments of equality and mutual exchange. These liminal moments within ritual place in perspective the more hierarchical and inhibited nature of ordinary relationships within the community. As such, for Turner, ritual's liminality re-creates and undergirds the most humane and mutually respectful dimensions of life together.

For Turner, then, ritual inherently structures into a group or society's life crucial occasions for freedom, mutuality, cathartic blowing off of steam, and truth telling. Ritual gives access to *communitas*, a universal substructure for the experience of community in human life. This experience of *communitas* nourishes the ordinary relationships, structures, and assumptions of groups so that they do not stray radically from the life-giving values of freedom, honesty, and mutuality. Turner is not, however, romantic in his analysis of ritual's *communitas*. He recognizes clearly that the liminal performances that exhibit *communitas* in ritual do not resolve the overall social tension between "*communitas* and difference, homogeneity and differentiation, equality and inequality," but rather reflect and make more conscious the "dialectical process" of "structure and anti-structure" in social life itself.[44]

Although Bell and J. Z. Smith resist—appropriately, in my opinion—Turner's universalizing vocabulary about ritual, the concepts of liminality and *communitas* can help elaborate and deepen a Bell and J. Z. Smith framework for how ritual helps groups think about, deploy, and embody problematic and crucial schemata of their life together.

The liminality within Ndembu ritual that Turner observed (and projected onto all ritual) is quite close to Bell's focus on how ritualization plays off a larger basic scheme. The importance of liminality in ritual for Turner has everything to do with Bell's sense that ritualized action gains significance by virtue of its belonging to larger basic schemes—that is, the reason that the uninhibited, free, and mutual behaviors of Ndembu ritual have meaning (for Turner) is that they play off the larger and daily relational fields of Ndembu society, where one is not so free and mutual.

Liminality need not be applied to all ritualization, in my opinion. But as a concept it helps to understand how some ritualization creates a space of less inhibited freedom, expressiveness, and mutuality. For Turner, this liminality is a goal in itself of ritual, while for Bell this liminality would be yet another strategy for playing several basic schemes off one another in order to reproduce and deploy them in adjusted forms. Similarly, from the perspective of J. Z. Smith, it is easy to see how Turner's description of liminality in Ndembu ritual could help them mark and think about differences in their experience—that is, the freer (liminal) experience in the Ndembu ritual could help them notice and reflect on the more rigid relationalities and behaviors in their ordinary life.

Turner's *communitas* has a similar, although not identical, relationship to the ritual theories of Bell and J. Z. Smith. Turner's examples of *communitas*, especially in the Ndembu, illustrate J. Z. Smith's proposal that ritual helps communities think about certain larger tensions and problems in their lives. The mutuality of the Ndembu in ritual helps them reflect on, and perhaps occasionally perfect, their ordinary experiences of the values and limits of social structure and inhibition. Similarly, the descriptions of *communitas*, along with Turner's overall notions of "structure and anti-structure" within ritual, cohere closely with Bell's sense that ritualization opposes basic social schemes to one another in order to reproduce them for the current moment and communal moment.

Liminality and *communitas* help one to understand the social negotiation done ritually in Hellenistic meals. These meals often put people together as a social unit that differed from the normal social intercourse in ordinary life. Mixes of men and women, slaves and free, and various ethnicities and classes occurred often in these meals in ways that required different kinds of relationships at the meal. The festivities of the meals regularly threatened to break out into relatively unruly behavior, as indicated by the plethora of association rules barring or punishing such behavior. As already noted at the beginning of this section, the Hellenistic meals consistently structured the antithetical goals of social bonding and social boundaries, as well as social equality and social stratification, into the same meal occasion. Turner's concept of ritual liminality applies clearly to these somewhat volatile mixes of people, behavior, and purposes. It shows how the Hellenistic meal fits into a larger pattern of ritual events in which uninhibited behavior allows for otherwise less easily accessed social and communal productivity.

Similarly, the notion of *communitas* illuminates Hellenistic meal behavior. Especially among Hellenistic associations, the liminal mix of behavior, people, and purposes of these meals was a primary element in hundreds of thousands of persons' allegiance to relatively new community forms. The *communitas* of the meal became a creative dimension of group coherence as it played off against the hierarchies and dominations of the larger Hellenistic society.

Mary Douglas

Mary Douglas's extended examination of meals' ritual significance acts as an applied subset of the theoretical framework of J. Z. Smith, Bourdieu, and Turner for this application of ritual theory to Hellenistic meals. In addition, because Douglas addresses meals per se as ritual, her work is especially useful in seeing how Hellenistic meals as mainstream, nonesoteric events are highly socially coded.

Douglas's study of meals is useful to this study of Hellenistic meals inasmuch as it brings the rigor of ritual analysis to events similar to those this book examines during the Hellenistic era. Douglas's essay "On Deciphering a Meal" is part of her larger polemic against earlier anthropological truisms that rituals and modernism were basically antithetical. Her examination of meals is an extended illustration of how what appear to be secular meals are highly coded rituals. She demonstrates how who attends, what is eaten, where the meal occurs, and when each food is eaten signify the social relations of the group meal—for instance, which moderns have hors d'oeuvres and what kind has a great deal to do with social coding rather than simple preference for certain foodstuffs.

Although Bell and J. Z. Smith have some reservations about the "functionalist"[45] simplicity of ritual reproducing social relations, their overall understanding of meal as ritual fits tightly together. Indeed, the way Douglas shows how modern meals' order reflects social dynamics is a near perfect example of Bell's larger point that ritualization places basic social schemes alongside one another for a larger cultural production and signification. Similarly, both the variations in and loyalty to meal forms within modern society identified by Douglas illustrate J. Z. Smith's larger interest in how rituals mark difference. Douglas's insights into the ways meal order, foodstuffs, and constituencies carry major ritual (and therefore social) meaning complement the other ritual studies on Hellenistic meals. It need not be that the realia of modern meals ritually signify the same social dynamics as they might in the ancient world.

Summary

The last two generations of ritual theory have gone beyond seeing ritual as primarily metaphysical, psychological, or socially functional. Without rejecting these dimensions of ritual, these theorists have pointed to the ways ritual plays key roles in addressing the complexities of the particular society. In this way, ritual is not so much a thing in itself but a way human groups approach problematic realities of their lives. In contrast to earlier scholarship, these last two generations of ritual theorists have not generally found ritual addressing the same subject matter (for example, cosmic beginnings, key transitions in life, religious questions) around the world. Rather, the core dimension of ritual has had to do with how each group approaches a more or less local complexity.

Ritual is, in this framework, a kind of social intelligence, often reserved for subject matter that has proved too complex for individual discernment, too frightening for more direct address, or attached to vying long-term social loyalties. Whether it be the complex relationship between a giver and a receiver, the rivalry between the Israelite king and the high priest, the conflicts inherent in the geographical location and the social needs of an Algerian ethnicity, the contradiction of the simultaneous benefits and harmfulness of Ndembu hierarchy, or the class distinctions in modern democratic society, ritual is a primary way groups of people "perform" an approach to these relatively intractable issues. Performing a ritual then becomes a way of reframing various difficult issues of the specific ritualizing group so that they can be seen in different ways. These performances are seldom seen as a realistic solution to the intractable issues. They do, however, in their performative address to these complex issues, give perspective on and allow thought about the difficult issues.

Regularly, ritual seems simply to place or reproduce the difficult issue in a safe and constructed environment. Sometimes this reproduction of the issue in a stable environment occasions thoughtfulness and insight about the issue itself. Occasionally, ritual seems to help these groups deploy new resources toward the issue. All of this happens in a curiously implicit, semiconscious manner. The importance of doing the ritual is almost always obvious to the group, but the issue addressed is also almost always too volatile to be acknowledged directly. The oblique, performed quality of the ritual and the separate safe environment shield the group from too direct a consciousness of the pressing character of the issue itself. This distance from the issue itself and the oblique approach that ritual makes to issues allow for a kind of productive address to the otherwise too intimidating and complex subject matter.

The Hellenistic Mediterranean was waist deep in such intractable issues. The values of classical Greece were allegedly still at the heart of culture, and indeed the Roman Empire was forcefully and ironically expanding the scope of Hellenic/istic ways into additional locales. There was militarily enforced peace throughout the entire Mediterranean, which, in addition to being deeply ironic in itself, precipitated massive intermingling of previously separate cultures across the Mediterranean. Family and tribal structures lost many of their moorings within their former separate cultures. With the loss of regional cultural coherence and the insertion of new models, gender identities were in flux. Imperial economic confiscation brought devastating poverty to a wide range of persons. Massive imperial enslavement of both rich and poor conquered peoples dislocated and relocated entire segments of regional societies. Different cultural codes of honor and shame overlay one another, with confusing and contradictory results. Patron-client relationships took on governmental (imperial) and cross-cultural dimensions that infused new power dynamics into almost every locale.

It was in this larger (cross-)cultural situation that a common Mediterranean-wide meal practice emerged and commanded interest and allegiance. As noted earlier, it was not that the form was absolutely new but that the social freight and identity markers it carried increased drastically. The SBL Seminar on Greco-Roman Meals has shown how the Hellenistic association phenomenon used the meal as one of its primary components in trying to meet the identity needs of the new situations.[46] In the examination of the socially charged, identity-infused character of the Hellenistic meal, Dennis Smith's willingness to characterize its social dynamics in tensive, seemingly contradictory ways (for example, the meal effects both social equality and social stratification) now turns out to be a resource. Ritual theory's focus on the way ritualization takes on complexities for those participating now can prove directly helpful in thinking about the social and identity formation effected in those meals.

Similarly, ritual theory's attentiveness to events like Hellenistic meals that do not fit the conventional notions of esoteric ritual can help signify the ways that these meals functioned ritually for the reframing, insight, and deployment relative to the many problematic dimensions of Hellenistic life. The various categories in ritual theory (for example, ritualization, deployment, marking difference, perfecting, *habitus*, liminality, *communitas*, communication) summarized above make a striking match with the social dynamics and identity formation already observed in Hellenistic meals.

Ritual Theory and Hellenistic Meals

Recent ritual theory provides a lens through which to see how meals furnished the larger Hellenistic society with ways to think about, experiment with, and negotiate its social structures, personal relationships, and identity formations. The semiprivate, constructed setting of the Hellenistic meals provided a stable and protected setting in which participants could "perfect" (J. Z. Smith) the structures and relationships under more contingent construction in Hellenistic society itself.

The complex relationships, for instance, among slaves, slave owners, and free persons were "perfected" along the lines of the Hellenistic values of mutuality and friendship within the meal. The meal became a place in which slaves could be president of the association, and owners, slaves, and free persons could recline together in generous friendship, whereas outside the ritualized meal setting a much more rigid hierarchy among the same people was the rule. At the same time, the meals reproduced social boundaries and stratification in the ways of the hierarchy of reclining according to honorable societal status. This, too, could be seen as a ritual perfection of the contradictory values of equality and stratification, although Bell's term of reproduction probably makes the ritual function clearer.

The set, yet flexible, activities assumed to be a part of every Hellenistic meal became a *habitus* (Bourdieu) in which social bonding and boundaries gained both stability and pliability. For instance, the libation that opened the symposial part of the meal was always assumed as a gateway into the range of *symposion* activities, while the range of gods to whom one could dedicate that cup occasioned constant experimentation. This *habitus* of the meal allowed a certain "liminality" (Turner) in which new relational patterns and social structures could be risked without the larger consequences of everyday life. This created a larger affirmation of the values of friendship, care, and generosity and underwrote a societal project within the meal of *communitas* (Turner). The safe space the meals provided along with their incorporation of larger schemes of behavior (for example, serving/being served, orating, including/ excluding, working/relaxing) gave the meal participants a particularly strong sense of "objective reality" (Bell).

In this chapter, I examine five key elements of the Greco-Roman meal identified by both Matthias Klinghardt and Dennis Smith in order to demonstrate how thoroughly ritual theory applies to these meals. These elements are as follows:

1. The reclining of (more or less) all participants while eating and drinking together for several hours in the evening.
2. The order of a supper (*deipnon*) of eating, followed by an extended time (*symposion*) of drinking, conversation, and/or performance.
3. The marking of the transition from *deipnon* to *symposion* with a ceremonial libation.
4. The leadership by a "president" (*symposiarch* in Greek) of the meal, a person not always the same, and sometimes a role that was contingent or disputed.

5. A variety of marginal personages, often including servants, uninvited guests, "entertainers," and dogs.

The reclining of (more or less) all participants while eating and drinking together for several hours in the evening. The ethic of reclining together was continually emphasized in the Hellenistic literature. Indeed, the very name of these meals was "the reclining." This literature was very self-conscious about reclining together, at the same time admonishing the beauty and honorableness of such a gesture and being regularly astonished that it could happen. Reclining was a relative innovation. In Homeric Greece and ancient Israel, for example, the custom was to sit at a meal. Beginning in classical Greece and accelerating into Hellenistic times, reclining became increasingly the norm. Reclining signified leisure, and therefore reclining together expressed a community of leisure.

The norm of reclining stood in tension with one's experience in ordinary life, where very few people experienced much leisure, many lived in the middle of distress, and social tension was high. So reclining together at meals helped mark and notice differences (J. Z. Smith) in larger society. The larger societal differences of some people (the small patrician class) being able to enjoy leisure while the vast majority struggled to survive were renegotiated and perfected (J. Z. Smith) at meals in which (almost) "everyone" reclined.[47] A *communitas* (Turner) was formed over against the larger societal norms, making the meal into a social experiment relative to economic inequity. The "ritual" of reclining together posited a togetherness that was in the moment both ephemeral and actual.

Such a meal practice of reclining fits J. Z. Smith's interest in the ways ritual helps people think about and mark differences. The power of the "ritual" of reclining lay in its ability to have people who often were not equal outside of the banquet room reclining as equals within the meal. This allowed people to "think about" or "mark" the differences—that is, the reclining together of people who in public had substantially different statuses by virtue of their work relationship, their ethnicity, or the place they lived was actively noticed at the meal. The pointed reclining together of different ranks was noticed and thought about in the very act of the common reclining. The ephemeral reclining community helped people assess their larger world as well as express their hopes for a different world.

At the same time, reclining at meals underlined status and stratification. This was because there was always a distinct order of reclining, with the most honored position being the one on the right hand of the president/*symposiarch* and the least honored being the one at the other end of the circle who faced the *symposiarch*'s back. Almost always those with the places closest to the right hand of the *symposiarch* had the most prestige and honor in the larger society. But even when the order of reclining did not reflect societal status, there was still stratification.[48] Philo's description of the

Jewish group of Therapeutae in rural Egypt includes the following observation about a reclining order:

> After having offered up these prayers the elders recline, still observing the order in which they were previously arranged, for they do not necessarily designate as elders those who are advanced in years and very ancient, but in some cases they esteem those as very young men. (67.1,2)

That is, even while glorying in the koinonia/community of everyone reclining together, the reclining itself expressed a distinct stratification.

This contradiction initially seems hard to interpret. With the help of ritual theory, this practice of reclining that simultaneously celebrates overtly the expression of mutuality and the affirmation of societal rank can be seen as typical of the work ritual does. Holding up the values of equality and stratification at the same time ritually reproduces the tension of these two values in the society at large. It places this tension within a generally safe and controlled environment, which allows the participants to think about this contradiction in values. Indeed, occasionally Hellenistic literature pictures discussions at meals themselves about these contradictions. More often, the thought engendered is implicit, below the surface, with the analytical payoffs later or in different contexts.

But the "ritual" activity of reclining in some cases occasioned what Bell calls a deployment. This was the case relative to women at meals. While in the larger Greco-Roman society women were seldom allowed in public at all without explicit deference to men, in some cases (mostly in the western Mediterranean) this difference was ritually noticed and perfected as women reclined with men.[49] The habitus (Bourdieu) of reclining itself "produced" from the perspective of ritual theory a renegotiation of the general exclusive male prerogatives of society.

Of course, the occasional woman reclining accomplished such (re)thinking about males and females. But there were more intricate examples of this ritual reflection on and experimentation with the budding consciousness of a contradiction inherent in the way women were treated in the larger society. During the Hellenistic period, women were often found sitting at the feet of reclining men. It was from the position of sitting that some women could partake in the conversation and food of the meal. Lucian also mentioned the existence of a chair for women and contrasted it to the couch for reclining.[50] Such a positioning of women marked simultaneously the possibility of their participation in the generally male meal and their being marked as different from or somewhat inferior to the reclining men. The very act of a woman "ritually" sitting at the feet allowed the gathering to "think about" (J. Z. Smith) the male privilege in the larger society by simultaneously calling attention to male privilege and the possibility of women's participation in the meal setting.

Whether there were women occasionally reclining with men, women sitting in a somewhat segregated manner, or women sitting at the feet of men, these meals reproduced the tension around women's rights in the larger society in a way that allowed for retrenchment, insight, or social change. Here, the meal "ritual" produced a kind of liminal (Turner) situation in which the moorings of patriarchal order were slightly loosened during the meal. This loosening of male privilege was not so much an act of rebellion as an occasion for thinking about the difference, both between the outside world and that of the meal and between men and women. At most, it was a social experiment; at least, it was a rumination on difference. In Bourdieu's terms, it was a brief challenge to the *habitus* to allow the possibility of the *habitus* itself to shift slightly.

In the cases of differing status and gender politics, the meals actively reproduced in a heightened manner implicit tensions in the larger society in ways that occasioned semiconscious acknowledgment of the tensions, insight into those tensions, and occasional redeployment of either the meal structure itself or some part of the issue in another societal location. Such adjustments to the meal or society sometimes reaffirmed established stratification and sometimes changed toward mutuality.

This ritual theory explanation of the dynamics of meal reclining in relationship to larger societal issues of status and gender meshes with the earlier characterizations of symbolic gestures at these meals. Matthias Klinghardt identified the "utopian" character of the meals, while Dennis Smith paid attention to the way meal gestures and vocabulary seemed to have an "idealized" character to them. This lines up well with J. Z. Smith's understanding of ritual as "perfection," Bourdieu's sense that ritual breaks the ordinary boundaries of social order, and Turner's ritual liminality that leads to *communitas*. That Klinghardt and Dennis Smith have observed this utopian or idealized dimension to Hellenistic meal gesture confirms in another way the aptness of using ritual theory to understand the meals. On the other hand, the terminology of "utopian/idealized" does not do complete justice to the deep ambivalence and contradictory representations within the meal. Only ritual theory can explain both the utopian hopes and the contradictory values within these meals.

The order of a supper (deipnon) *of eating, followed by an extended time* (symposion) *of drinking, conversation, and/or performance.* This second basic element of the meals is so wide reaching that it cannot be comprehensively analyzed in this chapter. This chapter contents itself with treatment of one aspect of the *deipnon*. Some aspects of both the *deipnon* and the *symposion* that are ripe for ritual analysis must remain unaddressed.

Because the *deipnon* was the eating part of the meal, it could be assumed that it was more straightforwardly just a matter of nourishment and less susceptible to ritual analysis. It is, however, a tribute to the charged character of the whole meal that the *deipnon* attracted major attention on a symbolic level. It turns out that even this seemingly straightforward dimension of the meal carried serious social freight. One of these dimensions was dramatic tension about the food itself. Klinghardt summarizes the various tensions within these meals relative to the amounts of food and situations in which there did not seem to be enough.[51] Paul in Romans 14 and 15 addressed a major controversy about whether to eat meat or not.

In the extended discussions of Plutarch and Pliny, it becomes clear that tensions around food at the meals seem quite similar to some of the questions about who reclined where. The questions included the following: Should everyone receive the same amount and the same quality of food? If not, how is this justified? If so, how is it decided and regulated? These problematic situations were not just about whether the person with more status received the most or the better food. Pliny detailed a situation in which the amount of food to be given to each person raised the question of who was more important: the honored guests or the business clients.[52] Pliny reported a solution to this dilemma of all receiving equal portions. This seems to correspond to what Plutarch in his many discussions of this situation preferred. But that the question attracted so much attention in the literature is a sign that in the meals themselves the question was not resolved simply but posed over and over again.

Other meals entailed people bringing their own portion from their own home and eating what they had brought from home. The associations' meals seem to have had somewhat less controversy about the amount of food, although the issue of ranking was still quite present. For the associations, the rules stated fairly consistently that the office holders of the association received more and better portions of food. Everyone else received equal portions. Paul also wrote about a similar controversy in Corinth in which the amount of food people did or did not have was a problem.[53]

Mary Douglas's basic premise in "Deciphering a Meal" holds for this discussion. What one eats at a meal is not only about taste and nourishment. It also communicates social order. Although it takes Douglas to convince modern readers of this, it was assumed in the Hellenistic Mediterranean. The lack of resolve about who received how much food is best seen through the lens of ritual theory in a way quite similar to the above treatment of reclining. The social values of *isonomia* and *philia* required that everyone received the same amount of food. The existing social stratification demanded that some people receive more than others in recognition of their status. The meal, as any good ritual, first simply used the amount of food to reproduce a larger social tension. This gave a group the chance to observe the tension in a relatively protected environment. It elicited thought about the tension. And in some cases, it prompted action both within the meal and beyond it.

The amount of food at the *deipnon* and who received how much was perhaps a main dimension of ritualization of complex issues in the Hellenistic Mediterranean. But it was far from being the only one discussed in the literature. In Romans 14 and 15, Paul portrayed a situation in which what foods one did and did not eat at the *deipnon* became an object of ritualization. The community to which Paul's letter was addressed consisted of both Jews and gentiles. They gathered primarily for meals together, and the dietary proscriptions for these Jews prevented them from eating the meat that was available.[54] It appears also that these Jewish members of this "Christ" community were hesitant and worried about eating with those who ate meat. Paul described the situation: "Some believe in eating anything, while the weak eat only vegetables. . . . If your brother or sister is being injured by what you eat, you are no longer walking in love. Do not let what you eat cause the ruin of one for whom Christ died. . . . Let us then pursue what makes for peace and for mutual upbuilding. . . . It is wrong for you to make others fall by what you eat; it is not good to eat meat . . . or do anything that makes your brother or sister stumble" (14:2, 15, 19, 20b, 21). Paul's proposed solution seems to be for the gentiles to abstain from eating meat at these common meals in deference to the meal's significance in mutual upbuilding and Jewish (the "weak") dietary proscriptions.

This letter is important for this study not so much for Paul's argument or position but for what it reveals about the complex ritual function of the meal.[55] It is clear that Paul was addressing an ongoing meal practice that had heightened tensions because of the difference in the diets of the Jews and gentiles in the group(s).[56] One must surmise that at these meals, most (if not all) Jews ate only vegetables. One must also surmise that many (if not all) gentiles continued to eat meat. From other literature, it is clear that some Hellenistic Jews felt comfortable with gentiles eating meat while limiting their own diet to vegetables.[57] It seems possible that some Jews may have on occasion eaten meat with the gentiles as an expression of community solidarity and then afterward had regrets. It also seems possible that some gentiles may have abstained from eating meat in deference to Jewish worries. And it is likely (since Paul had heard about it) that some Jewish members had expressed their discomfort. It also seems clear that these meals (and these different behaviors) had been going on for some time. Although the question of community meal diet was not resolved, one must surmise that these meals continued to be attractive to the Jewish members, even though a number of the gentiles were eating meat.

It is understandable that Paul would have wanted this "Christ" community to overcome its dietary disagreements. It is clear from some of his argument that he valued the community more than any particular party's dietary practices ("For the kingdom of God is not food and drink, but justice and peace and joy in the Holy Spirit," 14:17).

Nevertheless, it appears that Paul missed both the important performative reflection that the meal was working on and the difficulty of the larger issue of Jews and gentiles in the broader environment. I suggest that the meals in the community to which Paul was writing were in the process of working creatively on complicated and intractable issues. As good rituals do, these meals were reproducing for reflection and eventual deployment complex tensions in the larger situation. Paul thought that the question was mostly about whose food customs would prevail. Instead, it was about the deeper problems of being a community of Jews and gentiles under the theological assumptions of Israel's faith and the sociopolitical domination of Rome. In the optic of ritual theory, these meals used food types to reproduce the larger drama of how to be a socially inclusive Jew in Christ in a society where only Rome was allowed to represent everyone. In hindsight, this early project of having Jews and gentiles in Christ claim the same identity appears much more complicated than Paul (and other early "Christian" leaders) had thought. Indeed, having a meal in which most Jews were eating only vegetables, most gentiles were eating vegetables and meat, some Jews and some gentiles were accommodating each other's diets, and some Jews were accepting the diversity of diets may have been the most "perfect" meal such a community could have had under the religious and political circumstances of that day.

Although Paul's desire for resolution in a common diet for this community meal is understandable, it ignored the deep work ritual negotiation does for complex social situations. He missed the power of meals—as good rituals—to place tensive basic schemes alongside one another and allow a shifting *habitus* to develop. He did not recognize the value of liminality for *communitas*. It is somewhat surprising that he did not recognize this power of the meal, since in other situations (for example, in Gal. 2:11-14, his encouragement of disagreeing Jews and gentiles to eat together at Antioch) he knew of the meal's power to work for the integration of differences.

Because only Paul's description and polemic concerning the meals of this community are available to scholarship, it is not possible to know how productive these meals were in addressing the complexity of Jew and gentile together in Christ under Roman domination and Jewish theology. Thanks to this letter, it is possible to see how a dimension of *deipnon* practice exhibited typical ritual power and carried enormous social freight for emerging identities, even if Paul himself did not understand the contributions of the ritual tension in the meal.

The marking of the transition from deipnon *to* symposion *with a ceremonial libation.*
At the end of the *deipnon*, the president/*symposiarch* led the meal participants in the pivotal performance of the meal. It marked an end to eating and the beginning of the richly textured *symposion*. It was a libation or series of libations, almost always accompanied by a paean (a unison song of hymn or chantlike quality). The action of a libation generally included the *symposiarch* pouring a small bit of wine into a cup, dedicating the cup to a god, pouring some of the wine on the ground or into a fire, taking a sip of the wine, and passing the cup around to all those reclining, who also took a sip.

The libation was positioned then as the pivotal performance by virtue of its concluding gesture of the *deipnon* and the beginning of the *symposion*'s extensive period of drinking, talking, entertainment, singing, and drama. Its centrality also drew from the ceremonial passing of the libation cup around to all those reclining and its relationship to the sung paean. It would be inaccurate to say that the libation was either the most attractive or the most dramatic part of the meal. Although centrally positioned and dramatically highlighted by both the ceremonial passing and the paean, the libation received much less attention and energy than the *symposion*. It was the *symposion* that participants cared about most, whether that be in terms of the serious teaching and discussion possible at some meals or the hilarity and entertainment at others. Indeed, Klinghardt takes note of how the libation was often treated as a pro forma necessity.[58]

This action, however, had many variations.[59] Much of the Hellenistic literature prescribed that the cup be dedicated to three gods. In addition, there were often cups drunk at this point dedicated to honored guests. After Caesar Augustus's military victory in Egypt, all meals were also to have included a libation in honor of the genius of the emperor. Associations regularly dedicated their libations to the particular patron deity of their group, while many other meals' constituencies would vary the god(s) to whom the meal was dedicated. Often, the libation included a prayer to Zeus Soter. A frequent libation prayer would be simply "to the good god." As the god of order, Apollo was one of the most frequent gods to whom libation was made, and this libation often was conflated with the dedication to the emperor. The prayer accompanying the libation asked the particular god for help, especially healing. Other libation prayers were more prayers of thanksgiving, often for victory. Sometimes, the libation prayer and the paean were the same thing.

Ritual theorizing about libation at the meals must take a number of elements into account: (1) the "centrality" of the libation in the meal structure; (2) the fluidity of the practice of this pivotal element (for example, how many libations? To gods and guests? To which god or gods?); and (3) the simultaneous formality and inattentiveness of the libation(s). Whatever the meaning of the early Christian cup at the meal, the meaning of libation in the more inclusive category of Hellenistic meals plays an important role in that early Christian meaning making.

Summarizing two aspects of life in the Hellenistic Mediterranean is necessary at this point in order to consider what the libation(s) at the center of the meal might have been reproducing, reflecting on, communicating, or deploying. These two aspects are religion and identity formation. Ritual theorizing about libation also calls for a conceptual relationship between the two. Both topics obviously require book-length treatments. Here, brief summaries with bibliographical footnotes must suffice, to be followed by some suggestions about their interrelationship.

Religion in the Hellenistic Mediterranean was in major flux.[60] In obvious relationship to this era's turmoil and the emerging polyglot described above, religion was remaking itself.[61] The pantheons of Greece and Rome still continued to attract attention and devotion,[62] and they were actively hybridized in a number of settings. At the same time, both polytheism per se and the specific Greco-Roman pantheons were coming under substantial critique from Greco-Roman philosophers,[63] from various conquered cultures with different religious traditions, and especially from the ever more popular Judaism. Judaism's growth outside of Israel seems to have had to do with both its diaspora and the appeal of its ethics and monotheism to many gentiles.

But Judaism was not the only "new" religion appearing. Very significant religious movements involving other "foreign" gods also were growing. Isis, Mithra, Osiris, and Eleusis all had adherent communities throughout the Mediterranean.[64] Finally, the Roman Empire increasingly saw itself as a religious option related closely to its political and cultural domination.[65] As noted above, the imperial cult often was also attached to devotion to Apollo.[66] In thinking about Hellenistic religion, it helps to recall the injunctions of Philip Harland that religion in that era was thoroughly integrated into a wide variety of what moderns would call secular settings.[67] In addition, Hellenistic religion generally needs to be seen in a much more hybrid fashion than is generally understood in contemporary Western society. Hellenistic persons did not necessarily "belong" to one religion, as is the case today. It was much more likely that one could attend the temple of one god one day, invoke the help of another the next, and raise a cup to a third god on yet another day.

Identity in the Hellenistic Mediterranean also was a work in progress. The term *Hellenistic* itself reflects the curious identity formation occurring in this period in which classical Greece had disappeared yet remained a cultural ideal. Roman identity itself was in many ways a curious copy of classical Greek culture. In addition, of course, Roman political rule brought with it an aggressive agenda for imposing a Greco-Roman mix on cultures as diverse as North Africa, Egypt, Israel, and Britain. As noted earlier, such Roman domination did major damage to people's ability to identify themselves with their tribal and family groupings. Finally, the militarily enforced pax romana enabled massive economic trade throughout the Mediterranean, and subsequent and equally massive migration in all directions. Rome encouraged identity formation in imperial and binary terms in which all people were either Roman or "barbarians."[68]

It is impossible not to relate these respective volatilities of religion and identity formation in the Hellenistic Mediterranean. On the one hand, it is important to see how the emergence of "new"[69] religions contributed to the complex demands of identity formation for those in the Mediterranean crucible. For instance, it seems relatively clear that adhering to a religion from another culture (for example, Isis of Egypt, Mithra of Persia, Jesus of Israel) helped many culturally displaced persons feel as if they belonged to the new and bigger world with a complex ethnic mix. This possibility of choosing a god for oneself or one's family had deeper roots in the ways Greeks and Romans had related to their own pantheons.

On the other hand, new constructions of identity often provided a home for emerging religious practice. For instance, the associations' relationships to identity and religion were complex and creative. Often, an association gave a set of people a new sense of belonging and identity by virtue of their bond together as carpenters or shipbuilders. While the crucial creativity in this new (and somewhat provisional) identity rested primarily on the gathering together (association) of people of the same trade, often a trade association would also choose a god or two to which to attach itself. On the other hand, certain family-based associations would take on the name of a god as the primary designation of their association. In the volatile and complicated Mediterranean mix, identity and religious formation were tightly, but not always predictably, related.

Returning to the possibility of ritually analyzing libation(s), the fragility and fluctuation of Hellenistic identity and the creative contributions religion seems to have made to identity formation may help understand the ways libation(s) were done in Hellenistic meals. When one made a libation to a particular god, that act may have reinforced one's identification with one's family, who had traditionally been attached to that god. A libation to another god might have connected such an individual to their profession. Or it might have provisionally identified one with a neighborhood association whose patron god was the one saluted with the cup. That is, the volatility of which god received libation(s) that is problematic in Klinghardt and Dennis Smith may in fact have been a ritual reproduction of the pervasive tenuousness of identity in Hellenistic times. The multiplicity of gods, each of which may have characterized one's particular Hellenistic identity, may indeed have communicated for those participating the larger multiplicity of identities with which one was struggling. So to make a libation to Bacchus in one circumstance, to the divine emperor in another circumstance, and to Isis in yet another may have been a perfecting of one's volatile identity. It is not at all beyond reason to think that some individuals raised a cup to Bacchus one night and to Jesus the next. And while the exclusiveness of most Jesus groups may have objected to such multiplicity, the broad practice of libation at many different kinds of suppers demonstrates that the Hellenistic meal was doing important ritual work concerning the complexities of identity in that era. Libations to multiple gods represented both the contingencies and the possibilities of emerging identity for people in the Hellenistic mix. It is no wonder that in some quarters a libation to multiple gods was considered the correct libational way.

This also helps explain the curious ambivalence of placing the libation at the most pivotal moment of the meal and at the same time underplaying its performance. It was crucial for people to understand who they were in this tumultuous and multivalent era. Inasmuch as they could craft an identity, they were less buffeted by the complex forces beyond their control. So who you were (or, in the case of libation, whom you saluted) was pivotal. And even while trying out various libations for an eventual deployment of one's identity helped in the long term, a strong and steady belonging was desired. Hence, the central placement of the libation, accompanied by the serious singing of a *paean* and the obligatory passing of the cup to everyone, signaled the importance of belonging. So the fact that the libation was pivotal but uninspired corresponded to the process of forging identity. One should not have forgotten that it was pivotal, but on the other hand, it was nearly impossible to resolve in the near term. Engaging questions of identity too strongly brought only frustration, and the way the libation was performed enacted the ambivalence and complexity of the task of identity formation in that era.

Looking at the multiplicity of gods receiving libations as reproductive of the larger quest for identity can help one understand the conflation of libations to gods and libations to guests of honor at the meal. Associating oneself libationally with an important personage at the meal itself communicated important aspects of identity— that is, if one sees the pivotal libations as subliminal explorations of identity (to whom do you belong?), raising a cup to a person of honor at the meal one was attending encouraged a sense that one and the honored person belonged together, that the respective identities reinforced each other.

Most easily understood in this ritual theory perspective is the libation to the genius of the Roman emperor. Although officially required of all meals since Augustus's Egyptian victory, it is not reflected consistently in the literature of the time. Even beyond Jewish practice (which was exempted from the required libation), it is fairly clear that some meals included such a libation and others did not. As noted earlier, in some quarters a libation to Apollo, both Augustus's (mythical) father and the god of order, qualified as a libation to the emperor. Again, here the multiplicity of practice relative to the libation to the emperor reflects effective ritual productivity. Making a libation to the emperor of the occupying Roman invader and occupier, making a libation to Apollo as a sometimes implicit symbol of the Roman occupying power, or avoiding a libation to the emperor as ritual choices reproduces dramatically the dilemma of living under a foreign power. It was an intractable dilemma, and in the meal's libation lay the chance for effective ritual processing of this difficult problem.

It was clear to most practitioners of the meal that no imperial power could control who made libation to the emperor and who did not. Indeed, in most cases, there was little danger that someone would report a meal host or president to imperial authorities for not having done the libation to the emperor. Occasionally, it was likely that an imperial guest of one sort or another made the libation more necessary. So the range of libational options actually extended further from refusal through occasional compliance to regular salute to the emperor. Here, too, meal participants most likely made use of the range of choices. It seems plausible that someone whose own meals with friends and family did not include the imperial libation would also participate in such a libation when the host was imperially related. In all cases, the moment of libation reproduced the drama of real life in which collaboration with the occupying power, tacit cooperation, occasional resistance, and steadfast resistance were real and costly choices. For most people, their behavior in real life lay in the area between tacit cooperation and occasional resistance. And it was almost impossible to move too close to consistent collaboration or thorough resistance to Rome.

In other words, the choices in real life kept coming up. The ritual of libation provided people a protected environment in which the relationship to the occupying empire could be reflected on in a visceral manner but without the high stakes of life outside the meal. At the meal, one had a chance to see how making the libation to the emperor felt, even when one had suffered at the hands of the occupation. Or, conversely, one could have a sense of how wise it seemed to resist the libation to the emperor, even when one knew that in the larger world that entailed more risks. Such acts of protected resistance and collaboration would have been available in multiple forms at the moment of libation. If one wanted to try out resistance, one could simply not drink the imperial cup when it was passed around. Or one could change one's libation from being to the emperor to the more implicit Apollonian form. In all variations of the libation, the possibilities for such ritual experiences to inform one's actions (what Bell calls "deployment") in the real world were also multiple.

The leadership by a "president" (symposiarch in Greek) of the meal, a person not always the same, and sometimes a role that was contingent or disputed. On a formal level, meals were led by the president/*symposiarch*. A *symposiarch* was selected prior to the meal, although often only just prior. When the meal was in the home of someone, it was not at all presupposed that the host and the *symposiarch* were the same person. The host guarded the prerogative of inviting guests and selecting the *symposiarch*. This leadership position gave that person the privilege/obligation of selecting the guest of honor to recline at the right hand of the president. Similarly, the *symposiarch* gave instructions for the proportions for mixing of wine with water. At least one, although not always all, of the libations was done by the *symposiarch*. Some introductions also were made by the *symposiarch* throughout the evening. Since many meals included rowdy behavior, an enforcer of civility was often necessary. This role, as well as the leading of discussion, was sometimes performed by the *symposiarch* and sometimes by someone else. In the more philosophical and religious meals, a teacher (not the *symposiarch*) would often lead the discussion. At many meals, discussion was spontaneously begun by a participant. Indeed, Plutarch—who elevated or even hyperbolized the role of the *symposiarch*—acknowledges that some thought that in philosophical meals a *symposiarch* was not necessary because behavior was so exemplary.[70] In the gospels, for instance, Jesus was constantly pictured as leading discussion and teaching at meals, but (with the exception of the last supper) he was never pictured as the *symposiarch*. The equality of those reclining was obvious in the right of everyone to speak. Singing was led by a variety of persons.

The president/*symposiarch* actually had a relatively limited leadership role. What determined the events of the meal depended much more on the culture-wide consensus on the structure and character of the meal than on individual leadership— that is, listing symposiarchal leadership as a basic element in the meal is a way of noticing that the structure of the meal and the cultural agreement about its character were much more determinative than any personal leadership. This was obvious both in the order and in the chaos of the Hellenistic meal. That everyone respected the basic meal order and followed the ethics of reclining by rank, libation, and *symposion* reflected the strength of the structure itself. That meals were also known for their disorderly character, their permeability to uninvited guests, and their debates about procedures revealed how weak the element of personal leadership was in the meal.

It is important to muse about this curious and major characteristic of these meals, which were so attractive and representative of the Hellenistic culture itself. Why did such a central cultural practice structure itself away from strong personal leadership? Especially given the hierarchical and patriarchal models of leadership in the rest of the culture (for example, emperor, patron, paterfamilias), why did this evocative and attractive cultural institution of meals rely so heavily on a flexible structure for authority? This musing deserves attention from several perspectives. For instance, one would need to test whether the dominant forces of the culture (for example, Roman imperial power) worked to make the meal an event without strong leadership. And one might explore the power roles of the behind-the-scenes personae of patron and host.

A ritual theory perspective, on the other hand, can integrate two main aspects of Hellenistic meals in the broader culture: (1) the dependence on a flexible structure rather than on personal leadership, and (2) the popularity and creativity of the meals. From a ritual theory perspective, the meal's flexible structure reproduces one of the deepest problems of the Hellenistic age—that of leadership. This makes what seems at first the curiosity of the meal's minimal personal leadership and reliance on a strong yet flexible structure into a coherent ritual achievement.

Although Roman (and, before it, Seleucid and Ptolemaic) imperial power certainly dominated the Hellenistic landscape politically, the experience of direction and leadership by the populace throughout the empire(s) was deeply ambiguous. Few, if any, conquered populations found themselves buying into the imperial power's agenda. Even the long-term and intense efforts of Rome to transform the varied Mediterranean into its Greco-Roman ideal did not convince its colonized territorial populations to cooperate by their own free will.

At the same time, the powerful new cultural mixes resulting from extensive international commerce and migration prompted unlikely grassroots initiatives in many arenas. The flourishing of new religious movements throughout the Mediterranean was accompanied by the powerful emergence of guilds of workers and neighborhood associations. Widespread educational initiatives—such as the desert schools of learning, the popular Cynics, and the Alexandrian Jewish schools and libraries—sprang up in many locales. Women's rights progressed more in this time than in any other in the ancient Mediterranean. Economically, patronage networks unassociated with the empire thrived alongside the massive patronage endeavor of the empire itself. The populace saw, in countless ways, grassroots creativity throughout the empire without any imperial encouragement and occasionally even with imperial opposition. Although the society's economic resources went in an overwhelming mass toward the imperial agenda, local and regional initiatives proved able to sustain themselves.

This experience of dominant imperial leadership determining a great deal while grassroots impulses also flourished was confusing and disorienting. Although the empire represented itself as the only power and even attempted to supplant or redirect most indigenous authority, its dominance was far from complete and other functioning power centers in people's lives were obvious. The leadership of the empire was neither total nor avoidable. Nonimperial leadership impulses regularly succeeded and failed.

The limited role of the *symposiarch* in the context of a strong yet flexible meal order can be seen as a reproduction of the dilemma of leadership and power for Hellenistic populations. The relatively ostentatious positioning of the *symposiarch* (as keystone to the reclining order) along with his role in the libation presented him as an apparent power figure. However, his actual leadership was much more limited than the assumed structural order of the meal and the creative initiatives of other participants during the *symposion*. That the *symposiarch* was rarely the same in subsequent meals made sure that too much power could not accrue to one person.

The meal reproduced a power structure with a superficial leader and an unpredictable yet active constituency. The powerful allegiance of the general population to the meal order (without much attention to the *symposiarch*) wrote into the power dynamics of the meal a stable and safe environment, which could test the reliability of spontaneous and diffuse leadership in the presence of an artificial authority figure. The strength and safety of the meal order allowed multiple and regular initiatives by the regular populace. It allowed the inspired yet unofficial impulses to temporary leadership to succeed and fail on their own merit and reception. The formalized role of the *symposiarch*, even though weak, prevented any natural leadership from the participants to have sustained success.

This power structure within the meal delicately reproduced the ironies, chronic contradictions, potential, and long-term instability of grassroots leadership in the Hellenistic era.[71] It allowed constant and varied perfections within a safe environment. Individuals could test their own leadership charisma without taking too many social risks or having too much chance of long-term success and affirmation. The associations even legislated some of these leadership roles within the meal, allowing them to perfect group leadership process within the meal but without much recourse to leadership in everyday life.

It is tempting to see this relatively shared and spontaneous power balance in the meal as the evolution of a more democratic model of leadership. It is clear that the meal allowed a variety of leadership to emerge and that power was regularly shared in ways that evoked skills within a range of participants. That the associations took the next step in creating a legislative process to refine the governance of the meal cannot be overlooked.

On the other hand, I want to issue a caution for reading too much political and social modeling into this power structure of the meal. Rather, it seems to me that ritual theory is a much more cogent framework in which to see the meal's power structure. The way leadership and power were structured in the meal seems more like ritual's social intelligence of reproducing an intractable problem from the larger society for the attention of the meal participants. This longer-term wisdom of ritual dynamics that helps groups examine the problematics of their larger situation seems to be much more the case than the meal being a primary mechanism for democratic-style leadership. It is not at all clear that the meal power structure was a good model for governance. The *symposiarch* was somewhat of a stereotype, and the regular tendency of the meals to dissolve into temporary chaos had few merits for the larger Hellenistic society. Rather, the stereotypical *symposiarch* provided a foil for ritual reflection and perfection, and the temporary chaos illustrated the creative character of liminality for ritual process. This does not mean that the ritual perfection going on in the meal did not include some democratic explorations. It simply means that the overall structure of the meal was probably due more to the ritual dynamic of the meal than to explicit sociopolitical explorations. The intersection of social and political experimentation with ritual perfection is discussed in more detail in chapter 8 on meals as a key to early Christian social experiments.

A variety of marginal personages, often including servants, uninvited guests, "entertainers," and dogs. A great deal of ancient literature about meals treated in some detail the personages beyond those reclining. Crucial to the *deipnon* were the servants. Although a few exceptions in this regard are quite interesting,[72] the Hellenistic meal more or less required servants to bring the food into the *deipnon*, to clean up before the *symposion*, and—to a lesser extent—to serve wine at the *symposion*. In the less wealthy circumstances, there were fewer servants. In the associations (probably the place where the greatest number of poor people partook of such a meal), either the association hired servants using the dues collected or some members of the association rotated these duties while the others reclined. The presence of dogs at the meals had mostly to do with their ability to help in the cleanup after the *deipnon* by eating the food (especially the bread used as napkins or utensils) thrown on the floor.

During the *symposion*, another kind of hired personnel appeared: the entertainers. These entertainers were generally of three types: instrumental musicians (primarily, but not exclusively, flute players, who were primarily women), singers, and speakers (teachers/sages or orators). Not all entertainers were paid, and some of the sages and singers came simply for the opportunity to have an audience. Often, both singing and teaching were also done by those reclining as invited guests. Although too much to consider in this chapter, thinking about the ritual dimension(s) of this constant and necessary servant/employee presence at the meal is likely promising.

A focus for this part of the meal can be ritual analysis of the major phenomenon of uninvited guests. Although noticed occasionally in the literature of classical Greece about meals, the theme of uninvited guests became major in the Hellenistic literature. Klinghardt identifies in this literature three different kinds of uninvited guests: the *akletos* (one who crashed the party without any invitation); the guest who was invited but came late, usually only for the *symposion*; and the *epikletos* (someone invited secondhand by another invited guest).[73] Although both Plato, from the earlier period, and Plutarch, more extensively from the Hellenistic era, tended to present the uninvited guests as caricatures (in these two authors, the uninvited guests regularly provide a key contribution to the overall event), their existence is quite clear from the massive attention paid to the problems created by them. Even Plutarch had to address them as a problem in that in *Questiones Convivales* he went to some length to propose five different ways invited guests can help with the problem of uninvited guests (for example, don't invite someone who is a troublemaker).

Uninvited guests of all three types nevertheless appeared in the literature as troublemakers.[74] They interrupted the discussion, sometimes intentionally. Much of the literature cited Cynics as especially regular uninvited and provocative guests. Both the *akletos* and the *epikletos* burdened the host with the need to provide additional food and drink. Some of them stood at the meal because all of the couches were taken, while others demanded a couch and even one higher up in the order of reclining. Some of them made fun of the host or *symposiarch*. Others started fights. Lucian told the story of one Cynic who came uninvited, started a fight, extinguished the light in the room, tried to rape one of the flute girls, and because he refused to leave even after everyone else had left, slept off his hangover on the couch he had not been successful in claiming for himself during the meal.[75]

The increasing attention paid to the uninvited and late guests by the Hellenistic literature invites ritual theorizing. One could suggest that this is a perfect example of Turner's ritual liminality, which leads to *communitas*. The curious tolerance of such misbehavior by the Hellenistic meals certainly suggests that there is a quasi-intentionality about these guests' inclusion.

I suspect, however, that the situation is a bit more complex ritually. On some level, the discord created by the uninvited and late guests belonged to the meal. Although it might be said that the Hellenistic era simply could not control people well enough, the other ways that the meal maintained discipline (for example, invited guests reclined in a designated order) make this unlikely. Rather, the threat to the order of the meal through the uninvited guests was more a performance of a deeper set of issues worthy of reflection. So it is appropriate to analyze this complexity of late and uninvited guests as a ritualization.

A striking parallel exists between the messy constituency of the meal (given the regularity of late and uninvited guests) and the polyglot Hellenistic society. It very well could be that the surprising tolerance by the meal for these intruders was a reproduction of the messy societal makeup throughout the Hellenistic Mediterranean. The social intelligence of ritual process continually creates safe places (the meal order) for which to think through and perfect the major anomalies of the larger environment. In the case of the Hellenistic Mediterranean, one persistent dilemma was the new, unpredictable, enriching, destabilizing, and growing social mix of people. Inasmuch as the meal allowed some occasional surprising constituency into it, it ritually helped people to think about how to deploy resources in the broader social mix of the Mediterranean. Within this larger Bell and J. Z. Smith framework, it is also appropriate to notice the liminality of the uninvited guests.

Ritual analysis of the uninvited guests points to a more extensive dynamic of the meal in a similar regard. Klinghardt has noted how much of the literature concerning the uninvited or late guests traded in stereotypes—that is, the source of upheaval was consistently the uninvited or late guest(s). One could think then that the uninvited guest is simply a literary type and is not reliable as a source for the historical phenomenon of meals.[76] However, both the plethora of references and the way even Plutarch, who idealized the meal for its orderliness, described these disturbances support the reality of the uninvited guests.

One can also challenge the ancient literature's straightforwardness in another regard. I wonder whether one can take its representation of the late and uninvited guests as being the only (or even primary) disturbers of order. It may very well be that the literature's worry about disorder had also to do with the behavior of invited guests. It seems likely to me that the idealization of the meal and meal invitees could have very well reoriented the blame for disorder onto a caricature of the uninvited or late guest. Certainly, the likes of Plutarch, Cicero, and Lucian all also portray disruptive behavior by invited guests. It is also clear from the several manuals of rules from associations that rowdiness by the invited members occurred regularly at their meals. Paul's complaints about the Corinthian meals (1 Cor. 11:17-23; 11:27-34; 14:26-40) fit into this larger genre of literature about regular diners making trouble at the meals.

This complication concerning a possible caricature of uninvited guests as the source of meal disorder actually does not limit, but rather expands, the ritual analysis of the phenomenon of disorder at the meal. It seems that the larger tolerance of some disturbance, especially in the *symposion*, is explained most clearly as a ritual liminality that helps reproduce the larger tensive mix of people in Hellenistic society. The ultimately trustable established order of the meal allowed certain portions of the meal to descend into near chaos, since the ritualized experience of such social disorder helped perfect it for the ordinary life experiences of the diners. The ways the meals tolerated, or even elicited, these disorders created ritual space in which to reflect on the larger societal conflicts about "uninvited" ethnicities and migrants.

This chapter has made clear the importance of understanding Hellenistic meals within the optic of ritual theory. This ritual analysis has revealed the creative social practice of the meals themselves, showing that they are not incidental to the social dynamics of the Hellenistic era but rather a key dynamic in negotiating certain key social issues of Mediterranean society. Such ritual analysis of Hellenistic meals and their importance for the larger Mediterranean populace is foundational to any understanding of the contribution of Christian meals of the period. It is to these tasks that the next chapters turn.

CHAPTER FIVE
THE **Expansive Character** OF **Early Christian Meals**

BOTH THE BASIC SHAPE AND DYNAMICS of early Christian meals have now been established. The character of Hellenistic festive meals is clear, and the intensity of early Christian participation in such meals has been demonstrated. As this book now turns to elaborating the ways early Christians' meals became a primary social practice, two major questions about the scope of these meals relative to the larger Mediterranean society must be addressed:

1. *How broad was the social and economic reach of the festive meals in the Hellenistic Mediterranean?* Especially since much of the classic literature on these meals comes from the literate elite, it is very important to investigate whether these festive meals really occurred throughout Hellenistic society beyond these elite literary circles. This question matters a great deal, since much scholarship of the past twenty years has increasingly suggested that early Christians came substantially from poor classes.[1]

2. *How much did larger society matter to early Christians gathered at meals?* Because of their very marginal political power and relatively insignificant numbers in the first 150 years, one could imagine that early Christian meals might be relatively sectarian in character, with little interest in the larger society. Even given chapter 4's discovery that the Hellenistic meal dynamics ritually addressed a number of important social questions of that day, the societal stances of early Christians at festive meals need to be assessed.

This chapter examines both of these significant questions in order to fill out a picture of the place of early Christian meals in the larger Hellenistic society.

Did Poor Early Christians Gather at Festive Meals?

One might think that the answer to this question is obvious, since the New Testament and other early Christian literature clearly portray poor followers of Jesus gathering together for meals. However, almost all literary efforts in the first and second centuries must be related in some way to the elite, in that probably no more than 5 percent of the population was literate.[2] These writings, then, cannot be taken at face value and must be submitted to the same suspicion as is the more obviously elite literature about meals that has made up much previous scholarship on Hellenistic meals.

Key to understanding the central role meals played in the emergence of early Christianity is another field of new research that has come into its own in the past twenty years.[3] This recent research has significantly deepened some research done in the nineteenth and early twentieth century. It is the study of what have come to be called the associations of the Hellenistic Mediterranean. The picture this recent research paints of Hellenistic associations shows the vast majority of these organizations gathering principally at meals. The most recent reflections on the associations research by the leading researchers themselves have drawn close analogies among associations, early Christian congregations, and synagogues of that time—in this way placing all three allegedly separate institutions in close relationship with the Hellenistic festive meal.[4]

For the purposes of this investigation, these studies are especially important in thinking about what classes participated in the festive meals, since much of the evidence is from epigraphic (and therefore not purely literary) sources and since many associations had membership of common laborers. First, I summarize the research about the Hellenistic associations and, then I examine the linkages between associations research, Hellenistic meals, and early Christian social formation.

THE HELLENISTIC ASSOCIATIONS

Associations is the current English word used by scholars for a prevalent kind of social organization of the Hellenistic era. It is generally acknowledged as the best translation for the groups who called themselves by a wide assortment of Greek, Latin, and Hebrew names.[5] There is good reason to connect all of these different Hellenistic groups under the twenty-first-century label of "associations." But perhaps the easiest moniker for them for the reader not familiar with the technical research is *club*, a term also used by Dennis Smith and others.[6] Indeed, from the perspective of this book, one might even best call them "supper clubs."

This plethora of small groups gathering at meals was a Hellenistic innovation. Although such groups did exist in pre-Hellenistic times, there was an explosive interest in them in the Hellenistic era that made them as organizations a major society-wide phenomenon. These groups met regularly (usually monthly) in numbers as small as

10 and as large as 150;[7] they tended to be somewhere between 15 and 50 in size.[8] "The associations made various kinds of provisions for how the food was to be provided. Sometimes the banquet was held in the vicinity of a local temple, where banquet rooms could be rented and meat could be obtained from sacrifices. Sometimes a patron would host such a meal in an aristocratic home."[9] Sometimes the group rented a nontemple dining space, and occasionally an association became strong enough to purchase a building for its meetings.[10]

The constituency of these associations was particularly striking. As G. E. M. de Ste. Croix has emphasized, a great many of the associations had a primarily working-class membership.[11] On the other hand, the ancient literature on the "collegia" tended to concentrate on the influential persons who belonged to or sponsored the groups.[12] But in new research, it is clear that an unusually wide spectrum of persons belonged.[13] "Slaves could be leaders in such groups. The mix of slaves and free in this protected environment was frequent. Similarly men and women associated in these settings far more than in public."[14] Although many of these associations' memberships had familial or ethnic bases, others breached traditional family and ethnic boundaries.

The mood of association meetings generally reflected the larger atmosphere of the meals described earlier. Joy, humor, friendship, mutuality, and conversation were sustaining characterizations of the associations. It was, however, also the case that the unusually broad constituency created tensions. For instance, the rules of the Iabakchoi took great pains to prescribe goodwill and to punish conflict among its membership.

This Hellenistic culturewide organizational innovation of eclectic and relatively small groups gathering regularly

> was precipitated by the long-term dominance of imperial rule in the Mediterranean. Tribal and national cohesion and identity entered a dramatic period of decline after Alexander the Great conquered so much of the Mediterranean and Near East and the subsequent invasions and rule by the Seleucids, the Egyptians, and then most ambitiously, the Romans. These centuries of imperial domination dealt mortal blows to many of the ways extended families, clans, tribes, and nations gathered people together. The oppression of the various empires seriously undermined the ways people gathered in traditional associations based on blood and geography.
>
> Many of the empires attempted to replace traditional social groupings with their own organization. There were constant attempts to impose new kinds of social organization on the conquered peoples. Perhaps the most dramatic example of this in the long Roman rule of the Mediterranean was the wildly ambitious attempts of Rome to build complete new cities, based supposedly on the ideals of classic Greece and imposed on

almost every area by conquest. These imperial attempts to replace many traditional groups of kinship and nationality with their own had limited success.

The combination then of the destruction of traditional groups and the resistance to imperially imposed institutions resulted in a lack of social cohesion and identity among the populace throughout the Roman Empire. In the wake of these combined forces of social chaos, a new kind of social association emerged.[15]

This new organization of the Hellenistic association blossomed. It elaborated itself with groups forming around work roles, such as the associations of craftspersons and builders. Other associations came into existence with an impetus from entertainment and music. Religion was often a convening energy, with many of the associations taking on the names of gods. Many associations provided a guarantee of burial for their members, since—with the weakening of family and ethnic ties and a growing impoverishment in urban settings—many people lacked the means, land, or connections for a proper burial.[16] In all these contexts, the associations grew during the Hellenistic era.[17]

Kinds of Associations

Even in this brief introduction, it is already obvious that there were different kinds of associations. While it is clear that all of them shared an emphasis on group loyalty within a relatively small constituency, on gathering for meals, and on associational membership as a new and strong component of identity, substantial differences among the associations remain. Scholarship has been creating typologies for these differences since the nineteenth century.[18]

Echoing some earlier work but addressing more directly the possibility of a new typology, John Kloppenborg noted in 1996 that "it is especially difficult to arrive at a clear taxonomy of associations in the Hellenistic and imperial periods."[19] As an alternative to functionalism,[20] Kloppenborg suggested that there are three membership bases for associations: household, occupation, and cultic.[21] Harland follows Kloppenborg's suggestion and looks for common social networks that associations created. Harland proposes a typology of five different social network–based associations: "(1) household connections, (2) ethnic or geographic connections, (3) neighborhood connections, (4) occupational connections, and (5) cult or temple connections."[22]

Harland's shift to the association as social network directly promotes this book's interest in understanding the (meal-based) associations as a Hellenistic innovation of social formation. It underlines the importance of recognizing how the Hellenistic era abounded in enthusiasm for the creation of alternative social networks. The massive political, social, and cultural changes during the Hellenistic period required this kind of social productivity. The destabilization of group loyalty patterns by the new global power structure, the pervasive new economic patterns enabled by the ways the empires linked nations, and the rupture of old tribal and clan loyalties called for a new way of people gathering and identifying themselves. The Hellenistic associations were a major means for such new collective identity.

ASSOCIATIONS AND MEALS

The connection between associations and meals is obvious on a surface level. Matthias Klinghardt declares: "The meal of the associations was the most important and in many cases the only form of ancient association life," and the associations were "always a meal oriented community."[23] In his introductory essay to the seminal volume that he coedited with John Kloppenborg, Stephen G. Wilson also says that "communal eating and drinking are a fairly constant feature of life in associations."[24]

As a part of his study of the buildings that many associations owned, Harland summarizes archaeological scholarship on the few known buildings owned by associations, observing that they "often included both sanctuaries and banquet facilities."[25] The builders association of Ostia owned a structure that contained four dining rooms with built-in couches.[26] Rich in actual visuals from the Hellenistic period, Harland's book contains two reliefs from Asia Minor that show both reclining and gathering for a meal as a part of different associations' practices. In keeping with his insistence that religion was not segregated from much of the rest of Hellenistic life (see chapter 3), Harland also maintains that associations' "banqueting activities could be infused with varying degrees of religious significance for the participants, being viewed as a means of honoring or communing with the gods."[27]

For this book, it is also important to see how meals played a crucial role in the substantial development of Hellenistic associations. It is not just that the associations as major Hellenistic organizations had meals as a central element. The ways that the already developed meal practice helped these associations become a significant agent for bringing people in the Hellenistic era together cannot be overlooked. The symposial traditions of substantial and leisurely personal interaction after the *deipnon* allowed the associations to become organizations in which a new kind of grouping developed allegiance among its members. The Hellenistic age was a time when old ways of convening people were deteriorating or being actively undermined. The cities in which Hellenistic associations became so strong were often a jumble of dissimilarity and disjunction. That the associations were able to rely on the institution of the meal and did not have to develop a new form of regular and extended conviviality jumpstarted their abilities to convene neighbors, colleagues, and ethnicities.

Conversely, the associations contributed a larger organizational and communal structure in which meals became the primary Hellenistic medium for social expression and social experimentation. The ongoing organization of associations provided an expansive and stable social framework in which the variety and depth of human interaction at meals were extensively elaborated. This combination of the long-standing Near Eastern meal practice and the predominant organization of the associations in Hellenistic times made for a wide and strong platform for social formation and experimentation.

"Voluntary" Associations

Associations did represent a significant and widespread social formation in the Hellenistic era. The relatively new kind of grouping they represented has been studied in both nineteenth-century and current research.[28] In both phases of this research, part of the associations' significance has been pictured in the relatively strong role the formerly unassociated individual played in the group. It is clear that to a certain extent, such individuals chose to associate with these groups, in contrast to the ways most groups in previous eras were constituted through already established social classes, tribes, or families.

The Hellenistic associations' memberships seem to have depended much more on the will of the individual.[29] For instance, much has been made of the ways associations ensured that an individual who otherwise might not have the means or connection would receive a dignified burial and be honored posthumously at an association meal. It is quite clear that this assurance spurred certain individuals to join an association. Even more significant, as mentioned earlier, is that these associations also seemed to attract individuals just because of the appeal of their particular social dynamics, with perhaps the assurance of a funeral being only a superficial excuse for joining.

Similarly, in the case of ethnic associations, these groups were formed in explicit response to the various elements of Hellenistic society that threatened the dissolution of ethnic solidarity. Three specific forces of the time made it increasingly difficult for an ethnicity to hold together: (1) the Roman imperial pressure to be loyal to the empire and to see the banding together of ethnic groups as a threat; (2) the dispersion of ethnic groups throughout the Mediterranean due to commerce, immigrations, and forced labor and enslavement of conquered peoples; and (3) the ethnic tensions within the multiethnic cities of the Mediterranean. This meant that individuals were placed in larger social situations where their own ethnic loyalties could be reinforced by choosing to join an ethnic association.

The occupational associations also had a voluntary dimension to them in that becoming a member of such an association was not attached to the employment itself or to the employer. A builder, for instance, joined an association in solidarity with his fellow workers and occasionally even over against his employer(s).

All of this has led recent scholarship to the nomenclature of "voluntary associations."[30] But even more recently, doubts have been expressed about this label.[31]

A range of scholars have worried that this "voluntary" label too strongly connotes a kind of "modern" social model in which the individual is seen as largely autonomous. It is indeed the case that individuals in the Hellenistic era were far less autonomous than in the twentieth and twenty-first centuries. The examples of both the ethnic and the occupational associations illustrate at least as much social pressure from others to join an association as individual voluntary will. The idea of voluntary autonomy even in modern/postmodern society, of course, may also be more of a state of mind than a sociological datum.

However the field sorts out the label of "voluntary," it is in any case clear both that Hellenistic associations had a new dimension of individual choice about them and that the will of the modern individual could not have existed in that era. For the purposes of this study, both edges of the debate are appropriate. The Hellenistic nexus of meals and associations needs to be acknowledged as a new kind of broad-based social impulse in which individuals exercised a significant amount of choice, both in joining associations and in interacting within the meal of the association. On the other hand, the combination of ancient Mediterranean culture and small-group life has to be seen as full of collective forces bringing people together in unconscious ways involving feelings of cultural obligation quite foreign to the modern notion of choice. The meal in the associations had the peculiar advantages of a heightened sense of choice combined with deep and ingrained collective impulses.

ASSOCIATIONS, SYNAGOGUES, AND CONGREGATIONS

For over a century, some historians have proposed that Hellenistic associations were similar to and often confused with Christian churches in the first two centuries. A number of the researchers of the late nineteenth and early twentieth centuries suggested strong similarities.[32] The recent research of the past two decades has renewed this proposal.[33] It is necessary to set this analogy in a larger context of historical reflection on the origins of the social form of Christian churches/congregations in order to appreciate it fully and to assess its current significance for the study of Christian beginnings and this particular meal's approach to the larger issue.

On one level, even the most conventional perspectives on Christian beginnings have realized that early Christianity did not have "churches" in any sense that resembles twenty-first-century Christian congregations or, for that matter, monastic groups, Reformation churches, or medieval parishes. And so, the conventional imagination of the beginnings of "churches" or "congregations" has had to rely on the unlikely idea that churches/congregations appeared in the first century *ex nihilo* as a new Christian invention. This idea, often implicit in even more sophisticated scholarship,[34] not only is unlikely because such social forms do not spring into existence all at once. It also is at odds with the standard imagination of Jesus as the heroic innovator of Christianity, since there are no New Testament texts that portray Jesus as founding, or even interested in founding, churches or any social organization. Much of the master narrative and conventional imagination of the origins of churches in the first or second century then has rested on crude and unexamined presuppositions.

Somewhat less crudely, but with a basically similar idea, some historians of the past several generations have suggested that early Christian congregations were a new social form inherently derivative from new and unique Christian insights, theology, and social vision. These ideas of a new Christian social genius go as far back as Adolf Deissmann in Germany and Josiah Royce in the United States.[35]

More recent versions of this theory of how early Christian churches came into being have sometimes referenced Hellenistic associations, but mainly as organizations contrasted to the social visionary form of Christian congregations. In the 1980s, Wayne Meeks's pioneering introduction of sociological perspectives on early Christianity, *The First Urban Christians*, basically proposed—after reviewing organizations that may be considered similar—that there were more differences than similarities between congregations and associations.[36] As Philip Harland worries: "One begins to get the impression that Meeks views Christian groups not only as distinctive but as unique in the sense that they are incomparable."[37] Proposing that Christian congregations were essentially not comparable to any other institution only slightly veils the basic proposal that the Christian groups were a totally new social formation, dramatically appearing alongside of ingenious Christian beliefs per the master narrative.

Given the unlikely scenario of early Christian congregations appearing *ex nihilo*, some historians have suggested that the early Christian organizations were some variation on synagogues.[38] Since Jesus was a Jew and since the gospels portray Jesus as attending synagogues, this rationale goes, early Christian gatherings must have been some form of synagogue, even if an odd kind that welcomed gentiles. Although less obvious as flawed proposal, this imagination of the basic social formation of early Christianity also seems improbable. This is not because it would have been unlikely that a number of Jesus followers would have continued Jesus' practices after his death. The larger problem with seeing the first or second layer of Christian social formation as synagogues is that, upon closer historical investigation, it is not at all clear what a synagogue was during the first century.

The word itself is a Greek word, *synagoge*, which simply means "meeting," "assembly," "meeting place," or, most literally, "coming together." This Greek word is used throughout the Mediterranean for a wide variety of get-togethers. Most of its usages have nothing to do with a religious gathering, much less a Jewish one. It is the case that the term *synagoge* was used prior to the destruction of the Jerusalem Temple by Jews and their proximates for gatherings of Jews in geographic locales that were too far from Jerusalem to permit regular temple attendance. In the Hellenistic era, therefore, the wide diaspora of Jews throughout the Mediterranean were known to have gathered for "synagoge." In some cases—but by no means all—the buildings where these diaspora get-togethers occurred were also called "synagoge." Often, the word simply seems to have designated the "meeting" itself.

Nor is it clear what first-century diaspora Jews did at these meetings. There are a number of indications that practices varied at these meetings.[39] A wide variety of accounts of diaspora Jews gathering include descriptions of meals.[40] It is the case that after the destruction of the Jerusalem Temple in 70 CE, rabbinic Judaism slowly took shape, and this rabbinic Judaism created a mostly new organization of "synagogue" as a primary facet of its self-understanding. But this process needed at least two centuries to solidify itself and should not be confused with what was called "synagogue" in the diaspora of the first century. There are very few sources that provide any sense of overview of what these prerabbinic synagogues did, and the variety of partial sources that exist can (and perhaps should) be read as reflecting different practices in different parts of the Mediterranean. In addition, as Wayne O. McCready has recently noted, "there is minimal evidence in the New Testament showing an effort to imitate synagogue structure and organization."[41] In other words, even if one wants to propose that some early Christians met for some kind of synagogue, this does not solve the question as to what this practice was. As what follows will show, a number of historians are now thinking that associations research may actually be an important source for what these prerabbinic synagogues did. This only underlines the lack of sustained reflection on what kind of organization early Christian churches were and what practice they undertook.

Matthias Klinghardt has proposed: "That in their organization and even in their group dynamics the early Christian congregations are comparable in some aspects to Hellenistic associations is an old insight, which only recently has again slowly reached appreciation. Certainly it could lead to still much more fruitful results."[42] Klinghardt's hope on this front is being confirmed by much of the recent research that he cites and that has appeared since his 1996 assessment.

Wayne O. McCready's focused essay "Ekklesia and Voluntary Associations" concludes (after some hesitation):

> Early churches shared significant common features with voluntary associations, with the consequence that they were viewed as such, certainly by outsiders, and to a degree by insiders. . . . Research by Wilken, Malherbe, and Meeks confirms that voluntary associations are productive resources for investigating what others thought about early Christian assemblies, as well as what Christians believed and how they practiced their religion. It makes eminent sense that voluntary associations offered an initial reference point that placed churches comfortably within the parameters of Graeco-Roman society. . . . Indeed the diversity of voluntary associations was an attractive feature, for it allowed experimentation and development by the ekklesiai while at the same time providing a special

type of belonging that created a form of community definition that was distinct from the larger society.[43]

Reference has already been made to the ways G. E. M. de Ste. Croix places early Christian groups within the proletarian movement of associations in the Hellenistic era. Similarly, John Kloppenborg's essay in his 1996 edited volume with Stephen Wilson makes note of how a Christian theologian as late as Tertullian is referring to Christian gatherings with the vocabulary of associations.[44] Wilson himself presents an extended comparison of membership, activities, organization, exclusivity, burial activity, gender roles, class, and structure between associations and early Christian churches, generally affirming "a connection between Christian groups and collegia."[45]

In the past decade, both Richard Ascough and Philip Harland have produced specialized studies on the intersection of associations and Christian congregations that both confirm the similarities and complicate the enterprise. First, both Ascough and Harland have wisely decided to delimit these studies to particular locales—Ascough to the cities of Thessalonica and Philippi, and Harland to Asia Minor. Second, each of these studies has taken on a particular question about the connections between congregations and associations. Harland, as noted earlier, is most interested in the relationship between Christian congregations and Roman imperial authority. Ascough has linked the specifics of occupational associations and the early Thessalonian Christian assembly.

Ascough's 2003 book, *Paul's Macedonian Associations: The Social Context of Philippians and 1 Thessalonians*, undertook an in-depth analysis of the similarities between associations and the groups Paul related to in Philippi and Thessalonica. Ascough's conclusions in part were as follows:

> In our discussion we showed that aspects of Paul's understanding of the Macedonian communities can be found in the inscriptions of the voluntary associations. . . . In some cases Paul uses the practices of the associations in his attempts to nuance the Macedonians' self-understanding as communities. In doing so Paul's starting point is voluntary association language and organization. All of this suggests that both Paul and the Macedonian Christian communities share the same discursive field as the voluntary associations. . . . The comparative process reveals that on the social map of antiquity the associations provide a ready analogue for understanding the community structure of the [*sic*] Paul's Macedonian Christian communities.[46]

Harland's own 2003 book never directly renders a final judgment on how much associations and congregations can be seen as the same thing. However, on his Web site, Harland is a bit more direct:

According to standard views, Jews and Christians set themselves completely apart from Greco-Roman society, and avoided any participation in surrounding culture. It is indeed true, that from a bird's eye of culture in the Roman empire, synagogues and congregations stand together as minority cultural groups. This is primarily because of their monotheism . . . in a polytheistic culture. . . . Yet, at the same time, a closer look at synagogues and congregations within the context of associations in Asia Minor begins to draw attention to the many ways in which gatherings of Jews and Christians, like other "pagan" associations, could claim a place for themselves and find a home within ancient Mediterranean society. . . . Comparing associations with both Jewish and Christian groups can provide new, even revolutionary, perspectives on Christian origins and the New Testament. . . . Archeological evidence from the cities of Asia Minor provides a new vantage point from which to reassess our understanding of social and religious life in the Roman empire among Jews, Christians, and other Greeks and Romans.[47]

Despite his somewhat elliptical conclusions in the book, Harland lays out the most thorough set of similarities among Hellenistic associations, synagogues, and congregations in the past ten years of associations research. In his concluding chapter, he summarizes the main similarities presented throughout the book:

We have seen the value in comparing associations with both synagogues and congregations on a regional basis. . . . Inscriptions and archeology shed new light on Paul and his communities . . . including issues of identity in Pauline circles. Occupational identity and networks were an important basis of association in the ancient world. Paul often expressed his own identity in terms of his occupation as a handworker (tent maker), and we found that the workshop and its networks were a significant social context for early Christian preaching. . . . Furthermore the importance of fictive kin language within some associations, including the use of the term "brothers" for fellow members and "mother" or "father" for leaders, provided a new framework for understanding the use of this language within some Pauline groups as well. . . . The Pauline correspondence also evinces the ongoing negotiation of group-society relations and the definition of group boundaries. Interactions between congregations and surrounding society could be far more complex than common sectarian approaches often suggest. It is in light of the banqueting purposes of associations and the potential for multiple affiliations that we can better grasp the issue of eating idol food at Corinth (1 Cor 8–10), for example. Christian leaders such as Paul would need to decide what they felt was acceptable practice in relation to the broader cultural world.[48]

Although, as noted earlier, Harland's book often seems to be working at the cross purposes of studying the links between associations and congregations and combating the impression that associations were not generally anti-imperial, this is only a problem of the book's organization and style. In fact, the two purposes are meant to be entirely complementary. For Harland, the point about associations not being generally anti-imperial in fact is meant to serve his larger point that Christian congregations are very much like Hellenistic associations. Harland is aware that he must combat a long history of Christian interpretation that simplistically took the many New Testament affirmations of not being "of this world" to mean that all early Christian communities were "sectarian" and therefore intentionally contrasting themselves to Hellenistic organizations like the associations.[49] Harland therefore seems to need above all to undermine these traditions of interpretation and scholarship, so that they do not blind others to the important and pervasive similarities between Hellenistic associations and Christian congregations. His final paragraph shows how important this challenge to the "sectarian" scholarship is to his larger concern for the closeness of congregation and association:

> Most importantly, though, our case study of imperial dimensions of civic life specifically helped us to comprehend the place of Jews and Christians within society in Roman Asia Minor. In this regard, associations provided instructive models for comparison with both synagogues and congregations. Such a comparison employing inscriptional evidence rooted this study firmly in the social and cultural realities of life in the world of polis and empire. The results problematized the widespread sectarian reading of these groups. There was a range of attitudes and practices among Jews and Christians with respect to imperial and other dimensions of the polis, reflecting variant opinions on where and how starkly the line between group and society was to be drawn.[50]

For our purposes, it is crucial to honor Harland's main concern: early Christian congregations were almost certainly modeled on associations. The central dependency of the organization of congregations on the model of association is to help elaborate this book's larger portrait of early Christian (meal) dynamics emerging from an already formed set of social forms and functions.

This strong similarity between associations and early churches cannot be understood completely without accounting for a third term proposed by Harland and already marginally part of this chapter. That term/organization is synagogue. Earlier in this chapter, the ambiguity of synagogue as a term for the first-century Jewish diaspora has been noted. Here, it is noteworthy that synagogue belongs to the analogy of association and congregation proposed above.[51] In other words, as Klinghardt asserts, in thinking about organizational forms, "basically no difference between Hellenistic-pagan and Jewish communities is presupposed."[52] Similarly,

Harland concludes that "both Jews and Christians, too, identified their groups using common terminology for associations."[53]

In summary, then, the terms synagogue, congregation, and association seem to have substantially overlapped in the Hellenistic world. Certainly within early Christian groups, each of these notions seems to have been in play. More to the point, these three terms were also all used in synonymous or complementary manners throughout the Hellenistic era for a wide range of groups, whether they were "Christian" or not.[54] The idea that Hellenistic churches and synagogues had their own respective distinct organizational forms, as they have had for the past sixteen hundred years, is not tenable. It is more accurate to think of them as belonging to a larger organizational category, to which this chapter and the recent research it has summarized have referred to as "associations."

Whatever the missing nuances in the comparison of early churches and associations may be,[55] it should be clear that this comparison provides a much more solid base for thinking about the provenance of early Christian congregations than any of the other, relatively crude and simplistic proposed origins outlined earlier in this chapter. Only uncritical thinking with a strong loyalty to the master narrative of Christian origins can entertain that churches appeared ex nihilo in the first century or as a commission (which does not exist in the New Testament) by Jesus.

That early Christian congregations emerged organizationally as a part of a larger and longer associations phenomenon helps elaborate the central role of meals in the development of Christianity itself (see this chapter's conclusion). At least as important is the picture of early Christianity's emergence within and as a part of existing organizational structures of the larger society. Understanding the wide range of associations in the Hellenistic world (and early churches' part in that larger phenomenon) allows a less magical and more developmental understanding of Christian beginnings.

MEALS, ASSOCIATIONS, AND EARLY CHRISTIANS

With a clear overview of the powerful and extensively institutionalized social practice of meals in the Hellenistic Mediterranean, and a general understanding of the association as a growing and pervasive organization of that era, it is now possible to see the crucial ways these existing societal elements helped form early Christianity.

Chapter 3 presented the widespread social practice of meals in the Hellenistic era, including the deep social values the meals promulgated and the dynamics of social experimentation they fostered. That chapter reviewed the centrality of these same meals in early Christian literature, confirming the significant similarity of social values and experimentation both in that literature and in Hellenistic meals. This survey of Hellenistic associations has demonstrated both the strong organizational similarities between associations and early churches, and the centrality of meals for each of them.

The social experimentation and values of early Christianity were shaped, then, primarily at their meals, and a large proportion of those meals occurred in association-like "Christian" groups. Of course, from this point of view, it is also easy to observe how closely many of the early Christian social values and experiments were shared by the larger swath of Hellenistic associations. As noted earlier in this chapter's study of the relationship between meals and associations, combining the social practice of meals with the organizational structure of associations quantumly increased the social power of both. The creative and formative dynamics of small-group life in the Hellenistic era depended on both the highly institutionalized social practice of meals and the organizational attractiveness of associations. The emergence of early Christianity is impossible to contemplate without the meal and the organizational form of Hellenistic associations. The creativity and sustaining power of the early churches depended crucially on the meal dynamics. The organizational spread of the early churches was unthinkable without the model of the associations. Although this does not mean to eliminate the role of new "Christian" ideas or personalities in Christianity's emergence, it clearly relativizes their importance vis-à-vis the power of the meal and the association.

ASSOCIATIONS, EARLY CHRISTIANS, AND POOR PEOPLE

For this chapter, the most crucial perspective that the closeness between early Christians and the larger institution of associations brings is its picture of Hellenistic associations including many groups of poor people and slaves. The associations were often guilds of lowly workers. They often included slaves not only as members but as leaders. The intense similarity between associations and early Christian groups at festive meals is a powerful indication that such early Christian gatherings were not an elite assembly but most likely included—perhaps even predominantly—many laborers with few resources, women of similar means, and slaves.

Crucial to these conclusions are the sources of the newest round of research on associations. The work of Ascough, Harland, Kloppenborg, and Wilson has depended much less on literary sources (of the elite) and much more on inscriptions written into buildings, columns, and public signage. It is widespread, often more primitive than the literary works, and signals the ways associational meals were held across a very wide social and economic spectrum.

OTHER EARLY CHRISTIAN POOR PEOPLE AT MEALS

After crediting the powerful social combination of meals, early Christians, and associations, one must also note that a number of important early Christian meals must have occurred in settings that had little to do with associations; that is, the highly institutionalized social practice of Hellenistic meals extended significantly beyond association settings in general and in early Christianity. Interestingly enough, some of these other meal settings have strong indications of both early Christian presence and poor people.

Perhaps one of the clearest instances of early "Christian" meal gatherings in nonassociational settings is that of some of the earliest wandering "Christian" sages. This practice of sages traveling itinerantly[56] from place to place, seeking to be hosted at a meal of some kind (for example, neighborhood, extended family, a gathering of friends) is evident in the Revelation to John,[57] the Didache,[58] and the letters of Paul.[59] Most scholars see the so-called "mission instructions" for the twelve or the seventy who go out to proclaim the reign of God in Matthew, Mark, Luke, and Thomas as reflecting the practices of itinerant sages in Galilee. These texts portray a practice of coming to a village to proclaim the nearness of God's reign, seeking out a house where one could stay and eat, and staying there until the work was done.[60] Some scholars think of these instructions as primarily descriptive of the practices of the Q movement after Jesus' death,[61] others see them as exclusively the practices of Jesus' followers during his own teaching career,[62] and still others see them as descriptive of a movement that spanned both periods.[63]

The meals at which these very early "Christian" sages taught were most likely of several kinds as described in the works of Dennis Smith and Matthias Klinghardt. These meals could have been on the occasion of someone inviting neighbors, friends, and extended family to gather for a meal. Smith and Klinghardt have documented this as an extensive practice in the Hellenistic Mediterranean. Here, the invited (and perhaps a few uninvited) persons gathered for the purposes of social bonding and mutuality described in chapter 3, but not as a part of the associations described in this current chapter. These meals were more occasional, initiated upon the wish of the host or the birthday of someone. It would then be at such a meal that a sage (invited or uninvited) might present some teaching during the *symposion*. It most likely was the case that many of the social values and a good deal of the social experimentation described in chapter 3 also occurred at such meals. And it is quite clear from the descriptions of visiting sages—honored or disdained, invited or uninvited[64]—in both the early Christian and broader literature[65] that these sages played a substantial role in the emergence of early Christianity in the 30s and 40s CE.[66]

That the early sages had to cajole invitations to festive meals, as is clear from the above descriptions, indicates the poverty of these itinerant Christian sages. The stark descriptions of this itinerancy in early Christian accounts attest to such poverty, although they do not make particularly clear whether that poverty was circumstantial or voluntary: "Take no purse with you, no sack, no sandals. . . . Whatever house you enter, let your first words be, 'Peace to this house.' . . . Stay in that same house, taking what food and drink they offer. . . . Wherever you go into a town where they make you welcome, eat what is put before you."

The point of this investigation is not to claim necessarily that early Christian meal gatherings were always only of poor laborers, outcast women, and slaves. Such a picture would be far too romantic and would not fit much of the data even in this study. Rather, the critique of earlier meal scholarship that meals may have been only for elite Christian gatherings no longer holds. The types of early Christians at meals expanded across a wide number of social and economic demographics, including a very substantial number of poor people.

How Much Did Larger Society Matter to Early Christians Gathered at Meals?

In chapter 4, ritual analysis of the Hellenistic meal and its early Christian elaborations pointed to the powerful socially formational dynamics of this major social practice. From these studies, it is evident that the meal's semiprivate location in Hellenistic culture became pivotal for the imagination of alternative worlds. Inasmuch as these meals were more or less protected private space, they allowed the imagination of and experimentation with alternate relationships and social constellations. The relative privacy permitted meal participants to muse in gestures and words about what the world might look like other than its current state, without being subjected to the rough-and-tumble interaction of the larger society in crisis. As the ritual analysis demonstrated, sometimes this protected imagination was reactionary, nostalgic, and conservative in response to the changing landscapes of Hellenistic society. Sometimes this private imagination prompted either timid new adjustments or bold social adventures within the meal world. Chapter 6 describes ways that this private protection evoked gestures of resistance to Roman power over other Mediterranean cultures.

How men and women related, who was in charge, how wealth was distributed, what ethnicity did and did not mean, how work and leisure fit together, who belonged to society, what roles families and tribes could play, and what to make of the complex social mix of Hellenistic society all became topics of reimagination, thanks to the meal's ritual vocabulary and the protection of the private dining space.

But the dining was not just private. The dining spaces were actually semiprivate. There was almost always a window open toward the larger society. David Balch and Michael White have shown how the dining rooms in the villas of the Greco-Roman era—indeed, in many ways, how the villas themselves—were architecturally open to the world for display.[67] The more plebian associational meals occurred either in rooms that were rented by the public or in association houses with a great deal of coming and going. Hellenistic temples almost always had many dining rooms around the altar and were used for a wide variety of social functions, from birthday parties to welcoming of important intellectuals. Laborers and even slaves were able to find dining rooms in the cities to rent for an evening. In all of these spaces—whether in private homes or in rented rooms for a general public—there was always a good possibility that strangers would wander in uninvited. (Indeed, as discussed in chapter 4, it seems as if these meals were subliminally structured to be open to such disturbances.)

So the meals—while taking advantage of a certain protected private character— also were occasions for some display to a wider society. That which was said, sung, or shown at a meal had a somewhat unpredictable and volatile audience. This kind of presentational consciousness was normal throughout the meal and was perhaps best characterized by the libation, which simultaneously proclaimed to an audience and bonded a group together.

This mix of private and public encouraged the imagination of alternate worlds. The opening to the larger society forced the presentational consciousness, while the security of the closed walls and the intimacy of reclining together invited a kind of longing not allowed in blatantly public settings. The meals invited participants to live in an imagined world constituted by the meal's formal stability, a certain longing for something different occasioned by the meal's intimacy, and a vague awareness of the world peeking into the room. Although ritual theory has helped show that this imagination within the meal was always open to revision and was—by the very constitution of the main meal elements—unstable, these banquets also generated material that imagined alternate worlds.

It is possible to explore ambitious, fanciful, and cosmic imaginations of early Christians and set them firmly within the meal. How appropriate was the meal for Christians to generate magnificent visions of alternate worlds fueled by some cosmic imaginations from the Israelite and Greco-Roman legacies can now be assessed. And— perhaps most tellingly—the social power of both the cosmic imaginations and the meal itself can be tested. The function of the grandiose cosmic vocabulary of these small Christian cells might be seen when viewed in the context of the social reimaginations of the meal; that is, the cosmic vocabulary of much of early Christian literature—when situated socially in the meal context—may be understood more clearly as helping early Christians envision and celebrate a new social world. Placing the cosmic vocabulary in the meal explains much more than any other scholarly speculation has why these cosmic visions of early Christians were almost always in the present tense. The socially visionary purpose of the cosmic language of much of early Christianity might be understood as a component of the already charged and socially evocative meal. In turn, the meal's social implications are then also quantumly multiplied by the largeness of the cosmic language. The meal's already established importance in reimagining and adjusting social relations may have been augmented by the cosmic imagination of early Christians.

This hypothesis is tested in two stages. First, specific formal connections between certain kinds of early Christian literature and the Hellenistic meal are explored. After suggesting connections between early Christian cosmic imagination and specific parts of the meal itself, the possibility that other forms of early Christian literature might have been read, performed, or generated during these meals is also proposed.

COSMIC HYMNIC IMAGINATIONS
OF EARLY CHRISTIANITY AT THE HELLENISTIC MEAL

Chapter 1 described several scenes of elaborate singing at Hellenistic meals. Chapter 3 described how the standard meal often included a great deal of singing, especially during the *symposion*. Chapter 4's ritual analysis of the libation of wine between the *deipnon* and the *symposion* demonstrated the importance of singing a paean or hymn during the libation. Paul writes to the Corinthians: "When you come together, each one has a hymn, a lesson, a tongue, or an interpretation" (1 Cor. 14:26), almost certainly referring to the range of activities during a *symposion*.

Study of the many existing texts of songs in classical and Koine Greek has helped identify some standard forms of song of the ancient Mediterranean. New Testament scholarship has pointed out that this song form is found relatively frequently in the New Testament and other early Christian literature. This scholarship discovered songs embedded within the letters, the gospels, and even the apocalypse of the New Testament through the formal literary character of ancient hymns. It is perhaps the standard failure of New Testament form criticism to ask social questions of its literary discoveries that accounts for this same scholarship not having asked why there were songs in the middle of these early Christian texts and where such songs were sung. For the purposes of this book, this now highly recognized form of critical detection confirms a close connection between early Christian literature and the meal, where songs were so much a part of the standard symposial activities. Indeed, it would be unclear where else early Christians would have sung songs if not at the meals.[68]

Scholarly studies of these early Christian hymns have observed that the songs' language is strikingly cosmic.[69] Typical of the eras in which form criticism was accomplished, more attention was paid to the theological implications of this cosmic language than to the social purposes of such cosmic hymns. Hence, the ways in which these songs made Christ a more cosmic figure have been treated in earlier scholarship. This chapter turns to a reading of the socially formative dimension of these cosmic songs,[70] now more addressable because of the Smith and Klinghardt research on the exact character of early Christian meals and specifically the extensive use of songs at those meals.[71]

Examples of these early Christian hymns illustrate the prevalence of their cosmic language. Perhaps best known is the hymn embedded in the prologue of John's gospel (John 1:1-4, 8-14, 16-18, author's translation):

In the beginning was the word [Gr., *logos*];
The word was with God
And the word was God.
It was with God in the beginning.
Through it all things came into being,

Nothing came into being except through it.
What came into being through this word was life,
Life that was the light of humans;
And that light shines in the darkness,
But darkness could not overpower it. . . .
The word was the true light
Which gives light to everyone;
It came into the world.
The word was in the world
Which had come into being through it,
And the world did not recognize the word.
It came to its own
And its own people did not accept it.
But to those who did accept the word,
It gave power to become children of God,
To those who trusted in his name
Who were born not from humankind,
Nor human desire
Nor human will
But from God.
The word became flesh,
It pitched its tent among us,
And we saw its glory,
The glory that it has from the Father
As only Son of the Father,
Full of grace and truth. . . .
Indeed from its fullness all of us have received,
Grace succeeding grace.
For the law was given through Moses,
Grace and truth have come through Jesus Christ.
No one has ever seen God;
Only the Son,
Who is close to the heart of the Father,
Has made God known.[72]

This song was clearly cosmic and might even be considered a cosmogony, with its celebration of the beginning of all things in the preexistent Logos. The portrait of this preexistent Logos almost certainly depended both on Neoplatonist philosophical notions of the Logos and on the treatment of the preexistent Wisdom/Sophia in Prov. 8:22-31; Ben Sira 24:1-18; and Wis. 7:12-8:4. The light vocabulary also fit a wide range of cosmic language of the day and quite certainly was a part of an intentional evocation of Genesis 1. Both the content and the verb itself in verse 14 (for example, "the word pitched its tent—Gr. *skeneo*—among us") reflect strong dependence on the cosmic drama of Wisdom leaving her heavenly home, searching for a home on earth, and finding one in Israel.

Very similar content exists in the hymn found in Col. 1:15-20 (author's translation):

> He is the image of the unseen God,
> The first-born of all creation,
> For in him all things were created
> In heaven and on earth:
> All things visible and all things invisible,
> Thrones, ruling forces, principalities, and powers,
> All things have been created through him and for him.
> He exists before all things
> And in him all things hold together,
> And he is the head of the body,
> Which the assembly is.
> He is the beginning,
> The first-born of the dead,
> So that he is superior in all things;
> Because God wanted all fullness to be found in him
> That all things might be reconciled through and in him,
> All things in heaven and all things on earth,
> By making peace through his death on the cross.[73]

Christ's existence here was almost entirely in a cosmic realm. Here also, much attention was focused on the beginning and the foundation of all existence in Christ. Indeed, it used many of the same cosmic vocabulary and sources that the Gospel of John did. This hymn emphasized the surprising status of Christ by the way it twice piled on the cosmic superlatives and then twice ended the cosmic flourish with direct references to very concrete historical realities of the early "Christian" assemblies and Jesus' tragic death on the cross. He is, in quick succession, the image of the unseen God, the firstborn of all creation, the creator of all things everywhere, preexistent, holding everything together, the head of the body, and, in an odd and surprising climax, the head of the Christian assemblies. The second time around, Christ is the beginning, the firstborn of the dead, the supreme one, the one in whom everything becomes full, the one who reconciles everything, the one who brings peace, and, once again in an odd and surprising climax, the one who was crucified. This song hails in the languages of cosmic superlatives Jesus, the surprising chief of all things in the entire universe.

A similar vision of the universe in surprising submission to the crucified Jesus occurs in Phil. 2:6-11 (author's translation):

Christ Jesus,
Who being in the form of God,
Did not count equality with God
Something to be held on to.
But he emptied himself,
Taking on the form of a slave,
Becoming as humans are,
And being in all ways like a human
Was even more humble,
Accepting even death, death on a cross.
And for this God raised him up
And gave him the name
Which is above all other names,
So that all things
In the heavens,
On earth,
And under the earth
Should bend the knee at the name of Jesus
And that every tongue should acknowledge
Jesus Christ as Lord
To the glory of God the Father.

Here also, Christ Jesus was sung about as equal to God and reigning over everything in the universe. Like the Colossians hymn, the cosmic reign is placed in ironic tension with the humiliation of Jesus, especially in his crucifixion. The cosmic character of these three hymns is also found in a number of other pieces of early Christian literature (for example, Luke 1:67-79; 2:29-32; Rom. 11:33-36; 1 Tim. 3:16; 6:15, 16; and Rev. 4:11).[74]

Burton Mack comments at length on how this cosmic picture of these hymns functioned in the social imagination of early Christians:

> This is mythmaking on the cosmic scale. Throughout the Greco-Roman world lord meant sovereign. One needed only to know the name of the lord in question in order to locate his or her domain. The God of Israel was the lord for Jews. Serapis was the lord of his mystery cult. Other gods were lords of their people. Egyptian kings and queens ruled as lords by virtue of their divinity. And the Roman emperors were also encouraging obeisance and allowing themselves to be addressed as lords. The poem[75] says that Jesus Christ is the name of the lord that is above every other lord. That is an absolutely stupendous claim. Just the thought is mind-boggling. Think of every knee bowing, every tongue confessing, that the Christians' martyr by

the name of Iesous Christos was lord of all, and that if such bondage should happen throughout the cosmos, including the heavens and the underworld, God the Father would be pleased to receive the glory for it. . . .

What the Christ hymn reveals, then, is that Christians had taken themselves very seriously as an alternative society. They had thought about the ways in which their congregations differed from other social formations, and had looked for ways to say how much better their vision of human community was for people to live together in the world. . . . The Christ hymn was the result of a Christian protestation to have no king but Jesus.

But what an audacious claim! Compared with other kingdoms of the world, or even with other groups in ancient ethnic, national, or religious traditions . . . these Christians were nothing more than little ad hoc cells of unlikely people experimenting with a novel social notion. They had no status, no power, no cultural tradition of their own. . . . They were thinking of themselves as congregations that belonged to a kingdom, one that was independent from and superior to all the other kingdoms of the world. . . . With a lord more exalted than the Roman emperor . . .

To consider belonging to such a kingdom may have been a very attractive option for dislocated and disenfranchised people. Christian congregations provided a place for excited debates about the significance of this newly imagined cosmic kingdom. . . . It was a marvelous forum for intellectuals and poets to share creative thoughts and compositions about the event of its revelation.[76]

Mack does not explicitly mention the meal as the location for these hymns, even though the section directly before this treatment of the cosmic hymns of early Christians focuses on what he calls "the ritual meal."[77] The explicit details concerning singing at meals in the research of Smith and Klinghardt allow this chapter to place Mack's elaboration of the social meaning of early Christian hymns at the meal.[78]

As the cosmic character of early Christian songs is fit into the social practice of meals and the social re-visioning that these cosmic songs expressed is acknowledged, it is important to link this cosmic and social character of the meal to the ritual analysis of chapter 4. The medium of the meal—especially as it is analyzed as performance and ritual—underlines and goes beyond the social meaning of cosmic language in the early Christian hymns. One aspect of the meal already ritually analyzed in chapter 4 (singing at the libation) and two aspects of the meal not ritually analyzed in chapter 4 (making libation to a crucified Jesus and singing throughout the *symposion*) complement the above analysis of social meaning in the cosmic Christian hymn vocabulary.

The analysis of the libation between the *deipnon* and the *symposion* pointed to two dramatic negotiations of social meaning. Both of these performed social meanings are enhanced and nuanced by the fact that hymns were sung at the libation, as shown in chapter 4.

1. *The ways the libation in Hellenistic meals called forth and helped negotiate social identity through the mixing and selection of various (or one) god(s) as subject of the libation itself.* Close analysis of the wide range of gods to whom the libation could be dedicated made clear that various (relatively new) identities were being negotiated as different meals focused on or left open to whom the cup would be raised. As such, the choice of which god should be honored in the libation helped those at the meal practice their own emerging social loyalties. That some associations came to raise the cup only to a certain god helped them develop a certain social identity in the confusing Hellenistic polyglot. That extended family or neighborhood meals often experienced a confusing range of gods to whom they could make libation at the meal reflected the identity tensions that existed in this Hellenistic mix of cultures, defeated nations, ethnicities, religions, and empire. As will be discussed in chapter 6, that the emperor pressed meal associations to make libation to him indicates that something was at stake socially in deciding to whom the libation was made. That early Christians raised the cup uniquely to Jesus or to Christ was done against the backdrop of other meals' experimentation and tension with the libation as identity marker. Early Christians' libation to Jesus/Christ in this setting provided a strong assertion of social identity. Making a libation at a meal enacted the threats and affirmations of identity tension in this era of complex and still forming social mixes.

That songs were sung by all the meal participants during the libation and passing of the libational cup made the issue of social identity all the more dramatic and pointed. That early Christian songs were cosmic and, as such, carried a social vision of a new alternative world lent major significance to both the libation performance and the words of the Christ hymns. When the songs about Christ ruling the universe were sung exactly at the point of the meal where identity ambivalence and contestation of authority were high, the drama of making libation and the content of the hymn's words worked together in dramatic fashion. The libation exclusively to Jesus/Christ at early Christian meals performed the social utopian loyalty outlined by Mack above.

2. *The ways the libation elicited a relatively safe set of choices on how one positioned oneself relative to the occupying Roman Empire.* The (at least nominally) official requirement that libations be given at all meals to the emperor provided a ritual opportunity to experiment with both acquiescence and resistance to the emperor. Since such a requirement was impossible to enforce, the way each meal performed the libation was always a ritual exercise in identity relative to the imperial power. Since Jewish resistance to this requirement had succeeded

and Jews were exempted from it, every time Jews did a libation at a meal, they ritually affirmed a very important identity of resistance. Inasmuch as early Christians were Jews, they also participated in this crucial meaning of a libation that was never to the empire. Inasmuch as early Christians were not (considered) Jewish, their libation to Jesus/Christ experimented with a much riskier identity.

The singing of cosmic songs celebrating Jesus/Christ's reign over the whole universe at the moment of libation in the context of the requirement to give libation to the emperor and the Roman rule over the known world became a strong ritual performance of early Christian resistance. As noted above, the very act of raising the cup to Jesus had elements of resistance. But doing so while singing of Jesus/Christ's universal rule ritually dramatized the profile of emerging Christian identity and resistance to Rome.

The awareness of cosmic songs to Christ at the libation then augments chapter 4's ritual analysis of libation. But there are two other striking ritual connections between cosmic Christ hymns and the meal. One also concerns a particular function of meals for a particular Hellenistic constituency. The other has to do with the singing of songs during the *symposion* proper.

The first additional ritual significance of cosmic Christ hymns and meals lies in a particular social function Hellenistic meals took on for persons worried that they would not be remembered (or buried) when they died. Most Hellenistic associations included in their membership covenant a promise to bury one another in case of death and to have a memorial meal in honor of the deceased.[79] This component of membership in an association came by and large from the economic vulnerability of the population that often made the financing of funerals improbable. Associations used their membership dues to finance both the funerals and the memorial meals for each member who died. This connection between dying and meals among the commoners may account for the interesting confluence of ritual meal practice and Christ hymn language, while at the same time adding profile to the new social identity affirmed in the early Christian meals.

Two of the three early Christian hymns examined here (and others not included in this overview)[80] make pointed references to the crucifixion of Jesus. The ironic tension between Jesus' cosmic reign and his execution as an enemy of the empire by crucifixion will be examined at some length in chapter 6 in elucidating the resistance to Rome being experimented with in many early Christian meals. But here, libation and cosmic hymns in relationship to the death of those attending early Christian meals also needs to be explored in terms of social bonding and identity. The Colossians hymn proclaimed Jesus as "the firstborn of the dead." Inasmuch as this hymn was sung at an early Christian meal, it most likely needs to be seen as identifying Jesus as the first in a long line of "association" members to be remembered at their meal. In this regard, the early Christian diners would have been claiming both their bond to Jesus as one of their own remembered after death and their bond with one another in facing their own eventual deaths. The cosmic character of the hymn—especially with its direct reference to Jesus' crucifixion—evokes then a counterworld over which Jesus is reigning and a counteridentity that transcends death.

The Philippians hymn seems to have made a similar point in describing "Christ Jesus" as "being in all ways like a human [who] was even more humble, accepting even death, death on a cross." The insistence of the hymn on Jesus "being in all ways like a human" almost certainly evoked much more the bond of the meal community around being remembered after their respective deaths in the manner of the associations than the tortured connection later theology makes to atonement theology, which is not evoked at all in the hymn imagery. So the Philippians hymn celebrated a new cosmic belonging for those at the meal singing of Jesus' cosmic triumph. At the same time, those singing were claiming a standard associational bond with one another as they faced the eventuality of their own deaths. Their social identity—as sung in the cosmic hymn—was beyond death and the difficult circumstances that often caused death.

This connection among libation, death, and cosmic songs has deeper roots in the standard associations' meals for their members who had died.[81] Often at these particular associational meals that honored a member who had recently died, the libation itself evoked the person who had died. So the connection of cosmic belonging and death in the hymns themselves most likely made specific libational reference. While noting this connection among early Christian hymns, death, and libation, it becomes necessary to treat—at least briefly—another set of texts that link libation and death. This discussion, however, must be done cautiously and must avoid conflation of early Christian texts.

This set of texts includes those linking the dedication (libation) of the cup to Jesus' death. This connection is done in two different ways in the New Testament. In the earlier text(s) from Paul, a tradition he received about Jesus instructed the taking of the "cup after supper" as a "covenant in my blood" in memorial of Jesus (1 Cor. 11:25). Located clearly at the typical juncture of the libation, this practice linked the libation to remembering Jesus' death and instructed diners in this tradition to repeat this libational memory of and bond with the dying Jesus. Paul went on to write that "whenever . . . you drink this cup, you are proclaiming the Lord's death until he comes" (11:26, NJB). In 1 Cor. 10:16, Paul insisted that "the blessing cup that we bless, is it not a communing in the blood of Christ?" A similar connection between Jesus' death and the cup is made in the Synoptic Gospels. Although neither Mark nor Matthew[82] has Jesus instructing followers to "do this in memory of me," some of the force of the connection between libation and death still presents itself in the saying of Jesus about the cup and his blood being pictured at his last supper directly before the narration of his trial and crucifixion.

The caution necessary in linking these Last Supper libational traditions to the cosmic hymns has mostly to do with the presumptions of earlier scholarship about the ubiquity of the Last Supper traditions. Conventional Christian imagination, along with much previous scholarship, has assumed that the nexus of texts around the Last Supper, the bread, and the cup was almost universally observed in early Christianity.

However, this assumption has been called starkly into question by the past generation of meal scholarship.[83] It is not responsible to assume that the libational connection between Jesus' death and cosmic reign in the hymns necessarily happened at the same meals where the Last Supper trajectory also connects the cup and Jesus' death. It may be more probable that the hymns and the Last Supper sayings were working in their own respective ways on making the connection between Jesus' death and the libational cup. It is, however, possible that in some cases the Last Supper libational dedication of the cup was said before or at the same time as the cosmic hymns to Christ that called attention to Jesus' death. This set of libational connections to Jesus' death will be explored further in chapter 6's discussion of early Christian meals and resistance to the Roman Empire.

These cosmic hymns were not, however, sung just at the point of libation. Rather, as noted earlier in the general descriptions of the Hellenistic meal and of the songs' place at the meal, such songs were sung in many parts of the *symposion*—that is, this singing celebration of the cosmic reign of Jesus/Christ continued in the longer, leisurely portion of the meal, in which often teaching was done, discussion among the participants occurred, some performances may have been presented, occasional ecstatic speaking erupted, and general festivity prevailed.

Singing of Jesus' cosmic reign during this extended *symposion* almost certainly connected the community experience of participants at the meal with the alternative vision of Jesus' reign. It seems likely that the meal participants would have understood their own social grouping at the meal as tied to the subject matter of the cosmic songs themselves. Here then, as Mack noted earlier, through the cosmic hymns those at the meals most likely saw their own meal society as a real alternative to the larger world beyond the meal setting.

Early Christian Texts, Meals, and Expansive Visioning

Chapter 3 hinted that one might think of many stories about Jesus and others, sayings attributed to Jesus, letters from Paul and others, arguments for certain points of view, and poems about Jesus and others that may well have been told, taught, read, or recited at festive meals. Certainly, the *symposion* in general was known for its storytelling, poetry, debate, readings, recitations, and even dramatic performances. Chapter 8 takes an extended look at how such a mix may have happened, may have generated texts that eventually became a part of the New Testament or other collections, and may have shaped the social character of early Christianity.

At the end of this current chapter on the social expanse of early Christian meals and the broad societal vision of hymns sung at the meals, it is appropriate to take note of the match forming between the risky, adventuresome, and socially charged vocabulary of early Christian texts and the social dynamics of the meal. The specific link of hymns embedded within the New Testament with the expansive practice of singing such hymns at meals blazes the way toward such a possibility.

The ways the Hellenistic meal ritually addressed difficult issues of social identity in the Mediterranean have now been complemented by a range of early Christian imaginations of how the world could be different. The implicit ways that the ritual dimensions of the meal raise social questions have been dramatically expanded by the explicit socially visionary hymns found in the New Testament and sung at the meals. This has suggested an even wider possibility of early Christian stories, teachings, and letters in dynamic interaction with the social mix at the meal. As this exploration turns to the specific social challenges to early Christians from the imperial domination of Rome, the match of texts and meal claims deeper roots and more expanse.

CHAPTER SIX
Meals OF Resistance
TO Roman Imperial Power

O NE OF THE MOST NOTABLE ASPECTS of New Testament scholarship in the past
decade is the more pointed interest in early Christian literature within the context
of Roman imperial power. The emerging understanding that the letters of Paul, the
gospels, and a wide range of other early Christian works can be seen as evocatively
resistant to Roman oppression, imperial idolatry, and economic exploitation must
now be accounted for in all articulations of research concerning early Christianity.

After a brief summary of this new research and interpretation, this chapter
examines the relationship between early Christian meals and Roman imperial power.
Such an examination produces rather astonishing results. This chapter makes the
case that the social practice of early Christian meals was central to early Christian
resistance to Rome. Although other scholars have suspected the importance of meals
in early Christianity's relationship to Roman power,[1] this chapter outlines the manner
in which these meals became the central early Christian acts of resistance to Rome. It
charts both the specific dimensions of the meals themselves, which were expressively
resistant, and the early Christian texts that confirm this link between meals and
resistance. Although this chapter does not propose that all of early Christianity or all
of its meals resisted imperial power, it does show ways the meals played important
roles in the resistance that existed.

Summary of Recent Empire-Critical
New Testament Studies

Scholars are now placing the affirmations of early Christianity in the context of
the domination of the Mediterranean world of the first and second centuries by
Rome. Although much information about Rome's complete control of the entirety
of its known world has been known for quite some time, New Testament and early
Christian studies have only recently placed the literature and lives of early Christians

actively in this context. But since this contextualization has begun, the contrast between the early Christians and the Roman apparatus of military occupation, economic domination and exploitation, massive taxation and enslavement, cultural imperialism, and proactive religious reinforcement of the imperial divine right to all of the above has become striking and obvious.

This new scholarship on the antipathy between first-century Christianity and the Roman Empire has quickly taken hold. Not only have bold new scholars, such as Brigitte Kahl and Warren Carter, emerged, but other established contributors to New Testament studies, such as Elisabeth Schüssler Fiorenza, Dieter Georgi, and Richard Horsley, have also made major contributions. Even such conservative scholars as N. T. Wright have come into "more or less complete agreement with the thesis" that the authors of the New Testament need to be seen "as subversive to the whole edifice of the Roman Empire."[2]

At the heart of this new awareness is the centrality of the crucifixion for much meaning making in early Christian literature. Richard Horsley summarizes the anti-Roman meaning of the crucifixion for Paul:

> Surely the most blatantly anti-Roman imperial aspect of his gospel was its focus on the crucified Christ. . . . Crucifixion, of course, was the distinctively horrendous means by which the Romans tortured to death subject people who resisted the Roman order for its "demonstration effect" on others. . . . The rest of Paul's fundamental gospel, of course, was that the political insurrectionary crucified by the Romans had then been enthroned as the true Lord of the world and was imminently to return in *the* (eschatological) *parousia* (a reference to an imperial entrance to a subject city). The one crucified by the Roman rulers was now the Lord who would soon subject "all things," presumably including the Roman rulers.[3]

That crucifixion was the Roman punishment for insurrection against the empire made Jesus on the cross a blatant emblem of early Christian resistance to Rome.

It was not just that Jesus was crucified by Rome (since tens of thousands were crucified for relatively arbitrary reasons by Rome). Rather, Jesus' crucifixion corresponded in many ways to Jesus' own teaching about the presence of the "imperial rule of God" over against Roman rule.[4] Indeed, scholars now agree that the values in most of early Christian literature are formulated in explicit tension with Rome's claims. As Warren Carter summarizes: "Rome asserted divine sanction for its empire, claiming that the gods had chosen Rome to manifest the gods' sovereignty, presence, agency, and blessings on the earth. New Testament writings dispute Rome's claim, asserting over against them that God's purposes will eventually hold sway."[5] Early Christians gathering together in Jesus' name, says Brigitte Kahl, represented "a new age and world order where Jews and Gentiles, Greeks and barbarians, free and slave, male and female . . . ate together."[6] "Rome," says Kahl, "and its local agents understood that something was seriously wrong with this message of a disorderly inclusive table."[7] The values of Rome and early Christianity were diametrically opposed.

To express resistance to Rome's oppression, domination, and blasphemous claim to divine rule of the known world, early Christians began to use Rome's own terms against the empire. What Dieter Georgi called such "loaded terms as *euangelion* [the 'gospel' of the imperial Savior], *pistis* [the 'loyalty' or faithfulness of Caesar/Rome, to be reciprocated by the 'loyalty' of her subjects], *dikaiosyne* [the 'justice' imposed by Caesar], and *eirene* [the 'peace' of good order secured by Roman conquest] as central concepts" were used by early Christians to express their loyalty to the executed Jesus and the values he represented.[8] Richard Horsley asserts that "insofar as Paul deliberately used language closely associated with the imperial religion, he was presenting his gospel as a direct competitor of the gospel of Caesar."[9] N. T. Wright elaborates this New Testament theme: "'Our citizenship is in heaven, and from it we await the Saviour, the Lord Jesus, the Messiah.' . . . Jesus is Lord, and Caesar isn't. Caesar's empire . . . is the parody; Jesus' empire . . . is the reality."[10]

This pointed challenge by the small Christian movement to Rome's domination was dangerous. Karen King's description of this danger is apt: "To worship the local gods was the duty of every citizen and subject, for these were the gods that supported the Empire and their own cities. As Christians knew, to refuse this duty was considered treason, so that when Christians call these gods 'demons' and 'fallen angels' they had launched no less than a full attack on the mythic foundations of the Roman state and the very fabric of the social order."[11]

Perhaps the most consistent expressions of counterimperial values occurred in the early Christians' intention to build models that point toward different relationships and behavior. As Warren Carter notes:

> New Testament texts often urge readers to form alternate communities with practices that provide life-giving alternatives to the empire's ways. . . . Paul, for example, urges the churches in Rome, in a city full of displays of the elite's power and privileges: "Do not be conformed to this world, but be transformed by the renewing of your minds . . ." (Romans 12:2). . . . Paul instructs them to form communities of mutual support, to love one another, to not be haughty with one another, and to feed rather than avenge their enemies (chap 12). Clearly these practices differ vastly from the indebtedness and dependency of patron-client relations, from the empire's hierarchy and domination, and the execution of military retaliation. They create a very different societal experience and very different ways of being human. . . . Paul also gathers a collection among his Gentile communities to alleviate the suffering of believers in Jerusalem.[12]

This new impetus in New Testament and early Christian studies relative to the above themes of resistance to Rome may not be the only way of understanding this literature, but it now is clear that it must be taken into account in explorations of the character of early Christianity.

Early Christian Meals and Roman Empire

With this new understanding of early Christian resistance to Roman imperial power in the first one hundred years of "Christianity" summarized, this chapter now turns to the role of early Christian meals as a factor in this resistance. Dimensions of this resistant strain in Greco-Roman meals—and particularly early Christian meals—have already appeared at the periphery of several earlier chapters. But this chapter now tests the question of how central meals were to early Christian resistance to Rome.

This examination of the resistant character of these meals follows the same pattern as the book itself. First, the question of Greco-Roman meals in general as resistant to the Roman Empire is addressed. Then the subset of early Christian meals' resistance follows, first examining the role of meals as imaginal counter-societies and, second, exploring the ritual and literary relationship between crucifixion and the meals. In conclusion, this investigation takes a look at the strong possibility that meals were, in fact, the major form of early Christian resistance to Rome and explores what that might have meant.

Roman Imperial Worry about Associations Gathering for Meals

The Hellenistic era knew major controversy concerning a particular kind of meal gathering that has already been discussed in chapter 2. There is substantial evidence that the imperial governments saw associations' meal gatherings as suspicious, mainly in relationship to the possibility of their becoming occasions for sedition or planning for sedition. This tension has been studied in recent times by two different scholars with somewhat different results. In both cases, these two scholars make reference to and attempt to update the nineteenth-century studies, particularly those of J. P. Waltzing.

Wendy Cotter's 1996 study "The Collegia and Roman Law: State Restrictions on Voluntary Associations, 64 BCE–200 CE" reviews the history of Roman bans on associations from the Republic through the second-century imperial state.[13] Philip Harland's *Associations, Synagogues, and Congregations: Claiming a Place in Ancient Mediterranean Society*, an original study based mainly on new epigraphic research by the author in eastern Asia Minor, sees itself as a corrective to the general assumption of studies (including Cotter's) that portrayed thoroughgoing tension between associations and levels of Roman government.[14]

Cotter paints a clear picture of Roman anxiety concerning the possible seditious intentions of the associations' gathering at meals. She traces the worry about sedition back to the Roman civil war period, when the senate in 64 BCE took the step of abolishing all associations "which appeared to be in conflict with the public interest" as the first Roman general governmental action against the associations.[15] She goes on to note that the same civil war period seemed to validate such worry in that Clodius did indeed use his own removal of the ban against associations to foment his own attempt to seize power.[16] This resulted in two additional decrees against associations "between 58 BCE and the beginning of Julius Caesar's dictatorship in 49 BCE."[17] Julius Caesar also reinforced these bans, allowing only the "most ancient" to function.

Cotter goes on to document official action against association gatherings by most of the emperors of the first century CE (Augustus, Tiberius, Claudius, and Nero) on an empire-wide basis. She does note that documentation of action in the provinces is sparse, but that the more extensive records of Egypt tend to confirm imperial hostility to such gatherings.[18] It is important to note here that these bans on association gatherings are worded as such, not just against the meals of the associations. However, as noted in chapter 5, the meal/banquet was the common way associations did gather.

The early-second-century emperors discussed by Cotter reflect a slightly more nuanced approach to associations.[19] Both Trajan and Hadrian generally disapproved of the associations and took actions against them, but they did discuss in some depth some exceptions to this general disapproval. The existence of this more detailed material most likely helps explain a deeper dilemma of which Cotter is aware and which must be taken very seriously: "If Claudius, Nero and Trajan are seen to suppress the collegia, it is because these clubs continued to spring up and grow."[20] In other words, assessing the Roman suppression of the associations needs to take seriously both the steady imperial opposition and the obvious social success of these associations despite the repression by the government. Indeed, as seen in chapter 5, the very period of this imperial opposition to the associations is exactly the period of growth of associations in general and of Christian associations in particular.

Cotter's portrait of the imperial opposition to associations attends to two particular constituencies of interest to the study of early "Christianity." First, she describes in some detail the consistent tolerance of Jewish gatherings around the empire as an explicit exception to these more general bans of associations. Acknowledging that "to the Romans, Jewish synagogues would have appeared very much like other religious collegia," Cotter shows that the Romans regularly explicitly exempted the Jews' meal gatherings from this ban.[21] She cites Cicero, Julius Caesar, and Josephus in support of this exemption and points out that even in the cases where Claudius banned Jewish gatherings, this policy was quickly reversed by the subsequent authorities.[22]

In addition to this attention to the legality of Jewish association/synagogue meal gatherings, Cotter also takes note (as Harland's work quoted in chapter 2 also did) of the wide economic range of association meal gatherings. She shows that the laws were indeed quite conscious of the irony of the many bans on associations even while they were thriving, especially in her discussion of laws controlling membership in the associations. Specifically, she describes how, simultaneous to the bans, the emperors themselves and their governors explicitly allowed both poor people and slaves to join associations. This, of course, confirms chapter 2's portrait of the associations as having many poor members and often having slaves as meal "symposiarchs." As Cotter concludes, "There was good evidence for the existence of clubs of poor people."[23]

Cotter's strong conclusions help situate this picture of the empire's consistent attempts at suppression of highly successful associations in relationship to our interest in early Christian meals:

> The prohibition against and dissolution of voluntary societies was an unquestioned right and frequently employed policy of the Romans. . . . Thus the examination of the suppression of these clubs shows how important they were to the people of the Mediterranean world. Modern scholarship needs to address more closely the reasons for the continued interest in collegia, despite their politically illicit character.
>
> Second, the Roman restrictions on voluntary associations must be seen as part of the backdrop of early Christian communities. Did Christians pass "informal" scrutiny by city officials because their Jewish hero and their appeal to Jewish tradition cloaked them as a Jewish society? . . .
>
> The very real dangers in belonging to an unrecognized society during the imperial period are usually ignored in any reconstruction of the first generation Christian reality, as it is in the exegesis of the Christian texts themselves. Yet the clear evidence of Roman prohibition of such societies and the constant threat of their sudden investigation and dissolution must become incorporated into both aspects of our exegetical enterprise.[24]

Philip Harland cautions against assuming a general antagonism between associations and the Roman Empire and bases his case on his own detailed study of epigraphic evidence from Asia Minor. Although never going beyond "society in Roman Asia Minor," he concludes that "in general, associations were not anti-Roman or subversive groups."[25] He bases this assertion on epigraphic "evidence from Asia Minor that suggests that religious rites for imperial gods, which paralleled the sacrifices, mysteries, and other rituals directed at traditional deities, were a significant component within numerous associations."[26] Similarly, "involvement in imperial dimensions of the polis was one of the ways in which an association could claim a space for itself within society and cosmos."[27] In other words, Harland does not directly dispute the general tension between associations and Rome found by Cotter and her predecessors,[28] but he finds additional indications of cooperation and acceptance of Roman power in and around the associations.

Like Cotter, Harland is explicitly interested in extending this conclusion to both Jewish and Christian associations of Asia Minor.[29] He proposes that "many Jews and Christians viewed the emperors as important figures within the cosmic order of things, figures deserving of special respect and honors."[30] Although he does acknowledge some explicit Jewish and Christian opposition to Roman imperial rule,[31] his overall conclusion resists the anti-imperial conclusions of many authors cited at the beginning of this chapter inasmuch as—according to Harland—"there was a range of attitudes and practices among Jews and Christians with respect to imperial . . . dimensions of the polis."[32]

Harland's contribution is an important qualification. Especially since epigraphic evidence is often closer to the rhythms and phenomena of everyday life, that associations—even Jewish and Christian ones—sometimes consciously and voluntarily acknowledged Roman power must be accepted as historical reality. Finally, however, Harland's work needs to function to nuance the larger tension between the associations (especially the Jewish and Christian ones) and the Roman Empire. His important epigraphic evidence fits best within the following larger aspects of the issue of (early Christian) associations and imperial power:

1. There is relatively strong evidence of early Christian resistance to Rome in Asia Minor. The explicit opposition found in the Revelation to John was not the only example of a conflictual relationship. Horsley's and others' work on Paul shows a number of resistant efforts in Asia Minor.[33]

2. The geographical territory Harland surveys was a part of the Mediterranean under Roman control for a much longer time than many other parts of the first-century empire. Although it may be that Asia Minor more frequently observed the terms of Roman rule than other parts of the empire did, it is very important not to apply this characterization of Asia Minor to the rest of the occupied and colonized territories.

3. Cotter's (and others') review of the active antagonism of the empire to associations cannot be ignored. Harland does not even mention this broad swath of legal steps by Rome taken against associations' gathering.

4. Harland's own language is curiously twisted. He urges one to read the Revelation to John as rhetorical strategy,[34] but he seems to take the less

empire-hostile rhetoric of pastoral epistles and other early Christian literature more straightforwardly.[35]

5. Harland's point that associations, early Christian or not, made accommodations to Roman power must be acknowledged. That certain of these associations did bow to Roman authority from time to time cannot be disputed. Nor can it be disputed that certain early Christian communities instructed their members to obey the imperial government (1 Peter 2, Romans 12).

Overall, then, even Harland's strong effort to show that "there was a range of attitudes and practices among Jews and Christians with respect to imperial . . . dimensions of the polis" needs to be seen as indicative that many associations, and even more Jewish and Christian associations in particular, experienced tension with Rome.[36] When they gathered for a meal, they did so with a range of implicit challenges from Rome to their gathering. These challenges included—depending on the time and place—explicit bans from the emperor himself, explicit bans from the senate or provincial authorities, a range of Roman laws and edicts on who could and could not belong to associations, insistence that every meal gathering include a libation to the emperor, decisions on whether one should eat the meat at the meal in case it had been part of a sacrifice honoring the emperor or imperially connected god (for example, Apollo, Aphrodite, and Zeus), and the porous boundaries of the meal allowing imperial spies to inform on the meal activities.

With this general antipathy between Rome and the meals of Hellenistic associations noted, it is also important to note the aspects of the meal itself that, in a ritual manner, negotiated space for meal participants in relationship to Roman control. Although not highlighted in their particular character of resistance to empire, these aspects were studied in some detail in chapter 4's ritual analysis of the meal. Many of them demonstrated how a number of aspects of the semiprivate, semipublic meals provided the participants with opportunities to negotiate their identity with added reflection, resistance, and nuance not present in public arenas, where imperial power was more overt. The particular aspects of the meal creating this range of imaginative power in relationship to imperial domination included the following:

1. A "perfection" of the inequities of the larger society of slaves (often made by Roman conquering armies), freedmen, and slave owners occurred when these three unequal classes found themselves reclining together at meals. The meal provided the occasion and structure for small groups to recast their social order in a way counter to the domination system set up by Rome.

2. The *habitus*, or established cultural pattern, of the meal allowed a certain "liminality" in the meal times in which new relational patterns and social structures could be risked without the larger consequences incurred because of imperial domination in the public sphere. The stability and safety of the meal structure became a primary milieu in which to imagine different relationships emphasizing the qualities of *philia*, *koinonia*, and *charis*.

3. The larger economic differences of some people (the small patrician class) being able to enjoy leisure while the vast majority struggled[37] to survive were renegotiated and "perfected" at the meals in which (almost) "everyone" across class boundaries reclined together.

4. Holding up the values of equality (for example, "everyone" reclines at the meals) and stratification (for example, there is an order of status among those reclining) at the same time ritually reproduced the tension of these two values in the society at large. This tension provided a microcosm of the much more volatile tensions of the outside world in which slaves and free, men and women, Romans and colonized/occupied, educated and illiterate, and wealthy and poor were alienated from one another. This ritual reproduction of the contradictory values of the larger society in the safer space of the meals allowed for a mutual interrogation of each respective value.

5. The social values of *isonomia* and *philia* required that everyone receive the same amount of food. The existing social stratification demanded that some people receive more than others in recognition of their status. The dramatic discrepancies of food to be had in the larger society alongside of the pretense of that same society toward justice were played out in the less risky and safer meal environment. The meal, as with any good ritual, first simply used the amount of food to reproduce a larger social tension. This gave a group the chance to observe the tension in a relatively protected environment, place it in perspective, and in some cases enact the values of *isonomia* and *philia* relative to the food served.

6. The ritual of libation provided people a protected environment in which the relationship to the occupying empire could be reflected on in a visceral manner but without the high stakes of life outside the meal. At the meal, one had a chance to see how making the libation to the emperor felt, even when one had suffered at the hands of the occupation. Or conversely, one could have a sense of how wise it seemed to resist the libation to

the emperor, even when one knew that in the larger world resistance to the emperor entailed more risks. Such acts of protected resistance and collaboration would have been available in multiple forms at the moment of libation. If one wanted to try out resistance, one could simply not drink the imperial cup when it was passed around. Or one could change one's libation from being to the emperor to taking on the more implicit Apollonian form. Or one could propose a libation to Jesus, the God of Israel, or Isis and thereby ignore the imperial libation.

7. The meal reproduced a power structure with a superficial leader and an unpredictable yet active constituency. The powerful allegiance of the general population to the meal order (without much attention to the leadership of the *symposiarch*) wrote into the power dynamics of the meal a stable and safe environment, which could test the reliability of spontaneous and diffuse leadership in the presence of an artificial authority figure—that is, the viability of the meal's structure with weak formal leadership encouraged meal participants to flirt with other kinds of (shared) power than the imperial model. The strength and safety of the meal order allowed multiple and regular initiatives by the regular populace. It allowed the inspired yet unofficial impulses to temporary leadership to succeed and fail on their own merit and reception.

8. The larger tolerance of some disturbance, especially in the *symposion* (such as uninvited guests, late guests, and arguments), is explained most clearly as a ritual liminality that helped reproduce the larger tensive mix of people in Hellenistic society. The ultimately trustable established order of the meal allowed certain portions of the meal to descend into near chaos, since the ritualized experience of such social disorder helped perfect it for the ordinary life experiences of the diners. In this manner, the meal helped to model ways diverse populations could relate to one another without depending on the orders or power of the emperor.

The Hellenistic meal, then, both as a central part of the regular activities of the numerous—but often imperially questioned—associations and as a "ritual" containing numerous possibilities of anti-imperial gestures and imagination, functioned in many cases as a deeply embedded social practice that stood in tension with Roman imperial power. Plutarch's Timon expressed this tension explicitly: "If in other matters we are to preserve equality among people, why not begin with this first and accustom them to take their places without vanity and ostentation, because they understand as soon as they enter the door that the dinner is a democratic affair and has no outstanding place like an acropolis where the rich man is to recline and lord it over meaner folk."[38] Such a position of the associations vis-à-vis the empire fits almost exactly with what James C. Scott has named the "hidden transcripts" of the "arts of resistance" of grassroots folk and religious expression.[39]

Specific Aspects of Early Christian Meals and Resistance to Empire

As noted by Cotter and many others, that early Christian groups gathered regularly at Hellenistic meals put them in likely tension with Roman domination. That these early Christian meal gatherings did little to allay Roman general fears about associational meals (since they made libations regularly to a savior or lord other than Caesar) redoubled the regular tension between associational meals per se and Rome. The general prevalence and growth of these meals in Hellenistic culture resulted in two mutually tensive additional dynamics: (1) fueling the Roman paranoia and (2) providing a certain level of protection from Roman antagonism by virtue of the meal's pervasive success despite Roman worries.

The monotheistic positions of early "Christians"[40] at meals exacerbated this friction in that this monotheism stood in tension with the emperor's assertion of divinity or at least a divine right to rule the "world."[41] Because of earlier successful negotiations with the empire, Jewish meals were by and large exempt from similar Roman suspicion. Inasmuch as Christian meal gatherings were seen as something other than Jewish,[42] the Christian meals lay then under a double Roman suspicion of being a monotheistic association event. As noted at the beginning of this chapter, the blatant early Christian counterassertions (or caricatures) of Jesus (instead of Caesar) as Savior, Lord, or bringer of peace would have also drawn some worried attention from the Romans. As shown in the last chapter, the pivotal use of early Christian hymns to Jesus as anointed Savior and Lord, especially during the meal libation where one was supposed to salute the emperor, must have been seen from the outside as provocative of Roman ire.

Since, however, there is little evidence of widespread Roman action against the early Christians per se in the first two generations of their movement,[43] this chapter's exploration of early Christian meals as resistance to Rome concentrates more on the self-understanding of these meal groups as countering Roman oppression, idolatry, and pretension. In other words, the chapter explores the ways that these meals fostered and expressed a vision and self-understanding of counterimperial hope for the participants.

EARLY CHRISTIAN MEAL AS COUNTERSOCIETY TO ROME

That Hellenistic meals in general functioned as a way that groups and individuals expressed their "utopian" hopes is treated in this book's third chapter. There,

Klinghardt's extensive case for the meal value of *charis* makes clear the meal's capacity to have provided an experience for its participants that elicited a sense that how one behaved at the meal represented a model for society and the world.[44]

Chapter 5's portrait of the cosmic dimension of early Christian meals complements this utopian character. In locating first on technical literary grounds early Christian cosmic hymns and visions within the meal itself and second, by implication, much other early Christian oral and proto-literary expressions in the meal, analysis showed how hopes for a different world permeated the early Christian meals. The ways these cosmic hopes were ingested/internalized by the meal participants and transformed into social modeling within the meal itself became clear in chapter 5. This modeling was on the levels of individual behavior, social solidarity of the meals associations, and explicit consciousness of opposition and condemnation to the way the world was now. When the early Christian penchant for cosmic vocabulary was placed in the context of early Christian meals, it became clear that the meals imaged and imagined an alternate social world and at least semiconsciously provided ways of tasting that other social world.

This now allows placement of this early Christian cosmic rhetoric in a clearer social context. Once one understands the meal context of much of this Christian cosmic rhetoric and the ways Hellenistic meals were already negotiating alternatives to Roman imperial views of the world, the new *kosmos* imagined in early Christian literature can be seen as at least implicitly and often explicitly an anti-imperial one. Klinghardt's observation of the Hellenistic meal's resistant character applies directly to a meal contextualization of early Christian cosmic literature: "In Hellenism . . . the exemplary function of the meal community was not at all reduced, but rather placed much more in effect. The meal is a concrete utopia for the community. The idealization of this community in the meal serves as the basis for theorizing about governance."[45]

Singing about Jesus having "the name which is above all other names" and about "all beings in the heavens, on the earth, and under the earth bending the knee at the name of Jesus" (Phil. 2:9, 10) at the meal, then, must make the early Christian meal at Philippi an act of resistance to the Roman world and an assertion of an alternate "meal world" in its place. The Lukan literature contained material both against and for the empire. Nevertheless, the picture in Acts 2:44-46, "All who shared the faith owned everything in common and sold their goods and possessions and distributed the proceeds among themselves relative to what each person needed," connected to "meeting in their houses for the breaking of bread," makes for a nearly explicit political and economic challenge to the Roman rule.[46] Even reading passages like Matthew's story of Jesus being acclaimed as king when entering Jerusalem (21:1-11) at a meal becomes a way of imagining and expressing the longing for a ruler other than the emperor.

Adela Yarbro Collins has noted the important expressive character of the Revelation to John in the context of these meals:

It is likely that the Apocalypse was read aloud before the assembled Christians of a given locality, perhaps at regular intervals. . . . For this reason it is better to speak of the first "hearers" of Revelation rather than the "readers."

The Apocalypse is as evocative as it is expressive. Not only does it display attitudes and feelings; it elicits them. . . . The Apocalypse handles skillfully the hearers' thoughts, attitudes, and feelings by the use of effective symbols and a narrative plot that invites imaginative participation. . . . The emotions of the audience are purged in the sense that their feelings of fear and pity are intensified and given objective expression. The feelings are thus brought to consciousness and become less threatening. . . . Fear of Roman power is evoked and intensified. In various symbolic narratives, conflicts are described, each of which is a paradigm of the hearers' situation. . . . The hearers' destiny is symbolized by the story of the two witnesses in ch. 11 and the woman in ch. 12. The powers that threaten them are symbolized by the beast from the abyss and the dragon. These vivid images are certainly designed more to evoke terror than to allay it. Nevertheless, the projection of the conflict onto a cosmic screen, as it were, is cathartic in the sense that it clarifies and objectifies the conflict. Fearful feelings are vented by the very act of expressing them, especially in this larger-than-life and exaggerated way.

Resentment of Roman wealth and power is evoked or intensified especially in chs. 17 and 18. . . . All these alluring, unattainable goods are to be destroyed by divine wrath. . . . Feelings of fear and resentment are released by the book's repeated presentation of the destruction of the hearers' enemies. The element of persecution represents the present, conflict-ridden, and threatened situation in which the author invites the hearers to see themselves. The second two elements of the plot, judgment and salvation, represent the resolution of that situation: the persecutors are destroyed by divine wrath and the persecuted are exalted to a new, glorious mode of existence.[47]

The resistance to Rome in this cathartic expression was clear.

Similar, although more anachronistic, conclusions were drawn from Massey Shepherd's much earlier study *The Paschal Liturgy and the Apocalypse*. Although Shepherd was not privy to the major progress made on the character of first- and second-century Christian "worship" within the paradigm of the Hellenistic meals, his 1960 book made important notice of the ways the Revelation to John corresponded to early Christian worship. He constructed a "theory about the structure of Revelation . . ." provided by the use of the Hallel psalms (113–118) in chapter 19 immediately preceding the "marriage supper of the Lamb."[48] He went on to say that "this in turn fits with the Seer's statement that his vision was experienced 'on the Lord's day' (1:10)," noting that this is the earliest mention of Christians gathering on the "Lord's day."[49]

In somewhat overly churched language, Shepherd proceeded to make the point emphasized here about the function of Revelation's cosmic vision in relationship to the meal and the experience within it of another societal model other than Rome:

> The consummation of the Paschal liturgy is the eucharistic banquet in the presence of Christ, as He holds intimate communion with His Church, giving it light and life. One needs only to recall the gospel parables of the Messianic banquet, and the kingdom sayings of the Lord at the Last Supper, to realize the Eucharistic associations of the great eschatological theme of the Seer's supper of the Lamb. . . . The worship of the Church on earth is really a participation in and an anticipation of the worship of heaven. The Eucharist is the earnest of the final consummation of the age to come. . . . A very real clue to the basic structure of Revelation is to be found in the Paschal liturgy of the Church.[50]

If one overlooks the triumphalist capitalizations, the narrow liturgical categories, the anachronistic projection of later conceptualities, and the wooden (nonsocial) overtheologized assumptions, Shepherd's study of Revelation underlines strongly the way the meal structure, the Revelation text, and the experience of an alternative society coalesce, as elaborated by Collins and in chapter 5 of this book. The contribution of Shepherd's study to this chapter on the meal resistance to the Roman Empire is to note the close parallels among the Revelation text, the hope for an alternate world, and the ritual life of early Christians.[51]

Shepherd's work belongs to a much larger set of scholarly works throughout the twentieth and twenty-first centuries that ponders the "liturgical" forms within the Revelation text.[52] As noted in the previous chapter, much of this attention concentrates on the hymns within Revelation. Some also draw attention to the invitation in 3:20 to join the Christ figure of chapters 1–3 in a *deipnon*.[53] The function of hymns within the Hellenistic meal and in direct relationship to the libation weaves the Revelation text not only into some kind of ritual or "liturgical" fabric but directly into the meal itself. The explicit reference to the supper in 3:20 and 19:9 confirms that this is a Hellenistic meal with its typical negotiations of power made much edgier by the explicit longing for another world.

Revelation was dramatically clear about its resistance to Rome and its hope for an alternative. The above strong connections between the meal and Revelation must have been part of an explicit resistance to Roman imperial power. After all, the laments of Revelation 18 proclaiming the imminent destruction of "this great city whose lavish living has made a fortune," whose "traders were the princes of the earth," and by whom "all the nations were led astray" (18:19, 23) were perfect fits for the songs of the utopian meal. The explicit identification of the "seven heads" of the beast as both the "seven hills" of Rome and the "seven emperors" (17:9, 10) makes a meal in which Revelation is read (or, as Yarbro Collins would have it, enacted) a dramatic act of resistance against the empire.

A similar explicit match between meals and hope for a counter-empire occurred in Q/Luke 13:28-30 (Matt. 8:12) about all those who "come from the east and west, north and south, and recline at the feast in the kingdom/empire of God."[54] Why this saying pointed to reclining at a meal as a counter-empire event (rather than to a more explicitly political occasion, such as a court scene, a forum, or a palace) can be understood only through the experiential modeling that occurred at the meals. Indeed, the plethora of gospel scenarios (for example,, Luke 14:15-24; Mark 2:15-17; GThom 61; John 13:12-15; Matt. 14:13-21) in which the countercultural behavior of the kingdom/empire of God occurred at meals points directly to the function of meal experience for those opposing the oppression and injustice of the Roman Empire.

The meal was understood as behavior emblematic of ideal society. Even when early Christian literature did not picture meal behavior as modeling explicit political or cosmic ideals, the general principle of these actions as ideal still held. By implication, the behavior had societal import. In Warren Carter's study of the empire-critical character of the Gospel of Matthew, he proposes that the character of Matthean community life represented the main alternative to Roman imperial domination. He emphasizes

> signs of God's empire that are evident in the present, especially through the formation of an alternative community. This community of disciples of Jesus is marked by its commitment to him and by an alternative set of practices and lifestyles that challenge practices and values of the imperial world. . . . The existence and practices of this alternative inclusive, more egalitarian community were key aspects in the appeal of the early Christian movement's resistance to the empire. In addition to its theological challenge, Matthew's Gospel thus also presents a social challenge to the empire.[55]

The complex of sayings about servanthood in the Synoptics contains references to both meal modeling and the arrogance of rulers without addressing explicit societal or political issues. Here, it seems to have been a case of meal models exhibiting a behavior counter to that of (almost certainly Roman) political leaders, but with no direct societal or political applications. Luke's version—whose setting during Jesus' Last Supper makes it the most explicitly meal related—drew the following contrast: "Among the gentiles it is the rulers[56] who lord it over others, and those who are given the title of Benefactor. With you this must not be the case. No, the greatest among you must act as if he were the youngest, the leader must behave as if he were the one who serves. For who is greater: the one reclining or the one serving? Surely it is the one reclining? Yet I am among you as the one serving" (22:25-27, author's translation). Here, service at the meal acted as model behavior. Interestingly, Luke did not compare the way the rulers and early Christians ate. Rather, the political behavior of the rulers was contrasted with the meal behavior of the Christians, making clear the way what Klinghardt calls the meal value of *charis* functioned for visionary political and societal purposes, without an exact one-to-one comparison of political behaviors.[57]

This early Christian challenge to Roman cultural domination through emphasis of mutual service to one another at meals mirrored another earlier such contrast in the diaspora Jewish author Philo's description of the Therapeutae. There, Philo portrayed the Therapeutae as examples at meals who were not at all like the Greeks and the Romans.[58] One of the most assertive claims of such difference was that, in contrast to the Greeks and Romans, at the banquet of the Therapeutae "there is no slave, but the services are rendered by free men who perform their tasks . . . with deliberate good will. . . . For it is not just any free men . . . but young members of the association. . . . They give their services gladly and proudly like sons to their real fathers and mothers."[59] This portrait of a meal ethic of service to one another that contrasted to the existing domination model was so evocative to the fourth-century church historian Eusebius that he claimed that the Therapeutae must have been Christian.[60]

Dennis Smith points out that Mark pictured the service and hospitality of early Christian meals as "a primary form of honoring one's neighbors" and a gesture "to offer to them a place in one's social world."[61] Without noticing the dimension of Roman domination inherent in the text, Smith also notes that this Markan service and hospitality at meals was contrasted to "the yeast of the Pharisees and Herod" in Mark 8:15.[62] For Mark, then, the meal's societal vision supplanted the rule of the Roman governor. Although not as explicit in its contrast to Roman governance, Luke's version of the parable of the feast in 14:12-14, with its invitation to "the poor, the crippled, the lame and the blind," exhibited a similar contrast.

EARLY CHRISTIAN MEALS AND THE CROSS

A second major explicit connection between early Christian meals and resistance to the Roman Empire has to do with the importance of the powerful ways many early Christians referenced the crucifixion within their meals. Remembering that crucifixion was an imperial punishment for insurrection, it is striking that many (but not all) early Christian associations emphasized the crucifixion in their meals. Such referencing could have been understood only as an act of explicit challenge to Rome. Ritualizing the death by crucifixion of Jesus in meals had to be a self-conscious challenge to Roman authority, especially since—as noted earlier in this chapter— associational meals lay under suspicion from Rome in any case.

The textual connection between meals and Jesus' crucifixion was—if not ubiquitous—prominent. With the background of the meal paradigm established by Smith and Klinghardt, it can now be seen in what meal contexts these references to Jesus' crucifixion functioned. Four different components of the meal match the textual treatments of the crucifixion: (1) the libations, (2) the songs, (3) the blessing of the bread, and (4) the storytelling and teaching during the *symposion*. They are laid out in that order below.

The libations. There are three relatively separate elements of libations in Paul and the gospels within the Lord's/Last Supper texts that associate the cup with Jesus' death on the cross. They are (1) the persistent trajectory (pre-Paul/1 Corinthians/Mark/Matthew/secondary Luke) of the libation that associated the cup after the *deipnon* with Jesus' blood; (2) the command to remember Jesus in the libation, which is found only in the earliest text of 1 Corinthians; and (3) the floating Synoptic libation tradition about not drinking wine again until the reign of God comes. Some of this material is treated at other points in this book, (Ch. 4's analysis based on ritual theory and Ch. 5's relating of cosmic hymns to the libation) so here only the connection between the libation and Jesus' death and, hence, resistance to the Roman Empire is addressed.

The beginning of the cup = Jesus' blood trajectory is found in 1 Cor. 11:23, 25-27: "'The tradition I received from the Lord and I also passed on to you is that on the night he was handed over . . . in the same manner with the cup after dinner, [the Lord Jesus] said, 'This cup is the new covenant in my blood. Whenever you drink it, do this remembering me. Whenever you eat this bread then and drink this cup, you are proclaiming the Lord's death until he comes'" (author's translation).

This text and the "tradition" (11:23) behind it identified in a classic libational moment the cup after the *deipnon* with Jesus' blood and proceeded to assert that drinking the cup proclaimed Jesus' death. The stark challenge to Rome in this libation could not be overlooked. It proposed a "new covenant in my blood" (11:25). The dense set of ironies and political terms made clear the challenge for the early followers of this "tradition." This was the moment when associations were to have made a libation to the emperor. Instead, this "tradition" made a libation to one who had been executed by the emperor as an enemy of the state. And the libation was not just to the executed one. Its language went out of its way to evoke the blood inherent in death on a cross. The proclamation of the "new covenant" was language of social and political solidarity. It asserted a social loyalty to the executed one. The term *covenant* evoked simultaneously the kind of worrisome loyalty of associations bonded together and the troublesome and numerically threatening "nation" of Israel spread throughout the Roman Empire. Israel—even in its conquered state—had already forced Rome into compromises that granted Jews exemptions from imperial sacrifice and libation by virtue of the many Jews around the Mediterranean. The libation in 1 Corinthians made a clarion call to resistance to Rome by an expanded Israel.

It is relatively clear that this tradition is pre-Pauline. Scholars have long puzzled about Paul's claim that he has received this tradition "from the Lord" (11:23). In no other letter did Paul claim to have direct personal access to Jesus concerning this practice. Not even the most conservative scholars posit Jesus telling Paul in a vision about the Last Supper.[63] By and large, then, this has been taken by scholars as Paul receiving the "tradition" from those who taught him. For the purposes of this study, it is most important to see how the libational challenge to Rome is pre-Pauline. A number of scholars in the past fifteen years, however, have suggested that the origins of this tradition go back to early gentile "Christian" practice, rather than to Jesus himself or to Palestinian traditions related to disciples.[64]

Mark seems to have integrated the 1 Corinthians story into his passion narrative with several adjustments to be considered below. In specific relationship to the libational equation of cup and blood, Mark made two significant adjustments in dropping the command to make this libation in memory of Jesus and in adding that it is "poured out for many" (14:24). In terms of resistance to Rome, the implications of a lack of command to repeat the libation in memory of Jesus are unclear. However, although rarely recognized in scholarship, the cup as being poured out for many emphasized the libational character of the act, since the act of libation within the Hellenistic meal paradigm included both pouring out and drinking the cup. The meaning of this phrase has been often (mis)understood through the later Matthean addition of "poured out for many for the forgiveness of sins" (26:28). Such a Matthean addition has prompted a number of atonement interpretations of the Markan version as well. Letting this interpretation of the Matthean addition redirect the meaning in Mark obscures a major possible Markan meaning, especially in relationship to resistance to Rome. A libation poured out was simply a full libation. The Markan libation for many in relation to a covenant (sociopolitical bond) of resistance (death by imperial execution) envisioned "many" challenging Rome.

This also fits the similar Markan connection (10:35-40) between Jesus' crucifixion and the drinking of the cup:

> James and John, the sons of Zebedee, came to him. "Master," they said to him, "please do us a favor." He responded, "What is it you want me to do for you?" They said, "Allow us to sit respectively at your right and left hand in your glory." But Jesus said to them, "You do not know what you are asking. Can you drink the cup that I shall drink, or be baptized with the baptism I shall have?" They replied, "We can." Jesus replied, "The cup that I shall drink you shall drink, and the baptism with which I shall be baptized you shall have. But as for the seats at my right or left hand, these are not mine to grant" (author's translation).

This additional combination of the libational cup with Jesus' death reflects Mark's affirmation of the libational challenge to Rome in his larger narrative.

Matthew followed suit in integrating the libational challenge to Rome into his passion narrative while characterizing the libation as "for the forgiveness of sins." Although the interpretational history of this addition has (even for Mark) tended toward an understanding of the cup as atoning, within the context of both the Hellenistic meal paradigm and the resistance motif of a libation for many, it is not at all clear that an atonement reading is appropriate for Mark. "Forgiveness of sins" can be read in conjunction with a libation poured out for many in the spirit of Jesus executed (as so many were) by Rome. The "many" for whom such a libation was made would have certainly included both Jew and gentile. In this case, it—like so many other metaphors of early Christian writings—would have enthusiastically "forgiven" the "sin" of being a gentile. In consonance with the Markan predecessor, this libation would have—with a distinctive Matthean twist—underlined the oneness of the resistance of many within the tradition of Israel. In this case, the Matthean addition would not have been so much a redirection of meaning as a (particularly Matthean) enhancement of Mark's challenging libation honoring the blood of the one executed by the empire.[65]

This entire libational trajectory is missing from some early manuscripts of Luke.[66] Combined with the existence of another completely different cup saying (to be treated below), this suggests that the cup equation with Jesus' blood has been added "in a later scribal conflation of Mark, Paul, and the shorter Lukan accounts in interest of agreement."[67] Inasmuch as one would include it in Luke, it had minor variations, returning to the "new" covenant of Paul (over against the covenant of Mark and Matthew) and making the libation for "you" rather than for "many." Neither of these changes would have made much difference in terms of a libation of resistance, especially since Luke assumed more than the other canonical gospels a predominantly gentile readership.

This overview of the libation comparing the wine to the blood of the executed Jesus has shown a strong interest in all three main levels of the textual trajectory in the libational cup as a gesture of resistance to Roman power. While taking this element of a strong trajectory of early Christian texts seriously and pointing to their underattended anti-imperial meanings, it is also important to maintain the perspective of chapters 4 and 5 in seeing these gestures as ritual negotiations of meaning and social experimentation within the relatively protected environment of the meal; that is, this resistance libation of a substantial part of early Christian associations was not explicit in its meaning but part of a larger cultural set of gestures whose social setting provided shelter and whose meaning remained communal.

The second libational tradition concerning Jesus' death and its implication for resistance to Rome is the (possibly pre-Pauline and Pauline) injunction to do the libation as a remembering of Jesus. As noted in chapter 5, this command stood as part of a larger associational obligation throughout the Hellenistic world to have a meal in honor/ remembrance of all association members who died. That this mutual associational obligation came into being in large part because of the vulnerable and impoverished finances of association members certainly was related to Roman economic exploitation of its conquered peoples. One factor for this financial vulnerability was Roman taxation and the unequal distribution of resources favoring Roman aristocrats.

In addition, inasmuch as this libational injunction was a companion of the wine = Jesus' blood words (as is the case at least in 1 Cor. 11:25, if not in its pre-Pauline form[68]), the injunction to have a libation in Jesus' memory made the words much more charged. The meaning of this libational combination would have been very strong in its anti-Roman character, both evoking the death of Jesus as a new sociopolitical bonding at the meal and promoting it as an ongoing practice.

The third libational trajectory concerns only the Synoptic texts, but it is nevertheless complicated. The declaration of the Markan Jesus that "I shall not drink again of the fruit of the vine until that day when I drink it anew in the reign of God" (14:25) came after the other libational words. This was also true of the Matthean version, which changed it only slightly by adding that Jesus' drinking would be "with you" and that it was the "Father's" reign. However, the meaning of Luke's version was somewhat different ("I shall not drink of the fruit of the vine until the reign of God comes," 22:18), and it also came before the bread sentences.

The Lukan placing of this saying over a cup before the saying over the bread raises two larger questions: (1) Are there two cups in the Lukan Last Supper? and (2) Is this (first?) cup a libation at all, since it does not occur after the *deipnon*? Without extended rationale, I propose the following adjudication of these questions: (1) the second (and libational) cup in Luke 22:19, 20 was added to the earlier Lukan manuscripts (which do not include it) in the interest of making Luke's Last Supper story coherent with Paul and Mark; and (2) the first (and more secure in the early manuscripts) cup could not have been meant as a libational cup in Luke, since it preceded the bread and the end of the *deipnon*.

For this examination of the relationship between this libational saying and resistance to Rome, only the Markan and very similar Matthean versions then remain, despite the evocative possible meaning the Lukan saying might have as a libational saying in elliptically positing the coming of the reign of God in the next time Jesus drinks wine. Exploring the significance of this saying as libational resistance depends on close study of the Markan complex of libational sayings in 14:23-25. It has been noted earlier that Mark seems to have dropped the injunction to drink the cup in remembrance of Jesus but has kept—with a few variations—the rest of the 1 Corinthians complex around the cup. This observation needs to be paired with the lack of the currently examined saying about not drinking the fruit of the vine in 1 Corinthians. This leads directly to the clear possibility that Mark replaced the command to drink the cup in remembrance of Jesus with the saying about Jesus not drinking wine until he drinks it again in the reign of God.

Inasmuch as this was the case, it is relatively easily explained with reference to Mark's persistent apocalyptic references—that is, in replacing the injunction to drink in Jesus' memory with the promise not to drink wine until the coming of the reign of God, Mark simultaneously rejected some notion that life will go on with some regularity (allowing people to follow the command to repeatedly drink in Jesus' memory) and placed the Last Supper in stark apocalyptic perspective. From this point of view, the Markan passion narrative (already dramatically framed by chapter 13's "little apocalypse" and only a secret resurrection) made the Last Supper an ominous (and, for the Markan secretly chosen ones, promising) bonding between the convict Jesus and his followers. Mark made the libation into a dramatic confrontation between the soon-to-be imperially condemned Jesus and the promised counter-reign of God. This final element of the Markan Last Supper libation threw down the gauntlet of a cup poured out for many and defiantly drunk by Jesus and his followers, all while explicitly evoking Jesus' death as an enemy of the state. As usual, Matthew followed Mark's apocalypticism with few revisions. Luke—also as usual—toned down the Markan apocalyptic perspective, both by removing it from the drama of the libation and by spiritualizing the coming of the reign of God.

This overview of the various early Christian libational sayings confirms their general interest in experimenting with resistance to Rome within the relatively protected space of the meal. As has been noted in chapter 4, this was by and large part of a larger negotiation vis-à-vis Roman oppression at the time of libation in Hellenistic meals.

The songs. As already noted in some detail in chapter 5, the substantial collection of songs embedded in early Christian literature was most likely sung either at the time of the libations or during the *symposion*. These songs, which tended to be quite cosmic, also showed consistent interest in the cosmic significance of Jesus' crucifixion. Philippians 2:6-11; Col. 1:15-20; and several of the songs in Revelation drew strong and explicit attention to Jesus' crucifixion as a cosmically pivotal event.

The songs accompanying or directly following the libations carried special tension with them relative to Roman power. This had to do with the pressure from Rome for all meals to include a libation to the emperor. Inasmuch as the early Christian songs at the libation proclaimed Jesus as Savior or Lord, they stood in direct opposition to Rome's project of praise for the emperor during the libation. As chapter 4 explained, this Roman requirement of libations to the emperor almost certainly helped make the Hellenistic libations moments of ritual negotiation. Quite quickly, a range of libational options were improvised. One could have done a libation to the gods Apollo or Zeus as an implicit libation to Caesar. Or one could have included these gods in libations to a number of gods, further diluting the salute. Or one could have—in the relative protection of the meal—skipped a libation to the emperor or tried out an occasional libation to the emperor. Chapter 4 also examined the curious inattentiveness to the libation that some Hellenistic literature noticed, and it speculated that this inattentiveness itself could have been a negotiation of the Roman pressure to salute Caesar libationally.

Singing the songs about the alternative cosmic reign of Jesus and the pivotal event of Jesus' crucifixion during either the libation or the *symposion* had to have been understood as a challenge to Rome. Evoking the death of anyone at the hands of the Romans as a crucial event in bringing about a new world and salvation contradicted the overarching and public assertions and assumptions that Caesar had saved the world as an act of (his own) divine benevolence.

The blessing of the bread. There were two different "Christian" blessings of the bread cited in the extant literature of the first century: (1) the saying that equated bread and Jesus' body in 1 Corinthians and the Synoptic Gospels and (2) the thanksgiving for life in the Didache. Only the bread and body sayings are germane to this discussion of crucifixion-related dimensions of early Christian meals.

The analogy of bread and body has been analyzed in an almost fetishistic manner by theologians, historians, and liturgical scholars. The range of meaning for this analogy over the past two thousand years cannot be considered here. It is nevertheless necessary to examine the analogy in two ways related to this portion of this chapter: (1) the analogy's first-century relationship to the crucifixion and (2) its relationship to resistance to Rome.

Of the four blessings of the bread in 1 Corinthians and the Synoptic Gospels, there are some differences but not any discernible trajectory. The earliest text, 1 Cor. 11:23-24, had Jesus taking bread on the night he was handed over, giving thanks, breaking it, and saying, "This is my body which is for you," followed by a command to remember Jesus. The first gospel text (Mark) placed it in the passion story but dropped both the command to remember Jesus and the phrase "which is for you." Matthew followed Mark almost exactly, while Luke added "which is given for you" after the bread and body analogy.

On the surface of these texts it is not particularly clear that the body = bread analogy references the crucifixion at all. The later liturgical formula "body broken for you" is not found in the gospels or 1 Corinthians. As Klinghardt notes: "The use of the metaphor of one loaf of bread to portray the unity of a group is not at all a Christian discovery."[69] He goes on to conclude about early Christian texts concerning bread that "all examples have in common that a loaf of bread represented the unity of a meal community."[70]

Similarly, the use of body/*soma* for a social body was common. Klinghardt's clear and detailed summary of a wide variety of Hellenistic sources shows that the use of the term *body* was extensive in four kinds of explicit social frameworks: (1) body as "corporate personality" in Jewish patriarch traditions; (2) Hellenistic examples of the political body; (3) use of the body metaphor for Hellenistic associations;[71] and (4) other early Christian meal and nonmeal uses of body/*soma* for community.[72] It is not completely clear that this saying itself referred analogically to Jesus' crucifixion, since none of the versions of the saying about the bread explicitly evoked the crucifixion and there was extensive use of body and bread for social bodies.[73]

However, the narrative context of this saying in both 1 Corinthians and the Synoptics gave an indisputable crucifixion meaning to it. First Corinthians has the saying "on the night that he was handed over" (11:23). The Synoptics placed the entire unit from 1 Corinthians within the passion narrative. In all these cases, then, the meaning of bread = body must take into account the crucified body—that is, the blessing of the bread in this tradition was explicitly linked to a communal integration of Jesus' crucifixion into early Christian identity.

It is at this point that the nexus of meal scholarship and (re)new(ed) attention in New Testament scholarship to early Christian resistance to the Roman Empire helps elucidate the bread/body/crucifixion complex. In other words, it is important to picture the early Christian meals that used the bread/body/crucifixion complex as asserting that their social unity was rooted in the crucifixion of Jesus. The background of Rome's understanding both of associational meals as threatening and of crucifixion as a punishment reserved for opponents of Rome cannot be ignored here. Such an evocation of Jesus' death in the blessing of the bread must have had very similar dangerously resistant meanings for those who gathered at the meals as the libations and songs discussed above did.[74]

Burton Mack's connection of this bread blessing to a larger literature of martyrdom contributes crucially to the meaning of the bread blessing. Mack points out that Hellenistic martyrdom (including Jewish stories in this era concerning tragic deaths of Jews at the hands of the Seleucids and Romans) is based on the larger Greek tradition of noble death.[75] These Jewish and Hellenistic martyrs were understood as dying for their particular people. Their deaths, like those of the original Greek military heroes and subsequently Socrates and other dead leaders, were pictured in this larger body of literature as "for" their peoplehood and community. The term *body* was developed in this literature, since "it was the body, and only the body (not the person, soul, or flesh) over which the tyrant had any power."[76] Writes Mack: "The martyr myth was in mind as the supper symbols evolved. 'My body for you' contains the telltale, kerygmatic phrase 'for you,' and it is precisely the body that martyrological literature focused upon."[77]

Mack then imagines this particular bread blessing tradition in relationship to the Hellenistic meal paradigm where there was "connection made between the two special moments of the meal and the death of Christ according to the myth of the martyr."[78] His portrait notes that

this would not be inappropriate for an association meeting in the name of Christ. All associations had patron deities. . . . Experimenting with the special moments of the common meal as proper occasion for acknowledging the Christ as the community's patron deity, early Christians chose to recall the two essential moments of the martyr myth. One was the death itself; the other was the resolve that turned the death into a founding event for the community. . . . The . . . thanksgiving and breaking of the bread as signal for the dinner-association to begin would have been the appropriate moment to remember the founding event. One could imagine an early thanksgiving to the effect that Christ handed his body over "for" the gathered community. At some points the breaking of the bread could be thought of as pointing in both directions, that which reminded of Christ's resolve and that which constituted the community as gathered.[79]

Much of Mack's work on the 1 Corinthians–based bread blessing was done before much of the new scholarship on early Christian resistance to Rome was published. But with the new scholarship now in place, Mack's establishment of the literary base of this bread blessing within martyrological traditions transforms the bread/body/crucifixion complex into a clear gesture of resistance. It connects the obvious resistant strains evoked by the crucifixion context to an explicit and longer tradition of martyrs founding communities of resistance.

Mack's suggestion that this mini-narrative on bread/body/crucifixion in 1 Corinthians was meant as a foundation event or "etiological myth" for either pre-Pauline or Pauline meal associations also has major implications for an understanding of these meals as acts of resistance.[80] In other words, this particular bread blessing tradition was meant to give communal thanks for the foundational resistance in Jesus' crucifixion. The bread blessing at the meal gathering itself then served as a reenactment of the founding of this community of resistance.

Matthias Klinghardt places this communal meal participation in Jesus' crucifixion in relationship to the other important textual reference in 1 Corinthians, that of 10:16-17. There, the loaf of bread was understood as "sharing in the body of Christ. And as there is one loaf, so we, although many, are a single body, for we all share in one loaf." Klinghardt notes that the "goal of this argumentation is—after having established a meaning of the participation in Christ—the community of the meal participants with one another. . . . The 'koinonia' is participation in the body of the cross."[81]

What is striking here is that two key scholars of early Christian meals help elucidate the critical meaning of resistance to Rome in the bread/body/crucifixion blessing without having had access to or seeming interest in the larger scholarship about early Christian resistance to the empire. Their careful analysis of the literature from the perspective of the Hellenistic meal paradigm underlines this blessing of bread complex as resistant to Rome.

The storytelling and teaching during the symposion. As has been suggested in several portions of this book, the prevalence of storytelling and teaching in the

Hellenistic meals' *symposion* made it likely that many of the teachings and narratives in the early Christian literature were at some point in their development a part of *symposion* events. These (eventually written) teachings and narratives could have been parts of *symposion* teachings and stories at oral stages of development (for example, generated or retold at the meals), at oral-scribal[82] stages (for example, revised orally from documents read at the meal or documents at the base of performance or ritual events[83]), or as written letters or narratives read at meals. This opens the entire corpus of early Christian literature up to having been told, read, or performed during meal *symposia*.

This is germane to this chapter's investigation of early Christian meals of resistance since there were numerous teachings, stories, and letter segments about Jesus' crucifixion. Indeed, almost certainly more than 30 percent of early Christian literature involved reflection on Jesus' death. In other words, that many stories, teachings, and letter segments about Jesus' death on a cross were told at early Christian meals must also be seen as a significant part of the resistant character of those meals. As chapter 3 detailed and chapter 4 analyzed in terms of ritual theory, the *symposion* was the dominant and climactic portion of the meal, defining the overall character of the event. To have a substantial portion of the *symposion* concentrating on the crucifixion of Jesus was an act of resistance in and of itself. With the added power of the meal's ability to project a sense of community and a utopian world, substantial storytelling and teaching about the defining character of Jesus' crucifixion must have made these meals a powerful expression of resistance to Roman arrogance and imperiousness.

Libations, songs, bread blessing, and teachings and stories in the *symposion* all evoked explicitly the death of Jesus by crucifixion at the hands of the Roman emperor. The density of attention in early Christian meals to this inflammatory event of the cross made tension with Rome unavoidable. This confrontational subject matter near the heart of most early Christian meals combined with the major interest of these meals in representing an alternative world and its attendant behavior to mark them as events of substantial resistance to Rome. These explicit dimensions of resistance in the name of Jesus/Christ added to the already tensive relationship Rome had with associations in general.

What Was the Character of Early Christian Resistance to the Roman Empire?

With the rise in attention to themes of resistance in early Christian literature must come an obvious—but basically so far unaddressed—question. What behavior did the early Christians exhibit against Rome? Did they revolt as did some peoples, including the people of Israel twice in a span of seventy years? Were there public assertions of their opposition to the empire? Did they refuse to pay taxes to Rome? It has been clear for some time that early Christians did not do any of these explicit acts of resistance. Yet, as noticed at the beginning of this chapter, there is clear written evidence of early Christian opposition to Rome. What, then, were the corresponding actions of resistance?

This question becomes all the more pointed inasmuch as one assumes—as I do—that most early Christian associations were regarded at least for the first one hundred years for the most part as Jewish associations.[84] Since Jews were exempted by Rome from the public demonstrations of piety toward the emperor, it is unlikely that early Christians refusing to participate in public festivals in honor of the emperor would have been punished inasmuch as they (as "Jews") were exempted from these requirements. Such an assumption is further confirmed by the complete lack of controversy in early Christian literature and Roman records of early Christians being accused of such open resistance. So what early Christian behavior prompted both the occasional imperial accusations against Christians and the strong sense in early Christian literature that Roman imperial authority was antithetical to Christ?

This chapter has provided the obvious—but not yet stated in empire-critical New Testament studies—answer. The behavior that generated both the early Christian resistance and the occasional imperial accusations was simply the meal gatherings by early Christians. For the early Christians, the experience of an alternative societal model, the bonding in community, and the many evocations of Jesus' resistance on the cross at the meals made clear to them that they belonged to a counterimperial entity. For the Romans, their general worry about all associational meals combined with occasional knowledge of the more provocative libations, songs, and stories at the early Christian meals probably was reason enough for the occasional accusations or arrests. So, from both the external and internal perspectives, it was the meal behavior that was at the heart of the emerging opposition between early Christians and Roman imperial power.

It might be said that if these meals were the major behavior of resistance, it was a negligible resistance, not worthy of much attention. If, as has been confirmed, more explicit and public resistance to Rome was not practiced by early Christians, the meals as resistance seem to have had no discernible political or social effect, and to have appeared even silly or impotent. On the other hand, recent writings of James C. Scott have helped see the political power of this kind of resistance. In his *Domination and the Arts of Resistance: Hidden Transcripts*, Scott shows that effective political resistance in peasant and proletarian settings often takes forms of expression that—although not traditionally political—are nevertheless efficacious. Scott points out that folk culture, religion, and subcultural behavior can often be strong political statements of resistance.

"Subordinate groups," he asserts, "manage to insinuate their resistance, in disguised form, into the public transcript."[85] Often, the political power of these groups is not recognized, Scott says, since "the realities of power for subordinate groups mean that much of their political action requires interpretation precisely because it is intended to be cryptic and opaque."[86] Scott writes: "These ambiguous, polysemic elements of folk culture mark off a relatively autonomous realm of discursive freedom on the condition that they declare no *direct* opposition to the public transcript as authorized by the dominant."[87] Klinghardt directly invokes this same insight in discussion of the utopian and explicitly political role of the Hellenistic meal paradigm: "The more public and 'political' life shifted into the associations and its meals (because societal unity and community had become consistently less and less realizable on the macro level), the more association life became public and 'political' and overarching societal problems pressed in on association life, even though the associations themselves were at the same time and in the long run less capable of portraying a convincing contrasting societal portrait."[88]

Scott's portrait of this significant, but opaque, kind of political resistance from these subordinate groups fits early Christian meals very closely.

> The subordinate group must carve out for itself social spaces insulated from control and surveillance from above. If we are to understand the process by which resistance is developed and codified, the analysis of the creation of these offstage spaces becomes a vital task. Only by specifying how such social spaces are made and defended is it possible to move from the individual resisting subject—an abstract fiction—to the socialization of resistant practices and discourses.[89]

Throughout this book, the unique semiprivate station of early Christian (and all other Hellenistic) meals has been seen as particularly effective in providing social, political (utopian), and cosmic models in the midst of a repressive society.

> Social spaces of relative autonomy do not merely provide a neutral medium within which practical and discursive negations may grow. As domains of power relations in their own right, they serve to discipline as well as to formulate patterns of resistance. The process of socialization is much the same as with any stylized sentiment. If we can imagine, hypothetically, an unarticulated feeling of anger, the expression in language of that anger will necessarily impose a disciplined form to it. If this now-articulated anger is to become the property of the small group, it will be further disciplined by the shared experiences and power relations within that small group. If, then, it is to become the social property of a whole category of subordinates it must carry effective meaning for them and reflect the cultural meanings and distribution of power among them. In this hypothetical progression from "raw" anger to what we might call "cooked" indignation . . . the essential point is that a resistant subculture or countermores among subordinates is necessarily a product of mutuality. . . .

> The hidden transcript has no reality as pure thought; it exists only to the extent it is practiced, articulated, enacted, and disseminated within these offstage social sites.[90]

Early Christian meals have been shown in this book to have almost exactly this process of socializing resistance that Scott describes.

Scott goes on to describe further similarities. The Roman authorities' attempts to ban associational meals seems reminiscent of the following observation by Scott: "The strongest evidence for the vital importance of autonomous social sites in generating a hidden transcript is the strenuous effort made by dominant groups to abolish or control such sites."[91]

In describing this kind of resistance, Scott turns to an exact category of an analysis central to this book as he turns to "more complex and culturally elaborate forms of disguise found in oral culture, folktales, symbolic inversion, and finally in rituals of reversal."[92] His description of one such ritual of reversal (cults of spirit possession) resembles in many ways the semicovert gestures of early Christian meals.

> Where they exist, they frequently offer a ritual site at which otherwise dangerous expressions of hostility can be given comparatively free rein. I. M. Lewis, for example, argues persuasively that spirit possession in many societies represents a quasi-covert form of social protest for women and for marginal, oppressed groups of men for whom any open protest would be exceptionally dangerous. Ultimately Lewis's argument makes implicit use of the hydraulic metaphor . . . : the humiliations of domination produce a critique that, if it cannot be ventured openly and at the site at which it arises, will find a veiled, safe outlet. In the case of spirit possession, a woman seized by a spirit can openly make known her grievances against her husband and male relatives, curse them, make demands, and, in general, violate the powerful norms of male dominance. She may, while possessed, cease work, be given gifts, and generally be treated indulgently. Because it is not she who is acting, but rather the spirit that has seized her, she cannot be held responsible for her own words. The result is a kind of oblique protest that dares not speak its own name but that is often acceded to if only because its claims are seen to emanate from a powerful spirit and not from the woman herself.[93]

This analysis resembles in many ways the freedom of women to recline in some Hellenistic and early Christian meals with impunity in contrast to the shame they would have experienced in most public venues and even some private situations. More generally, this example shows similarity to the range of anti-imperial songs, libations, and stories that emerged from the Hellenistic and early Christian meals.

Scott's final assessment of a variety of rituals of reversal, including his major one of medieval "carnival," provides keen analytical help in categorizing early Christian meals as a particular kind of political and social resistance.[94] He writes: "I do not mean to imply that carnival or rituals of reversal cause revolt: they most certainly do not. The point is rather about the relation between symbolism and disguise. Carnival, in its ritual structure and anonymity, gives a privileged place to normally suppressed speech and aggression."[95] In almost exactly the same, if not more explicit, manner, early Christian meals gave "privileged place to normally suppressed speech and aggression." The ways early Christian meals imagined and modeled alternate societies, the manner in which the early Christian libations challenged the imperial edict to do a libation to the emperor, and the subversive implications of the stories and songs about Jesus' crucifixion all are major aspects of the meals' ritual of reversal of Roman authority.

Early Christian meals, then, were often very significant acts of resistance. On numerous levels, they regularly functioned for their participants as generative of opposition to Rome and models for alternative visions and behavior. It is, nevertheless, also important to remember—especially from the ritual analysis of these meals in chapter 4—that these meals produced other important effects in the lives of their participants beyond this significant resistance to Rome. (And it is clear that some early Christian meals had elements of complicity and collaboration with Roman power. For instance, the severe criticisms of Revelation 2 and 3 against certain Christian associations in Asia Minor make it relatively clear that some even made libations to the emperor alongside of the libations to Christ.) As Scott's example above of women's behavior in spirit possession indicates, the "hidden transcript" of resistance in the early Christian meals can also be resistance to powers other than Rome, such as the dominant and culturewide patriarchy of the Hellenistic era. Chapter 7 examines this kind of antipatriarchal resistance as a part of its overview of early Christian social experimentation at meals.

CHAPTER SEVEN

Meals AND Early Christian Social Experimentation

S EEING EARLY CHRISTIAN MEALS as a site of resistance to Roman imperial power is just one lens through which to decipher social gestures occurring at these meals. Ritual analysis has shown that many of the actions within the meal helped reproduce, negotiate, perfect, and think about difficult social issues of the Hellenistic era. This chapter examines further the social gestures within these meals and explores how much these ritualized social dynamics extended themselves into explicit engagement of social issues of that era. Such more explicit societal dimensions of these meals are designated here using Burton Mack's term "social experiments," which was examined in chapter 2.

Ritual Perfection or Social Experimentation or Both?

The relationship between social experimentation and ritual reflection, reproduction, perfection, and deployment needs to be clarified. As noted in chapter 4, ritual is engaged in the social realm not only tangentially but also primarily. On the other hand, even though ritual engages social dynamics so strongly, it almost never does so in direct address. It provides a somewhat removed and safe environment and usually in coded gesture and language reproduces a social conflict or problem. This indirect, veiled engagement of important social dynamics commonly provides a more effective address of intractable and frightening social issues.

These ritual/social achievements occurred within the basic elements of the Hellenistic meal. Such everyday actions as reclining and drinking became ritual frames of reference through which to engage important societal issues of status, diversity, gender, and identity. The ritual meal engagement of these social problems was characterized by the technical terms found in ritual and performance theory: reproduction, reflection, perfection, and deployment. That is, the meals reproduced in a safe environment and in coded manner intimidating social issues so that they could be thought about (reflected), made better in the meal setting than in the society at large (perfected), or addressed obliquely in the society itself (deployed). By and large, the meals' ritual component provided perspective and social intelligence for the longer-term address of an intractable social issue. Generally, meals' ritual address produced little or no direct solution to the societal issues. Rather, its power lay in the perspective it lent through longer-term reflection and the sense of processing such issues in the ritually subliminal frame.

When social experimentation is understood to have occurred in these meals, this includes the ritual address of societal issues but contains additional dynamics as well. Social experimentation not only reproduces and reflects on a complex societal problem. Nor does it simply perfect the particular social issue for the ritual moment or just deploy a ritually accrued insight to an occasional moment outside the ritual. Social experimentation is a relatively self-conscious behavior in the ritual with an explicit consciousness that this behavior should apply directly to a societal problem. In other words, when the ritual action takes on a relatively explicit and direct claim of relevance to the larger societal issue, I consider it social experimentation. This is not to say that ritual process does not complement social experimentation. The subliminal ritual process in the case of early Christian (and other Hellenistic) meals provides important access and sustained attention that undergird social experimentation.

For example, when a Hellenistic meal not only provided the experience of wealthy and poor reclining together (so that the intractable societal discrepancy of rich and poor could be reproduced and reflected upon) but also asserted explicitly that the wealthy should give money or goods to poor people, this would be considered a social experiment. Indeed, this did occur. Some Hellenistic meal groups did send food from their meals to people in need.[1] Although the ritual dimensions often generated such social experimentation through the implicit and indirect ways ritual raises difficult issues, some ritual behavior also became explicitly socially experimental. The cases of resistance to Rome at early Christian meals, outlined in chapter 6, serve as a first clear example. In the previous study of these cases, it was shown that subliminal ritual address to Roman dominion occurred in the tension of multiple libations intersecting with imperial insistence on a libation to the emperor. Subsequently, this study has shown that this creative ritual tension became explicit social experimentation when some early Christians started using libations to confront imperial oppression by raising a cup to Jesus and explicitly identifying his execution by the Romans in the libation.

Methodological Issues concerning Early Christian Societal Consciousness and Action

Social ranking, social identities, the possibilities of order and peace, gender contestations, economic need and affluence, leadership and authority, exclusiveness/

inclusiveness, ethnic tensions, and political privilege and oppression all were found to have been complexly raised to semiconsciousness through the ritual character of these meals.

This chapter builds on this awareness of the ritually addressed social issues in most Hellenistic meals. It assumes that early Christian meals were occasions for these same ritual negotiations of socially important issues and therefore rarely retraces the social meanings of the basic meal dynamics. Without pretending that early Christian meals were unique in this regard, it goes on to ask the specifics of early Christian negotiations on these various issues and the ways some early Christian meals introduced social experiments relative to many of these issues.

ANTHROPOLOGICAL LENS

Anthropological terms developed by the past two generations of New Testament scholarship for analyzing these social issues are important in that they provide frames of reference for non-Western, nonmodern societies like the Hellenistic Mediterranean. Systems of honor and shame have been identified in non-Western cultures of the recent past by anthropologists,[2] and these systems have been applied with some success to the Hellenistic age by New Testament scholars.[3] Similarly, the patron/client relationship has been studied by both ancient historians and anthropologists,[4] and these relationships have also helped make sense of a number of dynamics in early Christian literature.[5] The concepts of honor and shame and of patron/client indeed help in understanding how Hellenistic, and more specifically early Christian, meals addressed crucial social dynamics of that era. Both are crucial in seeing how meals directly reinforced and violated Hellenistic honor/shame codes and the patron/client ranking.

Meal reinforcement of Hellenistic honor and shame occurred regularly in the ranking of those reclined; the distinctions between reclining, sitting, and standing participants; the sometimes uneven distribution of food according to honor; and the distinction around invited and uninvited guests. Meal violation of honor and shame happened regularly in the enactment of equality, friendship, and mutuality among participants in tension with the various degrees of honor they had; the granting of equal voice to all those reclining even when they were clearly not of the same honor status outside of the meal; the introduction of reclining or sitting women as meal participants; the sometimes even distribution of food despite distinctions of honor; and the intentionally porous quality of the meal constituency in remaining relatively permeable to outsiders and uninvited guests. The particular ways various early Christian meals both reinforced and violated honor and shame codes (depending on the particular group) are elaborated below.

Similarly, meal reinforcement of Hellenistic patron and client status, a system that dominated much commerce and local government through placing a flexible cadre of agents (clients) at the disposal of a patron, often occurred by patron sponsorship of meals. In such meals, a range of deferential behavior toward the patron by clients was built into the meal by virtue of reclining order and invitation. Some—although not the majority of—associations also had patrons, who underwrote their meals and other activities.[6] In such associational meals, reproduction of the social privilege of patrons occurred in the reclining order, the list of guests, and the libations. On the other hand, many ongoing meal groups like the associations actively undercut the patron/client social order with the meal as a primary enactment of this defiance. The many associations that did not have patrons and instead constituted themselves socially and financially through membership and membership dues held meals in which unlikely personages played the role of *symposiarch*, honorees in the reclining order, and featured speakers during the *symposion*. Although direct evidence about patrons in the early Christian literature is meager, it is relatively clear that some regular Christian meals occurred under the sponsorship of a patron[7] and that other early Christian meal groups were more on the model of the patronless association.[8]

This chapter takes these anthropological lenses seriously as it examines ways that early Christian meals experimented with key societal issues. It addresses initially a set of texts reflecting direct address of a constellation of honor and shame issues through meal practice. It goes on to examine three examples of such social experimentation: gender contestation, ethnic tensions, and poverty and wealth.

Texts, Social Structures, and Method

Although much helpful information has been provided by archaeological sites and inscriptions, most material concerning early Christian meals and social concerns comes from texts. These texts cannot be taken at face value, however. Some of them are simply fictional. Some are relatively straightforward reports, but from a particular perspective. Many are comments or injunctions about someone else's behavior at a meal. Some use the important connections between meals and larger societal issues to promote a particular social agenda by telling a story about a meal.

Societal issues and meals can be approached both concurrently and as independent of each other. These texts are, however, not taken naively. A sole text cannot be assumed to be a direct record of either a meal or a social issue. Indeed, I assume that each text needs to be read as socially located and subject to ideologically active, relationally biased, and power-driven influences.

For this work, it is not necessary that these texts be accurate or unbiased. Rather, the main interest here has to do with demonstrating that they are engaged in a particular social dynamic or are connected to a meal, even if only imaginatively. The case for the vital place of meals in this era and within early Christianity does not depend so much on the accuracy or lack of prejudice of particular texts as on the thick set of Christian and non-Christian texts that overwhelmingly reflects the same dynamics.[9] That is, texts cited to support the connections between early Christian meals and societal issues are not assumed to be accurate; rather, they are used to indicate strong interest in meals and societal dynamics, and they are read critically to decipher the character of their connection to meals and society.

Social Experimentation with Honor and Shame in the Meals of a Galilean Jesus Movement

Literary analysis of pregospel traditions has isolated some collections of miracle stories most likely coming together in Galilee in the 50s and 60s CE.[10] In the first two-thirds of the twentieth century, this analysis focused on the miracle stories of the Gospel of John, which were seemingly distinct from the rest of the gospel in style and theology.[11] In the past thirty years, Antoinette Wire, Paul Achtemeier, and Burton Mack have done key additional work, combining the earlier work on John with pre-Markan studies and extending important socially analytical lenses to the studies.[12]

It appears that (depending on the scholar) there were one, two, or three (overlapping) collections of miracles stories that eventually made their way into the Gospels of Mark (and subsequently Matthew and Luke) and John. These stories have literary ties to one another. Wire, Achtemeier, and Mack all show a dependence on the miracles of Elijah and Elisha in many of the pre-Markan stories about Jesus as a miracle worker.[13] Dodd and Fortna demonstrate an interest in miracles as "signs" in the pre-Johannine collections.[14] Although not completely clear in the scholarship, none of the proposals for pregospel collections of miracle stories assumes that the collectors themselves composed each of the stories in the set. However, there are some intimations in the works of Achtemeier and Mack that these collectors could have added or composed some stories of their own to the larger collection.

For the purposes of this meals-related analysis, there are two additional, important aspects of this scholarship. First, all of the proposed sets of miracle stories include miraculous feedings. Second, the protagonists of these stories—especially the Markan ones—are marginalized persons who in one way or another carry cultural shame with them. Both Achtemeier and Mack have used these observations to propose social settings for the composers/collectors of these miracle stories. Achtemeier suggested that these stories came from a group or groups in Galilee that celebrated what Achtemeier called "eucharistic gathering."[15] Mack, who writes with knowledge of the work of Dennis Smith, eliminated the "eucharistic" vocabulary and changed the proposal into a group that gathered around meals.[16] Mack noticed that such group(s) gathering for meals must have had a substantially (if not entirely) marginalized constituency.[17] This suggestion derives from the predominance of protagonists from marginalized populations in the stories—that is, such groups most likely consisted of people with "shaming" diseases, people who consistently lacked enough food, and women and girls with questionable public presence or value.[18] Given the ways the miracle stories from this group were drawn from northern Israel miracle traditions of Elijah and Elisha, Mack proposes to call this (set of) group(s) the "Congregation of Israel."[19]

Mack suggests that the compilers of these miracle story collections used the occasion of a meal together to explore what it would be like for these marginalized persons to be in community together.

> The people who are healed are socially marginal by first-century standards, and they are ritually impure. Jesus' healings, then, are clearly understood to be an act of "cleansing" these people, but not for Levitical purposes. Instead, they illustrate the process of collecting candidates for the congregation that is constituted by the meal. One can easily imagine a storyteller with a twinkle in his [sic] eye taking this way to make a point about the unconventional mix of people who got together for talk about Jesus. . . . The really big miracle may simply have been that, within this group at least, differences in social background enhanced rather than hindered the spirit of the conversation about "congregation" at mealtime.[20]

Mack sees this group as actively experimenting with new kinds of social relationships, both among the marginalized participants and between them and the rest of society. What emerges then from this scholarship is not just a pregospel collection (or collections) of stories, but a collection of unlikely, "shameful" people who gathered at meals to affirm their belonging to God's realm, teased into a present reality by teachings and semiscandalous meal association(s). The tellers/collectors of the miracle stories were most likely themselves violators of Galilean honor shame codes. In their meals, these marginalized persons bonded together in mutual support. Their very coming together blatantly violated the honor shame code by placing "shameful" elements of the population at the center of a meal to highlight the ironic honor of reclining together.

These meals were indeed bold social experiments. Placing the Dennis Smith and Matthias Klinghardt research on meals and chapter 4's ritual analysis of these same meals at the service of this textual investigation makes it clear how such experimentation occurred. The meals both placed marginalized persons together and asked them to learn to relate to one another and to experiment in such a way that would make them behave much differently to one another. The meals also directly challenged the honor shame codes by enacting in a semipublic space the giving of honor to those considered "shameful." This most likely made these "shamed" meal participants think of themselves more positively in the larger world.

Calling the meals of this "Congregation of Israel" social experiments does not mean that they were not at the same time flourishing rituals of perfection (J. Z. Smith) and reproduction (Catherine Bell). In the ritual analysis of reclining, distribution of food at the *deipnon*, the weak role of the *symposiarch*, and the porous boundaries around uninvited guests, there is no better example of ritual effectiveness than the Congregation of Israel's meal of misfits. For instance, the miraculous feeding stories concentrated on the equal distribution of food with everyone eating his or her fill. This most likely reflected a fascination with the ways Hellenistic reclining meals ritually and creatively toyed with the contrast between enough food for everyone at these meals and the frequent experience of that day of many going hungry. The eloquence of these meal gestures by a group of marginalized Galileans was full of ritual reflection and renegotiation.

These "Congregation of Israel" meals also burst the bounds of ritual. As noted above, they had major effects beyond the meal proper on the people who participated in them. These "shamed" persons felt less shameful when they left the meal and entered their regular lives. The ways their meals gave them honor helped them feel and act less shameful in the rest of their lives. It also effected a loyalty among them beyond the confines of the meal, creating a community or congregation.

Here, however, caution is necessary in assessing the effects of the meals on the larger society. While these meals certainly made their sick, poor, women, and ethnically dubious participants less ashamed in their broader lives, it is not clear whether their "Congregation of Israel" changed the social order at all or even bothered anyone beyond the group(s). Mack has noticed that these collections of miracle stories lacked any of the antagonists of later gospel narratives or other early Jesus sayings collections, and he has proposed that these meal groups were most likely marginalized but uncontested gatherings.[21] That is, this "Congregation of Israel" may not have mattered at all to anyone beyond those who gathered at the meals. Surely, Mack wonders, if there had been opponents to this curious "congregation," the miracle stories that the group(s) compiled would have had antagonists similar to those of other Jesus traditions in their narratives.[22]

There is irony then in both noticing the ritual character of this "congregation's" meals and identifying the meals as so significantly socially experimental that they effect change beyond the meal itself. This irony comes mostly from the relative powerlessness of these marginalized people to change anything in their larger social setting except their own sense of identity. The meal practice in concert with the growing articulation of identity in the stories told at the meals gave these marginalized persons a different sense of themselves that they did take into the larger society. However, the structures of prejudice and power against them were so substantial that they could make very few actual societal changes relative to their marginalization. Given their own lack of influence, their new sense of possibility had to be referred back to the meal. To a certain extent, then, the ways the meal's social experimentation went beyond the boundaries of the meal itself actually resulted in the larger social identity of the group(s) depending even more on the meal.

The celebratory (and somewhat astonished) character of the miracle stories in these collections needs to be seen as the affirmation, joy, and inner liberation of this motley meal association's members. That such stories were composed and collected demonstrates a substantive social formation in pregospel and post-Jesus Galilee. That these stories had such a peculiarly consistent character of marginalized protagonists, miraculous meals, northern Israelite heroic traditions, and lack of antagonists points to the specific social position of the group(s) that compiled the stories. The meals of the "Congregation of Israel" socially experimented with the possibility of the "shamed" becoming honored by one another and by God.

The social experimentation at the meals had in the end only one major societal result: new identity for the meal participants. It did not produce shifts in the social status of these marginalized persons. Nor did it precipitate even the mildest social conflict. Nor did it create new behavioral independence for the Congregation of Israel. This, however, did not negate the pivotal creation of new identity for these shamed persons. The congregation's meal practice (with its culturally accepted ritual perfection already in place) experimented socially with new identities for these marginalized persons. The meal stage on which to play out these new identities grew larger through more intense loyalty to the meal and important elaboration of miracle stories about Jesus within the meal. The participants became more dependent on the meal for nourishment of their new identity. Although this "Congregation of Israel" social experiment differed substantively from other early "Christian" phenomena, this powerful and ironic combination of meal practice, relatively powerless social groupings, and gripping new identities experienced primarily within the meals will recur often in examples yet to be studied in this chapter and the next.

REPRISE OF METHODOLOGICAL CONSIDERATIONS OF THE RELATIONSHIP OF TEXT TO CULTURAL PRACTICE AND SOCIAL HISTORY

As crucial as this use of Achtemeier's and Mack's social reading of (a) hypothetical pregospel collection(s) of miracle stories is to this chapter, it cannot simply stand without a return to the methodological issues concerning the complex venture of reading ancient texts in relationship to cultural practice and social history. In this regard, three problems with the above portrait of the meals and texts of the Congregation of Israel must be identified, problematized, and addressed:

1. *The relationship of texts (in this case, the pregospel miracle story collections) to cultural practice and social history is never straightforward or uncomplicated.* Texts—even when read with a hermeneutic of suspicion—reflect only partially various cultural practices and historical phenomena. Mack and Achtemeier wrote in the heady early days of New Testament's venture into social history and cultural practice. The explorations of social readings in

the 1970s and 1980s were very important in breaking the stranglehold that theological, literary, and dogmatic studies had on scriptural scholarship. But the initial forays into translating ancient Christian texts into charts of early Christian social history and cultural practice have not stood up to subsequent rigorous critique.

Although Achtemeier's and/or Mack's scenarios for a pregospel Galilean meal community producing miracle story collections are entirely possible, this represents only one or two ways to think about the texts' relationship to first-century Galilean social practice. It very well could also be that the collection of miracle stories portrayed some author's (or authors') wishful thinking about how Galilean social practice should have looked. Indeed, most likely the relationship between the miracle story collection(s) and the social practice of that day was somewhere between Achtemeier's and Mack's hypotheses and the possibility that the collections' portrait was wishful thinking. It is, however, unclear and—at this stage of thinking about these issues—nearly impossible to decipher what the exact relationship is between a given text, the cultural practices around it, and the specific social history of the material evoked in the given text.

2. *Similarly, the Achtemeier/Mack supposition, which I support, that meals were necessarily the primary cultural context of these texts cannot be naively accepted.* The larger issue addressed at length in chapter 3 concerning the relationship between early Christian meals and texts has to be addressed. But for the treatment of the Congregation of Israel's meals/texts even beyond that more general question lies an entire set of possibilities. For instance, it could have been that the miracle story collection(s) used the very well-known social practice of meals to think about the place of marginalized people in Galilee without there ever having been an actual meal of marginalized persons. It could have been that the texts used meals "to think with" without ever having them. And again here, the most likely possibilities are that the miracle story texts' relationship to meals lay somewhere between the Achtemeier/Mack hypothesis and the possibility that the texts emerged without any relationship to actual meals of a motley collection of Galilean misfits.

3. *Although the literary studies by Wire, Achtemeier, and Mack are quite impressive in demonstrating commonalities among the set(s) of miracle stories, the existence of actual collections of these stories must be acknowledged as hypothetical.* The heyday of redactional and source criticism is finished. The assurance of the nineteenth and twentieth centuries' scholarship in

being able to determine literary trajectories has faltered. Beyond this general acknowledgment, the relatively new character of the Wire/ Achtemeier/Mack proposal must also be noticed. Here, a comparison to Q studies is in order. Although the identification of the hypothetical document Q is mostly accepted by contemporary scholarship, this (even now somewhat provisional) acceptance has required more than a century. The miracle storycollection hypothesis has not yet received or endured the critical attention Q experienced. Much of the above treatment of a Congregation of Israel's meals of the Galilean marginalized depends on the existence of this hypothetical collection of miracle stories.

How can these important methodological reservations be addressed in this chapter's exploration of the social experimentation of early Christian meals? Some more tolerant postmodern critics would suggest that this exploration be simply accepted provisionally as one of many possibilities. While willing to accept this tolerance, I want to take postmodern criticism more seriously. To my mind, the longer-term importance of interpreting New Testament and other early Christian texts will require rigorous efforts to integrate postmodern, literary, and historical-critical approaches to questions of textual interpretation and early Christian beginnings—that is, there is too much at stake for the respective insights of postmodern subjectivities, literary sensitivities, and historical analyses to remain at odds with one another. So, for this book, I aim for an integration of these contributions. And as for the particular three objections raised above concerning a portrait of meals in relationship to certain miracle stories in Mark and John, I take them seriously and claim them as resources in thinking about these texts' relationship to meals.

This study of Christian beginnings and meals does not depend on either historical certainty or exact correspondences between texts and social practices. The strong relationship between meals in the Hellenistic Mediterranean and early Christian texts does not rely on any one position on the three methodological issues raised above. It is important to examine the specifics of each methodological objection in the case of certain miracles stories in Mark and John.

The Achtemeier/Mack scenario developed above—although keen in its analysis— need not be free of error for this chapter's case for a telling relationship between Markan/ Johannine miracle stories and meals to be valid. For the moment, let completely contrary scenarios be entertained seriously: (1) the set of miracle stories identified by Achtemeier had nothing to do with an actual group of socially marginalized Galileans; and (2) these miracle stories were more likely to be simply the active imagination of one or several first-century authors, *or* the miracle stories were somewhat accurate reports of actual occurrences. Once the vocabulary of meal meaning making in the Hellenistic Mediterranean and the prevalence of these meals are clear, the basic conclusions about the connection between these particular miracle stories and meals still holds; that is, even if either of these relatively unlikely counter-scenarios is accepted alongside the knowledge of meals and the ways they provided meaning and identity for the general Hellenistic population and the specific early Christian movements, the conclusions about the connections between miracle stories and meals still apply.

Whether Achtemeier and Mack are correct or not about the existence of something like a "Congregation of Israel," the confluence of meal practices and these miracle texts still points to important early Christian social experimentation. Even if there was no "Congregation of Israel" and only an imaginative author making up stories, the set of stories points toward a sensitivity of including marginalized persons in the Jesus story and a strong dependence on meal imagery as a principal way of imagining an inclusive community or movement. Similarly, even if (although, to me, highly unlikely) these particular miracle stories were mostly accurate reports of real occurrences, then these stories are reporting on a movement that emphasized meals as central to those marginalized people who gathered around Jesus for healing. Adding knowledge of what happened at meals, how they occurred, how prevalent they were, and what functions they served in both the larger culture and the early Christian community propels interpretation of the miracle stories toward recognizing social experimentation in early Christian groups.

Most postmodern critics of the social reading of Achtemeier and Mack, however, would only posit scholarship's complete lack of a social context for the writing of these miracle stories as a rhetorical ploy. When pressed to think about what may have been the relationship between these miracle stories and Galilean social history and practice, they—like me—would opt for some complex combination of the relatively obvious rhetorical functions of such stories and an Achtemeier/Mack–like social speculation based on literary analysis and some historical information. My response to methodological questions about the miracle stories/social setting issue—which, I suspect, is finally relatively close to postmodern critique—is that it is indeed impossible to determine the exact relationship between the miracle stories and Galilean social history. It is, nevertheless, probable that the miracle stories were told by people who knew social settings where there were actual hungry people, women whose public presence was taboo, girls who did not matter in the public consciousness, blind men who lived at the edges of society, and other persons shamed by the honor shame code. It very well could have been that the authors and collectors of the miracles stories exaggerated or censored the behavior of marginalized persons (and others) for their own rhetorical purposes.

Although it is likely that the historical Jesus did have meaningful interactions with marginalized persons, the composers of these miracle stories almost certainly also hyperbolized the actions of both Jesus and the marginalized. Although "authorship" of most early Christian stories is nearly impossible to determine, it seems to me more likely that the miracle stories were composed and collected by a group of illiterate to semiliterate persons than that they were written by a single author with no connection to group life in Galilee. The proposal that the composing or collecting group or groups were something like the marginalized protagonists of the stories themselves is both plausible and creative but cannot be considered likely, due to a lack of enough detail in the stories and information about illiterate storytellers in Galilee.

The methodological issue about whether the major cultural context for the composing and collecting of these miracle stories was meals can be answered similarly. In agreement with postmodern critique, it is impossible to know with any certainty what the exact cultural context for any ancient storytelling was. And it is totally plausible that these miracle stories were composed by someone or a group of people who framed them to express more what they wished their community, society, or meals were like rather than what they actually resembled.

But here, too, whether the composers/collectors of these stories were using meals "to think with" rather than having them as actual contexts matters little for the overall point made in this chapter. Whether they were real or imagined meals, the point still holds that the social symbolism of meals, the prevalence of meals, and the important functions meals played in ordinary people's imagination of society made some meals an occasion for serious social experimentation. Telling an imaginary story about a meal in relationship to hungry and shamed people participated in the socially experimental vocabulary of the larger meal practice. It is the case, as has been demonstrated in chapter 4, that the actual practice of meals had a larger range of dynamics to effect ritual perfection and social experimentation than an imaginary story about a meal. But such imagined stories would have depended on the cultural and ritual vocabulary that spawned social experimentation and would have had similar—if derivative— results. In other words, the worst-case, postmodernist scenario (that the relationship between these miracle stories and meals was completely imagined) still makes the same general case that knowledge of Hellenistic meals places these miracle stories in a context of social experimentation.

But since this worst-case, postmodernist scenario is mostly a rhetorical (although valuable) one, what can be said about the likelihood of this set of miracle stories having been in active relationship to meals? It seems to me that it is probable that the miracle stories were composed with real meals (not massive feedings[23] or just vague imaginations of meals) in mind. This is a slight retreat from Achtemeier and Mack. Achtemeier's proposal of a "eucharistic" setting is clearly anachronistic, since the work of Klinghardt and Smith has demonstrated there was no such thing as "eucharist" in the first century. But even when one makes Mack's adjustment from eucharist to meal, the leap from the prevalence of feeding stories in the miracle collections to a meal community is a relatively large one. It is true that Dennis Smith's later work reinforces Mack and Achtemeier to a certain extent in showing that the feeding stories have the dining room–based vocabulary of reclining transposed into a field. And Achtemeier's literary parallels between the feeding stories' blessing of the bread and the later dining room–based blessings must be acknowledged as an important link between the stories and meals in dining rooms. Nevertheless, that this prevalence of feeding stories necessarily indicates a meal community cannot be assumed. On the other hand, it is likely that the many early Christian texts had a meal context in their compositional and collecting stages. In other words, the objection to the connection of these miracle stories with meal practice is—in my analysis—moot, since it should be assumed, until otherwise indicated, that most texts were connected in powerful ways to meal contexts.

The final methodological issue concerning the validity of source and redactional critical perspectives that suggest one or more pregospel collections of miracle stories is perhaps the least troubling for this chapter. While Dodd/Fortna/Achtemeier/Mack's case for such collections seems substantive and keenly observed on literary levels, I must return to the earlier conclusion that it cannot yet be accepted definitively. The Dodd and Fortna proposals for pre-Johannine collection(s) have existed for over half a century with some acceptance and some detractors.[24] The Wire/Achtemeier/Mack proposals for pre-Markan collection(s), although creative and convincing, have not yet had enough scholarly response.

The variations on miracle story chains, then, can stand as an imaginative possibility. Even if it cannot yet be thoroughly accepted, the literary observations need to be heeded—that is, the dependence of the number of miracles on the Elijah and Elisha traditions, the consistent use of marginalized protagonists in these stories, and the centrality of the feedings are characteristics of the stories and therefore are subject to analysis and interpretation, whether they existed as a pregospel collection or not. Even within the context of studying Mark or John as whole gospels, these above dimensions of a number of "gospel" miracle stories require interpretation. Even if—in the worst case—the proposal for pregospel miracle collection(s) is totally refuted, the bunched literary characteristics of these miracle stories within the gospels themselves demand attention. Placing these literary characteristics of miracle stories in the larger gospel context actually takes nothing away from this chapter's case that the miracle stories portray a community of marginalized persons with deep connections to meals. The Achtemeier/Mack hypothesis works as well on a gospel level as it does on a pregospel level.

Socially Experimenting with Gender at Early Christian Meals

The past thirty or so years have witnessed a great deal of important scholarship on the status of women in early Christianity. This scholarship has convinced the rest of New Testament studies and beyond that the texts of early Christianity were quite explicitly and consistently interested in questions about women's participation and leadership. Application of ritual theory to Hellenistic meals has already shown that those meals also actively engaged contestation about women's participation. This next section examines the nexus of early Christian literature's and meals' engagement with these gender contestations and explores how much social experimentation went on at meals relative to gender. Two major groups of literature (Paul and Luke) are surveyed, followed by an overview of the rest of early Christian literature on the subject.

PRE-PAULINE AND PAULINE GENDER CONTESTATIONS

The attention in Paul's letters to women's leadership and participation had almost exclusively to do with what happened at meals. The issue has rarely been formulated this way, and consequently such a framing of the questions hopes to contribute to the larger study of Paul and women by attending to what such contestation would mean in the meals.

As has been noticed before, explicit treatment of women's participation in the communities to which Paul wrote appears primarily in 1 Corinthians. This is also a primary site for the study of meals in Paul. In this chapter, it leads also to consideration of women's roles in pre-Pauline communities.

The explicit and long-debated texts in 1 Corinthians are 11:2-16 and 14:33-36.[25] In 11:2-16, Paul appealed to a larger gender typology concerning men and women's heads in addressing the current issue at stake in Corinth: What should a woman wear when praying or prophesying at a meal gathering of the group? Paul's opinion/command was that women must have their heads covered when praying or prophesying at the group's gatherings (which were meal gatherings, as the rest of 1 Corinthians 11 illustrates). In 14:33-36, a similar (or perhaps the same) issue was addressed: Should women speak at the meal? Here, Paul's opinion/command was that women should be silent at the meal. (For this study, it is not necessary to resolve the obvious contradictions in Paul between chapters 11 and 14, since the larger question here concerns the roles and status of women at the Corinthian meals, rather than Paul's consistency or complexity of thought.)

Antoinette Wire's classic work *The Corinthian Women Prophets* remains the most thorough address to gender in the Corinthian "Christian" assemblies. Her insistent rhetorical criticism has uncovered a rather full portrait of the Corinthian women, who were both opponents and colleagues of Paul. She focuses on those women who spoke prophetically and lived demonstrative lives beyond the community gatherings. Her portrait is of women who were articulate theologically and socially, who for the most part "have moved away from traditional sexual relationships to devote themselves to the Lord."[26] This Lord "does not call the women of Corinth to remain as they were when called but transforms their social lives through new sexual choices and responsibilities. . . . On this basis they reject every attempt to bring forward a God of past structures or future judgment to compromise the living God to whom they are consecrated in body and spirit."[27]

Although their lifestyle played a major role in their self-understanding, their prophetic speaking often occurred at meals of the early Christian community: "The food and drink are communal in a spiritual and liberating sense, drawing them into the new and inclusive identity in Christ where their own meals become the Lord's meal and celebration of life overcomes the memory of death. This releases women prophets to know themselves positively and to demonstrate in their eating and drinking the authority of free people."[28]

It does not take Wire's fine rhetorical analysis to note that Paul did not dispute that women were leaders in the Corinthian community (1 Cor. 1:11). He acknowledged explicitly—even while trying to control it—that women were present at the meal gatherings. It is probable that these women were reclining at the meals as full participants and leaders. Ritual analysis shows that this presence at meals by women functioned as a subliminal exploration of gender relations in this patriarchal culture.[29]

It is Paul's contestation of these women speaking at the meals that demonstrated the socially experimental character of the Corinthian meals—that is, Paul did not appeal to notions of propriety at the meal in order to limit or silence these women's speech at the meals. In 14:34-35, he appealed to both Torah and the ways husbands and wives related in society as the reason why women should not speak. In 11:2-16, he appeals to broader conventions of dress in Hellenistic society and to Genesis 2 as reasons why women should cover their heads when speaking. Clearly, what the Corinthian women were already doing at the community meals had (at least for Paul) implications for larger societal roles, making the ritually exploratory presence of women at the meals into a social experiment of broader import (which Paul disapproved of). This connected to the other social experiments beyond the meal that these women were obviously already participating in through their sexual choices.[30]

Methodologically, the existence of this social experiment about gender at the Corinthian meals seems surer than the meals of the "Congregation of Israel." The specific character of Paul's opposition to these women speaking at the meals makes it more likely that the meal behavior was actually happening. Paul's opposition was strong. It was articulate in that it opposed not the women's presence (and probably reclining) at the meal but only their speaking freely. Finally, Paul's opposition was somewhat flailing in that he offered two different countermeasures in chapters 11 and 14. Placed alongside Wire's work, social experimentation at Corinthian meals about women's leadership seems likely.

SOCIAL EXPERIMENTATION IN LUKE

Like 1 Corinthians, the Gospel of Luke has long been a text in which both meals and gender have been studied. Dennis Smith has summarized very clearly the central place of meals in Luke's rhetorical strategy.[31] Perhaps the most complex (although far from the only) book-length address to gender in Luke is Turid Karlsen Seim's *The Double Message: Patterns of Gender in Luke-Acts*. Seim's work advances this scholarship particularly by going beyond the initial enthusiasm of the 1980s concerning the frequent presence of women in Luke to address the places women are silenced and slotted in the same gospel. She finds an insistent ambivalence in Luke about women's participation and leadership.

It turns out that the Lukan meal has a similar contested character relative to gender. A classic site of study is Luke 10:38-42, concerning a meal of Jesus at the home of Martha and Mary. The roles of Martha as head of the household and Mary as studying with Jesus have long caught the attention of scholars relative to the heightened status of these women. They are not unlike the women in 8:1-3 who provide financial support for Jesus. On the other hand, the aggressive contrast of the relatively docile (and perhaps silent) Mary with the assertive, managerial Martha has raised questions about the attitude of Luke toward women's place. These doubts have been confirmed by several studies on the parallels between this text and the treatment by 1 Corinthians 7 of sexual activity by men and women.[32] These parallels show that the common use of "distracted" (*aperispastos*) and "better part" (*meris, merizo*) in both 1 Corinthians 7 and Luke 10:38-42 most probably references celibacy and marriage. It is then quite possible that Mary's "better part" was celibate and Martha's distraction was marriage or sexual activity. Here, then, Luke seems to have placed authentic participation in the meal as contingent on celibacy.

When one understands the dynamics of the Hellenistic meal, these gender valuations become clearer. Mary is not reclining but seated at the feet of Jesus. The larger Hellenistic literature considered sitting, rather than reclining, at the meal as a lower status and used this designation often to keep women from full recognition at the meal.[33] Luke's placing Mary at Jesus' feet both recognized her as a disciple and limited her recognition in contrast to those reclining. In a certain manner, this restriction on recognition parallels almost exactly the limits that seem to have been set on the women relative to celibacy. Luke seems to have restricted leadership or participation to the sitting position/celibate lifestyle.

The highly crafted character of 10:38-42 makes it unlikely that the text itself represented an actual meal; rather, it is most likely a literary articulation that depends on the meal dynamics for some of its rhetorical power. To a certain extent, this eliminates direct consideration of meals' ritual effects in subliminally addressing gender issues. Rather, here the passage seems to have known about the subtleties of meals' semiconscious signals and then to have used this dynamic literarily. The finely tuned comparison between the women's position at the meal and sexual lifestyles illustrates this composed quality.

Unlike the 1 Corinthian passage, in which actual disagreement about meal behavior (who speaks under what conditions) escalated into a broader societal arena, Luke's use of seating versus reclining acted as part of a clever literary design. It would not, however, discount that actual readers of Luke might not be confronted by important ritual or socially experimental effects of this meal dynamic. The text simply cannot be used nearly as directly as 1 Corinthians in thinking through ritual effect and social experimentation at a particular early Christian community meal.

The intensity, however, of the gender debate within Luke about the degree of women's participation and leadership does add to what 10:38-42 might say about Lukan meals and gender contestation—that is, the literary tension about women's status that Seim and others have so clearly traced indicates a profound debate in Lukan circles.[34] It also makes difficult any easy relegation of Luke to categories of women-friendliness or misogyny. In this regard, the picture of Mary seated—perhaps silently—but not reclining could serve well as an icon for the larger gender conflict within the Lukan milieu on a level beyond the gospel page or the meal. It also could indicate that the meal was indeed a place of particular gender experimentation. Indeed, women seated rather than reclining seems to have been a relatively widespread compromise position in the emerging Hellenistic exploration of women's place at meals. Whether this remained on the evocative but subliminal level of ritual perfection, or whether it was extended in some cases to explicit experimentation with a compromise "solution," is not clear. In the Lukan case, the highly designed text makes it impossible to explore this with much determinacy.

OTHER TEXTUAL SITES ABOUT MEALS AND GENDER EXPERIMENTATION

A widely studied set of passages relating gender to meals is the woman anointing Jesus' head and feet at a meal (Mark 14:3-9; Matt. 26:6-13; Luke 7:36-50; John 12:1-11). Some interpreters have seen especially the Markan version of this at the head of the trajectory with Jesus proclaiming her deed as memorable throughout the whole world as a dramatic assertion of some early Christian advocacy for women's participation.[35] Inasmuch as the somewhat different Lukan version belongs to this trajectory, it does represent a relatively unique (perhaps the only) set of texts affirming a woman's presence at a meal.

However, placed in the broader paradigm of Hellenistic meals, all these texts fit very well into the most conventional women's roles at meals, in which women come in for serving and entertainment purposes only. Social experimentation with gender, then, is quite far from this textual tradition, which assumed the most conventional pattern of women as not reclining but rather strictly subservient to the reclining men. Indeed, this set of texts seems to have used the conventional meal separation of men from women as normative, over against the relatively common exceptions one finds throughout Hellenistic literature and vases showing ritual play with women reclining.

But this conventional picture was used ironically to raise questions about women's importance. Mark's version indeed concluded with cosmic praise for the isolated, controversial, and nameless woman as one to be "remembered throughout the world"

(Mark 14:9). This text—like that of Luke 10—was a highly constructed literary address to (among other things) women's presence. Its complex literary design makes it difficult to take as any direct picture of Markan (or earlier) meal community. Its ironic treatment of an all-male meal with a courageous and insightful woman servant used meal imagery to raise questions about women's significance in community. Neither the literary use of meal ideology nor the conventional meal picture it deconstructed can be considered to be socially experimental or ritually effective.

One of these exceptions occurs in the *Gospel of Thomas* 61, picturing Salome reproaching Jesus as he climbs on her reclining couch. Placed in connection with Peter's objection to Mary Magdalene's association with Jesus and Jesus' promise to make Mary male in 114, this underinvestigated textual milieu appears to reference the kind of social tension where meals prompted ritual negotiation of and social experimentation with gender. In both 61 and 114, there is enough conscious conflict to merit further research on the possible character of social experimentation here.

Many texts without explicit mention of both gender and meals may actually provide complex linkages of gender and meals by virtue of the field of discussion in this book. An example of such a complex linkage is illustrated in my article "Dealing under the Table: Ritual Negotiation of Women's Power in the Syro-Phoenician Woman Pericope."[36] This essay needs a complex redaction critical approach, parallels with Cynic teaching, and ritual theory to relate Mark 7:24-30 to meals. It proposes a trajectory of contestations about women's roles in meal settings from two levels of pre-Markan formulation through Matthean stages of the story's development. This essay produced not a definitive trajectory toward or away from gender mutuality but rather a complex mix of meal negotiation of gender relationships.

Conclusions about Gender and Social Experimentation at Early Christian Meals

It has been noted numerous times in this book that women reclining or sitting at early Christian meals provided occasion for ritual reflection and perfection about the role of women in larger society. The increasing frequency with which women in Jewish, Christian, and gentile settings reclined or sat at meals helped people imagine and reflect on other issues of women's leadership and presence outside the meal.

This survey of early Christian texts that address women at meals shows clearly an entire spectrum of postures about women's leadership and participation in various social roles. This spectrum seems to run all the way from the absence of even ritual reflection in Mark's picture of the anointing woman through the active Lukan and Thomasine literary play with ritual negotiation of women's roles to the active social experimentation of the Corinthian Christ association. The Lukan and Thomasine meals could also have been socially experimental, but the texts are not clear enough for this to be determined.

Ethnic Tensions and Social Experimentation in Early Christian Meals

Jews and gentiles eating together was a major subject of early Christian literature. Although much New Testament scholarship has investigated these texts almost exclusively in terms of religion and theology, these controversies also need to be addressed in terms of the larger ethnic mixes and tensions within the Hellenistic era. Classic Christian arguments have mistakenly seen the controversies around Jews and gentiles eating together as a question of Christianity versus Judaism.[37] Krister Stendahl's pivotal work *Paul among Jews and Gentiles* helped New Testament scholarship begin a phase of reflection still in motion that corrects these notions and proposes to think about Paul as having a central investment in the relationship between Jew and gentile. Stendahl saw, for instance, the meal controversy between Peter and Paul not so much as a Judaizing tendency versus an emerging Christian position as an indication that "Paul was chiefly concerned about the relation between Jews and Gentiles."[38] Indeed, so much of conventional Christian interpretation of the Jew/gentile dynamics in early Christian literature appears quite different, if one understands three basic dimensions of ethnicities in the Hellenistic era. These dimensions are as follows:

1. *There was intense mixing of ethnicities throughout the Mediterranean during this period.* The successive imperial reigns that made up the Hellenistic period brought nations and tribes together in a long-term and heady mix of cultural traditions. The pax romana allowed massive commerce and migration throughout the Mediterranean, resulting in entire new cities of profoundly mixed ethnicities and long-term proximities of different cultures in every urban area. The wonder at and enthusiasm for this ethnic mix was reflected in the Acts of the Apostles' legend of Pentecost: "They were amazed and astonished. . . . Parthians, Medes, and Elamites; people from Mesopotomia, Judaea and Cappadocia, POntus and Asia, Phrygia and Pamphylia, Egypt and the parts of Libya round Cyrene, residents of Rome . . . Cretans and Arabs" (2:7, 9-11).

This was such an intense and dominant trend that most individual and social identities were profoundly challenged and changed. One simply could no longer continue to think of oneself as primarily identified with one tribe or nation. The long-term, intense, and daily interaction among diverse ethnicities, for at least most urban dwellers, made it impossible to hold on to former identities. It was an imposing problem, one that, as this chapter demonstrates, was addressed by early Christian meals in powerful and evocative ways.

2. *The stark and prejudicial ways in which the dominant Greco-Roman culture characterized this ethnic mix.* For the dominant culture, the enthusiasm for the great mix of peoples found in Acts 2 was an error. Rather, one needed—according to the Romans and Greeks—to think simply of Greeks/Romans and "barbarians." At the very same time that a grand conglomeration of peoples was coming into being around the Mediterranean, those who ruled this massive new mixed population moved aggressively to deny the heterogeneity, to erase the former identities of the vast majority, and to enthrone one dominant culture. One was simply part of an ignorant, uncultured mass, or one was Greco-Roman. This simultaneous creation of a potent new hybrid population and the rejection of all but one identity made the crisis of self-understanding for most in the Hellenistic Mediterranean even deeper.[39]

3. *Hellenistic Judaism witnessed a creative resistance strategy against the Greco-Roman cultural hegemony.* The Pharisees movement in particular elaborated a strategy of Jewish self-consciousness, which involved the transfer of many temple purity rites to the Jewish home. Heightening existing Jewish dietary distinctions, this innovative movement made separation of Jewish foods and separation of Jews from gentiles (both hallmarks of the Jerusalem Temple rites) into broad identity markers for Jews in their homes and, by extension, in their lives overall. Applying rigorous (temple) purity procedures to ordinary dietary practice allowed the Pharisees to construct an effective Jewish counteridentity to both the Hellenistic mix and the Greco-Roman slander of Judaism as barbaric.[40] The Pharisees movement, although initially rooted in Israel, experienced broad success throughout the Mediterranean. As a Jew from Asia Minor, Paul claimed to have been a Pharisee (Phil. 3:6), indicating how widespread the movement was.

In other words, the attentiveness of early Christian literature to Jews and gentiles eating together belonged to a larger set of societal issues concerning the tensive ethnic mix of the Mediterranean and the variety of identity problems it posed. In chapter 4, the problems of Jews and gentiles eating together in Romans 14 and 15 was analyzed with the help of ritual theory. That treatment is extended here with the examination of four other key New Testament texts concerning meals and ethnic mix. In each case, primary attention is paid to how much (or how little) these texts reflect consciousness of social experimentation around ethnic difference occurring at particular traditions of early Christian meals.

DEBATE ABOUT JEWS AND GENTILES EATING TOGETHER AT ANTIOCH (GAL. 2:11–14; ACTS 15:1, 2)

Paul indicated in his letter to the Galatians that Peter, as a Jew, participated in meals of Jews and gentiles at Antioch until James and the "party of circumcision" arrived, at which point Peter withdrew from the meals. Paul accused Peter of hypocrisy for these two different behaviors. Although not explicitly stated in Galatians, it can be assumed that Peter's and James's insistence on eating separately from gentiles had to do with a certain kind of Judean stance, possibly related to the Pharisaic program. It is not at all clear that all Jews throughout the Mediterranean had these same principles. That Peter participated in the mixed meals at Antioch was one indicator that such mixed eating was not unheard of. Philo discussed at some length the complexities of Jews eating separately or with gentiles in Alexandria in the same period.[41] Indeed, it could have been that James's and Peter's behavior was related to a particular kind of Judean or Pharisaic program of eating separately. Acts 15:5, although probably not historically reliable, indicates that the discussions by Peter, Paul, and James in Jerusalem about Jews and gentiles together were participated in by "some believers who belonged to the group of Pharisees."[42] At the same time, it is relatively clear that Jews and gentiles eating together in Antioch would also have been considered somewhat unusual, although perhaps not more unusual than the occasional slave and slave owner reclining together.

Reclining together at meals probably functioned as a ritual marking of difference in the eating principles of both James and Paul, although with different purposes. In the case of James (and Peter), reclining together only as Jews was a way of noticing the difference between the exclusive company of Jews at the meal and the invasion of gentiles into the lives of Judeans every day. In the case of Paul at Antioch, reclining together as Jew and gentile became ritual reflection on the tension and mutual fascination among various ethnic groups in that cosmopolitan city. In both cases, these meals' attentiveness to who was fully present at the meals participated in the larger ritual dynamic of the Hellenistic meal. Since the meals made a major point that all who reclined together formed a bond of friendship and equality, these meals continually played ritually with who was bonded to one another and who was not. Judean/Pharisaic insistence that this be only a Jewish bond was a way of playing with how it might be if the Romans and other foreigners would leave Judea or if Jews would really (no matter where in the Mediterranean) be in control of their own bonds with one another. Paul and his associates' celebration of "neither Jew nor Greek" (Gal. 3:28) at the meal contemplated playfully a united world based on principles other than Roman dominance.

Here, however, the question is more pointed. Were either or both of these meal pictures (Pharisaic/Judean exclusion, Pauline inclusion) of an ideal gathering part of an active social experiment? This distinction between social experimentation and the powerful, but mostly subliminal, ritual negotiation of differences has been discussed above, with the conclusion that when the ritual action takes on a relatively explicit and direct claim of relevance to the larger societal issue, it is "social experimentation."

To what extent, then, can respectively the Pharisaic interest in separation of Jews and gentiles at meals, James's (and Peter's) similar interest, the Antioch community of Gal. 2:11-14/Acts 15:1, 2's practice of Jews and gentiles eating together at meals, and Paul's active defense of that Antioch practice be considered social experimentation? In which cases are these meal constellations of ethnicities socially experimental, and in which cases are they mostly subliminal ritual reproduction and perfection of Hellenistic meals? Upon close examination, answers to these questions turn out to be somewhat surprising.

In many respects, the most evidence of social experimentation exists in the Pharisaic practice. Although it is important to note that the meals of the Pharisees almost certainly also depended heavily on the use of ritual perfection and reproduction, it also seems clear that the Pharisees' meals that dramatically separated Jews from gentiles were understood as proactive social wedges against the loss of Jewish identity in the larger, Roman-dominated society.[43] Jews eating separately from gentiles served as acts of resistance against the incursion of Greco-Roman–based influences and preemptions. Although, outside the meals, there were many limitations on how Jews could resist Roman-based influences and incursions, the Pharisaic meal became more than reflection on and intellectual negotiation of Jewish and gentile differences. It became first an active social experimentation, second a successful movement, and third a mainstay of proto-rabbinic Judaism.

As for the Antioch community to which Peter was invited for a meal, it is less clear that it went beyond ritual play with interethnic consciousness and into social experimentation. That Paul traveled to Jerusalem to discuss the differences between his work and that of "gentiles" and others (Gal. 2:1-11; Acts 15:3-29) indicates a relatively explicit concern on a more than subliminal ritual level. But neither Galatians nor Acts refers explicitly to Jews and gentiles eating together as a problem (as Gal. 2:11-14 does concerning the Antioch meal).[44] Nor does the explicit language about the meal conflict concerning Jews and gentiles eating together at Antioch in Gal. 2:11-14 refer to the Antiochian community practice in a way that would necessarily go beyond the implicit ritual address of ethnic mix.

It is at this juncture that Paul's response to Peter's withdrawal from the mixed ethnic company at the Antioch meal must be considered. Since it is rarely clear whether Paul's opinions represented more than him, the question is posed as to whether his insistence on mixed meal company at Antioch was his reactive opinion or the explicit (and socially experimental) practice of the "Christian" Antioch community. Both positions seem plausible. Unless Paul's role in Antioch was very marginal (a situation difficult to imagine), it is clear that the mixed meal practice at Antioch would have become a matter of social experimentation after the Paul-Peter conflict; that is, once the ethnic eating mix became explicit and entered arenas of behavior beyond the meal itself (for example, Paul's letters or Jerusalem debates), it became something more than ritual negotiation. It at that point could be considered social experimentation. By virtue of Paul's usage of the Jew/gentile mix theme in 1 Corinthians, mixed ethnic eating became a conscious social experiment within Paul's circles at some point. Whether that occurred at Antioch is less clear but is certainly quite plausible.

Analysis of this nexus of meals and ethnicity has been unable to pinpoint every place that these meals were socially experimenting with either ethnic purity or ethnic mix, but the overview does identify that at least some of these meals went from ritual negotiation to social experimentation.

EATING IN GENTILE TERRITORY WITH MARK (MARK 7:24–8:10)

The earlier section on the Syro-Phoenician woman examined the possibility that this Markan text exhibited consciousness of ritual negotiation and social experimentation in meals around gender. It is important now to examine that pericope and the neighboring passage on the feeding of four thousand people in terms of both events occurring outside of Israel. The Syro-Phoenician woman pericope was located in "the territory of Tyre" (7:24). The feeding, which is paired with a previous one within Galilee (6:30-44), was located somewhere in gentile territory.[45] The pairing of feedings in and outside of Galilee alongside of the meal motifs in 7:24-31 calls attention to ethnic mix and eating. It seems as if Mark was making a point to have Jesus at meals in both Jewish and gentile territory.[46]

There is good reason to take the feeding stories in Mark metaphorically.[47] The most blatant reason is that Mark's own material did so in having Jesus interpret the number of loaves broken in each of the feedings as representing an esoteric message (8:19-21): "'When I broke the five loaves for the five thousand, how many baskets full of leftovers did you collect?' They answered, 'Twelve.' 'And when I broke the seven loaves for the four thousand, how many baskets full of scraps did you collect?' And they answered, 'Seven.' Then he said to them, 'Do you still not realize?'"

The interpretational necessity of pairing the feedings is made explicit by Mark in this passage. The numerologic and vocabulary significance of this esoteric approach has been somewhat clearly ascertained by a number of scholars and indeed confirms that what was at stake in the pairing of the feedings is the mix of Jew and gentile.[48]

Such an intentional pairing of Jewish and Greek feedings was clearly a Markan literary address to meals and ethnic mix. It is also obvious that the stories were not meant to be historical allusions as much as literary integration of Jew and gentile within the meals metaphor. Inasmuch as the feedings themselves, then, could not have been meant as social experimentation, that these stories reference socially experimental mixes of Jew and gentile in the Markan context remains a real possibility.

The grandiose nature of these stories did indeed evoke a social application of the idea of mixed meals to a bigger societal arena. The stories, of course, could also reference a Markan dream of such mixed meals as grand experiment. It is unclear how much Markan literary awareness of Jew-gentile meals together also represented actual social experimentation with ethnic mixing in this particular proto-Christianity.

Food That Unifies and Differentiates (Romans 14 and 15; 1 Corinthians 8 and 10; Acts 10 and 15)

Sustained ritual analysis of Romans 14 and 15 in chapter 4 demonstrated to what extent eating meat or vegetables in mixed Jewish and gentile community functioned to negotiate ritually the ethnic mix. I suggested that what was a relatively successful subliminal ritual address to the complexities of ethnic mixes had been complicated at least by Paul (and perhaps other meal participants) trying to provide an ideological answer to the problem. The mix of Jewish and gentile food raised delicately the complications of being an ethnically mixed community. Paul's more ideological suggestion that everyone eat vegetables so that the gentiles would not mock the Jewish convictions would have definitely moved this meal dynamic from a ritual negotiation to social experimentation. But it is not clear to me that such explicit experimentation of everyone eating vegetables together (rather than some gentiles eating meat that was offensive to Jews) would have finally been more successful in addressing the complexities of ethnic mix. It could have been that continuing to quibble together over what to eat may have been a more thorough and long-term process for negotiating ethnic mix.

In 1 Corinthians 8 and 10, Paul makes a series of recommendations about whether the Corinthian assemblies should or should not eat meat that has been sacrificed to "false gods." That Paul's recommendations in these two chapters may not have been consistent in terms of whether one should eat this meat does not matter in this study.[49] The point of interest here is what social effect eating particular foods might have had. In this regard, Paul seemed to be quite consistent in that he did not want food to interfere with the relationships of those who eat together, even to the point of not wanting it to interfere with the relationship between a "believer" and a "nonbeliever." In 8:13, Paul said: "If food can be the cause of a brother's downfall, I will never eat any meat anymore, rather than cause my brother's downfall." In 10:26; 10:28; and 10:29, the criterion of whether to eat such sacrificed meat always depended on not offending those with whom one eats. And his vehement opposition to eating such meat occurred only in relationship to what he called "the Lord's table."

It is unclear whether Paul's opinions about whether to have meat at particular meals corresponded to what the Corinthians actually did. Nor is it clear whether the kind of food eaten in these various settings had similar ritual power to what it had in the Roman "Christian" communities to whom Paul wrote. It is, however, surprisingly clear that there was active social experimentation at meals in terms of this issue—that is, Paul's various scenarios depended on the actual reactions of different diners to different circumstances of specific kinds of shared food. The food eaten at meals (in this case, at meals among "Christians" and among a more diverse constituency) acted as barriers and cement to the dining relationship. It was not just the meal gestures and process at stake, but broader abilities of individuals to be in relationship. Eating meat sacrificed to other gods could bring people together (and Paul approved). Not eating meat together could also bring people together (and Paul approved). In each case, a social bond beyond the meal seemed to have been created by virtue of eating or not eating these meats.

In Acts 15 (vv. 22-23, 28-29), what to eat was portrayed as the primary and determinative element of all Christian meals:

> The apostles and elders, with the whole church . . . chose Judas, known as Barsabbas, and Silas . . . and gave them this letter to take with them (to Antioch): The apostles and elders, your brothers, send greetings. . . . It has been decided by the Holy Spirit and by ourselves not to impose on you any burden beyond these essentials: you are to abstain from food sacrificed to idols, from blood, and from the meat of strangled animals and from illicit marriages. Avoid these, and you will do what is right.

Although this text disagreed with the report of Paul in Gal. 2:1-10 about the results of this meeting in Jerusalem and cannot be considered historically accurate,[50] it is relevant to this study's interest in the ways early Christian meals negotiated ethnic differences.

This stands in interesting comparison with Acts 10, which described Peter as having a dream in which he was told to eat of "every kind of animal, reptile, and bird" (10:12). Two elements of comparison are worth noting here. In terms of what was allowed by early "Christians" to eat, the explicit instructions by the Jerusalem letter were quite different from the instructions to Peter in his dream. What unites these two passages is their obvious fictional character. Much scholarship, both recent and fifty years old, portrays Acts as highly polemical in its representing these early issues among early Christians.[51] Acts seems to have had its own complex agenda in representing this early "history."

For our purposes, neither of these Acts texts can be seen as representing actual social experimentation with interethnic relations at meals. The stories themselves are mostly fiction and polemic. However, both linked in very important ways relationships between Jews and gentiles to meals. Acts 10 portrayed Peter as abandoning Jewish practice not to eat pork and shellfish in order to relate to the Roman centurion, and Acts 15 showed the apostles and elders instructing everyone to be united by abiding by certain Jewish prohibitions of food (foods sacrificed to "idols" and blood).

The rhetoric in Acts about meals, interethnicity, and specific foods—although not historically accurate—was intensely invested in the larger social significance of what early Christians ate at meals. It is impossible to determine what actual meal practice the writers of Acts were using or proposing. Yet its rhetoric hints strongly that specific foods were considered important in social experimentation around interethnicity at meals. What one ate (both at the community meals and most likely at other times) had come to represent by the time of Acts' composition major social markers.

Food has been shown in this brief survey to have been interethnically uniting and differentiating in early Christianity. The range of ways food acted either to differentiate ethnicities or to cross ethnic boundaries included ritual negotiation at subliminal levels in common meals; social experimentation to demonstrate ethnic solidarity at common meals; a variety of social experimentation to demonstrate new ethnic mixes at common meals; and social experimentation beyond the scope of common meals.

Conclusions about Social Experimentation with Ethnic Mixes and Early Christian Meals

In cosmopolitan cities such as Antioch and Rome, which also had strong and diverse Jewish populations, it is unlikely that Jews and gentiles eating together as Jesus-people would have necessarily been experienced as social experimentation (at least not any more than the whole city was a social experiment). In many cases, ethnically mixed eating probably remained at the level of ritual deployment and reflection. On the other hand, it is clear from both Acts and Galatians that the Peter-Paul differences about eating were—at one point or another—dimensions of real social experimentation with ethnic mixes centered at meals.

Social Experimentation and Early Christian Meals

Early Christian meals' semiconscious ritual address to important social issues of the Hellenistic era can now be seen on a continuum that includes self-conscious social experimentation around issues of economic marginality, gender, and ethnic mix. Although this chapter's investigations have often found particular early Christian texts to be polemical and unreliable historically, the thick textual layering associating social experimentation with meals is undeniable. It is not necessary to insist on any particular historical accuracy of texts to conclude that meals were prominent in enabling early Christians to address significant social issues in their lives and larger society.

Chapter 6 noted that there are not many texts that reflect or invoke early Christian action in the Greco-Roman societies of their day. Almost all of subsequent Christian discussion about Christianity and social action at its beginning stages depends on the imaginative or rhetorical dimensions of texts, not on texts' description of early Christians exercising societal influences. That chapter on meals as resistance to Rome proposed that the semipublic meal gatherings may have been the primary expression of societal values for early Christians.

Discussion of other social experimentation by early Christians has often shown similar tendencies for primary early Christian action to have concentrated within the meal. However, there has not been so stark a distinction in arenas of economic marginality, gender, and ethnic mix. Resistance to Rome in society at large carried huge consequences. Experimenting with the social issues discussed in this chapter also carried major consequences, but perhaps not quite so severe as those for opposing Rome. So with these other issues, the meal does appear to have been the major, but not only, focus for social action. Social experimentation other than resistance to Rome was linked to the meal but also seems to have occurred outside the meal, as in the cases of celibacy, purchasing practices at the marketplace, and relationships with non-Christians.

The category of social experimentation must be considered as more centrally characteristic of early Christianity. Seeing early Christianity as socially experimental may be more adequately descriptive than previous attempts at describing Christianity as a certain set of beliefs, a certain liberative ideology, or a particular kind of devotion to the central figure of Jesus. When examining a wide range of early Christian texts from the perspective of the central social practice of festive meals, a possibility for imagining early Christianity emerges in which social experimentation becomes crucial. The texts and meals seem to interface in experimentation with a range of social possibilities that are alternative to the restrictive prescriptions of dominion, honor and shame, and patron and client. It may be that these early Christian alternatives were guided not only by essential beliefs or ideological determinations but also by experience of the possibility of significant experimentation in loosening and reshaping social bindings.

CHAPTER EIGHT

Identity Performance AS A New Paradigm FOR THE Study OF Christian Beginnings

H AVING STUDIED THE SOCIAL IMPLICATIONS of the intersection of the Hellenistic meal paradigm with early Christian scriptures, this book can step back and situate this discussion in the larger field of Christian beginnings. This is accomplished in four steps: (1) a review of the book's major conclusions so far; (2) an examination of the relationship among early Christian theologizing, meal practice, and Christian beginnings; (3) an application of the analytical category of "identity" to the study of Christian beginnings through the lens of early Christian meals; and (4) a reflection on what the analytical category of "performance" does to the notion of early Christian identities.

A Review

Knowing the character of the Hellenistic meal has opened new doors into the New Testament and other early Christian texts. A wide range of connections between social issues of the first two centuries CE and early Christian writings has become clearer by virtue of understanding the social dynamics of the meals at which early Christians often gathered. The ways early Christians constructed their communities, the approaches they took to address specific relationships among themselves, and the components and character of their larger social visions have all come into finer focus. Texts—both those that reflect actual meal settings and those that imagine new worlds—find a comfortable anchor in the larger paradigm of Hellenistic meals.

Ritual analysis of these meals has underlined the social dynamics and achievements of these meals, both in and without direct reference to early Christian texts. The Hellenistic meal per se now appears as an important social practice that helped all of its participants negotiate key issues in their lives. In particular, the emerging identities of early Christians have taken on particular profiles when seen at these meals. Oft-disputed relationships between Jew and Greek, slave and free, and male and female can now be seen much clearer through the meal lens. Leadership issues, the key relationship to Roman imperial domination, and wealth/poverty tensions for early Christians obtain sharper focus at the meal.

Once placed at the meal, early Christianities become much more like ongoing social experiments. When texts without which the meal seemed to be a series of contradictory social positions about slavery, Roman imperial domination, ethnicity, and gender are placed within the meal dynamic, these texts suddenly appear as parts of a larger set of social experiments. Since the meal itself provided an opportunity for all groups to act out provisional positions on these key social issues without necessarily committing to them, the various textual positions on these issues now can be seen as parts of this experimentation. Furthermore, as chapter 5's treatment of the cosmic vocabulary of many early Christian meals has shown, the active early Christian imagination of new societal change can now also be owned.

The Meal and Early Christian Theologizing

This book has actively questioned the central role Christian belief and theology have played in thinking about Christian beginnings. It has noted that a central flaw of the master narrative of Christian origins has been its concentration on the idea of a pure Christian belief handed down from Jesus to the apostles to the church fathers and the makers of creeds. Following others, I have suggested that, at least as a way of balancing the weight of this belief-centered notion of Christian beginnings, one might think about the social dimensions to early Christianities. As a complement to the work of Karen King, Burton Mack, Richard Horsley, and John Dominic Crossan, this work has done an in-depth study of a major social practice to advance social analysis of Christian beginnings.

The new scholarly perspectives of the past two decades on Christian beginnings summarized in chapter 2 point toward tasks of picturing a spectrum of early Christian experience as central to understanding the first 150 years of Christianity. While severely criticizing the master narrative based so thoroughly on unexamined creedal and heroic assumptions, these new perspectives, however, are not naive or even optimistic about being able to access human experience of two thousand years ago. They understand experience to be relatively inaccessible in all cases, since the notion of "experience" combines exterior "facts," inner impressions, cultural paradigms, and complex participation in social norms. In addition, these new perspectives on Christian beginnings work mostly with texts, and they understand that texts often cover up and adjust as much as describe and reveal human experience. Nevertheless, as alternatives to the master narrative are explored, these new perspectives insist on thinking about Christian beginnings in terms of the relationships, cultures, social dynamics, ideologies, and politics of early Christians.

This book's study of early Christian meals has provided another approach to these experiences in the first century. Instead of belief and theology as the only categories that mitigate human experience in the first 150 years, here the meal has become another phenomenon that integrated, characterized, and negotiated the array of human experience. Indeed, as many ritualizing activities, meals seem to have been for the Hellenistic age an important way of examining the more problematic human experiences. Especially in dialogue with early Christian texts narrating or coming from the meal paradigm, meals appear to have been a quasi-conscious method for participants to sort through and make sense of such pivotal experiences. No wonder that Jonathan Z. Smith says that such rituals play crucial roles for "thinking about" problematic experiences. Hellenistic meals, then, actively—if mostly on a subliminal level—ordered an important set of experiences of the first and second century CE. This study has shown that the social practice of meals makes meaning of human experience, especially the pivotal and problematic experience of a particular time and place. As such, the social practice of meals needs to be seen as similarly significant to theological ideas in making sense of human experience in the first 150 years of Christian beginnings.

Nevertheless, it would be reactionary to avoid theological discourse in reimagining Christian beginnings. As has been the case with the texts analyzed in chapters 2–7, theological analysis is enhanced through rigorous investigation of social practice. Here, the creative interaction of meals and key early "Christian" ideas becomes apparent. The ideas and meal dynamics indeed often turn out to be complementary.

Such intersections have occupied most of this book. Chapter 3 traced at length the ways early Christian ideas meshed with the core "values" of the Hellenistic meal, as outlined in Matthias Klinghardt's study *Gemeinschaftsmahl und Mahlgemeinschaft*. Chapter 4 used Romans 14 and 15 as a key illustration of how the performance and ritual dimensions of a particular early Christian meal setting clarified some of the key ideals of that community and Paul. Chapter 5 examined the broad swaths of cosmic vocabulary in the New Testament and saw how this vocabulary could have been elucidated and generated by certain standard aspects of the meal. Chapter 6 studied the ways the meals' tension with Roman authority could have been amplified and inspired by a broad range of New Testament texts. Chapter 7 examined New Testament texts about gender, ethnicity, and honor and shame, and found that the meals were both foundational to the ideas in the text and occasion for elaborating the ideas through action and additional teaching. Both chapters 6 and 7 discussed a plethora of references to the ways early Christians made meaning of the death of Jesus at the intersection of idea and meal.

The *Basileia* of God

This chapter complements the other intersections of early Christian ideas and meals with one additional early "Christian" idea: that of the kingdom/reign of God. Asking about the relationship of the kingdom/reign of God to early Christian meals seems important on at least two counts: (1) its very early prominence in the teachings in the pregospel "sayings of Jesus" and in the letters of Paul, and (2) the breadth of its occurrence throughout the first 150 years of early Christian ideas. By this choice, I do not mean to suggest that the "kingdom/reign of God" is the essence of early Christianity or the governing idea. Rather, its prominence serves here as an additional test case for the intersection of key early Christian ideas and meals.

The traditional interpretation of the Greek word *basileia* as the "kingdom" of God has run into problems on several fronts in the past twenty years.[1] For this treatment, I will simply keep the Greek word in the discussion of the meaning of this early Christian idea, rather than choose between the current spectrum of flawed translations. This use of *basileia* means to draw on the range of meanings this Greek word seems to have in early Christian writings, rather than choosing among "kingdom, "realm," "domain," "empire," "kin-dom," "imperial domain," and "reign."

The following basics and major ambivalences can be found in the first 150 years of Christian reflection on the *basileia* of God and are held by most scholars:

- Although not prominent in the Hebrew scriptures, the notion does occur there, mostly in the wisdom writings.[2] Some commentators have probably legitimately seen Israel itself as a "kingdom of God,"[3] although even here the possibility of Israel as not just a kingdom but a counter-empire also seems to have occurred to some writers of the Hebrew scriptures.[4]

- Similarly, the idea of an imaginally counter-*basileia* to the powers-that-be occurs in Hellenistic Cynic and Stoic teachings. In these teachings, *basileia* connotes mostly the realm of control established by a philosopher over against the nonreflective assumptions that cede such control to gods, cultural givens, and political power.[5]

- There is almost complete agreement that the historical Jesus used the *basileia* of God as a key concept. Even the minimalists[6] and the pessimists[7] about what one can say about the historical Jesus concede Jesus' use of this idea. More than a century of disagreement exists concerning what Jesus meant by this idea. The major disagreement, both in the nineteenth century and now, concerns whether the historical Jesus saw the *basileia* of God as a present reality or an apocalyptically future one.[8] One of the main clusters of this idea in sayings often attributed (by both camps) to the historical Jesus occurs in parables. In these parables, the *basileia* is often compared to an element of everyday life. The meaning of the *basileia* as a present reality compared to such everyday elements is usually seen as poetic paradox that expands both the notion of the *basileia* and the character of everyday life. The future meaning of such comparison with everyday life is usually interpreted allegorically, with the element of everyday life functioning to interpret either the end-time or the time of waiting.

• Although not occurring as densely as in the teachings of Jesus, Paul also used *basileia* eight times in four letters. Four of the eight uses are concerned with those who "will not inherit the *basileia* of God" and seem to be used as a phrase indicating moral corruptness and perhaps apocalyptic condemnation. Romans 14:17 used *basileia* also in a negative way in relationship to meal dynamics. The phrase "it is not eating and drinking that make the *basileia* of God" was deployed by Paul to indicate that the arguments about what food to eat were not the crucial concern.

• However one parses which *basileia* sayings go back to the historical Jesus, it is clear that the gospels, both canonical and noncanonical, actively make meaning of their own with the idea of the *basileia* of God. Mark clearly emphasizes an apocalyptic meaning. Thomas clearly rejects an apocalyptic meaning and often makes it a dramatically interior reality within humans. Matthew uses it in both apocalyptic and interior ways. Luke does as well and also tends to extend any eschatological implications into a more distant future.

It seems relatively certain that almost every meaning of the *basileia* of God noted above was actively discussed among some early "Christians" at a meal. Since the *symposion* part of the meal was a time for all kinds of discussions, songs, and drinking, early "Christians" as well as the historical Jesus himself—like the rest of their culture—used it for serious reflection, playful imagination, and enthusiastic affirmation. And since the larger picture we have of the *symposion* from both Christian and non-Christian literature also often portrays such discussion and imagination as contested, it seems likely that many other notions of the *basileia* of God were also discussed at the meals.

At least as significant for the intersection of early Christian ideas and meals is the way the *basileia* of God was used by Jesus and the generations that followed him to imagine social alternatives for themselves. As Burton Mack puts it: "The Jesus people said, in effect, 'Come on, you can do it, you can live as if you belonged to the kingdom of God,' and 'If you do, the kingdom of God will surely take place in this very world."[9] Whether one associates *basileia* (or its Aramaic equivalent of *malchuthah*) with kingdom, reign, domain, or empire, the word itself is about a social frame of reference. The *basileia* of God in some way or another signifies a group or mass of people together called into being by God. Thinking about it imaginally, as both the parables and hymns of the first 150 years of Christianity do, evokes a new societal vision of how people can live and thrive together.

This imaginally social character of *basileia* corresponds dramatically with the way the Hellenistic meal functioned, especially as analyzed in chapter 4. The Hellenistic meal through the variety of participatory activities in the *symposion*, the complex social symbolisms of reclining, the numerous significances of the libation, the variations in leadership and constituency, and the different meanings of food itself was continually giving opportunity for the diners to imagine society in slightly or extravagantly different ways. As has been seen throughout this book, the meal provided occasion for societal visioning. Discourse about the *basileia* of God could hardly have found a better context than the Hellenistic meal.

Chapter 7 outlined how the particular ways early Christians participated in the Hellenistic meal resulted in a wide range of social experimentation at the meal. The idea of the *basileia* of God both drew upon the social visioning at Christian meals and inspired this same visioning process. It is, however, important not to oversimplify this active collaboration between theologizing about the *basileia* of God and Christians eating together. First of all, noticing how the meals and the *basileia* of God complement each other in their social visioning does not imply any direct causalities between them. It cannot be said that either *basileia* of God discourse or Christian meals were the cause or origin of this social visioning by early Christians. Rather, the social practice of the meal and the imaginal discourse about the *basileia* of God interacted in complex ways, contributing energetically in their interaction to early Christian social visions. The earlier analysis of the complexity of the meals' social dynamics serves as a reminder that the causalities are complex and that the idea that one particular idea or activity originates early Christian consciousness is pretentious. Second, just because the meal and *basileia* of God theologizing both work on societal visioning does not mean that they do the same kind of work on societal visioning. It is clear that they do different kinds of work. Although both are quite imaginal in their approach, playing with "What is the *basileia* of God like?" as an idea is quite different from meal dynamics of negotiating whether to eat the same amount and kind of food or heartily singing a song that one has sung together thirty times before.

Christian Beginnings, Meals, and Theologizing

As noted throughout this book, the field of "Christian origins" has mostly proceeded with an unfortunately disembodied methodology based on the ideas and beliefs of the first 150 years. This book has been able to demonstrate how the study of a particular social practice of early Christians can bring another dimension to thinking about Christian beginnings. This has not been a romantic contrast between thinking and doing. There has been no assertion that "in the beginning was the deed" in the spirit of Wolfgang Goethe.[10] Rather, throughout the book the treatments, texts, theology, history, and social practice have been presented as complexly interrelated.

In addition to this chapter's brief examination of the meal and the proclamation of the *basileia* of God, different kinds of intersections between early theologizing and meals have been studied in this book. For instance, it became clear that Paul's understanding of the oneness in Christ was deeply rooted in actual experiences of deciding who ate what food (Romans 14 and 15), who wore what to dinner (1 Cor. 11:4-12), and who reclined with whom (Gal. 2:11-14). The meal experiences themselves shaped the complex turns in Paul's thinking about how united and differentiated people were in Christ. Assuming that Paul had a theological principle about what it meant to be "one in Christ" that he applied to different communities is a far more wooden approach than to feature the meal dynamics as shaping Paul's thinking about how Jews, gentiles, men, and women were complexly connected and differentiated "in Christ." The ways the hyperbolized level of awareness at meals served also to filter, adjust, idealize, ignore, and recalibrate Paul's everyday experience of men, women, Jews, and gentiles also become clear. Obviously, these everyday experiences of oneness and difference acted as strong anchors for Paul's sense of being "in Christ." And the meals' intimate tradition of focusing attention on relational issues among different kinds of people generally shaped, re-formed, and de-formed Paul's and other meal participants' everyday relational experiences. In these arenas, Christian beginnings formed substantially through meal dynamics and ritualization and were complemented and congealed by explicit theologizing.

As outlined in chapters 5–7, ideas and stories about Jesus' death were constructed at the intersection of theologizing and meals across a range of early Christian texts and social locations. Here, too, first a set of experiences needs to be considered in possible relationship to these stories and ideas. Because of the textual content and the fact that crucifixion was a practice of Roman authorities in first-century Israel, both chapters 5 and 6 considered experiences of oppression by the Roman Empire as related to particular stories and ideas about Jesus' death. In other words, ideas and stories about Jesus' death could have easily been interpreting experiences of the wide range of people taxed, imprisoned, executed, conscripted, harassed, and otherwise governed by Rome and its client states, not just Jesus' own experience of being crucified. For instance, in Gal. 3:1, Paul's statement that the Galatians have seen Jesus Christ crucified can most likely be understood as a metaphor for some experience of their own, since Jesus was not executed in Asia Minor. Volume-length treatments of Jesus' crucifixion understood as lenses for making sense of experiences by people other than Jesus include Ched Myers's *Binding the Strong Man*, Elizabeth Castelli's *Martyrdom and Memory: Early Christian Culture Making*, and David Seeley's *The Noble Death: Graeco-Roman Martyrology and Paul's Concept of Salvation*.

In addition, it is possible that the more universal experience of dying or having a loved one die could be referenced by ideas and stories of Jesus' own death.[11] Likewise, the frequent and devastating experience of sickness in the first and second centuries could have also been addressed through these same ideas and stories (as is explicitly the case in 1 Cor. 11:29). Or these ideas and stories could have been vehicles for thinking about other traumas in Hellenistic community or societal life. Paul's statement in Gal. 2:22 that he has been crucified with Christ seems to be an example of Jesus' death having been a metaphor for Paul's relationship with the law.[12] Peter's misunderstanding of Jesus' mission (Mark 8:27-33) and denial of Jesus as he is near death in Mark seem to have been seen at least in part as failing the (Markan) community, inasmuch as Matthew explicitly tries to correct this impression in 16:18-19 by giving him the keys to the *basileia* and granting him explicit leadership.

As discussed in chapters 5 and 6, early Christian meals did indeed seem to address such experiences of the lives of participants through stories and ideas about Jesus' death. In particular, both chapters have shown that the libation formula first occurring in 1 Cor. 11:23-25 that salutes Jesus while invoking his death must have been seen at least by some as a challenge to the Roman execution of Jesus, the execution of others, or other Roman abuse. As noted in chapters 5 and 6, offering a libation explicitly evoking Jesus' crucifixion was likely to have been seen as an especially pointed rejection of the injunction to offer a libation to the Roman emperor. The hymns evoking Jesus' crucifixion (especially Phil. 2:6-11) sung at the meals most likely carried similar expression of resistance to Roman power and pretense to imperial divinity. In these cases, then, the beginnings of Christian opposition to Roman power could have been "thought" through the meal ritualization of libation or hymn singing without much explicit theological conceptualization.

On the other hand, telling versions of the stories of the death of Jesus in the canonical gospels and the *Gospel of Peter* almost certainly depended on some levels of theologizing prior to their being told at meals. By this, I do not mean to suggest that it was impossible that such theologizing about Jesus' death occurred in its initial stages during meal *symposia*. Indeed, I suspect that *symposia* were a major location for earlier Christian theologizing, since so many early Christian leaders were illiterate. This suggestion that such stories of Jesus' death almost certainly depended on prior theologizing refers to clear literary studies that show both the gospel stories and Pauline ideas about Jesus' death as formally indebted to the literary genre of "noble death" stories.[13] That is, in this case, the stories of Jesus' death could not have been composed whole cloth in a meal *symposion*, since there existed prior to any such composition a basic story genre of the noble death of a protagonist. In these cases, Christian beginnings of opposition to Rome through ideas and stories of Jesus' death began not with the meal but with an already existing story typology.

These various examples of early Christian theologizing show that the meal could have often begun early Christian formation and reflection on a range of issues, but not always. The relationship between theological reflection and meals was complex, with multiple scenarios by which what came to be known as Christian ways came into being. What is new here is the establishment of meal dynamics per se as a source of Christian expression, behavior, reflection, and belief. Meals were another way of "thinking" about the *basileia* of God, relationships among men and women, Roman oppression, authority structures within early Christian communities, and conflicts between Jews and gentiles.

On the other hand, the meals must not be seen as the single frame of reference for Christian beginnings. Everyday experiences, serious theologizing, and prior cultural and literary paradigms also framed important dimensions of early Christianities. It seems likely that each of these other dynamics did play serious roles within the meals themselves but did not depend on the meal. The social practice of meals by early Christians was crucial to Christian beginnings and to their theology and beliefs but must not be seen outside of a complex of cultural paradigms, powerful prior teachings, enigmatic everyday experiences, and other ritualizations.[14]

Meals and the Analytical Category of Identity Applied to the Study of Christian Beginnings

Social practice is never something that has one origin. Social practice connotes continuity. It is consistently derivative of a host of inspirations, sources, and energies. It is never pure; it is regularly a mélange or hybrid of many different components. Nor does it remain the same; it changes often in response to any number of factors. As noted at the beginning of chapter 2, meals—at any time and in the particular case of the Hellenistic meal—are quintessentially derivative, with no claim to a real beginning. To connect Christian beginnings with this social practice of the Hellenistic festive meal underlines the ambiguities of those beginnings themselves. It raises further doubt about the possibility of tracing Christianity to any specific origins and of finding its essence. It places Christian beginnings not in one particular ideology, creed, ethic, set of ideals, or heroic figure. Having explored early Christian meals as a social practice and seen the plethora of connections they have to the range of ethics, teachings, and behavior of "Christians" in their first 150 years, this book is now in a position to ask after additional ways of thinking about Christian beginnings and to see how the notion of meals at these amorphous "beginnings" fits. This is done by consulting two key, relatively new analytical concepts.

Judith Lieu has mostly analyzed a period somewhat later than this book. In her several suggestive works, she has concentrated on the eras in which the term *Christian* came into explicit use by the people themselves who practiced Christianity.[15] Examining mostly second- and third-century realities, Lieu has pointed to the term *identity* as especially helpful in thinking about Christian beginnings. Identity, like social practice, implies a much less essentialized and much more composite notion of Christian beginnings. Based within several emerging schools of thought from beyond the study of early Christianity or theology about identity,[16] Lieu asserts: "The construction of Christian identity is much more fragile than much . . . contemporary analysis presupposes. Further, there are a number of variables in the formation of Christian identity, the interplay between which invites exploration. Most obvious are . . . those inner tensions provided by the Jewish origins of Christianity."[17]

Identity in this sense is more of a construction than an origin, more of a moving target than a fixed reality, and more of a hybrid than an essence. Lieu has asserted that talking of Christian identity preserves the possibility of speaking of Christianity as a particular phenomenon without requiring it to have an unchangeable or completely fixed definition. Karen King has taken up Lieu's vocabulary and shown how the term *identity* helps transcend the master narrative's dead-end categories of "orthodoxy" and "heresy" in thinking about early Christianity in ways that include its diversity.

This book sees its study of one central, pervasive early Christian practice as a part of this same task. Lieu herself calls for "a grammar of practice" in the study of early Christian identity, and this book's examination of the social practice of Hellenistic meals understands itself as a response to that call.[18] It takes on the delicate task of thinking about Christianity's beginnings in the first 150 years mostly before its explicit separation from various Judaisms and in stages when its experimentations were volatile and fragile. Asking questions about Christian identity in the first 150 years, eschews the quest for Christian origins. Instead, it looks for ways to characterize those first four or five generations in their distinctive hybridities and nascent particularities. The term *identity* is specifically helpful in examining those early proto-Christians as constructing a number of identities peculiar to themselves and connected to the broader trajectories of Christian beginnings.

The meal was a construction site for identity in the Hellenistic Mediterranean. I suspect that the particular form and dynamics of the meal observed in Dennis Smith and Matthias Klinghardt came in part from the intense needs of this age to sort out possible identities. In any case, meals became a place where the almost endless mix of national and ethnic identities in the Mediterranean was contested, expanded, rethought, and improvised on. It was a place where social honor and shame could be confirmed and renegotiated. The new and reactionary possibilities of gendered identity in the Hellenistic era tugged and pulled at one another at these meals, confirming, rejecting, and reshaping possibilities. Pressure from and resistance to Rome's attempt to impose identities of citizen, barbarian, and client were negotiated at meals. In a time when many new identities were in the making, the meals were a place for their construction.

When related to the meals, these aspects of identity construction flourished in the first 150 years. The Pauline negotiation of "Jew," "gentile," and "Roman" identity categories has been evident at the meal in Galatians 2 and Romans 14 and 15. The meal's power to reconstruct, confirm, and reframe honor and shame is easily seen in the gospel stories about tax collectors, prostitutes, and foreigners. The Luke 10:38-42 story of Mary and Martha and the instructions in 1 Cor. 11:2-15 about veils and head coverings for women demonstrate the significance of the meal in confirming, rejecting, and reframing gender identity. Chapter 6 has shown the spectrum of texts with meal-related resistance and accommodation to the identity pressures of imperial domination.

It is not that the meal provided ready-made identities for early Christians or any others in the complex Hellenistic mix. The meal's relatively stable form, however, did provide a safe space in which the contradictions, pressures, and possibilities of identity could be held. Its openness to disagreement, social experimentation, and expressiveness invited provisional reworkings of identity. From this perspective, the Hellenistic meal was relatively typical of the way social practices evoke identity, since, as Judith Lieu points out, "contradiction, conflict, and ambivalence are fundamental characteristics of. . . social practices in which they are instantiated."[19] The meal's semipublic social location allowed for a creative mix of new identity display and, at the same time, protection from the contingencies and perils of the street, marketplace, and civic discourse. The meal housed volatility of change and clashes of cultures comfortably within its established and flexible rhythms. As such, it held a variety of identity constructions graciously open. It allowed for tentative and complex identity. No wonder that on occasion a fight would break out at meals with so much in flux. No wonder that the participants consistently came back for more risk taking, confirmation, and negotiation of identity.

Meals, Identity, and Early Christian Rhetoric

This open-ended yet boundaried identity construction process has striking parallels in the literature of Christianity's first 150 years. Paul's rhetorical container for disputed (not yet explicitly) Christian identity was most often the phrase "in Christ." For Paul, one was "neither Jew nor Greek, slave nor free, male nor female, for you are all one in Christ Jesus" (Gal. 3:28). Romans 3:22-24 rejects distinctions, proclaiming that "all are . . . free in Christ Jesus." Nor does sin distort who they are, for "you must see yourselves as being dead to sin but alive for God in Christ Jesus" (Rom. 6:11). "In Christ Jesus," the Corinthians are "called to be God's holy people" (1 Cor. 1:3). The assembly in Corinth and Paul "have the mind of Christ" (1 Cor. 2:16). Paul says the Corinthians are "people in whom Jesus Christ is present" (2 Cor. 13:5). Similarly, for Paul, the "body of Christ" was an identity construction that recognized and united differences of status and ability in his extended presentation in 1 Corinthians 12. The figure of Christ Jesus was for Paul a source of identity that helped negotiate some of the major differences and tensions confronting Hellenistic Mediterranean populations (all translations this paragraph by the author with the exception of 1 Corinthians 2:16).

Although Paul clearly preceded the gospel writers and contributed ideas to at least some of them, most interpreters of Jesus in the gospels have not seen him primarily as a figure with whom to identify. Curiously, Jesus in conventional post-Reformation readings of the gospels has been mostly the unique appearance of God or an unattainable moral standard but not an identity model. This reading persists even though the Synoptic Gospels regularly call for people to "follow" Jesus, invite the reader to share secrets with Jesus that even the disciples did not know or that they misunderstood, and portray Jesus negotiating many of the complexities of Hellenistic identity. Similarly, the Gospel of John repeats the refrain for its readers to be "in the Son" as the Son is in the Father.

I suggest that the gospels—like Paul before them—portrayed Jesus as a figure through which to negotiate identity. The gospels persist in picturing Jesus in the middle of controversies of pure and impure, of honor and shame, right alongside consistent invitations to follow Jesus. These were indeed narratives for identity constructions in the first 150 years. In Jesus, the narrative gospels offer paths toward identity. Of course, each gospel had particular conditions in mind, and even when they addressed the same identity tensions, each often did it somewhat differently. For instance, Luke's identity issues seem to have been more for an economically privileged constituency and constructed a path toward identity less hostile to Roman dominion.

Overall, however, each of the narrative gospels—including Luke—designed a path toward identity in Jesus that traverses landscapes of dramatic differences of status, relational fields, economics, purity, health, ethnicity, and gender. Even while taking the diversity of the respective gospels into full account, the narratives of Jesus' (and the readers') identity generally negotiate a daring plethora of options. Identifying with Jesus in the gospels offered a generally risky and messy complexity, not too different from the identity "in Christ" of Paul.[20] The study of Jesus Christ in the first century, traditionally called "New Testament Christology," can legitimately also be seen as an address to the rigors of Hellenistic identity.[21]

Finding one's identity in Jesus and in early Christian meals was then quite similar. Knowing who one was through the inclusivity of being "in Christ" or by following Jesus through conflict-filled scenes in the gospels offers a dynamic and complex identity very similar to attendance at an early Christian meal. The literature and the meals of early Christianity delighted in a shifting and complicated identity.

Markan Rhetoric, Identity, and Loss

This complex mapping of identity construction in the gospels has been expanded by a recent essay by Maia Kotrosits on Mark and identity.[22] Kotrosits examines the disjunctions in Jesus' and therefore Markan identity. Her essay takes seriously these disjunctions as part of a larger Markan strategy to address identity in situations of horror and loss. In this way, she takes on not only the multiplicities and shifts in Hellenistic identity but also, and more particularly, the trauma and loss standing in the way of unproblematized identity. For Kotrosits, it is not so much that Mark dealt with trauma and loss as impediment to identity but that Mark actually was more interested in how identity happens when horror is taken seriously. She notes:

> There is not an uncomplicated mention of Jesus' identity in the entire gospel. There are indeed multiple identifications used for Jesus at various times with no clear distinctions about their use, from the fairly straightforward address "Rabbi," to the highly ambiguous self-declaration "son of Adam"/"son of Man," to the apparently related terms "son of David" and "Anointed," not to mention the indications of Jesus as God's son. For as often as Jesus is titled and called, it seems Mark does not know exactly what to call him.[23]

Not only is the identity through titles unstable, but Jesus' own speaking of his identity exhibits a similar alienation from it. Kotrosits notes:

> Jesus often refers to himself as the son of Man—whatever ambiguity of meaning this phrase contains, it is clear enough that Jesus is speaking of himself in the third person. . . . The effect of this circumlocution is one of Jesus modeling a way of speaking about oneself as another—a dislocation and displacement of the self that allows speaking about the self in a different mode.[24]

This also applies to another key Markan title for Jesus with a slightly different twist:

> "Son of God" is only slightly less ambiguous than "son of Man," since while it was broadly used in the ancient world, Mack writes that it contained different imaginations, including messenger of God or mediator between God and humans, king of Israel or true Israelite, or even the whole of Israel. Mack also importantly notes that Mark is quite able to re-describe such terms or figures for his own intentions. In this vein, the narrative can be read for how Mark re-invents the term son of God. The most notable aspect of the term "son of God" is that it occurs exclusively around liminal bodies. Aside from at the transfiguration, it is spoken by unclean spirits that Jesus casts out (3:10-12), by God at the baptism of Jesus, and then by a centurion at Jesus' death. These are all times in which bodies are in transition—in fact it seems that the defining detail of the term "son

of God" in Mark is bodily transition. This makes the other ambiguities of the phrase strategic, rather than problematic. Mark's refiguring of the term "son of God" in this frame is a way of thinking about identity that is both mobile and dislocated, but is also embedded in the horrors and hopes of physical unpredictability.[25]

This volatility of identity also applies to the exchanges about who Jesus is in Mark, Kotrosits says, especially in structurally key locations in the gospel:

Indeed, throughout Mark it seems there are a number of key declarations of Jesus' identity that are somehow impaired and major revelations that are diminished, either in the confession itself or elsewhere in the narrative. There are two trial scenes, one before the high priest, and one before Pilate. In the former, the high priest confronts Jesus and asks, "Are you the Anointed, the son of the Blessed One?" Jesus answers with the ego eimi, "I am." This "I am" is subverted in two ways. For one, this earlier trial and unqualified "I am" is part of an intercalation structure which has the episode enclosed by Peter's denial. Then it is followed by the second trial when Jesus is confronted again about who he is. He answers, "If you say so." The succession of events moves from Jesus' confession to Peter's denial to Jesus' deflated half-confession.

"If you say so" is an oddly resonant statement for the Gospel of Mark, since throughout the gospel identity statements are almost unilaterally conferred on Jesus, rather than confessed by him. A heavenly voice, a centurion, demons, disciples, and those Jesus heals confess (often differently) who he seems to be, and Jesus silences rather than explicitly confirms them. What Jesus seems to prefer to confess instead is the pain and torture he is about to endure. In 8:27–33, Jesus asks his disciples what people are saying about him, and then asks them who they think he is. When Peter blurts out, "You are the Anointed!" Jesus not only warns him to not tell anyone, but begins immediately speaking "openly" (parrhsia) about how the "son of Man" will be killed and raised, and that his disciples must pick up their crosses and follow him. Jesus repeats this same son of Man saying in 9:31, and both times his disciples don't understand. Peter scolds him in chapter eight, and in chapter nine the disciples "dreaded to ask him about it." The move to circumlocution in these two spots is itself compelling. Why is speaking openly about this death and resurrection, if even in the third person, preferable to these identity claims? Or is it the invocation of the third person that makes this openness possible in the first place? Is speaking of his body's troubled future too difficult to sustain an "I"?[26]

This instability of speech about Jesus is, according to Kotrosits, not at all the only Markan disjunction related to identity.

> The destruction of the Jerusalem temple (or the "devastating desecration" in Mark's words) was a defining horror for the Markan community that explicitly implied identity. The temple stood not only as an organizing principle for Jewish identity for both local and diaspora Jews, but also as a broader place of articulation and contestation of identity in the first century. Caligula's mid-century demand that his statue be placed in the temple, for example, was not just a violation for Jews, but signified a larger agenda: the vain and forceful ubiquity of Roman rule and religion, in which regional and inherited traditions of conquered nations were co-opted and recapitulated as symbols of belonging to Rome.[27]

Kotrosits shows then how Mark's various portrayals of Jesus' identity are not at all disorganized but rather are highly structured. It is not, however, just a literary design; it is also an address to the complexity of identity formation in the Markan situation.

> In the extreme, such complex and multiple identifications, such slippage between persons, could be considered dissociative. This would, in a certain way, fit very well with the excess of horror in Mark's immediate context. But the literary sophistication of Mark with its doubles, building suspense, and intercalations doesn't suggest total disintegration as much as it suggests construction, however urgent and disturbed the content. For Mark, identifying in ways that are numerous, simultaneous and contradictory, confronts a reality of horror but refuses to fall into total fragmentation or resort to defensive reprisal. It neither shatters completely nor tries to glue the pieces back together.[28]

This applies finally to the ambiguity of Jesus's death and the empty tomb in Mark, according to Kotrosits. There, Jesus' cry of abandonment and the fear and uncertainty at the empty tomb "is a revelation of rupture, a moment of irrecoverable loss" but "does not simply seal this loss. It also establishes a site for the re-articulation of this identity,[29] newly constituted through and with loss."[30]

Here, early Christian rhetoric not only narrates identity formation at a time of cultural change and diversity but also takes on identity formation in the most difficult stages of loss and trauma. Kotrosits's study of Mark is especially significant since Mark was so thoroughly followed by Matthew and Luke in the material examined by her.

Kotrosits's work with identity and loss in Mark can be compared closely to the almost endless trade-offs and risks invoked within the alleged "leisure" of early

Christian meals. In both cases, identity is provisional and deeply implicated in loss.

IDENTITY AT THE INTERSECTION OF MEALS
AND EARLY CHRISTIAN RHETORIC

Early Christian rhetoric and meals made a striking match for each other. They both offered dynamics that left open substantial room for provisional identity construction. Indeed, they both seemed to invite an identity of process rather than essence. They historicized identity construction, rejecting especially the Roman hyperbole of permanently secured and eternally guaranteed dominant identity. They both offered the possibilities for open-ended, provisional, and incomplete identities over against the pretense of conformist stability.

The meal and early Christian rhetoric fed each other. The safe space of the meal and especially the traditions of teaching, debate, and song in the *symposion* offered a stage for Christian rhetoric. Early Christian teaching, song, and debate fueled the meal with the kind of energy on which it thrived. Early Christian identities were nurtured—and boundaried—by both. This match, of course, did not solve all the problems of identity in a complex time filled with violence. Nor did it do justice to a number of constituencies, even those at the heart of the possibility. It did, however, provide a combination of dynamics that generated enthusiasm and persistence.

Meals and the Analytical Category of "Performance" Applied to the Notion of Early Christian Identities

In its summary of ritual theory, chapter 4 accepted Catherine Bell's discomfort with an essentialized notion of "ritual." Bell worried, appropriately, that ritual is less an entity per se and more a way of acting. "Ritualization" was her preferred term, and with some reservation[31] Bell has placed it in close association with "performance."[32] It is now possible to return to the ritual theory used in chapter 4 and apply it in thinking about the "performance" of early Christian identities in relationship to meals.

Chapter 4's summary of ritual/performance theory included the following:

> Ritual is not so much a thing in itself but a way human groups approach problematic realities of their lives. In contrast to earlier scholarship, these last two generations of ritual theorists have not generally found ritual addressing the same subject matter (for example, cosmic beginnings, key transitions in life, religious questions) around the world. Rather, the core dimension of ritual has had to do with how each group approaches a more or less local complexity.

Ritual is, in this framework, a kind of social intelligence, often reserved for subject matter that has proved too complex for individual discernment, too frightening for more direct address, or attached to vying long-term social loyalties. Whether it be the complex relationship between a giver and a receiver, the rivalry between the Israelite king and the high priest, the conflicts inherent in the geographical location and the social needs of an Algerian ethnicity, the contradiction of the simultaneous benefits and harmfulness of Ndembu hierarchy, or the class distinctions in modern democratic society, ritual is a primary way groups of people "perform" an approach to these relatively intractable issues. Performing a ritual then becomes a way of reframing various difficult issues of the specific ritualizing group so that they can be seen in different ways. These performances are seldom seen as a realistic solution to the intractable issues. They do, however, in their performative address to these complex issues, give perspective on and allow thought about the difficult issues.

The relationship described here between ritual and "matter that has proved too complex for individual discernment, too frightening for more direct address, or attached to vying long-term social loyalties" can be applied to the relationship between meals and early Christian identities. As noted in this chapter's previous discussion on identity, identity is not something that can be easily defined, constructed, or maintained. At its best, identity is fluid, often it is volatile, and sometimes it mocks its own name.[33] Early Christian identity faced into realities of almost indiscernible ethnic mixes, important transformations in gendered power, the tension between Roman models imposed from above and fragmented images of the past, and almost unthinkable losses on many fronts. Identity, then, certainly qualifies as an "intractable" issue.

Performing identity does not reveal identity as much as it plays with it. At its most constructive, one might say that performing identity elaborates it. At its most dynamic, performance provides a construct in which the fluidity of identity can be celebrated. The ever-changing character of performance—never standing still—both reinforces the provisional reality of identity and further frustrates its stability.

Stable identity is therefore both a goal and a pretense. Judith Butler has explained how closely performance and the construction of subjectivity are connected:

Performativity cannot be understood outside of a process of iterability, a regularized and constrained repetition of norms. And this repetition is not performed by a subject; this repetition is what enables a subject and constitutes the temporal condition for the subject. This iterability implies that "performance" is not a singular "act" or event, but a ritualized production, a ritual reiterated under and through constraint, under and through the force of prohibition and taboo, with the threat of ostracism and even death controlling and compelling the shape of the production, but not, I will insist, determining it fully in advance.[34]

Performing identity is not the repetition of a known quantity but the production of that which is known only in its performance. As Butler insists: "Identity is performatively constituted by the very 'expressions' that are said to be its results."[35]

Early Christian meals were rich occasions for repetition and improvisation of new group identity. They provided a regular loose structure in which a panoply of options existed for reinforcement, adjustment, challenge, and negotiation of identity through the foods eaten, the songs sung, the libations raised and poured, the debates, the teachings, the constituency, and leadership roles. The varied and risk-riddled rhetoric of early Christians has turned out to be a striking match for this performative meal event, suggesting that emerging Christian identities can be newly perceived at the nexus of social practice and text. Holding the texts within the more fluid frame of the meals helps account for the delicate first- and second-century balance of textual exuberance about emerging Christian identities, the pulsing encounters with loss and oppression experienced by the people themselves, and the amazing diversity of early Christian expression.

This delicate balance has not been embraced by the proponents or opponents of Christian origins. There has been a constant push by Christian origins scholars to identify baselines of belief, values, ideology, and identity. Scholarly (mostly postmodern) opponents of the possibility of studying Christian beginnings have insisted that nothing can be said with any certainty because the variety of evidence, expression, and phenomena makes everything indecipherable. This study of early Christian meals signals the emergence of a more modulated perspective in which the obvious vibrancy of early Christian identities comes not from a (finally undecipherable) definition but from collective openness to being in process. The social practice of the meal held the variety of expressions and the experience of loss in an ongoing elaboration. As a repeated phenomenon, it provided an illusion of permanent identity, even while it ensured its fluidity. As the study of early Christian cosmic language showed, the meal dynamics of song, debate, and libation supplied an improvisational context for the hyperbole and wild assertions of Christian rhetoric. Its protected environment allowed for often marginal and usually curiously composed Christian groups to try out ambitious claims to world power, social reversals, and cosmic hybrids, without being held much more accountable than an actor in a play.

These meal performances of elaborative identities demonstrated a trust that proved creative, inspiring, and audacious. If they were not so pathetic in their actual social power, they would have been seen as pretentious. The level of trust in risking an ongoing fluid identity through performance-like dynamics spread into the early Christian literature (and, of course, rebounded back into the meals). The strong presence of an early Christian vocabulary of *pistis*/trust/faith attests to the combination of risk and protection in the meal dynamics.

Performance is a category that may hold both the ways these meals evoked subliminal dynamics of social identity through ritualization and more explicitly conscious social experimentation. Ritual theory has shown how these meals merited the trust of their participants to play out semiconsciously important possibilities for their own identities. The meals also provided an atmosphere in which some of this emergence of identity could move from the shadows of semiconsciousness into obvious experimentation with particular social identities. In these latter cases, the meals were the platforms for trajectories of identity into portions of the larger world.

The ongoing performance of Christian identity hints at a broader characterization that is both social and theological. In both cases, it may be wiser to think of early Christianity as a spectrum of elaboratively performed identities in response to an imagined unfreezing of limits. Rather than achieving the essence of Christian belief or even the direction of its social values, one might think of emerging Christianity as a broad set of performed imaginations of identity less bound by honor/shame, patron/client, or dominion/oppression prescriptions.[36] The social practice of gathering at meals together would have provided substantial support for such performances of identity.

Social identities in this characterization of early Christianity can be seen along the following trajectory:

1. Subliminally ritual encounters at the meal with crucial intractable identity issues prompted a variety of mostly micro imaginations, negotiations, and adjustments. These ritualizations often used or prompted composition of early Christian rhetoric.

2. Where these ritual performances brought certain issues into clear consciousness, new social stances were taken or proposed more explicitly within the relatively protected environment of the meal. Here, too, this social experimentation within the meal both used and inspired early Christian rhetoric.

3. The social experimentation within the early Christian meal prompted similar, if generally less blatant, social experimentation within Hellenistic society. Here as well, some early Christian rhetoric came from this larger social application or inspired it.

Theologically, trust in God as an imaginal category played a significant part in the performative imaginations of identity beyond previous bounds. Here, "God" can be seen as having acted as a creative empty space over against the overdeterminations of purity codes, imperial pretense, honor and shame, and cultural stagnancies. "Trusting

God" became the imagination of identity over against the existing determinations and without any alternative but emptiness. Perhaps even more, "trusting God" became the experience of claiming identity that was fluid, dangerous, and untethered from the presumptuous stability of purity and empire.

In this regard, Jesus as identity figure—especially in its multiplicity and fragmentations—complemented the performance of fluid identity with no final determination. The regular evocations of "freedom" within early Christian rhetoric were in this case more a trust in the ability to imagine identity from within emptiness and brokenness and in contrast to overdetermination. The freedom Jesus offered as an identity figure was not the pretense of dominion above the chaos but the claiming of partial and fluid identity within experiences of loss and trauma.

The meals of early Christianity offered social practice at trust, imagination, and freedom. Because social practice was also entwined in limits, prerogatives, and presumption, these meals could provide no essence, foundation, or purity. They simply offered practice at the performance of provisional identities.

Epilogue: Reflections ON Twenty-First-Century Christian Worship[1]

U NDER THE HIGH, ARCHED CEILING held up by massive stone pillars reminiscent of European cathedrals, worshippers sit around ten tables with decorative cloths holding a variety of food. Most everyone is eating and talking animatedly with one another around their respective tables. Although there is an impressive organ whose pipes are splayed across the front of the sanctuary, a jazz piano is playing in the background. Occasionally, someone will stand up from one or another table and ask everyone in the room to sing a song together or to speak of something on his or her heart. At one point during the thirty-minute gathering, a story is told to everyone and is referred to each table for conversation and response.

Since 2003, this chapel service at Union Theological Seminary in New York has happened monthly during the school year. In this service dubbed "At Table," students and faculty have gathered under the direction of worship professor Janet Walton, director of worship Troy Messenger, and me to eat together at midday. The songs vary from hymns to Broadway tunes, and the stories told by a variety of people come from contemporary events, noncanonical literature, and the Bible. There is a regular rhythm to each meal, to which—as the years have progressed—students and faculty have become accustomed.

Often, I will begin this meal with a sentence or two referencing the early Christian meal gatherings. Almost as often, I will be quick to add that we do not see ourselves as mimicking the early Christians and to reassure (or disappoint) those gathered that we won't ask them to recline together. Rather, the purpose here is to respond to this early Christian worship from within our own time and place.

The responses over the years to this chapel service have varied. Students and faculty are used to seminary chapel being a laboratory for all kinds of worship experiments. This leads some to attend with devotion to see what will happen that day and others to distance themselves because the rhythm of worship is less established for them than they need. "At Table," like other forms of worship at Union, has a solid constituency (perhaps attended slightly better than other services overall) and quite a few who come and go according to their more personal rhythms of study and work.

This Union experiment is, of course, not unique. A number of congregations across the country have regular worship that includes meals, although it is clearly more the exception than the rule. One can probably fairly assess at this juncture that meals and worship are a mix in twenty-first-century America that has little potential in the foreseeable future of becoming a widespread phenomenon but that may indeed continue to nourish and inspire some communities of faith.

This book—like my last one on early Christian meals[2]—can be seen as a recommendation to churches and other worshipping groups to consider worshipping while eating. That previous book, *Many Tables*, encouraged readers to be inspired by the diversity of early Christian responses to the Hellenistic meal and to create many diverse tables around which they might worship according to their own particular social circumstances. The last twenty-three pages of *Many Tables* sketched six different services using food. These ranged from relatively small variations of standard eucharistic services to relatively bold experiments, not unlike Union's "At Table" chapel service. These different examples included a eucharistic celebration of summer, an informal community potluck, a eucharistic celebration of African American history, a house eucharist, a feminist service, and a service of eucharistic presence for the Easter season.

Ritual Negotiation of Life Issues

Responding to early Christian meals by eating in worship today, however, touches only a small portion of the lessons to be learned from them. Taking seriously the substantial, although mostly subliminal, promise church ritual has for addressing crucial life issues of twenty-first-century persons cannot be underestimated. Here, I want to pursue what can be learned for twenty-first-century worship in American cultures, whether that involves eating or not.

Lest this be understood as an endorsement of the worship status quo, it is important to make clear my assessment of much church ritual today. Although there is substantial change also afoot,[3] the paralysis of much Christian worship must be acknowledged. Protestant worship is in many places still devastatingly captive of clergy leadership's incessant talking and domination.[4] In many places, the pastor gives long prayers and sermons, almost completely eliminating the voices and expression of the worshippers themselves. In Catholic circles, authoritarian posturing by both clergy and hierarchy has diminished the range of expression and participation substantially in what otherwise can be a rich panoply of the mass. I do not think that most Christian worship in America is trustworthy, transformative, or inspiring.

Nevertheless, worship in America is probably the most frequent occasion for Americans to come together for expression and interaction that is not primarily commercially motivated. Rivaled perhaps only by professional football and shopping malls, worship is a regular community event for a plurality of Americans, even though a good deal of it is incompetent, totalitarian, or corrupt. In this respect, it almost certainly represents the most persistent and widespread community ritualization in American cultures for purposes other than earning money.

It is indeed as a phenomenon comparable to Hellenistic meals in that it provides a regular, semipublic, protected space and time for groups to express themselves. As such, it—at least theoretically—offers many of the same ritualized possibilities that the Hellenistic meal did. Within the somewhat safe, somewhat on display space of worship, people may negotiate, perfect, deploy, and elaborate significant and intractable issues in their lives through a complex and mostly subliminal process. Worship "safety" lies primarily in its predictability and its less than fully public exposure. One can more or less know the broad outlines of what is going to happen in worship. There are singing, talking, sitting and standing, silence, and perhaps tiny bits of eating and drinking. At predictable times of the year, baptisms can occur, Christmas trees can appear, and processions can wind their way.

This relatively safe (predictable and regular) time and space is indeed a given "contribution" of American church worship.[5] Where, for many churches, the similarity to Hellenistic meals breaks down is in the flexibility and open structure of the Hellenistic meals. Whereas the meals were somewhat regularly occasions for vigorous debates, deep leisure, loud singing, a bit of inebriation, the barging in of uninvited guests, and even occasionally fights, church worship by and large is considerably more inflexible.[6]

Here I give some recommendations of adjustments to worship. I make them by and large by virtue of how some adjustments in American mainstream worship are already contributing to that worship's ability to ritually negotiate some important life issues for its participants.

I think that the flexibility and elaborative character of the Hellenistic meal can be quite easily extended into American worship. This does not mean changing major forms, since that often eliminates the feeling of safety. Rather, loosening up the structures so that variation and addition can happen, especially through the agency of those attending rather than leading, offers new chances for worship to provide the kind of mostly subliminal processing of life issues this book has found in Hellenistic meals.

Several examples of such flexibility may help:

- A major innovation in American worship of the past twenty-five years has been the introduction of a participatory prayer style often called "Prayers of Joy and Concern." In this form of prayer, the worship leader invites anyone in worship to speak a joy or concern in his or her life. Sometimes the individual expressions that come to the fore are followed by the congregation saying or singing a prayer response with words like "God, hear our prayer" or something more poetic. Often, these expressions do not use explicit prayer language but simply end up with the person talking about an illness, a societal issue of concern, a beautiful sunset, or a nagging worry. In the thousands of churches that have adopted this particular prayer style, this part of the worship may extend ten to twenty minutes and include ten to thirty persons speaking. Sometimes what is spoken is through tears or is met with a good deal of laughter. Sometimes it presents unsolvable and agonizing problems; other times, language that is halting or poetic; and still other times, stunning beauty. This style of worship does not usually involve any particular responses to that which is spoken, other than a musical or unison congregational response—that is, no one tries to solve the problems mentioned or think through the next steps of success. The wide-ranging life issues simply hang in the air without resolution.

The less flexible and conventional version of this Prayers of Joy and Concern time can be a relatively long pastoral prayer in which a clergyperson speaks to her or his best estimation of the issues in the lives of the congregation. Such a pastoral prayer offers much less chance for ritualized negotiation of the life issues of the congregation. The pastoral prayer for the most part wraps all of the joys and concerns into a rhetorical whole, often with reassurances of God's power and care, whereas the Prayers of Joy and Concern open up issues of both joy and pain about which the pastor would not dare speak. The pathos of people speaking their own gratitude, ecstasy, hurt, anger, and insight evokes a mostly subliminal negotiation of life issues by the persons speaking and hearing. The open-endedness of expression allows for a lack of resolution and invites a more partial and semiconscious "thinking about" the issues evoked.

- A similar kind of invitation concerning the physical makeup of the worship space can be equally evocative. One growing impulse in worship in this regard is the improvisational construction of altars within the worship space. In these exercises, a relatively central space is designated as a place where anyone can bring an object from their lives. Often, this invitation is framed as bringing an object that represents a blessing, a need for blessing, or a gift given or received. Usually, people are also invited to write something on a piece of paper and leave it on the "altar." Often, several leaders—artistic or not—take responsibility for putting the objects brought each week in some (perhaps aesthetic) order. Objects brought range from stones and shells found on vacation to pictures of loved ones to wedding rings to political bumper stickers.

The visual testimony of these altars can be moving and jagged. Having them in view of others and in the place of safety and prayer often serves as an invitation to the person who placed particular objects on the altar to see those objects in a new light. Again, this process is mostly subliminal and is registered more as a feeling than a thought. The people to whom the objects do not belong are often engaged as well to take the strengths and pains of others into account. This, too, rarely results in any action, because for the most part one does not know who placed what on the altar. Rather, a semiconscious shift happens within those viewing particular objects that are not theirs. A person views another's wedding ring and reflects on his or her own partnership, usually at a less than conceptual level. Another stares at someone else's photograph of a beach and thinks about a personal experience on another beach. Finally, people also see the altar as a whole and react at least subliminally. Sometimes this response can be an integration of disparate elements in one's own life. Other times, it can serve as a clarifying of one's relationship to the community who made the altar.

Shifting other physical objects within a worship space can also precipitate important negotiations. Moving an American flag from one place to another or removing such a flag from the worship space or bringing such a flag into the worship space can be a way for certain communities to act out their ambivalences and commitments around political loyalties. Many more than one congregation have engaged in such tussles, some more explicitly than others. These tensions brought to consciousness through the shift of objects in the worship space can serve a community's own process around its political or cultural directions. A painting added or removed, a flag displaced, or flowers brought or not represent more than the objects themselves. Ritualization hyperbolizes space and therefore implicitly requests that people care about what is present and how it is located. Some involved in such congregational tussles may assert that worship is not about such physical arrangements. This book's attention to the subliminal negotiation of life issues through ritual would suggest that worship is important because it generates such tension and helps people think about intractable matters.

- Various and exceptional modes of presentation can also contribute this same kind of healthy flexibility to worship's ritualization dynamics. Especially within the overall safety of predictable worship, the insertion of unusual media can invite people to engage difficult issues on a helpful yet subliminal level. Whereas usually most music in worship makes for safety, occasionally different kinds of music can remind worshippers of dimensions of life that need addressing, at least subliminally. Musical instruments from another culture can precipitate a semiconscious impulse to think about how much or how little one values the other cultures that are increasingly present in American lives. Rock music or drama presentations can sometimes access issues within one's body consciousness to which one otherwise remains oblivious.

This porousness and flexibility within the larger constructed character of ritualization brings issues into semiconsciousness. As noted throughout this book, such issues are often intractable and can only be treated obliquely and over a period of time. Worship's ritualization of such issues contributes to the longer-term processing of these issues.

Often, however, church leadership is too frightened to risk this flexibility and semiconsciousness of danger within the larger safety of worship's predictable and protected sequences. Here is where religious people are ignoring the contributions of their own religious forms. The subliminal character of so much worship language and the protected space of worship are an intentional mix, based on long acculturation, that makes for a longer-term strength for the worshipping community. If church leadership can trust its own worship dynamic enough to loosen its iron grip, its constituency will be able to begin to address important and intractable issues in their lives. In the long run, the strength of healthy ritualization to address difficult issues semiconsciously makes for a stronger community.

Part of the frightened reductionism in church leadership has turned worship's gift of ritualization on itself in harmful ways. This has happened in the following manner. Some Christian leadership has noted that an intractable issue for many within Christendom is the growing weakness of Christianity itself. These leaders have then referred this intractable problem to the worship service itself. The result has been to conflate preservation of one or another worship tradition with the preservation of Christianity itself—that is, the frightened leadership has signaled subliminally to the worshipping bodies to invest semiconsciously in keeping worship itself highly structured and safe as a way of "perfecting" Christianity's larger vulnerability. In these cases, then, worship does address an intractable issue ritually. But that ability to address the intractable issue of Christianity's growing weakness robs worship of the ability to address other intractable issues.

Early Christian meals trusted the larger dynamic of a well-structured meal practice interfacing with that same meal's flexibility. This provisional trust in ritualized address both invited and sparked energized speech and spirituality and provided a flexible strength to the social bodies emerging from this practice. Such a dynamic can still infuse worship today.

Notes

Chapter One: Experiencing the Meal

1. See also Dennis Smith, *From Symposium to Eucharist: The Banquet in the Early Christian World* (Minneapolis: Fortress Press, 2003), 97–101, 126–29, for references to birthday dinners in the Hellenistic world.

2. A clear description of supper clubs or "associations" formed around a trade guild or profession are described extensively in Richard S. Ascough, *Paul's Macedonian Associations: The Social Context of Philippians and 1 Thessalonians* (Tübingen: Mohr Siebeck, 2003), 16–19, 24–28.

3. This is a fictional portrait based on the extensive portrait of the Jewish group that Philo portrayed at length and called the "Therapeutae" or "the healers" in *The Contemplative Life*, (trans. F. H. Colson and G. H. Whitaker (Cambridge: Loeb Classical Library, 1929).

4. This sketch is based on the early Christian writings from the Synoptic Gospels, picturing persons in Jesus movements teaching at meals. See also the instructions to the twelve in Mark 6:7-13; Matt. 10:1-23; and Luke 9:1-6. See also Luke's instructions to seventy-two others in 10:1-12.

5. The term *Christian* is problematic when used with reference to the movements that associated themselves with Jesus or "Christ" for at least the first one hundred years of this phenomena. There is little sense that these various movements thought of themselves as a "religion" that later Christians represented. On the other hand, these movements were clearly the progenitors of what later became the Christian religion. In this regard, perhaps the clumsy term *proto-Christian* is the most accurate description. But such a notion leaves out important elements of these movements' self-understanding and implies a historical unity of Jesus and Christ movements that is not accurate. For the most part, most of these groups most likely understood themselves within the larger traditions of "Israel." But this needs important clarification as well. "Israel" represented more than a geography and something perhaps akin to a set of religious or social traditions (or both). And in the case of the early Jesus and Christ groups of the first one hundred years, it is probable that the majority of people claiming to belong to "Israel" as a part of a Jesus/Christ group were themselves gentiles. This complicated picture of proto-Christianity makes the term *Christian* very problematic. Hence, I have placed

the term in quotation marks at the beginning of significant sections of discussion to indicate its problematic character.

This complex and evolving identity of these various Jesus/Christ groups is, of course, symptomatic of the major questions surrounding Christian beginnings that this book wishes to address. When did "Christians" become Christians? It is clear that this question does not have one answer and that the term *Christian* was not even indigenous to all of the varieties of Jesus/Christ movements at these early stages.

6. See also Phil. 2:6-11 and extensive literature about this early Christian hymn cited in chapter 5.

7. A crucial distinction needs to be made between contemporary twenty-first-century meals and what scholars refer to as the meals of the ancient Hellenistic world. The ancient meals to which scholars refer were not simply the occasions for people of the first century to eat. Rather, in the Mediterranean society of the first century, a larger social convention of eating was in full swing. Perhaps the term *banquet* is more appropriate for this major institution of that time, if the term does not necessarily imply luxury. These banquets were pervasive among large swaths of Mediterranean society of the time, including but also extending far beyond early Christian gatherings. That these "meals" were part of a much larger social dynamic in the first centuries of Mediterranean society helps us to understand the emergence of early Christianity as a part of larger social patterns and dynamics. This larger banquet tradition of the Hellenistic Mediterranean is detailed in chapter 3, where a summary of two major recent scholarly works relating the banquet tradition to early Christian practice forms the core of the presentation.

8. A similar debate about eating together is addressed in Romans 14 and 15. This fictional sketch is meant to evoke such a dispute in another location. For a clear study of the Romans 14 and 15 conflict, see Jae Won Lee, "Paul and the Politics of Difference: A Contextual Study of the Jewish-Gentile Difference in Galatians and Romans" (Ph.D. diss., Union Theological Seminary, 2001).

9. The rest of the book cites in detail this research and its rationale for application.

Chapter Two: New Paradigms for the Study of Early Christian Identities

1. Chronologically considered from the latter part of the nineteenth century, major works include the following: Adolf von Harnack, *The Mission and Expansion of Christianity in the First Three Centuries* (London: Williams and Norgate, 1908), and Harnack, *History of Ancient Christian Literature to Eusebius* (Berlin: Akademie der Wissenschaften zu Berlin, 1900); Wilhelm Bousset, *Kyrios Christos: A History of the Belief in Christ from the Beginnings of Christianity to Irenaeus*, trans. John E. Steely (Nashville: Abingdon, 1970); Alfred Loisy, *The Birth of the Christian Religion* and *The Origins of the New Testament*, both translated by L. P. Jacks (New Hyde Park, N.Y.: University Books, 1962); Rudolf Bultmann, *Primitive*

Christianity in Its Contemporary Setting, trans. Reginald H. Fuller (Philadelphia: Fortress Press, 1956); James M. Robinson and Helmut Koester, *Trajectories through Early Christianity* (Philadelphia: Fortress Press, 1971); Burton Mack, *Who Wrote the New Testament? The Making of the Christian Myth* (San Francisco: HarperSanFrancisco, 1995); John Dominic Crossan, *The Birth of Christianity: Discovering What Happened in the Years Immediately after the Execution of Jesus* (San Francisco: HarperSanFrancisco, 1998); Elisabeth Schüssler Fiorenza, *In Memory of Her: A Feminist Theological Reconstruction of Christian Origins* (New York: Crossroad, 1994); and Rodney Stark, *The Rise of Christianity: A Sociologist Reconsiders History* (Princeton, N.J.: Princeton University Press, 1996).

2. The notion of master narrative derives from the work of postmodern literary critic Jean-Francois Lyotard, especially his introduction to *The Postmodern Condition: A Report on Knowledge* (Minneapolis: University of Minnesota Press, 1984), where he introduces the concept of "metanarrative" or "grand narrative": "I define postmodern as incredulity toward metanarratives. This incredulity is undoubtedly a product of progress in the sciences: but that progress in turn presupposes it. To the obsolescence of the metanarrative apparatus of legitimation corresponds, most notably, the crisis of metaphysical philosophy and of the university institution which in the past relied on it. The narrative function is losing its functors, its great hero, its great dangers, its great voyages, its great goal. It is being dispersed in clouds of narrative language elements—narrative, but also denotative, prescriptive, descriptive" (xiv–xv).

The application of this notion to Christian beginnings can be found in Halvor Moxnes, "The Historical Jesus: From Master Narrative to Cultural Context," *Biblical Theology Bulletin* 28 (1998): 135–49. Karen King uses the term *master story* in the same way. See King, *The Gospel of Mary of Magdala: Jesus and the First Woman Apostle* (Santa Rosa, Calif.: Polebridge, 2003), 158–63.

3. The master narrative does acknowledge that these church "fathers" were themselves far from perfect but credits them for transmitting the essentials of creed and sacramental practice.

4. See Robert Funk, *Honest to Jesus: Jesus for a New Millennium* (San Francisco: HarperSanFrancisco, 1996), 39–66.

5. See also the skepticism concerning the major proposals by Elisabeth Schüssler Fiorenza's *In Memory of Her* and Burton Mack's *A Myth of Innocence: Mark and Christian Origins* (Philadelphia: Fortress Press, 1988) and *Who Wrote the New Testament?* Similar skepticism has met John Dominic Crossan's *Birth of Christianity.*

6. See also Ward Blanton's critique of Christian origins in *Displacing Christian Origins: Philosophy, Secularity, and the New Testament* (Chicago: University of Chicago Press, 2007).

7. See the keen examination and critique of these questions in Judith Lieu, *Christian Identity in the Jewish and Graeco-Roman World* (New York: Oxford University Press, 2004). Also see Luke Timothy Johnson's assertions that history is not recoverable per se but that the most reliable way to deal with questions of origins is to consult the composite view of the canonical gospels, in *The Real Jesus: The Misguided Quest for the Historical Jesus and the Truth*

of the Traditional Gospels (San Francisco: HarperSanFrancisco, 1996), 1–27, 105–40. See also the many cogent works of Elizabeth A. Clark on the difficulties of determining early Christian historicities, especially *History, Theory, Text: Historians and the Linguistic Turn* (Cambridge, Mass.: Harvard University Press, 2004).

8. See Vincent Wimbush, *African Americans and the Bible: Sacred Texts and Social Textures* (New York: Continuum, 2000), 1–43; King, *Gospel of Mary of Magdala*, 155–90; Stephen D. Moore, *Poststructuralism and the New Testament: Derrida and Foucault at the Foot of the Cross* (Minneapolis: Fortress Press, 1994); R. S. Sugirtharajah, *The Bible and Empire: Postcolonial Explorations* (Cambridge: Cambridge University Press, 2005).

9. King, *Gospel of Mary of Magdala*, 158.

10. Perhaps the most persistent critical voice of the master narrative over the past twenty-five years has been that of Elisabeth Schüssler Fiorenza. Although the vocabulary of this critique has remained her own, the dimensions of her thinking have been sharp and expansive. See particularly the introduction and first three chapters of *In Memory of Her*.

11. Mack's work on Christian origins has spanned more than a decade and includes *A Myth of Innocence: Mark and Christian Origins*; *Who Wrote the New Testament? The Making of the Christian Myth*; and *The Christian Myth: Origins, Logic and Legacy* (New York: Continuum, 2001).

12. King's work has addressed issues of Christian origins from several angles. The works that address these questions are *The Gospel of Mary of Magdala*; *What Is Gnosticism?* (Cambridge, Mass.: Harvard University Press, 2003); and *The Secret Revelation to John* (Cambridge, Mass.: Harvard University Press, 2006). King's most direct essay on the subject is early and does not contain her bolder suggestions. See "Mackinations on Christian Origins," in *Reimagining Christian Origins: A Colloquium Honoring Burton L. Mack*, ed. Elizabeth A. Castelli and Hal Taussig (Valley Forge, Pa.: Trinity Press International, 1996), 157–72.

13. Ehrman is perhaps the only one of these scholars who holds firm to the notions of orthodoxy and heresy as the appropriate way of sorting through this diversity. See his plethora of books on this subject, including *Misquoting Jesus: The Story behind Who Changed the Bible and Why* (New York: HarperSanFrancisco, 2005); *Lost Christianities: The Battles for Scripture and the Faiths We Never Knew* (New York: Oxford University Press, 2003); and *The New Testament: A Historical Introduction to the Early Christian Writings* (New York: Oxford University Press, 2004), which have consistently taken this position. However, recently Ehrman has made public statements that he has "lost" his own Christian faith as a result of his work as a scholar of early Christianity. See the report in the *Washington Post*, March 5, 2006, by Neely Tucker, p. D1.

14. See the cogent illustration of this in Elaine Pagels and Karen King, *Reading Judas: The Gospel of Judas and the Shaping of Early Christianity* (New York: Viking, 2007), 33–42.

15. See Elisabeth Schüssler Fiorenza, *Jesus and the Politics of Interpretation* (New York: Continuum, 2000); and Hal Childs, *The Myth of the Historical Jesus and the Evolution of Consciousness* (Atlanta: Society of Biblical Literature, 2000).

16. The studies of Wayne Meeks and Gerd Theissen in the 1980s were some of the first to take this approach. See Meeks, *The First Urban Christians: The Social World of the Apostle Paul*

NOTES TO CHAPTER TWO 203

(New Haven, Conn.: Yale University Press, 2003), and Theissen, *The Social Setting of Pauline Christianity: Essays on Corinth* (Philadelphia: Fortress Press, 1982) and *The Sociology of Early Palestinian Christianity*, trans. John Bowden (Philadelphia: Fortress Press, 1978).

17. The scholarship in this regard has become so broad that it factors importantly in the work of a conservative scholar such as N. T. Wright (see *Paul: In Fresh Perspective* [Minneapolis: Fortress Press, 2005]) and a scholar of noncanonical documents such as Karen King. See the earlier notes in this chapter for King's works.

18. It is the master narrative's fiction that makes first-century Judaism into a corrupt religion. This was neither the first-century historical reality nor the viewpoint of most of the New Testament and early Christian literature. The Gospels of Matthew and Mark portray the dispute between Jesus and other parts of Judaism as an intra-Jewish dispute about a variety of issues. Since Krister Stendhal, most New Testament scholarship has also seen Paul as engaged in an intra-Jewish dispute. The theology of Luke/Acts, however, does seem to have been one of the first viewpoints that sought to portray Judaism as a corrupt tradition, which Christianity succeeded.

19. Mack, *Myth of Innocence*, 18, 19. More extensively, Mack also writes (*Myth of Innocence*, 10):

> There is, however, a burgeoning body of knowledge about the way in which symbol systems, myths, and rituals function in relation to social institutions and shared patterns of activity within groups. . . . In general, these recent approaches to the understanding of religious articulations see them as ordering activities involving the thoughtful observation, classification, and perfecting of systems of signs and practices fundamental to the operation of social units. Thus religious phenomena are intimately related to the construction and maintenance of social structures. Religious symbols function, however, at a certain distance from the actual state of affairs experienced in the daily round. They articulate a displaced system (imaginary, ideal, "sacred," marked off) as a counterpoint to the way things usually go. The inevitable incongruence between the symbol system and the daily round provides a space for discourse. It is the space within which the negotiations fundamental to social intercourse take place—reflection, critique, rationalization, compromise, play, humor, and so forth.

Mack also writes: "Social formation and mythmaking are group activities that go together, each stimulating the other in a kind of dynamic feedback system. Both speed up when new groups form in times of social disintegration and cultural change. Both are important indicators of the personal and intellectual energies invested in experimental movements" (*Who Wrote the New Testament?* 11).

20. Mack, *Myth of Innocence*, 123.

21. Mack, *Lost Gospel*, 8.

22. Ibid., 211.

23. Ibid., 9.

24. See Jonathan Z. Smith, *Drudgery Divine: On the Comparison of Early Christianities and the Religions of Late Antiquity* (Chicago: University of Chicago Press, 1990).

25. See Merrill P. Miller and Ron Cameron, eds., *Redescribing Christian Origins* (Boston: Brill, 2004). Prior to the seminar, see Castelli and Taussig, *Reimagining Christian Origins*.

26. Judith Lieu's theoretical case for a study of early Christian practice in *Christian Identity in the Jewish and Graeco-Roman World* is the most eloquent. See also Wayne Meeks, *First Urban Christians*; Douglas Oakman and K. C. Hanson, *Palestine in the Time of Jesus: Social Structures and Social Conflicts* (Minneapolis: Fortress Press, 1998). Without explicit address to Christian beginnings, see also the work of Talal Asad, *Genealogies of Religion: Discipline and Reasons of Power in Christianity and Islam* (Baltimore: Johns Hopkins University Press, 1993), and *Formations of the Secular: Christianity, Islam, Modernity* (Stanford, Calif.: Stanford University Press, 2003).

27. Lieu, *Christian Identity in the Jewish and Graeco-Roman World*, ch. 6.

28. "Identity" as a category did not surface primarily in the study of Christian beginnings. Rather, the category emerged intellectually from postmodern, feminist, and postcolonial reflection on the earlier period of "identity politics." See the works of Homi Bhabha and Judith Butler, particularly Bhabha, *Nation and Narration* (New York: Routledge, 1990) and *The Location of Culture* (New York: Routledge, 1994), as well as Butler, *Gender Trouble: Feminism and the Subversion of Identity* (New York: Routledge, 1990) and *Bodies That Matter: On the Discursive Limits of Sex* (New York: Routledge, 1993).

29. Lieu, *Christian Identity in the Jewish and Graeco-Roman World*, 6.

30. A number of American scholars bring strong postmodern background to this study. See Laura Nasrallah, *An Ecstasy of Folly: Prophecy and Authority in Early Christianity* (Cambridge, Mass.: Harvard University Press, 2003); Todd Penner, *Contextualizing Acts: Lukan Narrative and Greco-Roman Discourse* (Boston: Brill, 2004); and Melanie Johnson-Debaufre, *Jesus among Her Children: Q, Eschatology, and the Construction of Christian Origins* (Cambridge, Mass.: Harvard University Press, 2005). The Society of Biblical Literature section on "The Construction of Christian Identity" has a more conventional methodology and is rooted in European research, particularly Italian (e.g., Edmondo Lupieri, Mauro Pesce).

In relationship to collective memory, see the work of Alan Kirk and Tom Thatcher, eds., *Memory, Tradition, and Text* (Atlanta: Society of Biblical Literature, 2005); and Elizabeth Castelli, *Martyrdom and Memory* (New York: Columbia University Press, 2004).

Daniel Boyarin's work on the complex interactions of Judaisms and Christianities in the first three centuries contributed much to the notion of identities under construction. See *Dying for God: Martyrdom and the Making of Christianity and Judaism* (Stanford, Calif.: Stanford University Press, 1999) and *Border Lines: The Partition of Judaeo-Christianity* (Philadelphia: University of Pennsylvania Press, 2004). The work of Judith Lieu, cited earlier in these notes, is consulted by a variety of scholars and represents perhaps the most dedication to the term *identity* itself. See also, in specific relationship between identity and performance, Richard Horsley, ed., *Oral Performance, Popular Tradition, and Hidden Transcripts in Q* (Boston: Brill,

2006); John Dominic Crossan, *In Parables: The Challenge of the Historical Jesus* (New York: Harper & Row, 1973); Crossan, *The Dark Interval: Towards a Theology of Story* (Sonoma, Calif.: Polebridge, 1988); Crossan, *In Fragments: The Aphorisms of Jesus* (San Francisco: Harper & Row, 1983); and Stanley Stowers, "Elusive Coherence: Ritual and Rhetoric in 1 Corinthians 10–11," in Castelli and Taussig, *Reimagining Christian Origins*, 68–83.

31. The Munich Seminar for New Testament Exegesis has published a recent book, *Herrenmahl und Gruppenidentitaet* (Lord's Supper and Group Identity) (Freiburg im Breisgau: Herder, 2007), edited by Martin Ebner, which by virtue of its title should be almost the same project as this book. Perhaps, however, the title itself already betrays the severe limitations of the book. As has unfortunately been the case for the past thirty years or so, this German work has severe deficiencies in two regards: (1) it ignores almost all non-German scholarship, and (2) its devotion to traditional Christian theological positions limits the scope of its research. The work indeed raises very similar questions to my book here. It seeks to understand the role of "the Lord's supper" (seen as an overarching category for both early Christianity and contemporary Christianity) in the community identity of early Christians. Unfortunately, its methods of investigation remain almost entirely exegetical in its treatments of these questions. One essay (by Gerd Theissen) claims to pose the questions of ritual analysis but suffers an almost complete lack of knowledge of the field, citing primarily a narrow range of psychological studies of ritual. Finally, this entire study seems stunningly ignorant of the work of Matthias Klinghardt (a German scholar himself) and Dennis Smith. Klinghardt is mentioned in a few footnotes, but the overall hypothesis of Smith and Klinghardt seems unknown to this seminar and book, while it relies on much older typologies of mid-twentieth-century German scholarship.

32. The notion of performing identity is a relatively technical one, which will be discussed at length in chapter 8.

Chapter Three: The Hellenistic and Early Christian Social Practice of Festive Meals

1. A larger consciousness of the confluence of Klinghardt and Smith's work was the major impetus for the current Society of Biblical Literature's Seminar on Meals in the Greco-Roman World, which Dennis Smith and I cochair and on whose steering committee Klinghardt sits.

2. In addition, several other scholars in the past twenty-five years have placed meals near the heart of their portraits of early Christianity's emergence. James Breech's *The Silence of Jesus* (Philadelphia: Fortress Press, 1983), a pivotal work in the past three decades' reconsideration of the significance of the historical Jesus, placed Jesus' presence at meals central to his overall message. Similarly but in a much more elaborate manner, John Dominic Crossan's works on the historical Jesus, Paul, and early Christianity see what Crossan calls "commensality" at the heart of the social meaning of both Jesus and Paul. Burton Mack's several books on Christian origins have placed early Christian meal gatherings in important relationship to the emergent

movement's social experimentation, noted in this book's introduction. In many ways, it has been Mack's continued attention to meals as social experimentation that has nurtured the larger project of this book.

3. Here, too, the distinction made in chapter 1 needs to be reiterated. A crucial distinction needs to be made between contemporary twenty-first-century meals and what scholars refer to as the meals of the ancient Hellenistic world. The latter were not simply occasions for people of the first century to eat. Rather, in the Mediterranean society of the first century, a larger social convention of eating was in full swing. Perhaps the term *banquet* is more appropriate for this major institution of that time, if the term does not necessarily imply luxury. These banquets were pervasive among large swaths of Mediterranean society of the time, including but also extending far beyond early Christian gatherings. That these "meals" were a part of a much larger social dynamic in the first centuries of Mediterranean society helps us to understand the emergence of early Christianity as a part of larger social patterns and dynamics.

4. Plutarch, *Table Talk*, 1.

5. Those who were well known and of financial means were more likely to receive invitations the most frequently. A well-known teacher—even if not wealthy—would be a part of meals because notoriety and skill in entertaining made such a teacher an attractive guest. Chapter 7 examines the routine of sages receiving invitations and crashing meals. Wealthy persons participated in these meals more often than the poor, since their social circle possessed the readier means to host such events. Some scholarship on meals has suggested that these meals were actually only a custom of the wealthy. This has been proposed since most of the extensive classical literary sources (e.g., Plutarch's *Table Talk* or Plato's *Symposium*) are clearly documents of the wealthy class. This conclusion has become more suspect, however, since the discovery of literature and extensive epigraphic evidence of many of the associations in which ordinary workers and even slaves participated. This issue is addressed more directly in chapter 2.

6. Dennis Smith, *From Symposium to Eucharist: The Banquet in the Early Christian World* (Minneapolis: Fortress Press, 2003), 2.

7. Matthias Klinghardt, *Gemeinschaftsmahl und Mahlgemeinschaft: Soziologie und Liturgie Frühchristlicher Mahlfeiern* (Tübingen: Francke Verlag, 1996), 24–25 (my translation).

8. Klinghardt, *Gemeinschaftsmahl und Mahlgemeinschaft*, 45–152; Smith, *From Symposium to Eucharist*, 13–46.

9. Klinghardt, *Gemeinschaftsmahl und Mahlgemeinschaft*, 253–73; Smith, *From Symposium to Eucharist*, 8–12, 42–46.

10. Klinghardt, *Gemeinschaftsmahl und Mahlgemeinschaft*, 45–129; Smith, *From Symposium to Eucharist*, 13–46, 65–66, 84–87, 129–32.

11. Klinghardt, *Gemeinschaftsmahl und Mahlgemeinschaft*, 153–73.

12. Ibid., 153.

13. Ibid., 155.

14. Ibid., 155–56 (my translation).

15. It seems to me that this deterioration of community/*koinonia* at the level of the city-states themselves had much to do with imperial impositions on the city-states. Particularly, the

Roman overinvestment and twisting of the notion of the Greek city almost had to have effected a deterioration of *koinonia*.

16. Klinghardt, *Gemeinschaftsmahl und Mahlgemeinschaft*, 156.

17. See Aristotle, *Eth. nic.* 1168B, 6-9. For commentary on this proverbial equation, see J. Derbolav, "Das Problem der Verteilungsgerichtigkeit bei Aristotles und in unserer Zeit," in *Studien zu Platon und Aristoteles* (Stuttgart, 1979), 208-38. See also Klinghardt's review of primary and secondary references in *Gemeinschaftsmahl und Mahlgemeinschaft*, 158-63.

18. Plato proposes what he calls a proportional equality, which factors the quality of the person into the question of equality, both in meals and in society at large. See 757C, *Gemeinschaftsmahl und Mahlgemeinschaft*, 161. Plutarch chronicles extensive arguments on both issues but is especially eloquent on both sides of the food portions issue (see *Table Talk*). See also Pliny's pointed discussion in *Epistula* II 6; Klinghardt, *Gemeinschaftsmahl und Mahlgemeinschaft*, 160.

19. This dilemma occurs also in English.

20. Klinghardt, *Gemeinschaftsmahl und Mahlgemeinschaft*, 173 (my translation).

21. Ibid., 163 (my translation).

22. Ibid., 168 (my translation).

23. Klinghardt quotes ten ancient sources to this effect. Ibid., 168-71.

24. Fragment 43.10, Klinghardt, *Gemeinschaftsmahl und Mahlgemeinschaft*, 170 (my translation from Klinghardt).

25. At the end of a longer piece of Theognis, 757-64, quoted by Klinghardt. Klinghardt also cites Homer, Pindar, Pythogoras, and Alkaios. *Gemeinschaftsmahl und Mahlgemeinschaft*, 169 (my translation from Klinghardt).

26. Ode 19:11, as cited in Klinghardt, *Gemeinschaftsmahl und Mahlgemeinschaft*, 173.

27. Smith, *From Symposium to Eucharist*, 9.

28. Ibid., 9-10.

29. Ibid., 10.

30. Ibid., 10.

31. Ibid., 10.

32. Ibid., 11.

33. Ibid., 11.

34. Ibid., 11.

35. I object to this term "messianic banquet" and see it as a Christian retrojection on both scholarship itself and the early Christian situation. This category appeals to Hebrew scripture texts (e.g., Isa. 25:6-12) that do not use messianic vocabulary. Smith and Klinghardt in this regard would do well to retain their vocabulary of utopianism and idealization. Klinghardt, *Gemeinschaftsmahl und Mahlgemeinschaft*, 173; Smith, *From Symposium to Eucharist*, 9.

36. Philip A. Harland, *Associations, Synagogues, and Congregations: Claiming a Place in Ancient Mediterranean Society* (Minneapolis: Fortress Press, 2003), 61.

37. Since I wrote this in 2002, the study of Hellenistic associations has tended to drop the word *voluntary* and the oversimplified emphasis on individual choice in joining these

associations. Indeed, the notion that individuals in that day were able to exercise voluntary choice is most likely too modern an idea for that time. It is almost certain that deciding to join an association was also contingent on factors that were not purely voluntary. For example, a patron could exert influence over a client to become a part of a particular association. Or a person laboring in the building of ships would not be "free" to "choose" to be a part of the association of shipbuilders but would be under many kinds of social pressure to do so. Nevertheless, the word *voluntary* as applied to the associations does help underline the contrast between these associations and the tribal, extended family, and national obligations of other eras. See further discussion of this issue in chapter 2.

38. Hal Taussig and Catherine T. Nerney, *Re-Imagining Life Together in America: A New Gospel of Community* (Lanham, Md.: Sheed & Ward, 2002), 11–12.

39. See chapter 3's discussion of times when the Roman emperor did forbid the associations because of worries about their seditious character.

40. See the discussion in chapters 4 and 5 of ritual action and social order.

41. Previously, it has been asserted that the literature represents only the meals of the wealthy. This was the case but has been corrected in the past generation by Klinghardt's and others' work on the meal-based associations of workers. See the extensive discussion of this in chapter 5.

42. Many scholars doubt that 1 and 2 Peter were authored by Peter.

43. Many scholars doubt that 1, 2, and 3 John were written by any of the known New Testament characters named John. This includes the beloved disciple and John of Patmos. It is probable that the author—whoever he was—of the Gospel of John wrote at least 1 John, if not all three of the letters. The letter form for 1 John is somewhat disputed.

44. Smith, *From Symposium to Eucharist*, 201.

45. See the full discussion of this hymn and the scholarship that has identified it and other songs/hymns in early Christian literature in chapter 5.

46. Adela Yarbro Collins, *Crisis and Catharsis: The Power of the Apocalypse* (Philadelphia: Westminster, 1984).

47. For example, Xenophon, *Symposium* 9; Philostratus, *Vita Appollonae* 4; Lucian, *De Saltatione*.

48. See *Statutes of the Iobakchoi*, both 64 and 113. Also, in his study *Dionysiac Mysteries of the Hellenistic and Roman Age* (New York: Arno, 1975), 59–61, Martin P. Nilsson proposes a mime pattern for many of the Bacchic feasts.

49. *Statutes of the Iobakchoi*, 60–65, 109–20. Dennis Smith (*From Symposium to Eucharist*, 117) comments on the Iobakchoi:

> Participation in these rites was required of each member (lines 45–46), and if they performed their roles well, they received special honor. Roles were assigned by lot from the membership (lines 125–127), and whenever one's turn came to play such a role, he received a special portion from the sacrificial distribution as a symbol of the rank and status connected with these roles. The assigned roles that

are known to us are those of five officers and five deities as named in the sacrificial distribution list.... Probably only the names of the deities represented roles, with the actual officers taking their own parts in the ceremony. However, the plot of the mythic drama in which these characters played their roles is unknown to us. Dramatic presentations were, of course, not uncommon as a part of symposia entertainment.

50. By and large, early gospels seem to be written for the particular Christian communities. Mark, John, and Thomas all have literary markings of a highly boundaried audience. Matthew— although its boundaries seem somewhat more permeable—has perhaps the most articulated set of teachings about how to live together in community. But other gospels, such as Luke and Mary, seem occasionally to envision a broader audience.

51. See Ronald Hock and Edward N. O'Neill, eds., *The Chreia and Ancient Rhetoric*, vol. 1, *The Progymnasmata* (Atlanta: Scholars Press, 1986); and *Progymnasmata: Greek Textbooks of Prose Composition and Rhetoric*, trans. George A. Kennedy (Atlanta: Society of Biblical Literature, 2003). Also, Burton Mack, *Rhetoric and the New Testament* (Minneapolis: Augsburg Fortress, 1990), and Burton Mack and Vernon Robbins, *Patterns of Persuasion in the Gospels* (Sonoma, Calif.: Polebridge, 1989), apply these studies to gospel and pregospel formation.

52. For example, Plato's *Symposium*.

53. I have mapped out this elaborative process relative to the *Progymnasmata* and the meal in "Dealing under the Table: Ritual Negotiation of Women's Power in the Syro-Phoenician Woman Pericope," in *Reimagining Christian Origins: A Colloquium Honoring Burton L. Mack*, ed. Elizabeth A. Castelli and Hal Taussig (Valley Forge, Pa.: Trinity Press International, 1996), to be discussed further in chapter 4.

54. See, for instance, Joachim Jeremias, *The Parables of Jesus* (London: SCM, 1972), 95– 97; H. W. Kuhn, *Aeltere Sammlungen in Markusevangelium* (Göttingen: Vandenhoeck and Ruprecht, 1971), 20–45; Werner Kelber, *The Kingdom in Mark: A New Place and a New Time* (Philadelphia: Fortress Press, 1974), 25–43; and Mack and Robbins, *Patterns of Persuasion in the Gospels*, 16–24.

55. John Dominic Crossan, *The Historical Jesus: The Life of a Mediterranean Peasant* (San Francisco: HarperSanFrancisco, 1991), 261–64.

56. The other example, for Crossan, is exorcistic healing by the historical Jesus.

57. Burton Mack, *A Myth of Innocence: Mark and Christian Origins* (Philadelphia: Fortress Press, 1988), 114–22; Burton Mack, *Who Wrote the New Testament? The Making of the Christian Myth* (San Francisco: HarperSanFrancisco, 1995), 64–76.

58. Regarding social significance, see Mary Douglas, "Deciphering a Meal," in *Myth, Symbol and Culture*, ed. Clifford Geertz (New York: Norton, 1971), 61–81.

59. A number of scholars have questioned the historical accuracy of Acts 15. The most obvious reason for such doubt is occasioned by several differences between this text and Galatians 1, which is another account of the same encounter. See Dennis Smith, "What Do We Really Know about the Jerusalem Church? Christian Origins in Jerusalem according to

Acts and Paul," in *Redescribing Christian Origins*, ed. Ron Cameron and Merrill P. Miller (Atlanta: Society of Biblical Literature, 2004), 237–52; or Hal Taussig, "Jerusalem as Occasion for Conversation: The Intersection of Acts 15 and Galatians 2," *Forum*, n.s., 4.1.

60. First Corinthians 11:23 has Paul writing that he "received" this formula "from the Lord." This phrase is relatively similar to 1 Cor. 15:3: "I handed on to you as of first importance what I in turn had received." Most scholars understand 15:3 to be a quote of a previous formula that Paul had been taught by his mentors, and most likely as a community formula. The reception "from the Lord" could be a similar dynamic. On the other hand, Paul wrote to the Galatians (1:11-12): "The gospel that was proclaimed by me is not of human origin; for I did not receive it from a human source, nor was I taught it, but I received it through a revelation of Jesus Christ." Here, then, one could evoke the reception from the Lord in 11:23 as parallel to the "revelation of Jesus Christ," which Paul was not taught. Because 11:23 referred to a formula to be said during a somewhat ritualized meal, I suggest that the stronger parallel is between 11:23 and 15:3. For preferring the parallel between 1 Cor. 11:23 and Gal. 1:11-12, see Mack, *Myth of Innocence*, 98–99.

61. See Klinghardt, *Gemeinschaftsmahl und Mahlgemeinschaft*, 379–406, on how this Didache and Lukan pattern still fits the overall *deipnon-symposion* order.

62. See Susan Marks, "Jewish Weddings in the Greco-Roman Period: A Reconsideration of Received Ritual" (Ph.D. diss., University of Pennsylvania, 2003).

63. See Dennis E. Smith and Hal Taussig, *Many Tables: The Eucharist in the New Testament and Liturgy Today* (London: SCM, 1990), 56.

64. For samples of this critique, see Philo, *On the Contemplative Life*, 34–27, and Plutarch, *Table Talk* 1.2.615D—619C, and 1.4.620A—622C.

65. Smith, *From Symposium to Eucharist*, 240.

66. It is possible that reclining meals did also occur outside. Greco-Roman temple festivals often were so large that the temple dining rooms did not suffice, and people reclined in fields for festive meals. Similarly, second-century early Christian practice of having meals in cemeteries reflects banquet-style reclining out-of-doors.

67. Paul Achtemeier, "The Origin and Function of the Pre-Marcan Miracle Catenae," *JBL* 91, no. 22 (1972): 198–221; "Toward the Isolation of Pre-Markan Catenae," *JBL* 89, no. 3 (1970): 265–91.

68. It is true that, according to 1 Corinthians 8 and 10, some meats slaughtered and cooked at these temples were served at Corinthian Christian meals. Indeed, at points in chapter 10, Paul seems to approve of Christians eating such meat at their meals (see 10:25-27, 30).

69. No host is mentioned in this account, where hospitality turned out to be a key issue.

70. Paul instructed the Corinthians to "eat at home" if they were hungry, implying that their location was in a place not hosted by a particular person. It is, however, possible that this lack of mention of host is accidental or strategic, since Paul does mention prominently in the letter a number of (seemingly wealthy) leaders in the Corinthian correspondence.

71. See Marks, "Jewish Weddings in the Greco-Roman Period."

72. See, for instance, my "Ritual Perfection and/or Literary Idealization in Philo's *On the Contemplative Life* and Other Greco-Roman Symposia" (presentation to 2004 Society of

Biblical Literature Consultation on Meals in the Greco-Roman World, San Antonio, Texas). See also Smith, *From Symposium to Eucharist*, 6–9.

73. See, for instance, Robert Funk and the Jesus Seminar, *The Acts of Jesus* (Santa Rosa, Calif.: Polebridge, 1998), 90–91, which credits less than 20 percent of gospel texts on meals as historically probable. See also the complex analysis of this question in Breech, *Silence of Jesus*, 51–64.

74. *Klino, keimai* (Luke 12:19; John 21:9; Rev. 4:2), *keisthai*, and (occasionally) *pipto*, often as composite verbs with prepositional prefixes of *ana* (*anakeimai* = Matt. 9:10; 22:10, 11; 26:7, 20; Mark 6:26; 14:18; 16:14; Luke 22:27; John 6:11; 12:2, 3; 18:28) (*anaklino* = Matt. 8:11; 14:19; Mark 6:39; 12:37; 13:29) (*anapipto* = Matt. 15:35; Mk 6:40; 8:6; Luke 11:37; 14:10; 17:7; 22:14; John 6:10a, 10b; 13:12, 25; 21:20), *syna* (*synanakeimai* = Matt. 14:9; Mark 2:15; 6:22; Luke 14:10, 15), *kata* (*katakeimai* = Mark 2:15; 14:3; Luke 5:29; 7:37; 1 Cor. 8:10) (*kataklino* = Luke 7:36; 9:14, 15; 14:8; 24:30).

75. See Smith, *From Symposium to Eucharist*, 274.

76. One could even make a case for these foot washings to have occurred during the *symposion* part of the meal, since both occasion *symposion*-type discussion. Without implying any actual historicity of either event, both stories have the foot washing at their beginning, perhaps implying the *deipnon*.

77. See Klinghardt, *Gemeinschaftsmahl und Mahlgemeinschaft*, 373–488, concerning the curious order of the Didache's cup and bread instructions and the place of the libation and the blessing in the Didache meal.

78. See Iabakchoi, 1QS VI 9; VII 9.

79. See especially the discussion about how to treat uninvited guests in Klinghardt, *Gemeinschaftsmahl und Mahlgemeinschaft*, 84–90.

80. Actually, in some cases the texts themselves address more the opponents to such inclusion rather than the invitees. See Romans 14 and 15 for excluded Jews; Gal. 2:11-14 for excluded gentiles; and Luke 14:12-14.

81. Crossan, *Historical Jesus*, 261–64.

82. For the hidden meal dimension to this text, see Taussig, "Dealing under the Table."

83. With the study referenced in the previous note of the controversy sayings about Jesus eating with tax collectors and sinners, Matthew's Jesus teaching about the tax collectors and prostitutes preceding the chief priests and elders into the realm of God (21:31-32) also seems possible to be read as a subtextual case being made for the inclusion of women at meals. This is further supported by Kathleen Corley's excellent work on the subject of women at meals in the Synoptics, in which she identifies a longer Hellenistic tradition of slandering all women who attended meals by calling them prostitutes. Corley, *Private Women, Public Meals: Social Conflict in the Synoptic Tradition* (Peabody, Mass.: Hendrickson, 1993), 147–56.

84. Paul Achtemeier's studies in the early 1980s of these passages propose a pregospel formulation of this inclusiveness. See Achtemeier, "Origin and Function of the Pre-Markan Miracle Catenae," and "Toward the Isolation of Pre-Markan Cantenae."

85. Cf. above note 53 for the hidden meal dimension to this text. It is clear, however, that some versions of this text advocate for gentile as much as women's participation in the meal.

86. This Matthean version of the parable of the great supper appears to me and many other scholars (see Jeremias, *Parables of Jesus*, and John Dominic Crossan, *In Parables: The Challenge of the Historic Jesus* [Sonoma, Calif.: Polebridge, 1992]) as an allegory about the invitation of Jews to Jesus' meal, their rejection of Jesus' meal, and the subsequent inclusion of gentiles in that meal. This advocacy for gentile participation in the meals held even though Matthew was meant mainly for Jewish (i.e., nongentile) ears.

87. Although (like Matthew) the Didache addressed primarily staunchly Jewish Christian communities, its proud inclusion of gentiles is obvious from its prescribed prayer over the bread at meals: "As this broken bread is scattered upon the mountains, but was brought together and became one, so let your church be gathered together from the ends of the earth into your kingdom" (9:4).

88. See Sam K. Williams, *Jesus' Death as Saving Event: The Background and Origin of a Concept* (Missoula, Mont.: Scholars Press, 1975); David Seeley, *The Noble Death: Graeco-Roman Martyrology and Paul's Concept of Salvation* (Sheffield: JSOT, 1990); Mack, *Myth of Innocence*; Mack, *Who Wrote the New Testament?* and Stephen Patterson, *Beyond the Passion: Rethinking the Death and Life of Jesus* (Minneapolis: Fortress Press, 2004).

89. Justin, *Apology* 1.66.3.

90. Philo, *On the Contemplative Life*, 26–47.

91. Dennis Smith, "Table Fellowship as a Literary Motif in the Gospel of Luke," *JBL* 106, no. 4 (1987): 613–28, 623.

92. Massey Hamilton Shepherd. *The Paschal Liturgy and the Apocalypse* (Richmond, Va.: John Knox, 1960).

Chapter Four: Ritual Analysis: A New Method for the Study of Early Christian Meals

1. See chapter 3's summary of his thought.

2. See chapter 3's summary of his thought.

3. The work of Andrew McGowan is disparate but marks the only scholarly work that attempts to apply the Klinghardt and Smith paradigm to the second through fourth centuries of early Christianity. Almost entirely in periodical form, a full list of this creative work can be found in the "Works Consulted" section at the end of this book. The Society of Biblical Literature's Seminar on Meals in the Greco-Roman World has initiated an effort to bring together the thinking of McGowan in a full volume. Andrew McGowan, "Rethinking Agape and Eucharist in Early North African Christianity," *Studia Liturgica* 34 (2004): 165–76.

4. This means, of course, that there are still a substantial number of older or marginal scholars practicing today who give the impression that the first-century Christians actually said the prayers and did the gestures of the medieval mass in some form.

5. It is important to recognize that neither Smith nor Klinghardt are naive in the slightest about this relationship between text and meal. Both insist on complex historical-critical analysis of each text as a part of their respective portraits of Hellenistic meals.

6. See Harland's pioneering study *Associations, Synagogues, and Congregations: Claiming a Place in Ancient Mediterranean Society* (Minneapolis: Fortress Press, 2003).

7. The major nineteenth-century work of Emil Durkheim very proactively interpreted ritual socially. Durkheim's work fell out of favor for much of the twentieth century, but the thinkers under consideration in this chapter are in substantial debt to Durkheim.

8. See chapter 3's survey of Smith's and Klinghardt's respective work.

9. Bourdieu, Douglas, and Turner are deceased, while J. Z. Smith is still working.

10. Although J. Z. Smith's work is more or less a generation earlier than Bell's, J. Z. Smith is still working. Bell uses J. Z. Smith pivotally in her determination to see rituals "as situational as they are substantive . . . , a matter of what is selected to be done and how it is done in particular situations rather than fixed activities or even intrinsic principles that govern rituals everywhere." Catherine Bell, *Ritual: Perspectives and Dimensions* (New York: Oxford University Press, 1997), 91. On the back cover of Bell's *Ritual Theory, Ritual Practice* (New York: Oxford University Press, 1992), J. Z. Smith calls the book "the most important book on ritual in many a year . . . , the single most successful model for writing in the field of religious studies" and "a comprehensive and generous presentation of the state of the question."

11. Bell, *Ritual: Perspectives and Dimensions*, 91.

12. Ibid., 91.

13. Ibid., 91. See also Bell's defense of the relative merits of "ritual studies" in response to the important challenges of performance theory in "Performance and Other Analogies," in Henry Bial, *The Performance Studies Reader* (New York: Routledge, 2004), ch. 11.

14. Bell, *Ritual Theory, Ritual Practice*, 90.

15. Ibid., 91.

16. Ibid., 91.

17. Ibid., 91.

18. Ibid., 221.

19. Ibid., 140.

20. Ibid., 140–41.

21. Ibid., 140.

22. Bell, *Ritual: Perspectives and Dimensions*, 83.

23. J. Z. Smith's major work on ritual is *To Take Place: Toward Theory in Ritual* (Chicago: University of Chicago, 1987). Another important essay on the subject is "The Bare Facts of Ritual" in his earlier *Imagining Religion: From Babylon to Jonestown* (Chicago: University of Chicago Press, 1982). His edited *HarperCollins Dictionary of Religion* (San Francisco: Harper-SanFrancisco, 1995) is voluminous and useful in its treatment of a wide range of ritual-related subject matter. Perhaps the most systematic treatment of his work is in Burton Mack's summary of his thought in the essay "Introduction: Ritual and Religion," in *Violent Origins: Walter Burkert, René Girard, and Jonathan Z. Smith on Ritual Killing and Cultural Formation*, ed. Robert G. Hamerton-Kelly(Stanford, Calif.: Stanford University Press, 1987) .

24. See especially my use of J. Z. Smith in my ritual analysis of Mark 7 in "Dealing under the Table: Ritual Negotiation of Women's Power in the Syro-Phoenician Woman Pericope,"

in *Reimagining Christian Origins: A Colloquium Honoring Burton L. Mack*, ed. Elizabeth A. Castelli and Hal Taussig (Valley Forge, Pa.: Trinity Press International, 1996). Implicitly, Smith's work also dominates my approach in Dennis E. Smith and Hal Taussig, *Many Tables: The Eucharist in the New Testament and Liturgy Today* (London: SCM, 1990), and Catherine T. Nerney and Hal Taussig, *Re-imagining Life Together in America: A New Gospel of Community* (Lanham, Md.: Sheed & Ward, 2002).

25. Smith and Taussig, *Many Tables*.

26. J. Z. Smith, *To Take Place*, 100–101.

27. Ibid.

28. J. Z. Smith, *Imagining Religion*, 64.

29. J. Z. Smith, *To Take Place*, 101.

30. Bell, *Ritual: Perspectives and Dimensions*, 12.

31. J. Z. Smith, *Imagining Religion*, 63.

32. J. Z. Smith, *To Take Place*, 101.

33. Ibid., 131–62.

34. Smith and Taussig, *Many Tables*, 102–3.

35. It was also the case—as it has been in both Klinghardt and Smith—that in many meals the amount of food one received came in proportion to how close one reclined to the president or *symposiarch*. This also, almost certainly, needs to be seen as a ritual perfection relative to the fact that in society at large there were huge discrepancies of food amounts between the rich and the poor. In such cases, it is probable that the differing amounts were seen as a perfection or rectification (both J. Z. Smith terms) at the meal—that is, the distribution of food at the meal was meant at some level to signify that those with a certain kind of social honor deserved more food. See Matthias Klinghardt's summary of the debates about *meris*, or portion(s) of food, *Gemeinschaftsmahl und Mahlgemeinschaft: Soziologie und Liturgie Frühchristlicher Mahlfeiern* (Tübingen: Francke Verlag, 1996), 139–43.

36. Klinghardt summarizes this widespread practice of *apophoreta*, *Gemeinschaftsmahl und Mahlgemeinschaft*, 143–52. Klinghardt makes clear that this custom of distributing leftovers to those in need actually derives from similar, much more explicitly cultic practices concerning goods sacrificed in temples.

37. Pierre Bourdieu, *Outline of a Theory of Practice*, trans. Richard Nice (New York: Cambridge University Press, 1977). The title of this major work also remains the focus of his intellectual quest. Although his publications have been infrequent, he has persisted in the methodological quest for a theory of practice. His work has spawned a second generation of the pursuit in the works of Deborah Ortner, David Laiten, David Cannadine, and Simon Price.

38. Bourdieu, *Outline of a Theory of a Practice*, 133.

39. On the overall intellectual pursuit of a theory of practice, Bell (*Ritual Theory, Ritual Practice*, 76–77) says:

> As a term that represents a synthetic unity of consciousness and social being within human activity, "practice" appears to be a powerful tool with which to

embrace or transcend all analogous dichotomies. And that, of course, is one of its problems. Even in Marx's usage the terms comes to play two roles, encouraging a slip from one level of argument to another. In one role practice is seen as the synthetic unity and resolution of the dichotomy of consciousness and social being. Simultaneously, however, practice is also cast in a second role where, as synthetic practical activity, it is contrasted with theory as the *activity of consciousness* (or with "structure" as in Sahlin's analysis) with which it forms the poles of another dichotomy. This second dichotomy is frequently invoked in order to resolve it into a third term, the dialectical synthesis of "historical process" (or again, as in Sahlin's analysis, "cultural praxis".

40. See, for example, some of his major works: Victor Turner, *The Forest of Symbols: Aspects of Ndembu Ritual* (Ithaca, N.Y.: Cornell University Press, 1967); Victor Turner, *Ritual Process: Structure and Anti-Structure* (Chicago: Aldine, 1969); Victor Turner and Edith L. B. Turner, eds., *On the Edge of the Bush: Anthropology of Experience* (Tucson: University of Arizona Press, 1985).

41. For their critique of Turner, see J. Z. Smith, "The Domestication of Sacrifice," in Hamerton-Kelly, *Violent Origins*; and Bell, *Ritual: Perspectives and Dimensions*, 127–29.

42. See the chronicling and analysis of the Ndembu ritual of *chihamba* in Turner's *Revelation and Divination in Ndembu Society* (Ithaca, N.Y.: Cornell University Press, 1975).

43. It is to this application of liminality to all ritual that J. Z. Smith and Bell, among others, object. Smith would not at all deny that some rituals release some people from social inhibitions in order to help those people to think about the larger social institutions from which the ritual action departs or to mark differences between those larger social practices and other social possibilities. Nor would Bell see the phenomenon of liminality in Ndembu ritual as other than the juxtaposition of several basic schemes in order to "reproduce" culture and forge "individual categories of experience." But the characteristics of particular ritual for both Bell and Smith are not universalized. Indeed, both Bell and Smith could almost certainly find rituals in which the net effect is to inhibit freedom and mutuality or, in Turner's terms, to reduce liminality.

44. Turner, *Ritual Process*, 97. The phrase "structure and anti-structure" provided the subtitle of his 1969 book entitled *The Ritual Process*.

45. Bell, *Ritual Theory, Ritual Practice*, 180.

46. The 2005 session of this seminar was dedicated to this topic. For papers presented around this subject, see the seminar Web site: http://www.philipharland.com/meals/GrecoRomanMealsSeminar.htm#Seminar_Papers_Online_(for_2005).

47. See the massive study by G. E. M. de Ste. Croix, *The Class Struggle in the Ancient Greek World from the Archaic Age to the Arab Conquests* (Ithaca, N.Y.: Cornell University Press, 1981), 31–276.

48. See Philo's description of the way the reclining order among the Therapeutae corresponded not to societal rank but to the rank within the meal community.

49. See Kathleen E. Corley, *Private Women, Public Meals: Social Conflict in the Synoptic Tradition* (Peabody, Mass.: Hendrickson, 1993).

50. Lucian, *Conviviales*, 13–15.

51. Klinghardt's chapter "Phora and Apophoreton: Zur Oekonomie von Gemeinschaften" in *Gemeinschaftsmahl und Mahlgemeinschaft* not only provides a key overview but has an exhaustive bibliography in the chapter's footnotes.

52. Pliny, *Epistulae* 2.6.

53. 1 Cor. 11:20-22.

54. There was no Jewish dietary proscription that insisted on eating vegetables. It was just that the meats allowed for Jewish diet needed to be prepared in a certain manner that was most likely unavailable in the locale to which Paul wrote.

55. It is difficult to see how Paul's position is consistent. In 14:3, he wrote: "Those who eat must not despise those who abstain, and those who abstain must not pass judgment on those who eat," indicating a requirement that both parties respect each other's position. Similarly, in 14:6 his position was: "Those who eat, eat in honor of the Lord, since they give thanks to God; while those who abstain, abstain in honor of the Lord and give thanks to God." Nevertheless, his decisive instruction in 14:20-21 contradicts the above by directing the gentiles *not* to eat meat because it scandalizes the Jewish members of the community.

56. This is not a matter of differences between Jews and "Christians," but a difference between a proto-"Christian" community with both Jewish and gentile members. It is almost certain that at this early date all Christian communities were understood implicitly as Jewish. The diversity of Judaism in the Greco-Roman world was extensive, and "Christians" were almost certainly understood as some kind of Jewish. That these "Christians" welcomed gentiles into their Jewish community was one of its interesting markers.

57. See Prov. 23:3, 6; Ben Sira 31:14-22 (16-26); and Philo, *The Contemplative Life*, 53–55.

58. Klinghardt, *Gemeinschaftsmahl und Mahlgemeinschaft*, 102.

59. Both Smith and Klinghardt have summaries of these variations. Klinghardt attends to the many differences more extensively than does Smith. Both seem somewhat frustrated at the variations in the literature about how many libations occurred and to whom. See Klinghardt, *Gemeinschaftsmahl und Mahlgemeinschaft*, 101–11; and Dennis Smith, *From Symposium to Eucharist: The Banquet in the Early Christian World* (Minneapolis: Fortress Press, 2003), 28–31.

60. Two classic, yet not outdated, surveys are Helmut Koester's two-volume *Introduction to the New Testament* (Berlin: Walter de Gruyter, 1995) and Ramsay MacMullen, *Paganism in the Roman Empire* (New Haven, Conn.: Yale University Press, 1981). For a more theoretical perspective, see Jonathan Z. Smith, *Drudgery Divine: On the Comparison of Early Christianities and the Religions of Late Antiquity* (Chicago: University of Chicago Press, 1990).

61. See de Ste. Croix, *Class Struggle in the Ancient Greek World*, 278–326, 409–51. For the toll that imperial domination took on occupied territories, see the summaries in Warren Carter, *Matthew and Empire: Initial Explorations* (Harrisburg, Pa.: Trinity Press International, 2001), and Richard Horsley, ed., *A People's History of Christianity*, vol. 1, *Christian Origins* (Minneapolis: Fortress Press, 2005). See Burton Mack's summary description of cultural

diversity in *A Myth of Innocence: Mark and Christian Origins* (Philadelphia: Fortress Press, 1988), 1–45.

62. This is attested to historically in two primary ways: (1) the extensive references to these gods and goddesses in popular literature and (2) archaeological attestation of at least two kinds—actual Hellenistic temples devoted to these deities and extensive epigraphic reference to them. See Koester, *Introduction to the New Testament,* vol. 2.

63. See Gerald Downing's survey of these interactions in *Cynics and Christian Origins* (Edinburgh: T. & T. Clark, 1992), and Burton Mack's summary of how this critique created interest in Judaism throughout the empire in both *Who Wrote the New Testament? The Making of the Christian Myth* (San Francisco: HarperSanFrancisco, 1995) and his essay in *Redescribing Christian Origins,* ed. Ron Cameron and Merrill P. Miller (Atlanta: Society of Biblical Literature, 2004).

64. J. Z. Smith's *Drudgery Divine* provides a clear summary of these movements along with an important critique of the notion of "mystery religion" from the nineteenth and twentieth centuries.

65. Two key studies of the imperial cult are S. R. F. Price, *Rituals and Power: The Roman Imperial Cult in Asia Minor* (Cambridge: Cambridge University Press, 1984), and Duncan Fishwick, *The Imperial Cult in the Latin West: Studies in the Ruler Cult of the Western Provinces of the Roman Empire* (Leiden: Brill, 1987).

66. A broad-ranging review of the literature on this phenomenon is provided in Robert J. Miller, *Born Divine: The Births of Jesus and Other Sons of God* (Santa Rosa, Calif.: Polebridge, 2003) .

67. Harland insists (in *Associations, Synagogues, and Congregations,* 61):

> We need to realize that in employing terms such as "religious" and "religion" we are dealing with abstractions that allow us to conceptualize our subject; we are not dealing with objective realities that the groups and persons we are studying would necessarily isolate from other aspects of life. The modern compartmentalization of life into the political, economic, social, and religious does not apply to the ancient context, where "religion" was very much embedded within various dimensions of daily life of individuals, whose identities were inextricably bound up within social groupings or communities. Within the Greco-Roman context, we are dealing with a worldview and way of life centered on the maintenance of fitting relations among human groups, benefactors, and the gods within the webs of connections that constituted society and the cosmos. To provide a working definition, "religion" or piety in antiquity had to do with appropriately honoring the gods and goddesses (through rituals of various kinds, especially sacrificial offerings) in ways that ensured the safety and protection of human communities (or groups) and their members. Moreover, the forms that such cultic honors (or "worship" to use a more modern term) could take do not necessarily coincide with modern or Western preconceptions of what being religious should mean.

68. See Stamenka Antonova, *Barbarian or Greek: The Charge of Barbarism and Early Christian Apologetics* (Ph.D. diss., Columbia University, 2005).

69. Actually, the process by which new religious adherence to the figures of Isis, Mithra, Eleusis, Osiris, Jesus, and the God of Israel occurred appears to have had at least two criteria. One was that the "new" religious figure be from another part of the Mediterranean world than were the adherents themselves (e.g., Isis became popular in Greece rather than her native Egypt; Jesus became popular in Syria and Asia Minor rather than Israel). The other was that the figure herself or himself be a part of a long historical tradition—that is, it seems to have been important that the "new" religious figure be "old."

70. Plutarch, *Questiones Conviviales*, 176E. See also Horaz, *Saturnalia*, 2, 6, 67, for another assertion of the lack of necessity of a *symposiarch*.

71. Dennis Smith, whose formal response to this chapter at the November 2007 session of the Society of Biblical Literature's Seminar on Meals in the Greco-Roman World was highly appreciative and endorsed this ritual theory approach, has expressed reservations on the application of this reading concerning the *symposiarch* role in Hellenistic times. (Smith's comments are available at www.philipharland.com.) Smith doubted this interpretation inasmuch as—according to Smith—the weak *symposiarch* existed also in Hellenic and classic texts about the meal. If this were so, it would indeed undermine my interpretation. It is, however, not at all clear to me that Smith's assertion about the ironically weak *symposiarch* in classical Greece holds. A rhetorically critical reading of Plutarch on this subject (see Klinghardt, *Gemeinschaftsmahl und Mahlgemeinschaft*, 116–18 for a summary of Plutarch's position but not a rhetorical critique of Plutarch's insistence that a strong and responsible *symposiarch* was necessary for the Hellenistic meal) would show, I think, that there was substantial anxiety about the weak *symposiarch* in Hellenistic times; that is, Plutarch's idealization of the power of the *symposiarch* can be read as an indication of the inverse in reality. Indeed, Plutarch's own worry about disorder at the meal reveals this behavior. And both Plutarch (*Questiones Conviviales*, 176) and Horaz (*Saturnalia*, 2, 6, 67) cite a classical ideal of not needing a *symposiarch* because behavior was so civil.

72. Philo's extensive description of the Therapeutae in *The Contemplative Life* made much of this group's having no servants but rather, out of love for one another, taking turns alternately serving one another and reclining.

73. Klinghardt, *Gemeinschaftsmahl und Mahlgemeinschaft*, 84–97.

74. As noted above, Plutarch's stories never acknowledged these uninvited guests as problems, but his instructions on how invited guests can help straighten things out ended up being a clear recognition of the problems. Although Plato also idealized the uninvited and late guests, it is much less clear whether these guests disturbed the meals as much in classical Greece as they did in later Hellenistic times. It may well have been that Plato's time experienced substantially fewer of these uninvited or late guests.

75. *Conviviales*, 43–47.

76. This is the position of Dennis Smith in his November 2007 response to this chapter at the Society of Biblical Literature's Seminar on Meals in the Greco-Roman World. See his "A Response to Hal Taussig's Paper" at www.philipharland.com.

Chapter Five: The Expansive Character of Early Christian Meals

1. See the extensive studies of a variety of scholars, including Wayne A. Meeks, *The First Urban Christians: The Social World of the Apostle Paul* (New Haven, Conn.: Yale University Press, 1983); Gerd Theissen, *The Social Setting of Pauline Christianity: Essays on Corinth* (Philadelphia: Fortress Press, 1982); and John Dominic Crossan, *The Historical Jesus: The Life of a Mediterranean Peasant* (San Francisco: HarperSanFrancisco, 1991). See also John Dominic Crossan, *The Birth of Christianity: Discovering What Happened in the Years Immediately after the Execution of Jesus* (San Francisco: HarperSanFrancisco, 1998); and John Dominic Crossan and Jonathan Reed, *In Search of Paul: How Jesus's Apostle Opposed Rome's Empire with God's Kingdom: A New Vision of Paul's Words and World* (San Francisco: HarperSanFrancisco, 2004).

2. See William. V. Harris, *Ancient Literacy* (Cambridge, Mass.: Harvard University Press, 1989); and Alan Bowman and Greg Wolff, eds., *Literacy and Power in the Ancient World* (Cambridge: Cambridge University Press, 1994).

3. The substantial research of the past two decades came into focus through the sustained collaborative work of a seminar on associations sponsored by the Canadian Society of Biblical Studies from 1988 to 1993. Many of the results of that seminar are now available in a volume edited by John S. Kloppenborg and Stephen G. Wilson, *Voluntary Associations in the Graeco-Roman World* (New York: Routledge, 1996). Canada has remained the center of this research, in particular the University of Toronto. Richard Ascough's *Paul's Macedonian Associations: The Social Context of Philippians and 1 Thessalonians* (Tübingen: Mohr Siebeck, 2003) is perhaps the most thorough application of the term *associations* to New Testament studies. Matthias Klinghardt, *Gemeinschaftsmahl und Mahlgemeinschaft* (Tübingen: Francke Verlag, 1996), 29–43, reviews older and newer associations research and attends most closely to the connection between associations and meals. Philip Harland, *Associations, Synagogues, and Congregations: Claiming a Place in Ancient Mediterranean Society* (Minneapolis: Fortress Press, 2003), serves at the moment as the best example and summary of this research. This methodologically fine-tuned and carefully documented work provides an extraordinarily clear picture of associations. Its proposal for the ways early "synagogues" and "churches" belong to this larger social organizational model of associations is compelling, although the book's other focus on describing the complex relationship between imperial cults and associations in Asia Minor gives the book two major theses and as such can seem distracting to a full documentation of the associations-synagogues-congregations link. This chapter returns to the work of Ascough, Harland, and Klinghardt as it unfolds the ways the associations research dovetails with meals and early Christianity.

4. See, for instance, Harland, *Associations, Synagogues, and Congregations*.

5. They include *collegium* (Latin), *secta* (Latin), *factio* (Latin), *koinon* (Greek), *koinonia* (Greek), *thiasos* (Greek), *orgeones* (Greek), *ekklesia* (Greek), *synagoge* (Greek), *eranos* (Greek), *marzeach* (Hebrew), and *havurah* (Hebrew). As becomes evident in the presentation of this research, the enthusiasm for these groups so developed in the Hellenistic period that the

groups often invented their own unique names, such as *hierourgoi* (sacrificing priests), *synethei* (intimates), or *mystai* (initiates), for their particular groups.

6. Dennis Smith, *From Symposium to Eucharist: The Banquet in the Early Christian World* (Minneapolis: Fortress Press, 2003), 87–132.

7. Klinghardt, *Gemeinschaftsmahl und Mahlgemeinschaft*, 12–37.

8. See Wilson, "Voluntary Associations: An Overview," 8–15; and Kloppenborg, "Collegia and *Thiasoi*: Issues in Function, Taxonomy and Membership," 17–26, in Kloppenborg and Wilson, *Voluntary Associations*; Harland, *Associations, Synagogues, and Congregations*, 8–62; and Kloppenborg, *Voluntary Associations*, 8–18.

9. Catherine T. Nerney and Hal Taussig, *Re-imagining Life Together in America: A New Gospel of Community* (Lanham, Md.: Sheed & Ward, 2002), 12.

10. See Harland, *Associations, Synagogues, and Congregations*, 34–61.

11. G. E. M. de Ste. Croix, *The Class Struggle in the Ancient Greek World from the Archaic Age to the Arab Conquests* (Ithaca, N.Y.: Cornell University Press, 1981), 112–204, 278–326, 453–73.

12. See Jean-Pierre Waltzing, *Étude Historique sur les Corporations Professionnelles Chez les Romains Depuis les Origines Jusqu'à la Chute de l'Empire d'Occident* (Louvain: C. Peeters, 1895–1900), 62–89.

13. G. E. M. de Ste. Croix's original and sometimes polemical study *Class Struggle in the Ancient Greek World* portrays the Hellenistic associations as having a key role in organizing poor people against imperial oppression. De Ste. Croix pays close attention to the numerous riots that stemmed directly from associational activities and the empire's violent responses, 290–333, 512–40. Although his case for a strong subversive role of the associations is more pointed, de Ste. Croix is not alone in his sense of the associations as representing malaise. Most of the nineteenth- and early-twentieth-century research, as noted in this chapter, saw the associations as signs of discontent with the degenerating Hellenistic age.

14. Nerney and Taussig, *Re-imagining Life Together in America*, 12.

15. Ibid., 11.

16. Because of the prevalence of associations' interest in proper burial for their members, nineteenth-century scholarship generally held that a major type of association was funereal. See Waltzing, *Étude Historique*, 172–77.

17. My position concerning the strength of the associations during the Hellenistic period does not mean to imply that they were the consequences of decline in democracy or the life of the Greek *polis* itself, as has been classically argued by E. G. L. Ziebarth, *Das griechische Vereinswesen* (Stuttgart: S. Hirzel, 1896); William Tarn and G. T. Griffin, *Hellenistic Civilization* (London: Arnold, 1952); Claude Mosse, *Athens in Decline, 404–86 B.C.* (London: Routledge and Kegan Paul, 1973); and Heinz Kreissig, "Die Polis in Griechenland und im Orient in der hellenistichen Epoche," 1074–84 in *Hellenische Poleis: Kriseó Wandlungenó Wirkung*, ed. Elisabeth Charlotte Welskopf (Berlin: Akademie, 1974), or innovatively argued by de Ste. Croix (*Class Struggle in the Ancient Greek World*), whose important work on the ways associations literature provides key insight into the lower classes' collective expression still stands.

I am convinced by Harland (*Associations, Synagogues, and Congregations*, 89–112) that this alleged causality is yet to be proved and is perhaps even completely in error. The problems with this argument are that a decline in democracy during the Hellenistic era may not be so demonstrable at the local levels; that the literary hyperbole around classical Greek democracy is yet to be accounted for; that the vitality of the *polis* as a vital cultural, economic, and social institution in Hellenistic times is difficult to dispute; and that a causal link between any tendencies toward decline of democracy and the *polis* during the Hellenistic period seems presumptuous. However, Harland's critique seems to leave completely open the question of why the associations themselves became so vital in the Hellenistic era. Curiously, even while he is demonstrating the communal, civic, religious, and cultural vitality of the associations in the Hellenistic period, he does not theorize on the causes of this relatively new social form. As noted above and in my previous work (Nerney and Taussig, *Re-imagining Life Together in America*), I see the expansive consciousness and the imperial interruption of the Alexandrian, Seleucid, and Roman empires in some causal relationship to the emergence of the strong association life of the Hellenistic era.

18. Nineteenth- and early-twentieth-century scholarship seemed to see funeral associations as the dominant type. See Theodor Mommsen, *De Collegis et sodaliciis romanorum* (Kiliae: Libraria Schwersiana, 1843); Jean-Pierre Waltzing, *Étude Historique*; and George La Piana, "Foreign Groups in Rome during the First Century of the Empire," *Harvard Theological Review* 20 (1927): 183–354. These associations seem to have been formed initially to guarantee burial for poor persons whose families most likely would be unable to finance a proper burial. Waltzing's summary volume *Étude Historique* was typical of the opinion that the initial funereal purpose for such associations was quickly overtaken by the more general socializing function of these associations—that is, the new associational activities (gathering for meals and community) of these groups soon overshadowed the initial burial needs. This early scholarship also did note that there were associations whose primary focus was religious or occupational. And, although not always included in the early associational typologies, earlier scholarship also paid attention to groups that gathered for meals for philosophical and school purposes. Especially Waltzing concentrated on describing the ways many associations were formed around the work of Hellenistic laborers (e.g., shipbuilders, cow herders, potters, physicians, weavers, and bakers). As noted below, this typology seems to have held value even in twenty-first-century scholarship, which also pictures a major kind of Hellenistic association as a gathering of particular kinds of workers among themselves. Nineteenth- and early-twentieth-century studies were very impressed with the religious or cultic character of many of the associations and therefore saw them as a distinct kind of association. Still depending on some of this typology, but refining it in relationship to meal practice, Klinghardt proposes seven different kinds of associations.

In the past twenty-five years, this typology of associations has been challenged by Frank Ausbüttel, John Kloppenborg, and Philip Harland. On closer examination of the Hellenistic inscriptions and literature, Ausbüttel could not find associations that were dedicated only to funereal purposes. See his *Untersuchungen zu den Vereinen im Westen des Römischen Reiches* (Kallmünz: M. Lassleben, 1982), 21–24.

19. Kloppenborg, "Collegia and *Thiasoi*," in Kloppenborg and Wilson, *Voluntary Associations*, 18.

20. Kloppenborg proceeded in the same essay to suggest that "perhaps a better taxonomy of collegia would be based on the profile of their membership, especially since the actual functions of various collegia overlapped to a substantial degree" ("Collegia and *Thiasoi*," 23). Kloppenborg also worries about "the functional boundaries" as criteria for establishing types of associations, even though his own categories also depend relatively heavily on functions.

21. Kloppenborg and Wilson, *Voluntary Associations*, 23–25.

22. Harland, *Associations, Synagogues, and Congregations*, 25.

23. Klinghardt, *Gemeinschaftsmahl und Mahlgemeinschaft*, 33, 43 (my translation).

24. Stephen G. Wilson, "Voluntary Associations: An Overview," in Kloppenborg and Wilson, *Voluntary Associations*, 12.

25. Harland, *Associations, Synagogues, and Congregations*, 63.

26. Ibid., 65.

27. Ibid., 77.

28. See Franz Poland, *Geschicte des Griechisches Vereinswesen* (Leipzig: Teubner, 1909). See both Kloppenborg's and Wilson's introductory essays in their edited volume *Voluntary Associations in the Graeco-Roman World* (Kloppenborg, "Collegia and *Thiasoi*," and Wilson, "Voluntary Associations: An Overview.")

29. A range of older scholarship has demonstrated this. See Lewis Richard Farnell, *The Higher Aspects of Greek Religion* (London: Williams and Norgate, 1912); W. S. Ferguson, "The Leading Ideas of the New Period," in *The Hellenistic Monarchies and the Rise of Rome*, ed. S. A. Cook, F. E. Adcock, and M. P. Charlesworth (Cambridge: Cambridge University Press, 1964); Martin P. Nilsson, *A History of Greek Religion*, trans. F. J. Fielden (Oxford: Clarendon, 1925); and W. K. C. Guthrie, *The Greeks and Their Gods* (Boston: Beacon, 1950).

30. Pivotal, of course, is Kloppenborg and Wilson, *Voluntary Associations*. See also my own previous use in Nerney and Taussig, *Re-imagining Life Together in America*.

31. See Jonathan Z. Smith, "Dayyeinu," in *Redescribing Christian Origins*. See Ascough, *Paul's Macedonian Associations*. Although he does refer to the debate, Philip Harland's book does not use the term, even though his mentor Kloppenborg has entitled his own book with the label.

32. Perhaps the most explicit and pointed work of the nineteenth century was done by G. Heinrici in a series of articles (see Works Consulted) from 1876 to 1881 and followed by his book *Die Erste Brief an die Korinther* (Göttingen: Vandenhoeck & Ruprecht, 1896). In the English world, Edwin Hatch's *The Organization of the Early Christian Churches: Eight Lectures* (London: Rivingtons, 1888) made a similar explicit positive comparison, although Hatch's insistence on an exact match between funereal societies and Christian congregations made his overall proposals more subject to quick critique than they deserved. See also Waltzing, *Étude Historique*.

33. See Ascough, *Paul's Macedonian Associations*; Harland, *Associations, Synagogues, and Congregations*; and Kloppenborg and Wilson, *Voluntary Associations*. See also the 1978

Reallexikon fuer Antike und Christentum article by Peter Hermann, J. H. Waszink, Carsten Colpe, and B. Koetting, "Genossenschaft" (10:83–155); Peter Marshall, *Enmity in Corinth: Social Conventions in Paul's Relations with the Corinthians* (Tübingen: J. C. B. Mohr, 1987); and S. C. Barton and Richard Horsley, "A Hellenistic Cult Group and the New Testament Churches," *Jahrbuch für Antike und Christentum* 24 (1981): 7–41.

34. See Meeks, *The First Urban Christians*, and Raymond E. Brown, *The Community of the Beloved Disciple* (New York: Paulist, 1979).

35. See Adolf Deissmann, *Paul: A Study in Social and Religious History*, trans. William E. Wilson (London: Hodder & Stoughton, 1926); and *Light from the Ancient East: The New Testament Illustrated by Recently Discovered Texts of the Graeco-Roman World*, trans. Lionel R. M. Strachan (London: Hodder & Stoughton, 1927). See Josiah Royce, *The Problem of Christianity* (Chicago: University of Chicago Press, 1913).

36. Meeks, *First Urban Christians*, 74–83.

37. Harland, *Associations, Synagogues, and Congregations*, 210.

38. See, for instance, Oscar Cullmann, *Early Christian Worship*, trans. A. Stewart Todd and James B. Torrance (London: SCM, 1953), 14–34, 67–82.

39. It is probably safe to assume that almost all such meetings involved reading Torah and praying. In most cases, ritual sacrifice along the lines of the Jerusalem Temple did not occur. However, there is both literary and archaeological evidence of a Jewish gathering place near Leontopolis in Egypt where Jewish ritual sacrifice did occur.

40. See the wide variety of meal references in the Qumran literature. Another well-described example is found in Philo's treatise on the Egyptian Jewish group the Therapeutae (*On the Contemplative Life*, 17–52).

41. Wayne O. McCready, "Ekklesia and Voluntary Associations," in Kloppenborg and Wilson, *Voluntary Associations*, 62.

42. Klinghardt, *Gemeinschaftsmahl und Mahlgemeinschaft*, 25 (my translation).

43. McCready, "Ekklesia and Voluntary Associations," 69–70.

44. John Kloppenborg, "Collegia and *Thiasoi*," in Kloppenborg and Wilson, *Voluntary Associations*, 18.

45. Wilson, "Voluntary Associations: An Overview," in Kloppenborg and Wilson, *Voluntary Associations*, 3–13, 4.

46. Ascough, *Paul's Macedonian Associations*, 190.

47. See www.philipharland.com.

48. Harland, *Associations, Synagogues, and Congregations*, 267–68.

49. Ibid., 267.

50. Ibid., 268–269.

51. It is a mistake to think of Judaism and Christianity as separate during at least the first 150 years of what eventually became Christianity. It is most likely that most groups who gathered with reference to Jesus or Christ in the first century thought of themselves as some part of the spiritual community of "Israel," even if such belonging was debated by other Jews and included somewhat experimental ways of being a part of Judaism. In this

way, distinguishing synagogues from churches in the first century would have been almost impossible, and most probably anachronistic. For instance, the Revelation to John's letter to "the angel of the church in Smyrna" includes the following challenge: "I know the slander on the part of those who say that they are Jews and are not, but are a synagogue of Satan" (2:8-9). Although it is unclear exactly what was meant, it is quite possible that the words *church* (Gk., *ekklesia*) and *synagogue* were meant to be synonymous here. At any rate, it is almost certain that to be a Jew and a member of a synagogue was seen as good by the writer of Revelation (and perhaps the same as being a part of "the church in Smyrna"), and that the Smyrnans' "pretending" to be Jews when they really were not was the problem being addressed. Even when early Christian literature seems to have preferred the term *ekklesia* for their groups (which was far from the consensus point of view), it was not necessarily a term that was used to exclude thinking of themselves as a synagogue.

52. Klinghardt, *Gemeinschaftsmahl und Mahlgemeinschaft*, 11 (my translation).

53. Harland, *Associations, Synagogues, and Congregations*, 212. Harland cites Philo, *On the Contemplative Life*; *Special Laws* 2.145–46; *Embassy to Gaius* 312–13; *On Virtues* 33.178; Tertullian, *Apology* 38, 39; Eusebius, *H.E.* 10.1.8., 303.

54. In these texts, the Greek word for "association" would be *koinon*.

55. One must hasten to add, however, that the term *association* is a twentieth- and twenty-first-century term about the ancient Mediterranean rather than a label indigenous to the Hellenistic Mediterranean itself; that is, the current term *association* is being used for a wide range of names of groups, listed at the beginning of this chapter. And this might not be simply an issue of terminology. It is possible that the current scholarly term *association* is too vague or broad. While this chapter holds the new "associations" research as very valuable for grasping the larger organizational character of early Christian churches, reasons for scholarly reservations concerning this larger umbrella term of *association* are understandable.

With this appreciation for the nuances of associations research, what then can be said about how much early "Christian" congregations can be or could have been considered Hellenistic associations? In summarizing this possibility, one final caution also needs acknowledgment. It would be a mistake to assume that all Christian gatherings in the first 150 years looked the same. There was clearly quite a diversity in these groups in terms of constituency (e.g., gender, class, Jewish practice, and ethnicity seem to have varied a good deal in early "Christian" communities). The social structure of the early Christian groups also seems to have varied (e.g., some met as family groups, others as trade groups, some as somewhat secret groups, and others as part of larger neighborhood gatherings). Ironically, this diversity of constituency and social structures in early Christian groups corresponds almost entirely with the types of associations summarized earlier in this chapter.

This chapter has shown how the recent research of Wilson, Ascough, and Harland demonstrates extensive parallels in behavior, membership, terminology, and community roles between associations and churches. The entire range of research has pointed out the striking parallels of associations and early churches gathering primarily at meals, a similarity to which this chapter returns in its conclusion. The work of Kloppenborg, Klinghardt, and Wilson has also noted that both those outside and inside referred to Christian groups as *collegia*, funeral associations, or "communities" (Gk., *koinonia*). That both associations as an organizational form and early Christianity as a movement blossomed in the Hellenistic era cannot be overlooked as a link between the two.

56. Several works of Gerd Theissen describe this early itinerancy of early Christian sages, notably "Itinerant Radicalism: The Tradition of Jesus Sayings from the Perspective of the Sociology of Literature," *Radical Religion* 2, nos. 2–3 (1975): 84-93. See also Theissen, *The Sociology of Early Palestinian Christianity* (Philadelphia: Fortress Press, 1978). His work *The Social Setting of Pauline Christianity: Essays on Corinth* (Philadelphia: Fortress Press, 1982) takes account of this dynamic also in Greece and Asia Minor.

57. The dynamics between the "prophet Jezebel" and the church in Thyatira are described (negatively) like this (2:19-21). Although only implicit, actually the relationship between "John of Patmos" (using this name to designate the author of the Revelation to John, whoever that was) and the seven churches of Asia Minor seems to have been according to this pattern—that is, it seems as if the author of the Revelation has visited these groups, in some cases gaining authority and in others apparent hostility.

58. Didache 12:1-2 gives explicit instructions on how long such sages/prophets can remain and makes explicit reference to their eating and drinking with the community.

59. In some cases, Paul's letters propose a relationship to an existing "Christian" group as between a teacher (Paul) and pupils, even if Paul has never met them. This is most explicit in his letter to the Romans: "I remember you always in my prayers, asking that by God's will I may somehow at last succeed in coming to you. For I am longing to see you so that I may share with you some spiritual gifts to strengthen you" (1:10-11).

60. See Matt. 10:5-15; Mark 6:7-13; Luke 9:1-6; 10:1-12, and GThom 14:4-5.

61. See Burton Mack, *The Lost Gospel: The Book of Q and Christian Origins* (San Francisco: HarperSanFrancisco, 1993); and Leif Vaage, *Galilean Upstarts: Jesus' First Followers According to Q* (Valley Forge, Pa.: Trinity Press International, 1994).

62. See N. T. Wright, *Who Was Jesus?* (Grand Rapids: Eerdmans, 1993); and Marcus Borg, *Meeting Jesus Again for the First Time: The Historical Jesus and the Heart of Contemporary Faith* (San Francisco: HarperSanFrancisco, 1994).

63. See Crossan, *Historical Jesus*; *The Birth of Christianity* (New York: HarperCollins, 1998); and his "Itinerants and Householders in the Earliest Kingdom Movement," in *Reimagining Christian Origins: A Colloquium Honoring Burton L. Mack*, ed. Elizabeth A. Castelli and Hal Taussig (Valley Forge, Pa.: Trinity Press International, 1996), 113–29.

64. Not only the above cited commissioning of the twelve and the seventy-two (seventy) but also many texts representing Jesus as an invited or uninvited guest sage at a meal (e.g., Luke 19:1-10 and John 2:1-12) illustrate this dynamic. It is clear to me that many of the texts with Jesus in this role of sage at a meal may not be so much reports of Jesus as stories reflecting on this ongoing practice of sages at meals.

65. Of course, the broader Hellenistic literature on meals does not discuss the early Christian sages forging a larger movement at meals. Rather, knowing this literature (as is now

possible, thanks to Klinghardt and Smith) helps us more deeply understand the social process of sages at meals. See, for instance, the appearance of the Cynic sage Pancrates, *Ep.* 3, 19.5-9. Other such examples are collected in M. L. West, *Iambi et Elegi Graeci ante Alexandrrum cantati*, I/II, and Kloppenborg and Wilson, *Voluntary Associations*, 86. Of course, perhaps the best description of these dynamics occurs in Plutarch's *Questiones Convivales*.

66. It was also the case that such sages later visited the more association-based churches and their meals. This is made especially clear in Revelation 2 and 3 and Didache 13–16.

67. See David L. Balch, "Paul's Portrait of Christ Crucified (Gal. 3:1) in Light of Paintings and Sculptures of Suffering and Death in Pompeiian and Roman Houses," in *Early Christian Families in Context: An Interdisciplinary Dialogue*, ed. David L. Balch and Carolyn Osiek (Grand Rapids: Eerdmans, 2003), 84–109. Also see Michael L. White, *The Social Origins of Christian Architecture*, 2 vols. (Valley Forge, Pa.: Trinity Press International, 1996), which studies the place of the dining room in first- through fourth-century houses.

68. One other known early Christian activity could have been a likely occasion for singing. Baptism—with its obvious ritual character—may well have entailed singing. And the kinds of language used in the early Christian hymns surveyed in this chapter do match well with baptism's evocation of beginnings.

69. See Jack T. Sanders, *New Testament Christological Hymns: Their Historical Religious Background* (Cambridge: Cambridge University Press, 1971). Perhaps one of the only somewhat social studies of the cosmological language of these songs occurs in Burton Mack's *Logos und Sophia* (Gottingen: Vandenhoeck & Ruprecht, 1973), 11–18, 178–82.

70. The only major study of the social function of early Christian hymns is that of Burton Mack in both *A Myth of Innocence: Mark and Christian Origins* (Philadelphia: Fortress Press, 1988), 103–8, and *Who Wrote the New Testament? The Making of the Christian Myth* (San Francisco: HarperSanFrancisco, 1995), 91–96. Both of these works are consulted below. As is noted below, Mack makes the case that the hymns functioned socially, and even relates them directly to his treatment of meals. He, however, does not picture the hymns at the meals. Indeed, still typical of earlier scholarship on hymns, Mack does not propose any social location for the performance of these hymns.

71. Singing belonged to all Greco-Roman meals. The songs or hymns sung at a wide spectrum of these meals tended to have a cosmic flavor to them. Although this chapter focuses on the early Christian meals and cosmic songs, it is important to insist that it was not just the early Christians who sang cosmic songs at their meals. See Frederick Clifton Grant's treatment of Isis hymns in *Hellenistic Religions: The Age of Syncretism* (New York: Liberal Arts Press, 1953), 128–33, as well as Dennis Smith's (*From Symposium to Eucharist*, 206–14) and Klinghardt's (*Gemeinschaftsmahl und Mahlgemeinschaft*, 101–10) backgrounding.

72. Form critical studies have shown that verses 5–7 and 15 are not hymnic in cadence or form, matching the change also in subject matter from the word to John the Baptizer. See Sanders, *New Testament Christological Hymns*, and Mack, *Logos und Sophia*. Various theories exists on the exact hymnic text. Some theories hold that the hymn itself may very well be Jewish and without reference to Jesus in its original form; see Sanders, *New Testament Christological*

Hymns, 44–45. Sanders notes how several New Testament hymns focus on the figure of Wisdom, implying that Wisdom herself may have been a standard subject for such songs (*New Testament Christological Hymns*, 44–45). Most treatments (e.g., Schnackenburg), however, do see the original hymn with an explicitly Jesus-based christological focus. Still others (e.g., Raymond Brown) see only verse 17 as introduced later, given its change in subject.

73. Here, too, there is some discussion of a pre-Christian version of the hymn, since the two explicit Christian references come at the end of obvious stanzas (the *ekklesia* in verse 18d, and the death on the cross at the end of the whole song). Most commentators, however, note that these two "endings" are literarily climactic and make a very strong, if hyperbolic, connection between Jesus' small *ekklesia* and his humiliating death on the cross and his cosmic status. And here, too, the references to Wisdom/Sophia seem clear (e.g., "the first-born of all creation" in Prov. 8:22-26; "all things existing" in her/him in Wis. 7:26; her/his "existence before all things" also in Prov. 8:22-28). Scholarship has tended to be clearer on the breaks for stanzas for this hymn (after vv. 16, 18, and 20) than for John 1. See Sanders's summary, 75–87.

74. The song form in Revelation is more extensive and is discussed at greater length later in this chapter.

75. Mack acknowledges throughout his larger treatment that this is a "hymn" (*Who Wrote the New Testament?* 91–96). His reference to it here as a poem is a recognition of the poetic form of the language.

76. Mack, *Who Wrote the New Testament?* 92–96.

77. Ibid., 87–91. Mack does refer to a "marvelous forum" at which these hymns were composed.

78. Although the assertion that the cosmic Christ hymns were sung primarily at the meals does not exist explicitly in print, Mack himself has numerous times acknowledged in private to this author that he assumes the meals were the location for these hymns.

79. Wilson and Kloppenborg's *Voluntary Associations* corrects the conclusions of nineteenth-century scholarship on the associations relative to funerals and funeral meals. Whereas it was asserted in the earlier research that funeral associations were a certain kind of association, it now appears clear that a guarantee of a funeral and an honorific meal for the deceased association member were a general practice of almost all associations (12–16).

80. See Eph. 5:14b; Rev. 5:9-10.

81. See earlier in this chapter on this dimension of the associations. Early scholarship on the associations proposed that there were specific kinds of associations that focused on this bond around funerals (see Waltzing, *Étude Historique*). First John Kloppenborg and then more recently Philip Harland have suggested that almost all Hellenistic associations included an assurance that each of its members would be buried and feted at a memorial meal of the association.

82. The status of the scene in Luke is compromised by a somewhat garbled manuscript tradition, resulting in two different cups at the Lukan Last Supper, with the memorial cup belonging to the less secure manuscript tradition.

83. Both Dennis Smith (*From Symposium to Eucharist*, 225-27) and Klinghardt (*Gemeinschaftsmahl und Mahlgemeinschaft*, 286–91) reject this trajectory. Focusing on the

Didache's completely different cup saying that has no connection to the Last Supper, John Dominic Crossan's examination of the meal trajectories insists that there were a number of different kinds of early Christian words said around the cup (*Historical Jesus*, 1991:322–328). Burton Mack's study of the textual traditions around the meal propose a much more diverse set of libational sayings about the cup in early Christianity; see *Myth of Innocence*, 299–302 and 275–76. Finally, Dennis Smith and Hal Taussig, *Many Tables: The Eucharist in the New Testament and Liturgy Today* (London: SCM, 1990), 42–47, 72–81, propose a broad range of cup sayings in the early churches.

Chapter Six: Meals of Resistance to Roman Imperial Power

1. See Brigitte Kahl, "Reading Galatians and Empire at the Great Altar of Pergamon," *Union Seminary Quarterly Review* 59, nos. 3–4 (2005): 21–43; Warren Carter, *The Roman Empire and the New Testament: An Essential Guide* (Nashville: Abingdon, 2006); and Warren Carter, *Matthew and Empire: Initial Explorations* (Harrisburg, Pa.: Trinity Press International, 2001).

2. N. T. Wright, "Paul's Gospel and Caesar's Empire," *Reflections* 2 (1998).

3. Richard Horsley, ed., *Paul and Empire: Religion and Power in Roman Imperial Society* (Harrisburg, Pa.: Trinity Press International, 1997), 141–42.

4. This is the translation by the Scholars Bible of *basileia tou theou*. See the discussion of this translation in Robert Miller, ed., *The Complete Gospels* (Santa Rosa, Calif.: Polebridge, 1994), 12. See also the extended discussion of the *basileia tou theou* as an anti-Roman discussion in John Dominic Crossan, *The Historical Jesus: The Life of a Mediterranean Jewish Peasant* (San Francisco: HarperSanFrancisco, 1991), 265–302.

5. Carter, *Roman Empire and the New Testament*, 99.

6. Kahl, "Reading Galatians and Empire at the Great Altar of Pergamon," 40.

7. Ibid., 41.

8. Dieter Georgi, *Theocracy in Paul in Praxis and Theology* (Minneapolis: Fortress Press, 1991), 83.

9. Horsley, *Paul and Empire*, 140.

10. N. T. Wright, "Paul's Gospel and Caesar's Empire," *Reflections* 2 (1998).

11. Karen L. King, *The Secret Revelation of John* (Cambridge, Mass.: Harvard University Press, 2006), 168.

12. Carter, *Roman Empire and the New Testament*, 21.

13. Wendy Cotter, "The Collegia and Roman Law: State Restrictions on Voluntary Associations, 64 BCE–200 CE," in *Voluntary Associations in the Graeco-Roman World*, ed. John S. Kloppenborg and Stephen G. Wilson (London: Routledge, 1996).

14. Philip Harland, *Associations, Synagogues, and Congregations: Claiming a Place in Ancient Mediterranean Society* (Minneapolis: Fortress Press, 2003).

15. Cotter, "Collegia and Roman Law," 76, cites Asconius, *In Seantu contra L. Pisonem* 8.

16. Cotter, "Collegia and Roman Law," 76.

17. Ibid.

18. Ibid., 79.

19. Ibid., 82–86.

20. Ibid., 88.

21. Ibid., 77.

22. Ibid., 78.

23. Ibid., 87.

24. Ibid., 88.

25. Harland, *Associations, Synagogues, and Congregations*, 268, 173.

26. Ibid., 136.

27. Ibid., 160.

28. Chapters 6 and 9 of Harland's work actually proactively both recognize and downplay these association-empire tensions in their common title "Tensions in Perspective."

29. As noted in chapter 2 of this book, Harland's contribution to the identification of synagogues and "Christian" congregations with associations is a major achievement.

30. Harland, *Associations, Synagogues, and Congregations*, 237.

31. Harland devotes most of his last chapter to discussion of the highly anti-imperial language of the Revelation to John, which almost certainly was written to and/or in Asia Minor. This forces an acknowledgment of strong evidence of anti-imperial expression within early Christianity. Harland, however, mostly attributes this strong anti-Roman stance as either "rhetorical situation and strategy" or an unrealistic or untenable position by the author(s) of the Revelation to John (253). Since, finally, this current book concludes that Harland does not take anti-imperial dimensions of associations—Christian and otherwise—seriously enough (see the following pages) and since other dimensions of Harland's book are very valuable both for this current work and for the study of early Christianity's relationship to associations, a sustained citation of Harland's position on the Revelation to John is appropriate (*Associations, Synagogues, and Congregations*, 262):

> John calls on Christians to distance themselves from such aspects of civic life, but it is not always clear what, practically speaking, John expected these people living in the cities of Asia to do. He certainly wanted them to avoid sacrificial food that had been offered to imperial and other gods within any social context, including the communal meals of guilds. He also would want them to avoid the guilds altogether since imperial rituals and other practices he considered idolatrous took place in them. This would require that Christians limit social and business contacts with fellow workers and other merchants and traders. He also certainly did not approve of involvement in the production and trade of goods that contributed, in his view, to the well-being of an evil empire whose ultimate demise was imminent. How, then, did John expect Christians to make a living?

Were they to live in isolation from others? What occupations were acceptable? How would a local Christian merchant or dyer continue in his or her occupation without maintaining at least some friendly contacts with both fellow workers and with wealthier customers or patrons? How was one to avoid all contact with an imperialism that was embedded within virtually all of the polis? The Apocalypse does not provide clear answers to such questions, and we are left wondering.

32. Harland, *Associations, Synagogues, and Congregations*, 268–69.

33. See especially the work of Brigitte Kahl in her new book *Galatians Reimagined: Through the Eyes of the Vanquished* (Minneapolis: Fortress Press, 2008). See also Kahl, "Reading Galatians and Empire at the Great Altar of Pergamon."

34. Harland, *Associations, Synagogues, and Congregations*, 251–63.

35. Ibid., 231–37.

36. Ibid., 268, 269.

37. See G. E. M. de Ste. Croix, *The Class Struggle in the Ancient Greek World from the Archaic Age to the Arab Conquests* (Ithaca, N.Y.: Cornell University Press, 1981), 112–203.

38. Plutarch, *Questiones Conviviales* 616E–F.

39. James C. Scott, *Domination and the Arts of Resistance: Hidden Transcripts* (New Haven: Yale University Press, 1990).

40. Again here, the use of the term *Christian* must be acknowledged in general as anachronistic. The monotheism of many of these Christ or Jesus associations was almost certainly understood by both the meal participants and the outside observers as Jewish.

41. Recent scholarship proposing antagonism between early Christians and Rome often characterizes the tension in theological terms. This explanation would have it that early Christians' loyalty to one God or to Jesus as Savior and Lord created (and expressed) the antagonism. While this is undeniably the case, framing the antagonism simply as a theopolitical conflict ignores the embedded anti-imperial social visions entailed in gathering at a meal at all. From the Roman point of view, the overarching paranoia about whether any association was using the meal gathering for seditious planning illustrates that having this kind of meal in and of itself was problematic. In this light, current twentieth- and twenty-first-century scholarship's emphasis on a theological cause of Christian-Roman tension appears overly focused on the importance of ideology and not attentive enough to the political dimensions of (counter-) cultural practice.

42. As Cotter wonders, it is likely that the first two generations (and perhaps as long as the first two hundred years in some locations) of early Christian meals were understood as Jewish, both by their participants and by the Romans, and therefore were by and large exempt from Roman suspicion on the grounds of their monotheistic rejection of the emperor's divine right to rule the "world."

43. It is my position that the early Christians—even in the first several generations—were under quite regular pressure from Roman oppression—not because they were "Christians" per se but because all elements of the nonelite occupied populations were under pressure,

constraint, and random explicit oppression.

44. Matthias Klinghardt, *Gemeinschaftsmahl und Mahlgemeinschaft* (Tübingen: Francke Verlag, 1996), 163–74.

45. Ibid., 163 (my translation).

46. This Acts 2:44-46 text is not meant to be taken as historically accurate. It is cited here simply as an illustration of how Luke uses the link between meal behavior and sociopolitical models of resistance.

47. Adela Yarbro Collins, *Crisis and Catharsis: The Power of the Apocalypse* (Philadelphia: Westminster, 1984), 144–45, 153–54.

48. Massey Hamilton Shepherd, *The Paschal Liturgy and the Apocalypse* (Richmond, Va.: John Knox, 1960), 78.

49. Ibid., 78.

50. Ibid., 96–97.

51. Shepherd's overarching thesis, which drew parallels between third- to fifth-century paschal liturgies of early Christianity with Revelation, is, of course, with the advent of later studies on the Hellenistic meal as the primary modality of first-century Christian "worship" gatherings, no longer tenable. However, his study's emphasis on the Hallel psalms, hymnody, and ritual participation in relationship to a long list of Revelation passages is still usable with the newer data.

52. See Otto Piper, "The Apocalypse of John and Liturgy of the Ancient Church," *Church History* (1951): 10–22; and Colleen McDannell and Bernhard Lang, *Heaven: A History* (New Haven, Conn.: Yale University Press, 1988), 36–41.

53. "Look, I am standing at the door, knocking. If anyone answers and opens the door, I will come in and eat a meal at that person's side" (Rev. 3:20).

54. See Robert Miller's commentary on the translation of *basileia* as "empire" or "imperial rule" of God in *Complete Gospels*, 12.

55. Warren Carter, *Matthew and Empire*, 170.

56. The Greek is *basileis*, which can be translated "rulers," "kings," or "emperors."

57. Both Mark's (10:41-45) and Matthew's (20:20-24) versions of this saying were somewhat less explicit in their reference to meals. There was no reference to reclining and no narrative context of a meal, but the saying was immediately preceded by other meal vocabulary related to whether the disciples can drink Jesus' cup. Both Matthew's and Mark's versions of the saying use the Greek *diakoneo* (to serve) as the pivotal term in the saying. *Diakoneo* has a range of meanings, including "to manage." But this verb was the primary verb used for service at meals. Smith also thinks that the term *diakonos* in v. 43 is best translated as "table servant," although he—as I do—thinks that the prevalence of the term *kathizein* (to sit) most likely referred to a court setting, not a meal setting. Dennis Smith, *From Symposium to Eucharist: The Banquet in the Early Christian World* (Minneapolis: Fortress Press, 2003), 246.

58. Philo, *The Contemplative Life*, 48–64.

59. Ibid., 72.

60. Eusebius, *Ecclesiastical History*, 2:17, 18.

61. Smith, *From Symposium to Eucharist*, 245.

62. Ibid., 245.

63. Even the relatively conservative (Roman Catholic) *New Jerusalem Bible* (New York: Doubleday, 1985) comments in its textual notes: "Not by direct revelation, but from a tradition going back to the Lord. Here, as in 15:3-7, *see* 15:3b. Paul is using the technical terminology of the rabbis for the passing on of tradition: he seems to be quoting from the earliest Christian tradition about the Eucharist, couched in terms and phrases untypical of Paul" (p. 1903). See Burton Mack's more scholarly study of this "tradition" as an etiological legend in *A Myth of Innocence: Mark and Christian Origins* (Philadelphia: Fortress Press, 1988), 99–100, 116–20.

64. See Crossan, *Historical Jesus*, 360–67; Mack, *Myth of Innocence*, 118–20; and Hal Taussig, "The Meals of the Historical Jesus" (paper presented at Westar Institute Meeting, Spring 1992).

65. See Mack, *Myth of Innocence*, 105–8, 261–62, concerning the important Markan proclivity toward Jesus' death as a martyr. This reinforces the notion above that the libation focused on the meaning of Jesus' death as a resister.

66. An extended analysis of these very significant manuscript variations is found in Bruce M. Metzger, *A Textual Commentary on the Greek New Testament* (Stuttgart: United Bible Societies, 1971), 173–77, including a charting of the five significant manuscripts that do not have the "cup is my blood" work in Luke at all.

67. Mack, *Myth of Innocence*, 301.

68. Whether the injunction to repeat the libation in Jesus' memory was Paul's idea or one he inherited makes a great deal of difference in the way one positions Paul and his predecessors in relationship to the Roman Empire. If Paul innovated the command, it would make him a strong provocateur of Rome. If he inherited it, it might not make him less resistant to Rome, but it would position pre-Pauline "Christianity" as importantly anti-imperial.

69. Klinghardt, *Gemeinschaftsmahl und Mahlgemeinschaft*, 310 (my translation). Klinghardt lists a wide variety of Greek and Latin texts that use bread as a symbol for the unity of a group (see pp. 310–15).

70. Klinghardt, *Gemeinschaftsmahl und Mahlgemeinschaft*, 311 (my translation). Klinghardt's survey of these texts is on pp. 308–15.

71. Interestingly enough, Klinghardt's extensive review of literature on this finds the preponderance of body = association uses in the Latin rather than the Greek.

72. See Klinghardt, *Gemeinschaftsmahl und Mahlgemeinschaft*, 310–12, especially the extensive footnotes.

73. Construction of a first-century meaning of bread = body without significant reference to the crucifixion would depend on two additional elements: (1) a separation of the saying about bread and body from the narrative context, and (2) a comparison with the bread blessing in the Didache, which did not reference Jesus' death at all.

74. See also the implications of breaking the bread in relationship to the larger Hellenistic practice of discerning the future through examining the entrails of the sacrificed bodies of animals to be eaten at Hellenistic meals. Stanley Stowers's essay on the possibility that early

Christian breaking of bread was to be understood within this paradigm has implications for meanings concerning resistance—that is, inasmuch as one broke the bread and discerned Jesus' crucified body, this could have served these meal communities as a negotiation and contemplation of the possible consequences of their gathering around such a body. See Stowers, "Elusive Coherence: Ritual and Rhetoric in 1 Corinthians 10-11," in *Reimagining Christian Origins: A Colloquium Honoring Burton L. Mack*, ed. Elizabeth A. Castelli and Hal Taussig (Valley Forge, Pa.: Trinity Press International, 1996), 68–86.

75. See Mack, *Myth of Innocence*, 260–68.

76. Burton Mack, *Who Wrote the New Testament? The Making of the Christian Myth* (San Francisco: HarperSanFrancisco, 1995), 90.

77. Ibid., 90.

78. Mack, *Myth of Innocence*, 119.

79. Ibid., 119.

80. Ibid., 304. Mack has vacillated on whether this etiology happened at the pre-Pauline or Pauline level (116–21).

81. Klinghardt, *Gemeinschaftsmahl und Mahlgemeinschaft*, 308.

82. See Werner Kelber, *The Oral and the Written Gospel: The Hermeneutics of Speaking and Writing in the Synoptic Tradition, Mark, Paul and Q.* (Philadelphia: Fortress Press, 1983), xxii–xxiii.

83. It is now clear from a variety of scholarship that some early Christian literature served more as a tradition of ritual or entertainment performance than as simply written record. See Richard Pervo's fine analysis of the entertainment value of the textually volatile Acts of the Apostles and other early Christian Acts. Also, Adela Yarbro Collins's analysis of the cathartic function of the Revelation to John (*Crisis and Catharsis*) posits both drama and ritual at the heart of that document. See also Allan Callahan's keen and provocative analysis of the form of the *Gospel of Thomas* in "'No Rhyme or Reason': The Hidden Logia of the Gospel of Thomas," *Harvard Theological Review* 90, no. 4 (1997): 411–26.

84. See Philip Harland's position in this regard concerning the general assumption that congregations, synagogues, and associations in Asia Minor were most likely regarded as the same thing (*Associations, Synagogues and Congregations*, 177–270). Of course, this does not necessarily mean that the Jewish and Christian kinds of "associations" were necessarily all regarded as Jewish. For the larger question of the conflations of Jewish and Christian identity, see, among others, Daniel Boyarin, *Border Lines: The Partition of Judaeo-Christianity* (Philadelphia: University of Pennsylvania Press, 2004). See also Judith Lieu, *Neither Jew nor Greek? Constructing Early Christianity* (London: Clark, 2002), in which Lieu writes: "Some of the most important insights into the nature of 'early Christianity' in recent study have arisen out of a recognition of its Jewishness; continuities provide the framework within which discontinuity can be explored. Growing awareness of the rich variety of 'Judaism' at the end of the Second Temple period, an awareness fuelled by discoveries such as that of the Dead Sea Scrolls but also by renewed interest in literature other than that of developing rabbinic Judaism, has made it possible to locate the early 'Christians' within that diversity" (2).

85. James C. Scott, *Domination and the Arts of Resistance: Hidden Transcripts* (New Haven, Conn.: Yale University Press, 1990), 136.

86. Ibid., 137.

87. Ibid., 157.

88. Klinghardt, *Gemeinschaftsmahl und Mahlgemeinschaft*, 162, 163 (my translation).

89. Scott, *Domination and the Arts of Resistance*, 118.

90. Ibid., 118–19.

91. Ibid., 124.

92. Ibid., 138.

93. Ibid., 141.

94. Ibid., 172–86.

95. Ibid., 181.

Chapter Seven: Meals and Early Christian Social Experimentation

1. See Matthias Klinghardt, *Gemeinschaftsmahl und Mahlgemeinschaft* (Tübingen: Francke Verlag, 1996), 143–52.

2. See Mary Douglas, *Purity and Danger: An Analysis of Concepts of Pollution and Taboo* (Boston: K. Paul, 1966).

3. See Bruce J. Malina and Jerome H. Neyrey, *Portraits of Paul: An Archaeology of Ancient Personality* (Louisville, Ky.: Westminster John Knox, 1996); and Bruce J. Malina and Jerome H. Neyrey, *Calling Jesus Names: The Social Value of Labels in Matthew* (Sonoma, Calif.: Polebridge, 1988).

4. See K. C. Hanson and Douglas Oakman, *Palestine in the Time of Jesus: Social Structures and Social Conflicts* (Minneapolis: Fortress Press, 1998).

5. See Bruce J. Malina, *The New Testament World: Insights from Cultural Anthropology* (Atlanta: John Knox, 1981).

6. See Klinghardt, *Gemeinschaftsmahl und Mahlgemeinschaft*, 21–44; Richard Ascough, *Paul's Macedonian Associations: The Social Context of Philippians and 1 Thessalonians* (Tübingen: Mohr Siebeck, 2003), 28–46; Philip Harland, *Associations, Synagogues, and Congregations: Claiming a Place in Ancient Mediterranean Society* (Minneapolis: Fortress Press, 2003), 25–88, 137–60.

7. Luke/Acts has indirect evidence of a patron-based meal model. The list of (women) financial supporters of Jesus—while not to be taken seriously as a report of the historical Jesus' activity—may suggest a Lukan model of association based in an aristocratic family or group sponsorship. Michael White has demonstrated that Lukan vocabulary about houses indicates the villas of the wealthy; see *Building God's House in the Roman World: Architectural Adaptation among Pagans, Jews and Christians* (Baltimore: Johns Hopkins University Press, 1990). This would fit larger association models suggested by John S. Kloppenborg and Stephen G. Wilson (see *Voluntary Associations in the Graeco-Roman World* [London: Routledge, 1996], 10–26) in

which wealthy families both sponsored and provided much of the membership of such a group. Paul's attentiveness in the Corinthian correspondence to certain named individuals may also indicate the possibility of (a) patron(s) for the Corinthian group(s).

8. Paul's letters to Philippi and Thessalonica have strong intimations of non-patron-based associations. See Richard Ascough's studies in *Paul's Macedonian Associations*; Warren Carter's portrait of Matthean "community" (*Matthew and Empire: Initial Explorations* [Harrisburg, Pa.: Trinity Press International, 2001]) emphasizes its egalitarian structures and concerns.

9. Of course, the archaeological and epigraphic evidence that complements so closely the wide and deep range of texts has also been crucial in Dennis Smith and Klinghardt's independent confirmation of the substantial role of meals in Hellenistic culture.

10. The stories making up the collections are the healing of the woman with a flow of blood (Mark 5:25-34), healing of the blind (Mark 8:22-26; John 9:1-11), healing of the deaf man (Mark 7:31-37), raising of Jairus's daughter (Mark 5:22-24, 35-42), stilling of the storm (Mark 4:35-40), walking on the sea (Mark 6:47-50; John 6:16-21), feeding of the five thousand (Mark 6:33-44; John 6:1-13), feeding of the four thousand (Mark 8:1-9), healing of a man at the pool (John 5:2-9), raising of Lazarus (John 11:1-44), and turning of water into wine (John 2:1-10).

11. See initial work by C. H. Dodd, *Historical Tradition in the Fourth Gospel* (Cambridge: Cambridge University Press, 1963), and Rudolf Bultmann, *The Gospel of John: A Commentary*, trans. G. R. Beasley-Murray, ed. R. W. N. Hoare and J. K. Riches (Oxford: Blackwell, 1971). This was followed by nearly a half century of research and publication by Robert Fortna (e.g., *The Signs Gospel* and *The Fourth Gospel and Its Predecessor*), which has recently been resummarized and extended by Fortna in a 2005 book.

12. Achtemeier's series of articles in the early 1980s on what he calls the "miracle cantenae," or chains, has served as a pivotal analysis of the texts and a joining of the pre-Johannine and pre-Markan scholarship. Mack's *A Myth of Innocence: Mark and Christian Origins* (Philadelphia: Fortress Press, 1988), 92, and *Who Wrote the New Testament? The Making of the Christian Myth* (San Francisco: HarperSanFrancisco, 1995), 63–67, have followed Achtemeier's literary analysis and social sketches and placed them in a larger assessment of pregospel Galilean Jesus movements.

13. Also, there is dependence of some Exodus imagery. Achtemeier and Fortna have also proposed an internal organization to the collection of stories.

14. Fortna develops the initial proposal by Dodd and details a number of other literary characteristics shared by the various "signs" stories.

15. Achtemeier, "The Origin and Function of the Pre-Marcan Miracle Catenae," *Journal of Biblical Literature* 91, no. 22 (1972): 198–221.

16. Dennis Smith, in his more recent *From Symposium to Eucharist: The Banquet in the Early Christian World* (Minneapolis: Fortress Press, 2003), has confirmed Achtemeier's and Mack's sense that the feedings stories had to do with the gathering of a Galilean community at a special kind of meal. Analyzing the vocabulary of the miraculous feeding stories in relationship to Hellenistic meals, Smith concludes that the feeding stories are indeed meant to be reflections

on gatherings at meals (222).

17. Mack, *Myth of Innocence*, 92; Mack, *Who Wrote the New Testament?* 63–67.

18. This point is, of course, made by numerous commentators on the gospels' miracle stories and does not necessarily need a pregospel literary analysis for its validation. Perhaps the most assertive argument for this socially inclusive character of a gospel's notion of miracles is Ched Myers's treatment of Mark in *Binding the Strong Man: A Political Reading of Mark's Story of Jesus* (Maryknoll, N.Y.: Orbis, 1988).

19. Mack, *Myth of Innocence*, 91–93.

20. Ibid., 92–93.

21. Ibid., 67.

22. This is not to say that no miracles stories have antagonists. Indeed, there are a number of miracles stories that have strong antagonism near the heart of their narrative. For instance, the miracles in which the performing of a miracle on the Sabbath (e.g., John 9) are written around such antagonism. What is remarkable, however, is that the pre-Markan miracle chains identified by Achtemeier contain none of these miracles. Similarly, John 9, which belongs to the pregospel "signs" source, has this dimension only in its Johannine redacted form. Indeed, the entire miracle of the healing of the blind man is recounted without mentioning that it happened on the Sabbath. Only the Johannine redaction in 9:14 of the earlier story added that the healing was done on the Sabbath.

23. See Dennis Smith's analysis of the ways the vocabulary of the feeding stories mimics the logistics of the larger paradigm of meals in dining rooms (*From Symposium to Eucharist*, 240).

24. See R. Alan Culpepper, *Anatomy of the Fourth Gospel: A Study in Literary Design* (Philadelphia: Fortress Press, 1983), 162–74, for a critique of this hypothesis.

25. When this investigation explores the character of gendered participation in pre-Pauline meals, 1 Cor. 12:13, which may have left women out of its formula intentionally, is consulted as well.

26. Antoinette Clark Wire, *The Corinthian Women Prophets: A Reconstruction through Paul's Rhetoric* (Minneapolis: Fortress Press, 1990), 96.

27. Ibid., 96–97.

28. Ibid., 96–97.

29. See the thorough study by Kathleen Corley in *Private Women, Public Meals: Social Conflict in the Synoptic Tradition* (Peabody, Mass.: Hendrickson, 1993).

30. Wire, *Corinthian Women Prophets*, 72–97.

31. See Smith, *From Symposium to Eucharist*, and Dennis Smith, "Table Fellowship as a Literary Motif in the Gospel of Luke," *JBL* 106, no. 4D (1987): 613–28.

32. See Turid Seim, *The Double Message: Patterns of Gender in Luke and Acts* (Nashville: Abingdon, 1994), 112–18; Elisabeth Schüssler Fiorenza, "A Feminist Critical Interpretation for Liberation: Martha and Mary: Luke 10:38-42," *Religion and Intellectual Life* 3, no. 2 (Winter 1986): 21–36; Hal Taussig, "The Sexual Politics of Luke's Mary and Martha Account: An Evaluation of the Historicity of Luke 10:38-42," *Forum* 7, nos. 3–4 (1991): 317–19.

33. See Corley, *Private Women, Public Meals.*

34. See Barbara E. Reid, *Choosing the Better Part? Women in the Gospel of Luke* (Collegeville, Minn.: Liturgical Press, 1996); Elisabeth Schüssler Fiorenza, *In Memory of Her: A Feminist Theological Reconstruction of Christian Origins* (New York: Crossroad, 1994); and Robert Price, *The Widow Traditions in Luke-Acts: A Feminist Critical Scrutiny* (Atlanta: Scholars, 1997), all complement Seim's position.

35. Even while acknowledging some of the textually conservative dimensions, Elisabeth Schüssler Fiorenza claims this as a central moment, for which she names her pivotal book *In Memory of Her.*

36. Hal Taussig, "Dealing under the Table: Ritual Negotiation of Women's Power in the Syro-Phoenician Woman Pericope," in *Reimagining Christian Origins: A Colloquium Honoring Burton L. Mack*, ed. Elizabeth A. Castelli and Hal Taussig (Valley Forge, Pa.: Trinity Press International, 1996), 264–79.

37. An example already cited in the introduction is Adolf von Harnack, *Expansion of Early Christianity in the First Three Centuries* (New York: Putnam, 1904), 77–87. See also N. T. Wright, *The Resurrection of the Son of God* (Minneapolis: Augsburg Fortress, 2003).

38. "When he rebukes Peter in Antioch, it is not for Peter's practice of keeping a kosher table, but for Peter's changing his attitudes under pressure from Jerusalem." Krister Stendahl, *Paul among Jews and Gentiles and Other Essays* (Philadelphia: Fortress Press, 1976), 2–3.

39. Two new studies address this overarching Greco-Roman prejudice: Davina Lopez, *Apostle to the Conquered: Reimagining Paul's Mission*, Paul in Critical Contexts Series (Minneapolis: Fortress Press, 2008); and Stamenka Antonova, "Barbarian or Greek? The Charge of Barbarism and Early Christian Apologetics" (Ph.D. diss., Columbia University/Union Theological Seminary, 2005).

40. Characterizing Jews as barbaric was a common strategy of Hellenistic gentile rhetoricians. Circumcision was most often used as the example of Jewish barbarism. See William V. Harris, ed., *The Spread of Christianity in the First Four Centuries: Essays in Explanation* (Boston: Brill, 2005).

41. See Philo, *The Contemplative Life.*

42. See Hal Taussig, "Jerusalem as Occasion for Conversation: The Intersections of Acts 15 and Galatians 2," *Forum*, n.s., 4, no. 1 (2001): 89–104.

43. See Jacob Neusner's summary of the Pharisees as an "eating circle" in his *Neusner on Judaism* (Burlington, Vt.: Ashgate, 2004), 385–99. Neusner uses the term *ritual* in a very different way than this study does. He insists that Pharisees' meals were important identity markers but that they were not "rituals" like the meals of the Christians. There are almost certainly valid distinctions made by Neusner in this regard, but the distinctions cohabitate thoroughly with both his and my insistence that the Pharisaic meals were important in the establishment of Jewish identities. For the role of Rome in this dynamic, see Seth Schwarz, *Imperialism and Jewish Society, 200 B.C.E. to 640 C.E.* (Princeton, N.J.: Princeton University Press, 2001).

44. Acts and Galatians seem to reverse the sequence of controversy at Antioch and meeting in Jerusalem.

45. Mark 7:31 is confusing in that it places Jesus "by way of Sidon toward the sea of

Galilee, through the Decapolis territory." The problem here is that the three locations are in quite different areas. When put together, they at least suggest gentile territory.

46. This corresponds to another dimension of Mark 8 in that it is in this chapter that Peter confesses Jesus to be the anointed one near Caesarea Philippi (which is also outside of Israel).

47. Matthew 15:32-39 follows Mark quite closely but recognizes the problematic geography in Mark. Matthew has Jesus return to the sea of Galilee and go up on a mountain. This would be more likely on the gentile side of the sea, but it cannot be certain that Matthew, who corrects Mark in terms of the woman being a "Canaanite" rather than Syro-Phoenician, wants the second feeding on gentile territory.

48. See Werner Kelber, *Mark's Story of Jesus* (Philadelphia: Fortress Press, 1979), 40–42; Norman A. Beck, "Reclaiming a Biblical Text: The Mark 8:14-21 Discussion about Bread in a Boat," *Catholic Biblical Quarterly* 43, no. 1 (January 1981): 49–56; and Myers, *Binding the Strong Man*, 225–26. Beck summarizes (52): "The number 5 (5 loaves and 5,000 men), the number 12 (12 baskets) and the Hebrew name for basket (*kophinos*) belong to the Jewish circle; the number 7 (7 loaves and 7 baskets), the number 4 (4,000 men or people), and the Greek name for basket (*syris*) belong more specifically to the Greek."

49. In 10:21, Paul rejects eating such meat: "You cannot have a share at the Lord's table and the demons' table as well." In 10:25, Paul seems to say that eating such meat is acceptable: "Eat anything that is sold in the butchers' shops." In 10:26-28, Paul is equivocal: "If an unbeliever invites you to a meal, go if you want, and eat whatever is put before you; you need not ask questions of conscience first. But if someone says to you, 'This food has been offered in sacrifice,' do not eat it."

50. See Taussig, "Jerusalem as Occasion for Conversation."

51. For recent scholarship, see the important volumes by Joseph Tyson, *Marcion and Luke-Acts: A Defining Struggle* (Columbia: University of South Carolina Press, 2006); and Richard I. Pervo, *Dating Acts* (Santa Rosa, Calif.: Polebridge, 2006). A more established and proven study with the same position is Hans Conzelmann, *Acts of the Apostles: A Commentary on the Acts of the Apostles*, trans. James Limburg, A. Thomas Kraabel, and Donald H. Juel; ed. Eldon J. Epp with Christopher R. Matthews, Hermeneia Series (Philadelphia: Fortress Press, 1987).

Chapter Eight: Identity Performance as a New Paradigm for the Study of Christian Beginnings

1. Many scholars have noted that *basileia* was the Greek term used for "empire" as well as "kingdom" and have proposed accounting for that context and meaning in the translation of the *basileia* of God. Also, the term *kingdom* has not been received well in feminist circles because of its masculine valence. Finally, a number of translators have worried about the lack of "kingdom" as a social reality in the (post)modern world. This has led to such other translations as "kin-dom," "realm," "domain," "imperial domain," and "reign," all of which have problems.

2. See Burton Mack, *A Myth of Innocence: Mark and Christian Origins* (Philadelphia:

Fortress Press, 1988), 27–62.

3. John Bright, *The Kingdom of God* (Nashville: Abingdon, 1953), has traced this possibility thoroughly.

4 See Seth Schwarz, *Imperialism and Jewish Society, 200 B.C.E. to 640 C.E.* (Princeton, N.J.: Princeton University Press, 2001); and David Carr and Colleen Conway, *Introduction to the Bible* (forthcoming from Oxford Press).

5. For example, Cynic/Stoic *basileia* references. See the extensive studies by F. Gerald Downing and the ensuing uses of these references by Mack, *Myth of Innocence,* and Hal Taussig, "Jesus as Sage," in *Profiles of Jesus,* ed. Roy Hoover (Santa Rosa, Calif.: Polebridge, 2002).

6. For example, James Breech, *The Silence of Jesus: The Authentic Voice of the Historical Man* (Philadelphia: Fortress Press, 1983).

7. For example, Robert Price, *Deconstructing Jesus* (Amherst, Mass.: Prometheus, 2000).

8. Scholars proposing a present reality of the *basileia* of God in one way or another include John Dominic Crossan, Robert Funk, Marcus Borg, and Bernard Brandon Scott. Scholars proposing an apocalyptically future *basileia* of God include Albert Schweizer, Bart Ehrman, and Dale Allison.

9. Mack, *Who Wrote the New Testament? The Making of the Christian Myth* (San Francisco: HarperSanFrancisco, 1995), 43.

10. Wolfgang Goethe, *Faust,* pt. 1, 903.

11. See the work of Rodney Stark on Christian origins, *The Rise of Christianity: A Sociologist Reconsiders History* (Princeton, N.J.: Princeton University Press, 1996).

12. Whether this reference to law (*nomos*) is to the Jewish law or the Roman law is an important question. See Brigitte Kahl's important new presentation of *nomos* as Roman law in her *Galatians Reimagined* (Minneapolis: Fortress Press, 2009) as a counterproposal to almost all established scholarship, which sees it as Jewish Torah.

13. See David Seeley, *The Noble Death: Graeco-Roman Martyrology and Paul's Concept of Salvation* (Sheffield: JSOT, 1990); Stephen J. Patterson, *Beyond the Passion: Rethinking the Death and Life of Jesus* (Minneapolis: Fortress Press, 2004); John Dominic Crossan, *Who Killed Jesus?* (San Francisco: HarperSanFrancisco, 1995); Mack, *Myth of Innocence*; and the article by George Nickelsburg on which all the above studies depend, "The Genre and Function of the Markan Passion Narrative," *Harvard Theological Review* 73 (1980): 153–84.

14. Other ritualizations that seem to have been important for some segments of early Christianity include baptism and celibacy.

15. Judith M. Lieu, *Christian Identity in the Jewish and Graeco-Roman World* (Oxford: Oxford University Press, 2004); and Judith M. Lieu, *Neither Jew nor Greek? Constructing Early Christianity* (London: Clark, 2002).

16. The works of Pierre Bourdieu, Homi Bhabha, Julia Kristeva, Talal Asad, and Judith Butler provide a range of exposure to this literature.

17. Lieu, *Christian Identity in the Jewish and Graeco-Roman World,* 8.

18. Chapter 6 of Lieu's *Christian Identity in the Jewish and Graeco-Roman World* lays this proposal out in detail.

19. Lieu, *Christian Identity in the Jewish and Graeco-Roman World*, 164.

20. These discussions of identity must take into account both social and individual identity. It is clear that the Hellenistic Mediterranean and early Christians as a part of that larger cultural complex understood themselves to be part of a social body more than (post) modern Westerners do. Almost all of the texts of the first and second centuries discussed in this book use the plural "you" in negotiating identity, rather than the singular "you."

21. It is important not to idealize this function of Jesus/Christ in early Christianity, since it is also clear that the identities in play around the images and narratives about Jesus/Christ often violated the identity options of slaves, women, and Jewish, Greek, Egyptian, and other marginalized persons. Even though it seems clear that the new kinds of identity in Jesus/Christ made more room than many conventional or imperial identity options, it is equally clear that these identity processes also did injustice to a number of Hellenistic populations. Indeed, even the persons whose identities were opened up "in" Jesus/Christ were also damaged by the rhetoric "in" Jesus/Christ.

22. Maia Kotrosits, "Mark: Identity and Horror" (unpublished essay, 2007).

23. Ibid., 2.

24. Ibid., 4.

25. Ibid., 11–12.

26. Ibid., 10.

27. Ibid., 2.

28. Ibid., 6.

29. Kotrosits resists the Markan identity proposal being considered as either unexplainably mystical or some kind of final answer. She acknowledges her indebtedness to Werner Kelber, especially his essay "Narrative and Disclosure: Mechanisms of Concealing, Revealing, and Reveiling" (*Semeia* 43 (1988): 1–20) but does not agree with his seemingly religious endorsement. She writes:

> Kelber calls this crisis/apex moment the "epiphany at the point of absence" (17) but quickly revises this to mean the revelation of "parabolic mystery." Naming such a moment of cynical horror "parabolic mystery" though surely romanticizes it. That Mark's empty tomb narrative even ends with absence ("he is not here"), not to mention silence and fear (". . . and they didn't tell anyone, for they were terrified. . . .") expresses a narrative determination that chasm be embedded in the story. Indeed, the double use of forms of *scizw* (to tear, to divide) suggests that rupture is the hinge on which these revelations turn.

30. Kotrosits, "Mark, Identity and Horror," 16.

31. See Catherine Bell, "Performance and Other Analogies," in Henry Bial, ed., *The Performance Studies Reader* (New York: Routledge, 2004), ch. 11.

32. See Bell's introductory essay to "performance studies" in *Critical Terms for Religious Studies*, ed. Mark C. Taylor (Chicago: University of Chicago Press, 1998), 205–24.

33. In terms of the disappearance of subjectivity and identity, the work of Julia Kristeva is important.

34. Judith Butler, *Bodies That Matter: On the Discursive Limits of Sex* (New York: Routledge, 1993), 95.

35. Judith Butler, *Gender Trouble* (New York: Routledge, 1990), 25.

36. That which occasioned these performative imaginations of identities needs also to be subject of investigation and study but is beyond the scope of this book. It is appropriate to ask what occasioned such a sense of the unfreezing of particular limits. Such investigation requires a great deal of intellectual rigor, historical research, and imagination.

Epilogue: Reflections on Twenty-First-Century Christian Worship

1. In addition to having been a professor for the past twenty-five years, I have also during that entire time served part-time as pastor of three local churches.

2. Dennis E. Smith and Hal Taussig, *Many Tables: The Eucharist in the New Testament and Liturgy Today* (London: SCM, 1990).

3. See chapter 1 of my *A New Spiritual Home: Progressive Christianity at the Grass Roots* (Santa Rosa, Calif.: Polebridge, 2006) for a national survey of new initiatives in worship expression.

4. See my description of the damage done to worship by clergy wordiness and authoritarianism in Catherine T. Nerney and Hal Taussig, *Re-imagining Life Together in America: A New Gospel of Community* (Lanham, Md.: Sheed & Ward, 2002), 151–60.

5. All of this is also true, of course, of synagogues, mosques, and other places of worship.

6. It is interesting in this regard to consider the case of many kinds of African American and Pentecostal worship, where ecstatic ejaculations and even trances can occur with some regularity. To a certain extent, this worship simply needs to be considered an important exception to the predictability of worship (and in this way even closer to Hellenistic meals). On the other hand, regular attendance at these more ecstatic worship services can sometimes serve to show how the ecstatic expressions indeed are predictable in both timing and character.

Works Consulted

Achtemeier, Paul. "Toward the Isolation of Pre-Markan Catenae." *Journal of Biblical Literature* 89, no. 3 (1970): 265–91.

_____. "The Origin and Function of the Pre-Marcan Miracle Catenae." *Journal of Biblical Literature* 91, no. 22 (1972): 198–221.

Antonova, Stamenka. "Barbarian or Greek: The Charge of Barbarism and Early Christian Apologetics." Ph.D. diss., Columbia University, 2005.

Aristotle. *Ethica Nicomachea.*

Asad, Talal. *Genealogies of Religion: Discipline and Reasons of Power in Christianity and Islam.* Baltimore: Johns Hopkins University Press, 1993.

_____. *Formations of the Secular: Christianity, Islam, Modernity.* Stanford: Stanford University Press, 2003.

Ascough, Richard. *Paul's Macedonian Associations: The Social Context of Philippians and 1 Thessalonians.* Tübingen: Mohr Siebeck, 2003.

Ausbüttel, Frank. *Untersuchungen zu den Vereinen im Westen des Römischen Reiches.* Kallmünz: M. Lassleben, 1982.

Balch, David L. "Paul's Portrait of Christ Crucified (Gal. 3:1) in Light of Paintings and Sculptures of Suffering and Death in Pompeiian and Roman Houses," in *Early Christian Families in Context: An Interdisciplinary Dialogue*, ed. David L. Balch and Carolyn Osiek, 84–109. Grand Rapids: Eerdmans, 2003.

Barton, S. C., and Richard Horsley. "A Hellenistic Cult Group and the New Testament Churches." *Jahrbuch für Antike und Christentum* 24 (1981): 7–41.

Beck, Norman A. "Reclaiming a Biblical Text: The Mark 8:14-21 Discussion about Bread in a Boat." *Catholic Biblical Quarterly* 43, no. 1 (January 1981): 49–56.

Bell, Catherine. *Ritual Theory, Ritual Practice.* New York: Oxford University Press, 1992.

_____. *Ritual: Perspectives and Dimensions.* New York: Oxford University Press, 1997.

_____. Introduction to *Critical Terms* for Religious Studies, ed. Mark C. Taylor, 205–24. Chicago: University of Chicago Press, 1998.

_____. "Performance and Other Analogies," in *The Performance Studies Reader*, ed. Henry Bial. New York: Routledge, 2004.

Bhabha, Homi. *Nation and Narration.* New York: Routledge, 1990.

_____. *The Location of Culture*. New York: Routledge, 1994.

Blanton, Ward. *Displacing Christian Origins: Philosophy, Secularity, and the New Testament*. Chicago: University of Chicago Press, 2007.

Borg, Marcus. *Meeting Jesus Again for the First Time: The Historical Jesus and the Heart of Contemporary Faith*. San Francisco: HarperSanFrancisco, 1994.

Bourdieu, Pierre. *Outline of a Theory of Practice*. Translated by Richard Nice. New York: Cambridge University Press, 1977.

Bousset, Wilhelm. *Kyrios Christos: A History of the Belief in Christ from the Beginnings of Christianity to Irenaeus*. Translated by John E. Steely. Nashville, Abingdon, 1970.

Bowman, Alan, and Greg Wolff, eds. *Literacy and Power in the Ancient World*. Cambridge: Cambridge University Press, 1994.

Boyarin, Daniel. *Dying for God: Martyrdom and the Making of Christianity and Judaism*. Stanford: Stanford University Press, 1999.

_____. *Border Lines: The Partition of Judaeo-Christianity*. Philadelphia: University of Pennsylvania Press, 2004.

Breech, James. *The Silence of Jesus*. Philadelphia: Fortress Press, 1983.

Bright, John. *The Kingdom of God*. Nashville: Abingdon, 1953.

Brown, Raymond E. *The Community of the Beloved Disciple*. New York: Paulist, 1979.

Bultmann, Rudolf. *Primitive Christianity in Its Contemporary Setting*, Translated by Reginald H. Fuller. Philadelphia: Fortress Press, 1956.

_____. *The Gospel of John: A Commentary*. Translated by G. R. Beasley-Murray. Edited by R. W. N. Hoare and J. K. Riches. Oxford: Blackwell, 1971.

Butler, Judith. *Gender Trouble: Feminism and the Subversion of Identity*. New York: Routledge 1990.

_____. *Bodies That Matter: On the Discursive Limits of Sex*. New York: Routledge, 1993.

Callahan, Allan. "'No Rhyme or Reason':The Hidden Logia of the Gospel of Thomas." *Harvard Theological Review* 90, no. 4 (1997): 411–26.

Carr, David M., and Colleen Conway. *Introduction to the Bible*. New York: Oxford Press, forthcoming.

Carter, Warren. *Matthew and Empire: Initial Explorations*. Harrisburg, Pa.: Trinity Press International, 2001.

_____. *The Roman Empire and the New Testament: An Essential Guide*. Nashville: Abingdon, 2006.

Castelli, Elizabeth A., and Hal Taussig, eds. *Reimagining Christian Origins: A Colloquium Honoring Burton L. Mack*. Valley Forge, Pa.: Trinity Press International, 1996.

_____. *Martyrdom and Memory: Early Christian Culture Making*. New York: Columbia University Press, 2004.

Childs, Hal. *The Myth of the Historical Jesus and the Evolution of Consciousness*. Atlanta: Society of Biblical Literature, 2000.

Clark, Elizabeth A. *History, Theory, Text: Historians and the Linguistic Turn*. Cambridge: Harvard University Press, 2004.

Collins, Adela Yarbro. *Crisis and Catharsis: The Power of the Apocalypse.* Philadelphia: Westminster, 1984.

Conzelmann, Hans. *Acts of the Apostles: A Commentary on the Acts of the Apostles.* Edited by Eldon J. Epp with Christopher R. Matthews. Translated by James Limburg, A. Thomas Kraabel, and Donald H. Juel. Hermeneia Series. Philadelphia: Fortress Press, 1987.

Corley, Kathleen. *Private Women, Public Meals: Social Conflict in the Synoptic Tradition.* Peabody, Mass.: Hendrickson, 1993.

Crossan, John Dominic. *In Parables: The Challenge of the Historical Jesus.* New York: Harper & Row, 1973.

_____. *In Fragments: The Aphorisms of Jesus.* San Francisco: Harper & Row, 1983.

_____. *The Dark Interval: Towards a Theology of Story.* Sonoma, Calif.: Polebridge, 1988.

_____. *The Historical Jesus: The Life of a Mediterranean Peasant.* San Francisco: HarperSanFrancisco, 1991.

_____. "Itinerants and Householders in the Earliest Kingdom Movement," in *Reimagining Christian Origins: A Colloquium Honoring Burton L. Mack.* ed. Elizabeth A. Castelli and Hal Taussig, 113–29. Valley Forge: Trinity Press International, 1996.

_____. *Who Killed Jesus? Exploring the Roots of Anti-Semitism in the Gospel Story of the Death of Jesus.* San Francisco: HarperSanFrancisco, 1996.

_____. *The Birth of Christianity: Discovering What Happened in the Years Immediately After the Execution of Jesus.* San Francisco: HarperSanFrancisco, 1998.

Crossan, John Dominic, and Jonathan L. Reed. *In Search of Paul: How Jesus's Apostle Opposed Rome's Empire with God's Kingdom; A New Vision of Paul's Words and World.* San Francisco: HarperSanFrancisco, 2004.

Cullmann, Oscar. *Early Christian Worship.* Translated by A. Stewart Todd and James B. Torrance. London: SCM, 1953.

Culpepper, R. Alan. *A Commentary on the Fourth Gospel.*

Deissmann, Adolf. *Paul: A Study in Social and Religious History.* Translated by William E. Wilson. London: Hodder & Stoughton, 1926.

_____. *Light From the Ancient East: The New Testament Illustrated by Recently Discovered Texts of the Graeco-Roman World.* Translated by Lionel R. M. Strachan. London: Hodder & Stoughton, 1927.

Derbolav, J., "Das Problem der Verteilungsgerichtigkeit bei Aristotles und in unserer Zeit," 208–38 in *Herkunft und Prinzipien des platonischen Staatsdenken,* Studien zu Platon und Aristoteles, Stuttgart, 1979.

Dodd, C. H. *Historical Tradition in the Fourth Gospel.* Cambridge: Cambridge University Press, 1963.

Douglas, Mary. *Purity and Danger: An Analysis of Concepts of Pollution and Taboo.* Boston: K. Paul, 1966.

_____. "Deciphering a Meal," in *Myth, Symbol and Culture,* ed. Clifford Geertz, 61–81. New York: W. W. Norton, 1971.

Downing, Gerald. *Cynics and Christian Origins.* Edinburgh: T. & T. Clark, 1992.

Ebner, Martin, ed. *Herrenmahl und Gruppenidentität*. Freiburg im Breisgau: Herder, 2007.

Ehrman, Bart. *Lost Christianities: The Battles for Scripture and the Faiths We Never Knew*. New York: Oxford University Press, 2003.

_____. *The New Testament: A Historical Introduction to the Early Christian Writings*. New York: Oxford University Press, 2004.

_____. *Misquoting Jesus: The Story Behind Who Changed the Bible and Why*. New York: HarperSanFrancisco, 2005.

Farnell, Lewis Richard. *The Higher Aspects of Greek Religion*. London: Williams and Norgate, 1912.

Ferguson, W. S. "The Leading Ideas of the New Period," in *The Hellenistic Monarchies and the Rise of Rome*, ed. S. A. Cook, F. E. Adcock, and M. P. Charlesworth. Cambridge: Cambridge University Press, 1964.

Fishwick, Duncan. *The Imperial Cult in the Latin West: Studies in the Ruler Cult of the Western Provinces of the Roman Empire*. Leiden: Brill, 1987.

Funk, Robert. *Honest to Jesus: Jesus for a New Millenium*. San Francisco: HarperSanFrancisco, 1996.

Funk, Robert and the Jesus Seminar. *The Acts of Jesus*. Santa Rosa, Calif.: Polebridge, 1998.

Grant, Frederick Clifton. *Hellenistic Religions: The Age of Syncretism*. New York: Liberal Arts Press, 1953.

Guthrie, W. K. C. *The Greeks and Their Gods*. Boston: Beacon, 1950.

Harland, Philip. *Associations, Synagogues, and Congregations: Claiming a Place in Ancient Mediterranean Society*. Minneapolis: Fortress Press, 2003.

Harris, William V. *Ancient Literacy*. Cambridge, Mass.: Harvard University Press, 1989.

_____. *The Spread of Christianity in the First Four Centuries: Essays in Explanation*. Boston: Brill, 2005.

Hatch, Edwin. *The Organization of the Early Christian Churches: Eight Lectures*. London: Rivingtons, 1888.

Heinrici, G. *Die Erste Brief an die Korinther*. Göttingen: Vandenhoeck & Ruprecht, 1896.

_____. "Die Christengemeinden Korinths und die religioesen Genossenschaften der Griechen." *Zeitschrift fuer wissenschaftlichen Theologie* 19 (1876): 465–526.

_____. "Zur Geschichte der Anfaenge paulinischer Gemeinden." *Zeitschrift fuer wissenschaftlichen Theologie* 20 (1877): 89–130.

_____. "Zum genossenschaftlichen Charakterder paulinischen Christengemeinden." *Theologische Studien und Kritiken* 54 (1881): 505–24.

Hock, Ronald, and Edward N. O'Neill, eds. *The Chreia and Ancient Rhetoric*. Vol. 1, *The Progymnasmata*. Atlanta: Scholars Press, 1986.

Horsley, Richard. *Paul and Empire: Religion and Power in Roman Imperial Society*. Valley Forge, Pa.: Trinity Press International, 1997.

_____, ed. *A People's History of Christianity*. Vol. 1, *Christian Origins*. Minneapolis: Fortress Press, 2005.

Jeremias, Joachim. *The Parables of Jesus*. London: SCM, 1972.

Johnson, Luke Timothy. *The Real Jesus: The Misguided Quest for the Historical Jesus and the Truth of the Traditional Gospels*. San Francisco: HarperSanFrancisco, 1996.

Johnson-Debaufre, Melanie. *Jesus among Her Children: Q, Eschatology, and the Construction of Christian Origins*. Cambridge, Mass.: Harvard University Press, 2005.

Justin Martyr. *Apology*.

Kahl, Brigitte. "Reading Galatians and Empire at the Great Altar of Pergamon," *Union Seminary Quarterly Review* 59, nos. 3–4 (2005): 21–43.

_____. *Galatians Reimagined: Through the Eyes of the Vanquished*. Minneapolis: Fortress Press, 2008.

Kelber, Werner. *The Kingdom in Mark: A New Place and a New Time*. Philadelphia: Fortress Press, 1974.

_____. *Mark's Story of Jesus*. Philadelphia: Fortress Press, 1979.

_____. *The Oral and the Written Gospel: The Hermeneutics of Speaking and Writing in the Synoptic Tradition, Mark, Paul and Q*. Philadelphia: Fortress Press, 1983.

_____. "Narrative and Disclosure: Mechanisms of Concealing, Revealing, and Reveiling." *Semeia* no. 43 (1988): 1–20.

Kennedy, George A., trans. *Progymnasmata: Greek Textbooks of Prose Composition and Rhetoric*. Atlanta: Society of Biblical Literature, 2003.

King, Karen. *The Gospel of Mary of Magdala: Jesus and the First Woman Apostle*. Santa Rosa, Calif.: Polebridge, 2003.

_____. *What Is Gnosticism?* Cambridge, Mass.: Harvard University Press, 2003.

_____. *The Secret Revelation to John*. Cambridge, Mass.: Harvard University Press, 2006.

King, Karen, and Elaine Pagels. *Reading Judas: The Gospel of Judas and the Shaping of Early Christianity*. New York: Viking, 2007.

Kirk, Alan, and Tom Thatcher, eds. *Memory, Tradition and Text*. Atlanta: Society of Biblical Literature, 2005.

Klinghardt, Matthias. *Gemeinschaftsmahl und Mahlgemeinschaft: Soziologie und Liturgie Frühchristlicher Mahlfeiern*. Tübingen: Francke Verlag, 1996.

Kloppenborg, John S., and Stephen G. Wilson. *Voluntary Associations in the Graeco-Roman World*. New York: Routledge, 1996.

Koester, Helmut. *Introduction to the New Testament*. 2 vols. Berlin: Walter de Gruyter & Co., 1995.

Kotrosits, Maia. "Mark: Identity and Horror." Unpublished essay, 2007.

Kreissig, Heinz. "Die Polis in Griechenland und im Orient in der hellenistichen Epoche," in *Hellenische Poleis: Krise—Wandlungen—Wirkung*, ed. Elisabeth Charlotte Welskopf, 1074–84. Berlin: Akademie, 1974.

Kuhn, H. W. *Aeltere Sammlungen in Markusevangelium*. Göttingen: Vandenhoeck Ruprecht, 1971.

Lee, Jae Won. "Gentile Difference in Galatians and Romans." Ph.D. diss., Union Theological Seminary, 2001.

Lieu, Judith. *Neither Jew nor Greek? Constructing Early Christianity*. New York: T. & T. Clark, 2002.

_____. *Christian Identity in the Jewish and Graeco-Roman World*. New York: Oxford University Press, 2004.

Lopez, Davina C. *Apostle to the Conquered: Reimagining Paul*. Paul in Critical Contexts Series. Minneapolis: Fortress Press, 2008.

Loisy, Alfred. *The Birth of the Christian Religion and the Origins of the New Testament*. Translated by L. P. Jacks. New Hyde Park, N.Y.: University Books, 1962.

Lucian. *De Saltatione*.

Lyotard, Jean François. *The Postmodern Condition: A Report on Knowledge*. Translated by Geoff Bennington and Brian Massumi. Minneapolis: University of Minnesota Press, 1984.

Mack, Burton. *Logos und Sophia: Untersuchungen zur Weisheitstheologie im hellenistischen Judentum*. Göttingen: Vandenhoeck & Ruprecht, 1973.

_____. "Introduction: Ritual and Religion," in *Violent Origins: Walter Burkert, René Girard, and Jonathan Z. Smith on Ritual Killing and Cultural Formation*, ed. Robert G. Hamerton-Kelly, 1–72. Stanford: Stanford University Press, 1987.

_____. *A Myth of Innocence: Mark and Christian Origins*. Philadelphia: Fortress Press, 1988.

_____. *Rhetoric and the New Testament*. Minneapolis: Augsburg Fortress, 1990.

_____. *The Lost Gospel: The Book of Q and Christian Origins*. San Francisco: HarperSanFrancisco, 1994.

_____. *Who Wrote the New Testament? The Making of the Christian Myth*. San Francisco: HarperSanFrancisco, 1995.

_____. *The Christian Myth: Origins, Logic and Legacy*. New York: Continuum, 2001.

Mack, Burton, and Vernon Robbins. *Patterns of Persuasion in the Gospels*. Sonoma, Calif.: Polebridge, 1989.

MacMullen, Ramsay. *Paganism in the Roman Empire*. New Haven, Conn.: Yale University Press, 1981.

Malina, Bruce J. *The New Testament World: Insights from Cultural Anthropology*. Atlanta: John Knox, 1981.

Malina, Bruce J., and Jerome H. Neyrey. *Calling Jesus Names: The Social Value of Labels in Matthew*. Sonoma, Calif.: Polebridge, 1988.

Malina, Bruce J., and Jerome H. Neyrey. *Portraits of Paul: An Archaeology of Ancient Personality*. Louisville, Ky.: Westminster John Knox, 1996.

Marks, Susan. "Jewish Weddings in the Greco-Roman Period: A Reconsideration of Received Ritual." Ph. D. diss., University of Pennsylvania, 2003.

Marshall, Peter. *Enmity in Corinth: Social Conventions in Paul's Relations with the Corinthians*. Tübingen: J. C. B. Mohr, 1987.

McGowan, Andrew. "Eating People: Accusations of Cannibalism against Christians in the Second Century." *Journal of Early Christian Studies* 2 (1994): 413–42.

_____. "'First Regarding the Cup': Papias and the Diversity of Early Eucharistic Practice." *Journal of Theological Studies*, n.s. 46 (1995): 569–73.

_____. "Naming the Feast: The Agape and the Diversity of Early Christian Ritual Meals." *Studia Patristica* 30 (ed. E. Livingstone; Leuven: Peeters, 1997): 314–18.

_____. *Ascetic Eucharists: Food and Drink in Early Christian Ritual Meals.* Oxford: Clarendon, 1999.

_____. "'Is There a Liturgical Text in this Gospel?' The Institution Narratives and Their Early Interpretive Communities." *Journal of Biblical Literature* 118 (1999): 77–89.

_____. "Marcion's Love of Creation." *Journal of Early Christian Studies* 9 (2001): 295–311.

_____. "The Inordinate Cup: Issues of Order in Early Eucharistic Drinking." *Studia Patristica* 35 (2001): 283–91.

_____. "Discipline and Diet: Feeding the Martyrs in Roman Carthage." *Harvard Theological Review* 96 (2003): 455–76.

_____. "The Meals of Jesus and the Meals of the Church: Eucharistic Origins and Admission to Communion," in *Studia Liturgica Diversa: Essays in Honor of Paul F. Bradshaw*, ed. Maxwell E. Johnson and L. Edward Phillips, 101–15. Portland: Pastoral Press, 2003.

_____. "Rethinking Agape and Eucharist in Early North African Christianity," *Studia Liturgica* 34 (2004): 165–76.

_____. "Food, Ritual, and Power," in *A People's History of Christianity.* Vol. 2, *Late Ancient Christianity*, ed. Virginia Burrus, 145–64. Minneapolis: Fortress Press, 2005.

Meeks, Wayne. *The First Urban Christians: The Social World of the Apostle Paul.* New Haven, Conn.: Yale University Press, 2003.

Miller, Merrill P., and Ron Cameron. *Redescribing Christian Origins.* Boston: Brill, 2004.

Miller, Robert J., ed. *The Complete Gospels.* Santa Rosa, Calif.: Polebridge, 1994.

_____. *Born Divine: The Births of Jesus and Other Sons of God.* Santa Rosa, Calif.: Polebridge, 2003.

Moore, Stephen D. *Poststructuralism and the New Testament: Derrida and Foucault at the Foot of the Cross.* Minneapolis: Fortress Press, 1994.

Mosse, Claude. *Athens in Decline 404–86 B.C.* London: Routledge and Kegan Paul, 1973.

Moxnes, Halvor. "The Historical Jesus: From Master Narrative to Cultural Context." *Bibilical Theology Bulletin* 28 (Winter 1999): 135–49.

Myers, Ched. *Binding the Strong Man: A Political Reading of Mark's Story of Jesus.* Maryknoll, N.Y.: Orbis, 1988.

Nasrallah, Laura. *An Ecstasy of Folly: Prophecy and Authority in Early Christianity.* Cambridge, Mass.: Harvard University Press, 2003.

Neusner, Jacob. *Neusner on Judaism.* Burlington, Va.: Ashgate, 2004.

Nicklesburg, George. "The Genre and Function of the Markan Passion Narrative." *Harvard Theological Review* 73, nos. 1–2. (January–April 1980): 153–84.

Nilsson, Martin P. *A History of Greek Religion.* Translated by F. J. Fielden. Oxford: Clarendon, 1925.

_____. *Dionysiac Mysteries of the Hellenistic and Roman Age.* New York: Arno, 1975.

Oakman, Douglas, and K. C. Hanson. *Palestine in the Time of Jesus: Social Structures and Social Conflicts.* Minneapolis: Fortress Press, 1998.

Patterson, Stephen J. *Beyond the Passion: Rethinking the Death and Life of Jesus*. Minneapolis: Fortress Press, 2004.

Penner, Todd. *Contextualizing Acts: Lukan Narrative and Greco-Roman Discourse*. Boston: Brill, 2004.

Pervo, Richard I. *Dating Acts*. Santa Rosa, Calif.: Polebridge, 2006.

Philo. *The Contemplative Life*. Translated by F. H. Colson and G. H. Whitaker. Cambridge: Loeb Classical Library, 1929.

Philostratus. *Vita Appollonae*.

Plato. *The Symposium*.

Pliny. *Epistulae*.

Plutarch. *Table Talk*.

_____. *Quaestiones convivales*.

Poland, Franz. *Geschicte des Griechisches Vereinswesen*. Leipzig: B. G. Teubner, 1909.

Price, Robert. *The Widow Traditions in Luke-Acts: A Feminist Critical Scrutiny*. Altanta: Scholars Press, 1997.

_____. *Deconstructing Jesus*. Amherst: Prometheus, 2000.

Price, S. R. F. *Rituals and Power: The Roman Imperial Cult in Asia Minor*. Cambridge: Cambridge University Press, 1984.

Reid, Barbara E. *Choosing the Better Part? Women in the Gospel of Luke*. Collegeville, Minn.: Liturgical Press, 1996.

Robinson, James M., and Helmut Koester. *Trajectories through Early Christianity*. Philadelphia: Fortress Press, 1971.

Royce, Josiah. *The Problem of Christianity*. Chicago: University of Chicago Press, 1913.

Sanders, Jack T. *New Testament Christological Hymns: Their Historical Religious Background*. Cambridge: Cambridge University Press, 1971.

Schüssler Fiorenza, Elisabeth. "A Feminist Critical Interpretation for Liberation: Martha and Mary: Luke 10:38-42." *Religion and Intellectual Life* 3, no. 2 (Winter 1986): 21–36.

_____. *In Memory of Her: A Feminist Theological Reconstruction of Christian Origins*. New York: Crossroad, 1994.

_____. *Jesus and the Politics of Interpretation*. New York: Continuum, 2000.

Schwarz, Seth. *Imperialism and Jewish Society, 200 B.C.E. to 640 C.E.* Princeton, N.J.: Princeton University Press, 2001.

Scott, James C. *Domination and the Arts of Resistance*. New Haven, Conn.: Yale University Press, 1990.

Seeley, David. *The Noble Death: Graeco-Roman Martyrology and Paul's Concept of Salvation*. Sheffield: JSOT, 1990.

Seim, Turid Karlsen. *The Double Message: Patterns of Gender in Luke and Acts*. Nashville: Abingdon, 1994.

Shepherd, Massey Hamilton. *The Paschal Liturgy and the Apocalypse*. Richmond: John Knox, 1960.

Smith, Dennis E. "Table Fellowship as a Literary Motif in the Gospel of Luke." *Journal of Biblical Literature* 106, no. 4 (1987): 613–28.

_____. *From Symposium to Eucharist: The Banquet in the Early Christian World*. Minneapolis: Fortress Press, 2003.

_____. "What Do We Really Know about the Jerusalem Church?: Christian Origins in Jerusalem according to Acts and Paul," in *Redescribing Christian Origins*, ed. Ron Cameron and Merrill P. Miller, 237–52. Atlanta: Society of Biblical Literature, 2004.

_____. "A Response to Hal Taussig's Paper." Meals in the Greco-Roman World Seminar of the Society of Biblical Literature, November, 2007, San Diego. Available at www.philharland.com.

Smith, Jonathan Z. *Imagining Religion: From Babylon to Jonestown*. Chicago: University of Chicago Press, 1982.

_____. "The Domestication of Sacrifice," in *Violent Origins: Walter Burkert, René Girard, and Jonathan Z. Smith on Ritual Killing and Cultural Formation*, ed. Robert G. Hamerton-Kelly, 191–205. Stanford: Stanford University Press, 1987.

_____. *To Take Place: Toward Theory in Ritual*. Chicago: University of Chicago, 1987.

_____. *Drudgery Divine: On the Comparison of Early Christianities and the Religions of Late Antiquity*. Chicago: University of Chicago Press, 1990.

_____, general ed. *HarperCollins Dictionary of Religion*. San Francisco: HaperSanFrancisco, 1995.

Stark, Rodney. *The Rise of Christianity: A Sociologist Reconsiders History*. Princeton, N.J.: Princeton University Press, 1996.

de Ste. Croix, G. E. M. *The Class Struggle in the Ancient Greek World from the Archaic Age to the Arab Conquests*. Ithaca, N.Y.: Cornell University Press, 1981.

Stendahl, Krister. *Paul among Jews and Gentiles and Other Essays*. Philadelphia: Fortress Press, 1976.

Stowers, Stanley. "Elusive Coherence: Ritual and Rhetoric in 1 Corinthians 10–11," in *Reimagining Christian Origins: A Colloquium Honoring Burton L. Mack*, ed. Elizabeth A. Castelli and Hal Taussig, 68–83. Valley Forge, Pa.: Trinity Press International, 1996.

Sugirtharajah, R. S. *The Bible and Empire: Postcolonial Explorations*. Cambridge: Cambridge University Press, 2005.

Tarn, William, and G. T. Griffin. *Hellenistic Civilization*. London: Arnold, 1952.

Taussig, Hal. "The Sexual Politics of Luke's Mary and Martha Account: An Evaluation of the Historicity of Luke 10:38-42." *Forum* 7, nos. 3–4 (1991): 307–19.

_____. "Dealing under the Table: Ritual Negotiation of Women's Power in the Syrophoenician Woman Pericope," in *Reimagining Christian Origins: A Colloquim Honoring Burton L. Mack*, ed. Elizabeth A. Castelli and Hal Taussig. Valley Forge, Pa.: Trinity Press International, 1996.

_____. "Jerusalem as Occasion for Conversation: The Intersections of Acts 15 and Galations 2." *Forum*, n.s., 4, no. 1 (2001): 89–104.

_____. "Jesus as Sage," in *Profiles of Jesus*, ed. Roy Hoover. Santa Rosa, Calif.: Polebridge, 2002.

_____. "Ritual Perfection and/or Literary Idealization in Philo's 'On the Contemplative Life' and Other Greco-Roman Symposia." San Antonio: Society of Biblical Literature Consultation, Meals in the Greco-Roman World, 2004.

_____. *A New Spiritual Home: Progressive Christianity at the Grass Roots.* Santa Rosa, Calif.: Polebridge, 2006.

Taussig, Hal, and Catherine T. Nerney. *Re-imagining Life Together in America: A New Gospel of Community.* Lanham, Md.: Sheed & Ward, 2002.

Taussig, Hal, and Dennis E. Smith. *Many Tables: The Eucharist in the New Testament and Liturgy Today.* Philadelphia: Trinity Press International, 1990.

Theissen, Gerd. "Itinerant Radicalism: The Tradition of Jesus Sayings from the Perspective of the Sociology of Literature." *Radical Religion* 2, nos. 2–3 (1975): 84–93.

_____. *The Sociology of Early Palestinian Christianity.* Translated by John Bowden. Philadelphia: Fortress Press, 1978.

_____. *The Social Setting of Pauline Christianity: Essays on Corinth.* Philadelphia: Fortress Press, 1982.

Turner, Victor. *The Forest of Symbols: Aspects of Ndembu Ritual.* Ithaca, N.Y.: Cornell University Press, 1967.

_____. *Ritual Process: Structure and Anti-Structure.* Chicago: Aldine Publishing Company, 1969.

_____. *Revelation and Divination in Ndembu Society.* Ithaca, N.Y.: Cornell University Press, 1975.

Turner, Victor, and Edith L. B. Turner, eds. *On the Edge of the Bush: Anthropology of Experience.* Tuscon: University of Arizona Press, 1985.

Tyson, Joseph. *Marcion and Luke-Acts: A Defining Struggle.* Columbia: University of South Carolina Press, 2006.

Vaage, Leif. *Galilean Upstarts: Jesus' First Followers according to Q.* Valley Forge, Pa.: Trinity Press International, 1994.

von Harnack, Adolf. *Expansion of Early Christianity in the First Three Centuries.* New York: Putnam, 1904.

_____. *The Mission and Expansion of Christianity in the First Three Centuries.* London: Williams and Norgate, 1908.

Waltzing, Jean-Pierre. Étude Historique sur les Corporations Professionnelles Chez les Romains Depuis les Origines Jusqu'à la Chute de l'Empire d'Occident. Louvain: Peeters, 1895–1900.

West, M. L. *Iambi et Elegi Graeci ante Alexandrrum cantati,* I/II.

White, Michael L. *Building God's House in the Roman World: Architectural Adaptation among Pagans, Jews and Christians.* Baltimore: Johns Hopkins University Press, 1990.

_____. *The Social Origins of Christian Architecture.* 2 vols. Valley Forge, Pa.: Trinity Press International, 1996.

Williams, Sam K. *Jesus' Death as Saving Event: The Background and Origin of a Concept.* Missoula: Scholars Press, 1975.

Wimbush, Vincent. *African Americans and the Bible: Sacred Texts and Social Textures.* New York: Continuum, 2000.

Wire, Antoinette Clark. *The Corinthian Women Prophets: A Reconstruction through Paul's Rhetoric.* Minneapolis: Fortress Press, 1990.

Wright, N. T. *Who Was Jesus?* Grand Rapids: Eerdmans, 1993.

_____. *The Resurrection of the Son of God.* Minneapolis: Augsburg Fortress, 2003.

_____. *Paul: In Fresh Perspective.* Minneapolis: Fortress Press, 2005.

_____. "Paul's Gospel and Caesar's Empire." Lecture, Center of Theological Inquiry, Princeton.

Xenophon. *Synposium.*

Ziebarth, E. G. L. *Das griechische Vereinswesen.* Stuttgart: S. Hirzel, 1896.

Subject Index

Author Index

Scripture Index